Comparing Democracies **3**

Comparing Democracies 3

Elections and Voting in the 21st Century

edited by **Lawrence LeDuc,**
Richard G. Niemi, and Pippa Norris

Los Angeles | London | New Delhi
Singapore | Washington DC

© Lawrence LeDuc, Richard G. Niemi and Pippa Norris 2010

First published 2010

Reprinted 2010, 2011

SAGE Publications Ltd
1 Oliver's Yard
55 City Road
London EC1Y 1SP

SAGE Publications Inc.
2455 Teller Road
Thousand Oaks, California 91320

SAGE Publications India Pvt Ltd
B 1/I 1 Mohan Cooperative Industrial Area
Mathura Road
New Delhi 110 044

SAGE Publications Asia-Pacific Pte Ltd
33 Pekin Street #02-01
Far East Square
Singapore 048763

Library of Congress Control Number: 2009937880

British Library Cataloguing in Publication data

A catalogue record for this book is available from the British Library

ISBN 978-1-84787-503-7
ISBN 978-1-84787-504-4 (pbk)

Typeset by C&M Digitals (P) Ltd, Chennai, India
Printed in Great Britain by CPI Antony Rowe, Chippenham, Wiltshire
Printed on paper from sustainable resources

CONTENTS

ABOUT THE CONTRIBUTORS

Ingrid van Biezen is Professor of Comparative Politics at Leiden University. She has previously taught at the University of Birmingham and the Johns Hopkins University, and has held Visiting Fellowships at Yale University and the University of California, Irvine. She is the author of *Political Parties in New Democracies* and *Financing Political Parties and Election Campaigns* and has published widely on comparative party politics, political finance, and democratic theory in European and American journals.

André Blais is Professor of Political Science at the Université de Montréal. He is a fellow of the Royal Society of Canada, and a research fellow with the Centre for the Study of Democratic Citizenship, the Centre interuniversitaire de recherche en économie quantitative (CIREQ), and the Center for Interuniversity Research Analysis on Organizations (CIRANO). He is past president of the Canadian Political Science Association. His research interests are elections, electoral systems, turnout, public opinion, and methodology.

Elisabeth Carter is Lecturer in Politics at Keele University in the UK. Her research interests include political parties, electoral institutions, and electoral behaviour. Her articles on the impact of electoral institutions on small and extremist parties have been published in the *European Journal of Political Research*, *Representation*, and *West European Politics*. She is the author of *The Extreme Right in Western Europe: Success or Failure?* (2005) and the co-editor of *The Europeanization of National Political Parties: Power and Organizational Adaptation* (2007).

Russell J. Dalton is Professor of Political Science at the University of California, Irvine and was the founding director of the Center for the Study of Democracy. He has received a Fulbright Research Fellowship at the University of Mannheim, the Barbra Streisand Fellowship, a German Marshall Research Fellowship and a POSCO Fellowship at the East/West Center. His recent publications include *The Good Citizen* and *Democratic Challenges, Democratic Choices*; he is co-editor of *Party Politics in East Asia*, *The Oxford Handbook of Political Behavior* and *Citizens, Democracy and Markets around the Pacific Rim*, and *Parties without Partisans*.

David M. Farrell has recently taken up the position of chair of Politics at University College Dublin. Prior to that he was the Jean Monnet chair in European Politics at the University of Manchester. He is co-editor of the journal *Party Politics* and also of the ECPR/Oxford University Press book series on Comparative Politics. Recent publications include *Representing Europe's Citizens?* (2006) and *The Australian Electoral System* (2005). He is currently finalizing a revised edition of his long-standing textbook on *Electoral Systems*.

Timothy Hellwig is Assistant Professor of Political Science at Indiana University. He has published articles on economic voting, political account-ability, and the electoral consequences of globalization in journals such as the *British Journal of Political Science, Comparative Political Studies, International Studies Quarterly*, and the *Journal of Politics*. He is currently working on a book-length project, funded by the National Science Foundation, on eco-nomic globalization and mass politics in advanced industrial democracies.

Lawrence LeDuc is Professor of Political Science at the University of Toronto. His publications include *The Politics of Direct Democracy* (2003) and *Absent Mandate: Canadian Electoral Politics in an Era of Restructuring* (1996) as well as articles on voting, elections, and related topics in North American and European political science journals. His current research deals with electoral reform, political participation, and direct democracy.

Richard G. Niemi is Don Alonzo Watson Professor of Political Science at the University of Rochester. He is co-author or co-editor of *Vital Statistics on American Politics, 2009–2010* (2009), *Voting Technology: The Not-So-Simple Act of Casting a Ballot* (2008), *Institutional Change in American Politics: The Case of Term Limits* (2007), and other books. His current research includes voting, US ballots, and public opinion.

Pippa Norris is the McGuire Lecturer in Comparative Politics at the John F. Kennedy School of Government, Harvard University. She has also served as Director of the Democratic Governance Group at UNDP in New York. Her work compares democracy, elections and public opinion, politi-cal communications, and gender politics. Recent books are *Cosmopolitan Communications* (coauthored with Ronald Inglehart, 2009), and *Public Sentinel: The News Media and the Governance Agenda* (edited, 2009).

G. Bingham Powell, Jr. is Marie C. and Joseph C. Wilson Professor of Political Science at the University of Rochester. He is author of *Elections as Instruments of Democracy* (2000), *Contemporary Democracies* (1982) and co-author and co-editor of the textbook *Comparative Politics Today* (9th edn, 2008). His current research focuses on election rules, party systems, and political representation.

Marian Sawer is Adjunct Professor and Director of the Democratic Audit of Australia at the Australian National University. She has published 15 books, including the co-authored *Australia: The State of Democracy* (2009). Apart from electoral reform, her current research projects deal with the evolution of social movements and gender and multilevel governance.

Susan E. Scarrow is Professor of Political Science at the University of Houston. She is author of *Perspectives on Political Parties* (2002) and *Parties and Their Members* (1996), and co-editor of *Democracy Transformed?* (2003). Her main research interests are political parties, direct democracy, and political finance.

Claes H. de Vreese is Professor and Chair of Political Communication and Scientific Director of The Amsterdam School of Communication Research (ASCoR) at the University of Amsterdam. He is also Adjunct Professor of Political Science and Journalism at the University of Southern Denmark and Director of the Center for Politics and Communication (www.pol comm.org). He has published more than 50 peer-reviewed journal articles on political communication, media, public opinion, journalism, and European integration.

Christopher Wlezien is Professor of Political Science at Temple University. He is co-author of the forthcoming *Degrees of Democracy* (2010) and co-editor of *The Future of Election Studies* (2002) and *Britain Votes* (2005). He has published many articles on elections, public opinion and policy, and currently is co-editor of the *Journal of Elections, Public Opinion and Parties,* and the 'Poll-Reviews' section of *Public Opinion Quarterly*.

1

Introduction: Building and Sustaining Democracy

Lawrence LeDuc, Richard G. Niemi, and Pippa Norris

Elections and Democracy: Three cases

Belarus: Electoral Autocracy

President Alexander Lukashenko of Belarus has been dubbed "Europe's last dictator."[1] Ruling the country with an iron fist since 1994, his grip on power tightened further in 2004 when a controversial referendum abolished the constitution's two-term presidential limit. Leading opponents have been jailed, dissidents repressed, and many protesters arrested (Frear 2008; Way 2005). On 29 September, 2008 Belarusians had the opportunity to cast their ballots in elections for the 110-member House of Representatives, the third such contest held under the 1994 Constitution. Citizens had a choice of candidates, five dozen representing five opposition parties, competing alongside 183 independents. On election day, however, pro-Lukashenko deputies swept the board, taking 100% of the seats. The result generated scattered street protests in Minsk, but there was no "color revolution," such as those that occurred in Georgia (2003) or Ukraine (2004). Instead, long after the Soviet era had faded in neighboring Poland, Latvia, Lithuania, and Ukraine, the election consolidated Lukashenko's rule. Despite the periodic holding of elections, Freedom House, which rates all countries of the world annually on their record of political rights and civil liberties, continues to give Belarus its lowest ratings on these measures.[2]

The independent Office for Democratic Elections and Human Rights (OSCE) sent a team of observers to monitor the Belarusian elections. Their report documented a series of practices that restricted opposition forces from using elections as an effective mechanism to challenge Lukashenko's rule.[3] The state controlled the appointment of members of the Central Electoral Commission administering the process. Opposition parties faced severe legal limits in their capacity to organize and nominate candidates, and in communicating their message to voters. In practice, the campaign was barely visible to most citizens. All outdoor campaign rallies and meetings required prior authorization by the state, and state-owned newspapers showed a marked pro-government bias. Media monitoring by the OSCE showed that few dissenting views and alternative perspectives were presented in the state-controlled TV news. The threshold set by the two-round electoral system posed further hurdles, since independent and minor party candidates needed to gain a majority (50%+) of votes in each seat to win office.

All this did not deter people from casting a ballot; official figures suggest that 75% of the registered electorate voted. Once the campaign ended, however, several irregularities occurred. Ballot boxes used for early voting were not secured. Observers monitoring the election in many areas had limited or no access to the vote count, despite opposition reports of irregularities. Electoral complaints and legal appeals after polling day were rejected by the authorities without investigation. The multiparty contests, largely following prescribed legal processes, gave citizens a choice at the ballot box in nearly every seat, but the outcome further consolidated Lukashenko's grip on power. Foreign news coverage of these events was minimal.[4] The international community largely shrugged its shoulders and looked away, with more urgent problems calling for its attention. Belarus exemplifies what we will refer to in subsequent discussion in this chapter as an *electoral autocracy*, characterized by widespread abuses of human rights and a lack of any effective checks on executive power exercised by the president and the state bureaucracy (Eke 2000).

Ghana: Liberal Democracy

Contrast this situation with the multiparty elections held in Ghana just a few months later. The simultaneous presidential and parliamentary elections on 7, December 2008 were closely fought between the major parties, and the contest was largely peaceful, free, and fair. Parties mobilized supporters through party rallies and local canvassing, with news coverage reflecting diverse views and perspectives. After the event, and despite some tensions, the EU Election Observation Mission reported that the elections were conducted in an "open, transparent and competitive environment" respecting the right to stand for election and to vote, with widespread freedoms of assembly, expression, and movement.[5] The outcome was even more remarkable in a continent where experiments with democracy have too often failed (Bratton and Van de Walle 1997; Lindberg 2006).

The dangers of military coups remain real. The existence of predominant parties means that peaceful rotations of power from the government to opposition parties are relatively rare. But in Ghana, democratic processes triumphed, as the governing New Patriotic Party (NPP) stepped down after two terms in office, and the opposition National Democratic Congress (NDC) came peacefully to power. On the 2008 Freedom House measures, Ghana for the first time received the highest ratings – equivalent to those of Costa Rica, Greece, or Japan.[6]

A half-century ago Ghana was the first African state to achieve independence following colonial rule. In April 1992 a constitution allowing for a multiparty system was approved in a referendum, ushering in a sustained period of democracy. Presidential elections are held using the two-round majoritarian system, while the 230 members of parliament are elected for a four-year term in single-member constituencies using a first-past-the-post electoral system. The two largest political parties have both enjoyed two consecutive terms in presidential office and majorities in parliament – the NDC from 1992 to 2000 and the NPP from 2000 to 2008. In December 2000, John Kufuor was elected president, succeeding Jerry Rawlings in a peaceful transition of power (Aye 2000). Re-elected in 2004, President Kufuor stepped down voluntarily four years later, observing the constitutional two-term limit.

The 2008 campaign environment was lively and the parties canvassed voters door-to-door, holding a series of peaceful local rallies and town-hall meetings across Ghana, with the presidential candidates of the NPP and NDC touring the country. The parties published detailed policy manifestos. A series of independent polls were published in the media. Debates between the presidential candidates of the four parties with parliamentary representation were broadcast live via the major media outlets. Public and private sector broadcasting channels offered extensive news reporting about the campaign, and newspapers provided a diverse range of views and covered all of the major events organized by the parties during the campaign. The first round of the presidential contest ended on a knife-edge; the popular vote was evenly divided between the NPP candidate – Nana Akufo Addo – who received 49.1% of the vote and the NDC candidate – John Atta Mills – with 47.9%. As no single candidate gained an absolute majority, the outcome was decided by the second round contest between the two leading candidates. This round saw an extremely close contest where Atta Mills won a slender lead (50.2%) over the governing party's Akufo-Addo (49.8%). The parliamentary elections, held under plurality single member rules, proved equally competitive. The result saw the governing NPP fall to 107 parliamentary seats with 49% of the popular vote. It was overtaken in a tight race by the NDC, gaining 114 seats, with 47% of the national popular vote. Candidates of two minor parties and four independents were also returned as members of parliament.

Electoral observers and party agents were able to observe all stages of polling, vote counting, and aggregation. Disputes followed the second round of presidential voting, and tensions rose in the tight contest with some slight delays in announcing the vote, but these were resolved peacefully. The governing NPP stood down and President Atta Mills moved into Government House. The outcome is all the more remarkable because Ghana lacks many of the social and economic conditions which are commonly associated with stable democracies, and has many long-standing ethnic and religious divisions. Ghana is also one of the poorest countries in the world. One-third of the population lives below $1.25 a day.[7] Yet overall the Ghanaian elections were judged by both domestic and international observers to be a considerable success, another largely orderly and peaceful contest further consolidating Ghana's successive steps towards sustainable *liberal democracy*.

Venezuela: Electoral Democracy

Somewhere in between these two starkly contrasting examples of the differing contexts in which elections take place we find a country such as Venezuela. On 3 December 2006 Hugo Chavez was re-elected as president, receiving 63% of the vote. Turnout was a healthy 75% of the electorate. But all is not well with democracy in Venezuela. In 2007, Venezuelan authorities shut down the popular television station RCTV, generating student-led protests that continued for some months. However, when President Chavez tried to push through an extensive revision of the constitution that would have both consolidated and extended his power, voters narrowly rejected it in a referendum. Thus, Venezuelans in recent years have used the democratic institutions available to them to both support and constrain Chavez in varying degrees. The Freedom House ratings of Venezuela on the political rights and civil liberties indices, falling midway between those recorded by Belarus and Ghana, reflect this ambiguity. Venezuela is, in its terminology, "partly free" (Freedom House 2009).

Chavez came to power in December 1998, when he ran a populist-style anti-corruption campaign, using his candidacy to attack the entrenched political elites, and won the presidency democratically with 56% of the vote. Soon after his election, he embarked on a broad program of social, political, and economic change which he termed a "Bolivarian revolution" after the nineteenth-century liberator Simón de Bolivar. Drawing upon the country's burgeoning oil revenues, he introduced health care and literacy programs, as well as state subsidies for various consumer staples. A Constituent Assembly dominated by Chavez's Fifth Republic Movement (MVR) drafted a new constitution that strengthened the presidency and created a new unicameral National Assembly. Voters approved the new constitution in a December 1999 referendum with a 72% Yes vote. Following the adoption of the new constitution, the old bicameral Congress and the Supreme Court were dismissed, and new national elections were held in May 2000. Although Chavez was re-elected president (to a six-year term under the new constitution), with 60% of the vote, opposition parties won most of the country's governorships, about half of the mayoralties, and a significant share of National Assembly seats.

Following a failed coup attempt in 2002, Chavez moved swiftly to regain control of the military, dismissing dozens of generals and installing his own supporters in key positions. A short time later, a general strike that lasted 62 days increased the atmosphere of political instability. Anti-Chavez groups continued their agitation against the president and his controversial new regime. In addition to providing for a longer presidential term (but with a two-term limit), the new constitution also introduced a provision for recall. Opposition groups were quick to make use of this new provision, garnering more than the minimum 2.4 million signatures needed to initiate a recall referendum. Following a contentious campaign, Chavez easily survived the recall attempt. However, the referendum outcome did not put an end to the disputed nature of democracy in Venezuela. In the 2005 National Assembly elections, the main opposition parties, alleging irregularities in election administration and vote counting, staged a boycott of the election, allowing Chavez's MVR to obtain 116 of the 167 seats in the National Assembly. With only 25% turnout, opposition groups claimed that the elections demonstrated a "lack of legitimacy" in Chavez's government. However, Chavez himself was re-elected in the presidential election a year later with 63% of the vote and a reported turnout of 75%. Subsequently, in February 2009, another referendum was narrowly passed that abolished term limits for the president and other elected officials. The rejection by voters of Chavez's boldest attempt to consolidate both his power and his revolutionary social and economic agenda – the 2007 constitutional referendum – and the narrowness of the referendum win in 2009, show that democracy is more than alive in Venezuela, if not in the best of health. The fierce battles between Chavez and his opponents have been fought at least as much at the ballot box as in the streets or with the military. Venezuela is clearly an *electoral democracy*, but opponents of the regime operate under very difficult conditions. Voting in the 2006 presidential election was generally considered free and fair, but Chavez's use of state resources conferred a massive advantage in television exposure, and the promotion of social and infrastructure projects often blurred the line between his official role and his electoral campaign. It is not surprising that it has proven difficult, both for us and for other observers of elections, to decide how to categorize Venezuela in any comparative analysis of electoral democracies.

The Role of Elections

Multiparty elections following legal procedures are universally regarded as an essential institution of any democratic state, necessary but not in themselves sufficient for citizens to exercise power over their leaders. In the Schumpeterian tradition, the essence of democratic governance is, at a minimum, the competitive struggle for the people's vote (Schumpeter 1950). This idea continues to resonate widely today, leading researchers to continue to define democratic regimes as those cases where, if the governing party loses the popular vote, it abides by the rules and leaves office (Przeworski et al. 2000). But the differing outcomes and meaning of elections in Belarus, Venezuela, and Ghana raise many questions for understanding the not-so-simple relationship between elections and democratic governance. These contrasting cases highlight the importance and the complexity of the many issues regarding elections discussed throughout this volume. Before it is possible to evaluate with any confidence whether electoral contests in any country meet the requirements to qualify as genuinely "democratic," observers need to consider a series of detailed questions. Evaluations of the democratic quality of elections require difficult judgments about a wide range of practices. In particular, do the type of electoral system and administrative procedures strengthen electoral choice, fair outcomes, and effective party competition? What is the role of party systems and legal regulations in constraining and channeling the range of choices available at the ballot box? Do laws regulating campaign funding, advertising, and the mass media facilitate a genuinely level playing field and fair competition for all contestants? Who participates in parties and campaigns, who is excluded, and what are the deep drivers of electoral turnout? What are the major channels of information for citizens, including interpersonal and mass communications? The closure of a TV station in Venezuela clearly tells us something about the present state of democracy in that country. But so does the rejection by voters of the president's proposed new constitution. What laws regulate ballot access, including the selection and nomination process? Are candidates drawn from a diversity of social sectors, including women and ethnic minorities? Do parties and candidates offer a genuine choice of issues, platforms, and ideologies, and, in explaining the outcome, how did these factors shape voters' choices? How significant is the appeal of party leaders, and is this important for voting behavior, even in parliamentary systems? Does government performance matter for electoral outcomes, especially their handling of the economy? And lastly, what are the broader consequences of elections, both for democracy and for autocracy? Subsequent chapters will consider these sorts of complex issues and many more.

In the past, the assumption that multiparty elections are the foundation of democratic states was often treated as relatively unproblematic. This practice was particularly common when the study of elections and voting behavior was largely restricted to a limited number of Anglo-American and European countries. In these countries, democratic institutions typically evolved over many decades, or even over centuries. National election studies, based on surveys of the electorate, facilitating the systematic analysis of voting behavior, started in the United States in 1948. Subsequent decades saw a series of national election studies gradually develop in many other Anglo-American, Nordic, and European democracies (Thomassen 1994). The shared theoretical frameworks that anchor the sub-field of elections and voting behavior today are still derived from the classic studies of the 1950s and 1960s. The contemporary literature continues to build upon the foundations of the social psychological Michigan tradition established by *The American Voter* (Campbell et al. 1960), the structural approach to European voting behavior and party systems founded by Seymour Martin Lipset and Stein Rokkan (1967), and the rational choice perspective shaped by Anthony Downs (1957). The conventional approach to understanding the social and partisan roots of voting decisions, drawing upon these rich and deep intellectual roots, has been applied subsequently to a far wider range of contexts in recent decades, following the diffusion of national election surveys and public opinion polls to many other countries around the world. For example, today the Comparative Study of Electoral Systems (CSES) links together a network of national election studies in more than 50 countries, including Central and Eastern Europe, Latin America, Asia and Africa, as well as North America. The modern research literature seeks to test how far classical theories continue to apply in explaining voting behavior today. But, as the number of different electoral contexts has multiplied, understanding voting behavior and elections under conditions of restricted competition has become increasingly important, in part due to contemporary developments in many nations where democratic practices are still relatively new.

The Ghanaian case exemplifies the phenomenon of third-wave "*liberal democracies*," which is much discussed in the literature on democratic transitions.[8] Since the early 1990s, a series of elections held in this country have met international standards, and Ghana has made considerable progress in building the institutional capacity and effectiveness of other institutions of liberal democracy, including strengthening parliament, the judiciary, and public sector bureaucracy, as well as human rights, political parties, and civil society organizations (Boafo-Arthur 2007). Despite major challenges of development and deep-rooted poverty, and the existence of regional conflicts that occasionally spill across national borders, Ghana today can be regarded as one of the most successful third-wave liberal democracies in sub-Saharan Africa.

By contrast, Belarus exemplifies the phenomenon of "*electoral autocracy*"– countries that go through the formal rituals of voting, campaigns, and multiparty elections, but where such contests serve primarily to legitimate and reinforce the power of the ruling authorities. A series of constrained elections may provide opportunities for mobilizing civil society and strengthening opposition forces, although alternatively they may also demoralize and weaken reform movements, deflecting international and domestic pressures for regime change (Lindberg 2006). We regard the Belarus election as an egregious example of "electoral autocracy," but it is far from unique (Carothers 2002; Diamond 2002; Levitsky and Way 2002; Way and Levitsky 2006; Zakaria 1997). We could as easily cite cases such as Egypt, Gabon, or Kazakhstan – countries that regularly hold elections but in which the electoral process clearly does not determine who holds the real power. Venezuela is likewise not a unique case, but its complexity makes all of the categorizations discussed here more problematic. There are many other countries – Lebanon, Uganda, or Sri Lanka, for example – in which elections *can* provide a meaningful avenue of political participation but which cannot be classified as liberal democracies because some of the essential elements are missing or underdeveloped.

Classifying Elections as Instruments of Democracy

The contrasts between Belarus, Ghana, and Venezuela illustrate some of the major contemporary challenges to programs that advocate elections as the primary tool for strengthening democratic governance. Although widely regarded as essential institutions for any democratic state, it is far from the case that the existence of periodic multiparty elections *per se* is sufficient to guarantee democracy. Today few states are governed by absolute monarchies or by military juntas without the fig-leaf of a civilian executive; instead nearly all autocracies have learned to use the façade of elections as a way to legitimate ruling elites in the eyes of the international community. Elections, or the promise to hold them in the near future, may provide opportunities for mobilizing opposition forces, but they can also help to contain or suppress popular dissent at home.

What does this imply for this book, focusing on understanding elections and voting in *democratic* states? One consequence is that considerable care is needed to conceptualize and define the most appropriate universe of democratic elections prior to comparison. Before proceeding to examine the evidence, the notion of "democratic" elections, as well as the most appropriate operational measures of this concept, need to be considered and unpacked (Bollen 1990; Munck and Verkuilen 2002a, 2002b). What normative concepts of "democracy" underline alternative empirical indicators of democratic elections? Is it best to adopt a minimalist approach by selecting a few key indicators of democratic elections or is it preferable to provide a more comprehensive set of benchmarks? When operationalizing the concept of democratic elections, should our indicators be continuous, implying subtle gradations in levels of democratization? Or should they be categorical, suggesting that elections need to cross a specific threshold, such as holding a series of competitive multiparty contests, after which they can then be considered "democratic" (Collier and Adcock 1999; Elkins 2000)? Should the evidence for classifying democratic elections rest on observable regularities from "objective" data, such as official levels of voter turnout, the frequency of national votes, or the number of parties contesting legislative seats? Or should such benchmarks be supplemented by "subjective" evaluations, exemplified by the expert judgments used by Freedom House (or other similar agencies) to evaluate conditions of political rights and civil liberties? What are the major sources of random and non-random measurement error arising from each of these decisions that could potentially generate misleading comparisons? Multiple approaches to measuring democratic regimes and democratic elections exist in the literature and these broadly divide into either *minimalist* or *maximalist* conceptualizations, each with its own strengths and weaknesses.

Minimalist measures of democracy focus attention upon just one or two key benchmarks, notably by concentrating on the rules governing party competition for government office. In the well-known Schumpeterian conception, democracy is seen to exist in the competitive struggle for the people's vote (Schumpeter 1950). Building upon this tradition, Przeworski et al. (2000) argue that democratic states can be defined as those providing regular electoral opportunities for removing those in power (see also Cheibub and Gandhi 2004). This implies that an opposition party has to have some chance of winning elected office as a result of popular elections and there must be some uncertainty about the outcome, so that the incumbent party could conceivably lose power. If the incumbent party loses, there has to be the assurance that they will leave office and that the winning party will succeed them. Through this mechanism, governing parties can be held accountable for their actions and, if they fail to prove responsive to public concerns, they likewise face a realistic chance of being replaced in a regular and orderly constitutional process. Following this conceptualization, Przeworksi et al. classified all states from 1950 to 1990 as either a democracy or an autocracy according to several basic institutional rules.[9] Cheibub and Ghandi (2004) updated the series to 2000. This process is also easily replicable from published sources, allowing the dataset to be extended by other scholars to test their key findings in other contexts and time periods. The advantages of reducing the potential errors that arise from inconsistency and the misclassification of democratic elections are thought to outweigh the potential limitations of minimalist definitions.

The most commonly acknowledged danger of minimalist approaches is leaving out certain important dimensions of democracy which are included in more comprehensive measures. In the Belarus case, for example, the first-ever multiparty contests for the presidency occurred in 1994, where Lukashenko won with 80% of the vote. This outcome met the criteria of a peaceful transition following the electoral loss of the governing party or candidate. Since then, however, a series of legal multiparty elections have been won by Lukashenko in contests that can hardly be regarded as genuinely competitive elections. Belarus is far from alone in this regard. For example, Russia had a peaceful presidential transition of power from Boris Yeltsin to Vladimir Putin in 1999, followed by the subsequent shift in May 2008 from Putin to Dmitry Medvedev. But there are serious doubts on how well contemporary Russia meets the condition of democratic multiparty competition, in part because of imbalanced television coverage of parties during election campaigns and other constraints arising from a hegemonic party system and fragmented opposition (Colton and McCaul 2003). According to the strict minimalist definitions proposed by Przeworski et al., Russia should be classified today as a democratic regime, as many parties and candidates have contested office, and the outcome of elections has seen a peaceful and legal transition of executive officeholders. But this interpretation violates broader notions of the multiple conditions required for democratic and competitive elections.

A Typology of Electoral Regimes

The cases we have highlighted emphasize the need to think clearly when generalizing about elections and voting behavior among a wide variety of institutional contexts and types of societies. The common colloquial use of terms such as "transitional regimes," "consolidating democracies," or even the classification of "newer democracies," often turns out to be remarkably slippery and complicated in practice (Armony and Schamis 2005). Is the fact that periodic multiparty elections are now held in Belarus, Russia, and Ukraine, indicative of a democratic spring? Are such regimes seen as still in the process of "transitioning" towards democracy nearly two decades after the fall of the Berlin Wall? A clear analytical typology can help guide us here, sorting out different categories of regimes, each with divergent consequences for democratic governance. Figure 1.1 illustrates a proposed sequential classification of states used for the comparative framework in this book, employing a relatively simple and unambiguous decision-rule to help guide each stage of the process. This process helps to categorize states across a continuum from the most autocratic to the most democratic, while also facilitating the comparison of trends over time, and the use of progressively narrower and more restrictive notions of democracy.

Step 1: Is the territory an independent nation-state?
    The first and most basic distinction concerns the focus on comparing the world's 199 independent nation-states. This sets aside processes of

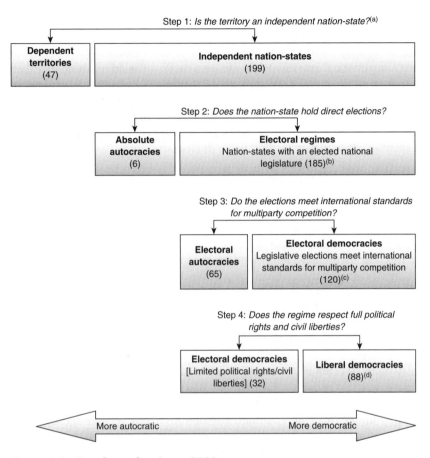

Figure 1.1   Typology of regimes, 2009

Notes: The classification of countries worldwide as of 1 January 2009 is operationalized as follows:

(a) The number of countries is defined by those territorial units recognized by the International Organization for Standardization (ISO-3166); www.iso.org/iso/country_codes. htm. "Independent nation-states" are classified as all member states recognized by the United Nations; www.un.org/members/list.shtml

(b) Nation-states with a functioning elected national parliament, as classified by Banks CNTS dataset, 1815–2007. We include here 191 cases on which there is sufficient current information and stability to make such a classification.

(c) "Electoral democracies" are states that the 2009 Freedom House *Freedom Around the World* (2009) survey classifies as those that hold elections with multiparty competition, a universal adult franchise, regularly contested and reasonably free and fair elections, a and open political campaigning. Freedom House collected data on 193 countries in its 2009 report.

(d) "Liberal democracies" are electoral democracies which the 2009 Freedom House *Freedom Around the World* survey classifies as "free" in terms of a wide range of political rights and civil liberties.

governance in almost 50 dependent territories and disputed regions which as of early 2009 had not yet achieved the status of becoming recognized by the international community as independent member states of the UN, including controversial cases which are in the process of seeking statehood, such as Kosovo, Kashmir, Kurdistan, the Palestinian Authority administered territories, and Tibet. All of these territories are important politically, and electoral contests within them have occasionally played a critical role, such as the Palestinian elections in 2006. But legally recognized statehood is an essential precondition for building a democratic state.

Step 2: Does the nation-state hold direct elections?

Independent nation-states can be further sub-divided into "electoral regimes" which periodically hold direct contests for the lower house of the national legislature and for executive office in presidential systems, and "absolute autocracies," which do not. The global spread of electoral regimes around the world has been extraordinary; in recent years more states worldwide have held elections than ever before.[10] If we compare all countries around the globe in early 2009, only six contemporary independent nation-states (see Table 1.1) continue to lack an elected parliament because they are headed by absolute rulers with appointed consultative assemblies.[11] It remains more difficult to clarify a few other residual cases where there is an elected parliamentary body specified in the constitution but the legislature has been "temporarily" suspended, whether by the military junta (Myanmar), or during conflict in fragile states (Somalia, Guinea, and Eritrea). Countries such as Bangladesh and Thailand, which have recently restored elected parliaments after a period of suspension, could qualify under this rule. It should be noted that this second decision-rule does not specify the degree of party competition; whether the elections allow voters to choose candidates from only one party (as in China and Cuba), or whether they have a genuine choice of multiparty candidates. Instead the rule emphasizes the prior condition of whether *any* bodies are elected or else filled by appointment, inheritance or patronage.

Step 3: Do the elections meet international standards for multiparty competition?

This third step, concerning whether there are effective conditions for multiparty competition in any elections, dividing electoral regimes into electoral autocracies and electoral democracies, requires more complex and subtle judgments. "Electoral autocracies" are understood here as regimes holding elections that fail to meet international standards, especially the need for multiparty competition, universal adult franchise, regular free and fair contests, and open political campaigning. One-party states that hold elections for the national legislature but have constitutional or legal bans on parties from organizing and from contesting elections clearly fail this criterion. In some cases, a limited degree of electoral choice is maintained where individual candidates from within the same party run for office, as exemplified by local elections among alternative Communist candidates in

China (Manion 1996), or among parliamentary candidates in Iran, all of whom must be approved by the ruling Guardian Council in order to be eligible to run. But, in general, the presence of competition from more than one party is widely regarded as essential for genuine electoral choice and democratic contestation; only parties can present voters with a choice of leadership teams and programs representing a coherent set of policies, and thus provide collective responsibility. As Schattschneider (1942) claimed, modern representative democracy is unworkable without political parties. But formal constitutional or legal opportunities for party competition do not, by themselves, guarantee *de facto* conditions of multiparty competition. Electoral autocracies typically use the façade of multiparty contests to legitimate their rule, while restricting opposition rights and activity.

International standards for elections have been debated and established by multilateral bodies, drawing upon core documents such as the 1948 Declaration of Human Rights and related internationally agreed conventions. These standards recognize that multiparty elections require, at a minimum, that opposition parties can appeal freely and fairly for the people's vote, without fear of legal restrictions on ballot access, overt campaign media bias, vote-rigging, or outright voter intimidation, manipulation and fraud. International standards also specify certain conditions for the role of election management bodies, voter registration processes, ballot access, election campaigns, media access, funding, balloting, vote counting, the role of election observers, and processes of dispute resolution (International IDEA 2002). According to these criteria, the number of electoral autocracies has expanded in recent years. Electoral contests with restricted multiparty competition have been adopted in some cases in response to international or domestic pressures, but this has not generally produced any effective challenge to autocratic rule.

Step 4: Does the regime respect a wide range of political rights and civil liberties?

Many electoral democracies holding periodic multiparty contests still continue to lack many basic human rights and fundamental freedoms. Hence electoral democracies can be further sub-divided into "liberal democracies," which respect the full panoply of civil liberties and political rights, and others, which do not, or do so only conditionally. The notion of "liberal democracy" has been most clearly articulated by Robert Dahl (1989), who argued that this type of regime is characterized by two main attributes – contestation and participation. In practice, to ensure that electoral competition is meaningful, liberal democracies allow freedom of expression, the availability of alternative sources of information (freedom of the media), and associational autonomy (freedom to organize political parties, interest groups, and social movements).

One of the best-known measures of liberal democracy, and one of the most widely used in the comparative literature, is the Gastil index of civil liberties and political rights produced annually by Freedom House. The measure has been widely employed by policymakers, and it has also been used by many comparative scholars (Barro 1999; Diamond 1996; Inglehart and Wlezien 2005). Freedom House, an independent think-tank based in the United States, first began to assess political trends regarding freedom of political expression in the 1950s with the results published as the *Balance Sheet of Freedom*. In 1972, Freedom House launched a new, more comprehensive annual study called *Freedom in the World*. Raymond Gastil developed the survey's methodology, which assigned ratings of their political rights and civil liberties for each independent nation-state (as well as for dependent territories). The survey continued to be produced by Gastil until 1989, when a larger team of in-house survey analysts was established. Subsequent editions of the survey have followed essentially the same format although more details have recently been released about the coding framework used for each assessment. We have employed the Freedom House measures as a means of selecting countries for analysis in all three editions of *Comparing Democracies*.

The index monitors the existence of political rights in terms of electoral processes, political pluralism, and the functioning of government. Civil liberties are defined by the existence of freedom of speech and association, rule of law, and personal rights. The Freedom House research team draws upon multiple sources of information to develop their classifications based on a checklist of questions, including ten separate items monitoring the existence of political rights and 15 on civil liberties. These items assess the presence of institutional checks and balances constraining the executive through the existence of a representative and inclusive legislature, an independent judiciary implementing the rule of law, and the existence of political rights and civil liberties, including participation by minorities, and the presence of free and fair election laws (Collier and Adcock 1999). Each item is allocated a score from 0 to 4 and each is given equal weight when aggregated. The raw scores for each country are then converted into a 7-point scale of political rights and a 7-point scale for civil liberties, and in turn these are collapsed to categorize each regime worldwide as either "free," "partly free," or "not free." The emphasis of this measure on a wide range of civil liberties, rights, and freedoms means that it most closely reflects notions of liberal democracy. At the same time, the process of classification involves more "subjective" evaluations than previous steps in this process, providing more detailed information but with some loss of replicability. The index also has the advantage of providing comprehensive coverage of nation-states and independent territories worldwide, as well as establishing a long time-series of observations conducted annually since 1972. Roughly two-thirds (120) of all electoral regimes were classified by Freedom House in 2009 as "electoral democracies," defined as those with multiparty competition, universal adult franchise, regular free and fair contests, and open political campaigning (Figure 1.1) (Freedom House 2009). The remaining 65 states were categorized as "electoral autocracies," failing to meet these interntional standards, exemplified by recent contests in Egypt, Uzbekistan, Cambodia, or Uganda, all of which use multiparty competitive elections for legislative and executive offices as a façade to legitimate autocratic regimes. Of those 120 "electoral democracies," Freedom House (2009) estimates that 88 nations can presently be classified as "liberal democracies" (categorized by the organization as "free," and rated as 3 or below on their 7-point scale of political rights and civil liberties). Thirty-four countries remain in the "grey zone" described earlier, including countries as diverse as Venezuela, Malaysia, and Nigeria. This represents a remarkable advance during the third wave era; compared with the situation in the early-1970s, the number of liberal democracies has doubled. Nevertheless progress has recently slowed and Freedom House now estimates that the balance of regime types has largely stabilized during the last decade.

TABLE 1.1 Classification of regimes, 2009, according to categories in Figure 1.1

Absolute autocracies (n=6)

Korea (North)
Libya Arab Jamahiriy
Myanmar (Burma)
Oman
Qatar
Saudi Arabia

Electoral autocracies (n=65)

Afghanistan	Djibouti	Morocco
Algeria	Egypt	Nepal
Angola	Equatorial Guinea	Pakistan
Armenia	Eritrea	Rwanda
Azerbaijan	Ethiopia	Singapore
Bahrain	Fiji	Somalia
Bangladesh	Gabon	Sudan
Belarus	Gambia	Swaziland
Bhutan	Guinea	Syrian Arab Republic
Bosnia & Herzegovina	Guinea-Bissau	Tajikistan
Brunei Darussalam	Haiti	Tanzania
Burkina Faso	Iran	Togo
Burundi	Iraq	Tonga
Cambodia	Jordan	Tunisia
Cameroon	Kazakhstan	Turkmenistan
Central African Rep	Kuwait	Uganda
Chad	Kyrgyzstan	United Arab Emirates
China	Laos	Uzbekistan
Comoros	Lebanon	Vietnam
Congo, Republic of	Malaysia	Yemen
Cote D'Ivoire	Maldives	Zimbabwe
Cuba	Mauritania	

(Continued)

TABLE 1.1 (Continued)

Electoral democracies with limited political rights/civil liberties (n=32)

Albania	Nicaragua
Antigua & Barbuda	Niger
Bolivia	Nigeria
Colombia	Papua New Guinea
Congo, Democratic Republic	Paraguay
Ecuador	Philippines
Georgia	Russian Federation
Guatemala	Seychelles
Honduras	Sierra Leone
Kenya	Solomon Islands
Liberia	Sri Lanka
Macedonia	Thailand
Madagascar	Trinidad & Tobago
Malawi	Turkey
Moldova	Venezuela
Mozambique	Zambia

Liberal democracies (n=88)

Andorra	Guyana	Norway
Argentina	Hungary	Palau
Australia	Iceland	Panama
Austria	India	Peru
Bahamas	Indonesia	Poland
Barbados	Ireland	Portugal
Belgium	Israel	Romania
Belize	Italy	Samoa
Benin	Jamaica	San Marino
Botswana	Japan	São Tomé & Príncipe
Brazil	Kiribati	Senegal
Bulgaria	Korea (South)	Serbia
Canada	Latvia	Slovakia
Cape Verde	Lesotho	Slovenia
Chile	Liechtenstein	South Africa
Costa Rica	Lithuania	Spain
Croatia	Luxembourg	St Kitts & Nevis
Cyprus	Mali	St Lucia
Czech Republic	Malta	St Vincent & Grenadine
Denmark	Marshall Islands	Suriname
Dominica	Mauritius	Sweden
Dominican Republic	Mexico	Switzerland
El Salvador	Micronesia, Federated States	Taiwan
Estonia	Monaco	Tuvalu
Finland	Mongolia	Ukraine
France	Namibia	United Kingdom
Germany	Nauru	United States
Ghana	Netherlands	Uruguay
Greece	New Zealand	Vanuatu
Grenada		

The Changing Face of Global Democracy

To examine long-term trends more systematically, Figure 1.2 illustrates the classification of liberal democracies in 1975, representing the start of the "third" wave of democracy, compared with the contemporary situation in 2008. The Freedom House index of civil liberties and political rights has been standardized to a 100-point scale, for ease of comparison. Countries located in the top-right corner of the scatter-gram have been rated as liberal democracies throughout this era, including many post-industrial economies such as Belgium, France, Ireland, and Australia, as well as some developing countries such as Trinidad & Tobago, India, Botswana, and Barbados. Other states falling into the bottom-left quadrant are consistent autocracies, with a diverse range of rulers, including Cuba under Presidents Fidel and Raul Castro, Libya under Colonel Maummar al-Gaddafi, Saudi Arabia under the House of Saud, and Communist China. Some autocracies are middle-income industrialized and oil-rich economies, while others are low-income developing nations, including many nations in sub-Saharan Africa. What is also apparent from the figure is the sheer number of states that have become far more democratic during the third-wave era, located in the top-left corner. Many of these are Latin American and Central European middle-income states, with these developments exemplified most dramatically by the changes registered in Lithuania, Estonia, the Czech Republic, Romania, South Korea, Panama, and Mongolia, as well as the case of Ghana already discussed. Lastly there are cases of reversal, often explained by particular events in each country, such as military coups occurring in Fiji, The Gambia, and Thailand, or the erosion of civil liberties in Venezuela and Sri Lanka.

To focus on shorter-term changes, we can follow a similar procedure to look at the contrasts between liberal democracy in 2000 and 2008, as illustrated in Figure 1.3. Here, as might be expected, the pattern shows far less dramatic change. During this period, there are a few cases of dramatic reversals falling underneath the diagonal line, notably the temporary suspension of parliament by the military coup in Thailand, and the more gradual deterioration in human rights in several other countries, such as Russia, Somalia, Zimbabwe, and Nigeria. But on balance far more countries fall above than below the diagonal line, suggesting gradually strengthening political rights and civil liberties during this period, notably in Liberia following the election of President Ellen Johnson-Sirleaf, in Ukraine following the "orange" revolution, and in Indonesia after the death of Suharto. On balance it seems too early to predict a new "reverse" wave or "democratic recession" as some observers suggest, but the overall pattern of both advances and reversals suggests that democratic governance today faces serious challenges (Diamond 2008; Puddington

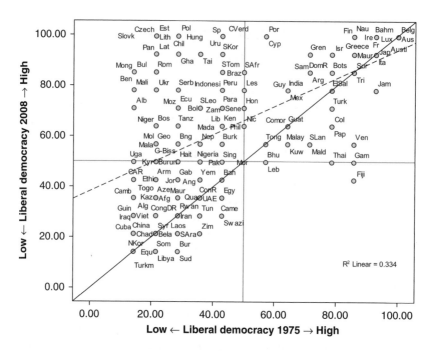

Figure 1.2   Long-term change in liberal democracy, 1975–2008

Notes: Liberal democracy is measured by the Freedom House Gastil 7-point index of political rights and civil liberties standardized to 100 points, where high = more democratic. The dotted line represents the regression across all observations.

Source: Calculated from Freedom House www.freedomhouse.org

2008). Regime transitions are triggered for diverse and highly contingent reasons; whether exemplified in the last few years by military coups suspending democratically elected governments (as in Pakistan, Thailand, and Mauritania); a sustained push-back by the executive gradually restricting human rights, opposition movements, and press freedoms (as in Putin's Russia); a close election result triggering a sudden outbreak of ethnic conflict and destabilizing violence (as in Kenya); or populist movements expanding the power of the executive (as in Chavez's Venezuela). Moreover, the current global economic recession, enduring problems of human development and poverty, and ongoing issues of violent conflict and the difficulties of peace-building in fragile states, may deepen some of these challenges. In today's circumstances, it has become increasingly important to understand the conditions that underpin the advance of electoral and liberal democracies, and the underlying factors that help to produce elections that can function as effective agents of democracy and democratization.

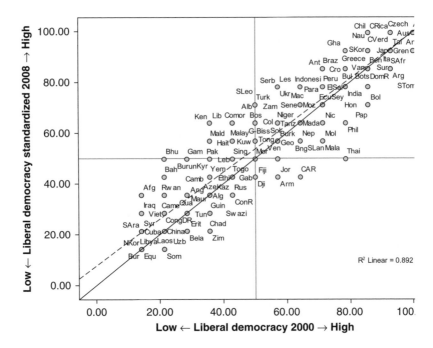

Figure 1.3   Short-term change in liberal democracy, 2000–2008

Notes: Liberal democracy is measured by the Freedom House Gastil 7-point index of political rights and civil liberties standardized to 100 points, where high = more democratic.

Source: Calculated from Freedom House www.freedomhouse.org

What is New in this Edition?

In the first edition of *Comparing Democracies* (published in 1996) we selected 53 countries for analysis based on the Freedom House ratings at that time and a minimum population of 3 million people. In this edition of the book we range more widely. Many of the world's smaller democracies have much to teach us about the role of elections in different types of political settings. Further, as we have argued in this chapter, democracy is a complex concept, and elements of it may survive and develop even in hostile political environments. Divisions of the world into categories of "large" and "small" or "democratic" and "authoritarian" no longer capture the many nuances of democratic practice found in the world of the twenty-first century. Still, it is worthwhile to revisit our original categorizations, as these also help to document the ways in which the political world has changed over the past two decades. What we find is that, particularly in those countries that do not have a long and well-established tradition of democratic practice, there is variation in both the political rights and civil liberties measures. In a few instances, the variation is extreme, due either to the outright suspension of democracy (Bangladesh, Thailand, Pakistan), or to the gradual erosion of civil liberties and/or political rights (Nepal, Russia, Venezuela). In a number of countries democracy has strengthened over this period (Brazil, Bulgaria, Chile, Turkey, Taiwan, Uruguay, India), while in others it has been weakened. Eight of the 53 countries considered in the first edition of *Comparing Democracies* could not be included on a comparable list today, due to the changes that have occurred.[12] Most encouragingly, there are many countries that *would* be included in such a list today that could not have been in 1996. Among these are Croatia, Ghana, Indonesia, Peru, and Senegal.

Of course, the study of elections is not only about classifications regarding the strength or weakness of democracy, or the role of elections in promoting or sustaining democracy. There are many topics of research that pertain to democracies at any stage of development that are important to consider in some depth. Institutional arrangements determine the manner in which elections are structured and the processes that take place within the framework of those institutions. We address issues related to this topic in the first half of this book. The choices that countries make with respect to electoral systems determine the types of choices that are available to voters when they cast their ballots in an election. If the choice is among parliamentary candidates, as in British-style first-past-the-post electoral systems, voters will have to choose between local candidates who are often surrogates for their parties or leaders; where the choice is between lists of candidates representing their parties, as in proportional systems, the choices presented to the voters are quite different. Elisabeth Carter and David Farrell, who have written extensively on electoral systems, explore these questions in Chapter 2 of this volume.

In Chapter 3 Susan Scarrow looks at the role of political parties and party systems, and the manner in which political parties structure voting choice and make it more meaningful for voters. Because political parties are an essential component of electoral democracy, the strength and stability of party systems remain a central concern in the process of democratic development. Ingrid van Biezen (Chapter 4) considers the financing of political parties and candidates, perhaps the least transparent of all political activities, and therefore one that has serious but often underappreciated implications for the sustainability of democracy. The question of how and why campaigns matter is addressed by Christopher Wlezien in Chapter 5. Campaigns convey the information to voters that they need in order to make informed decisions, but they do so in different ways, and the nature of campaigns has changed greatly with advancing technology. In Chapter 6 Claes de Vreese examines the role played by communications and media in election campaigns. We have noted in the earlier discussion the importance of the freedom of the mass media in determining the extent to which elections can affect the exercise of power in both new and more established democracies.

In the second section of the book, we turn our attention to public opinion and voting and the manner in which citizens make electoral decisions in a number of different institutional settings. Russell Dalton (Chapter 7) considers how social modernization and democratization transform the ideological basis of citizens' political orientations and affect partisan attitudes and voter choice. In Chapter 8 André Blais discusses political participation, both in the form of voter turnout and other mechanisms. Low and declining turnout has become a concern in many long-established democracies, and may also be of consequence in legitimizing democracy in new settings. Timothy Hellwig, in Chapter 9, examines the role that the economy may play in determining both voting choice and electoral outcomes. Might we expect that the current economic crisis will have consequences at the ballot box? In Chapter 10 Marian Sawer analyzes the increase of representation of women in many parliaments, and the implications of this trend for the effects that elections may have on public policy. The fact that women currently lead governments in Chile, Germany, and the Philippines, to mention only a few such instances, and occupy important cabinet positions in many other countries, raises a number of issues regarding the potential longer-term effects of the greater involvement of women in politics at all levels. Finally, in the concluding chapter of this volume, G. Bingham Powell returns to some of the themes addressed in this chapter. Can elections conducted in authoritarian states initiate a process of democratic change? What are the consequences of different types of electoral regimes for representation? For public policy? For the sustainability of liberal democracy?

This book is accompanied by a dedicated website (www.sagepub.co.uk. leduc3) that contains additional information on all of the topics addressed in this volume. Changing technology has meant that information on the ongoing conduct and outcomes of elections around the world is more readily kept current electronically than on the printed page. On the website will be found links to a number of sources that routinely collect and publish information on elections in most of the world's democracies. In addition, longer and more detailed versions of some of the tables in this volume are available on the website to accommodate those who may be seeking information on a larger set of countries than it is possible to include here. A dataset is also provided on the website that can be used to extend or test independently some of the arguments.

PART I
ELECTORAL INSTITUTIONS AND PROCESSES

2

Electoral Systems and Election Management

Elisabeth Carter and David M. Farrell

The *sine qua non* of representative democracies is a process of elections that is fair and competitive. This is the role of electoral institutions, which determine how elections are fought, how the act of voting results in the election of political representatives and the determination of which political leader (in a presidential system), or party or set of parties (in a parliamentary system), is to form the executive leadership for the next few years. Electoral institutions cover a multitude of responsibilities. This chapter deals with two: the electoral system, which is responsible for determining how the voting act translates into an election result; and election management bodies, providing the over-arching structure within which the electoral process occurs. We spend most time on the first of these issues, starting in the first section with a classification of the world's different electoral systems. This is followed by a review of the main political consequences of electoral systems. The third section deals with questions relating to electoral system design and reform. In the final section, our attention shifts to a focus on the issue of election management, with an overview of how this varies across our range of democracies.

Classifying Electoral Systems

The world of electoral systems is complex and becoming more so all the time.[1] The range of variations among the different electoral systems makes life quite difficult for the analyst seeking to produce an acceptable typology. One option might be simply to base a classification of the systems on their *outputs*, that is, with reference to the process of translating votes into seats where one distinguishes between those systems that have "proportional" outcomes and those with "non-proportional" outcomes. The essence of proportional systems is to ensure that the number of seats each party wins reflects as closely as possible the number of votes it received. In non-proportional systems, by contrast, greater importance is attached to ensuring that one party has a clear majority of seats over its competitors, thereby (hopefully) increasing the prospect of strong and stable government.

An alternative approach to classification – and the basis for most of the existing typologies – entails breaking the electoral system down into its component parts, focusing on the *mechanics* of how votes are translated into seats.[2] Douglas Rae (1967) was the first to distinguish three main components of an electoral system: "district magnitude," "electoral formula," and "ballot structure." District magnitude (M) refers to the size of the constituency (or "district"), measured in terms of the number of seats to be filled. For example, in the US and the UK, which both use the single member plurality system, each constituency elects just one legislator (M=1); by contrast, in Spain, which uses a list system of proportional representation, on average each region elects seven legislators (M=7).

The ballot structure determines how voters cast their votes. Here the common distinction is between *categorical* ballots, such as those used in the US or Brazil, where voters are given a simple either/or choice between the various candidates (in the US) or party lists (in Brazil) on the ballot paper, and *ordinal* ballots, such as in Ireland or Malta, where voters can vote for all the candidates, ranking them in order of preference. Finally, the electoral formula manages the translation of votes into seats. As we shall see, there is a large range of electoral formulas currently in operation (and theoretically a limitless supply of alternatives).

Having outlined the three main components of electoral systems, the next stage is to determine exactly how to use them in developing an appropriate classification of electoral systems. There has been a lot of discussion about the precise effects of the three components on the performance of electoral systems (Farrell 2001; Lijphart 1994). The general consensus is that district magnitude has the greatest effect on the overall proportionality of the result: the larger the district magnitude the more proportional the translation of votes to seats.[3] This might lead us to expect that a classification of electoral systems should base itself first and foremost on this component. However, most of the existing classifications tend to be based on the electoral formula first, only taking secondary account of the other features of electoral systems (Blais and Massicotte 2002; Bogdanor 1983).[4]

Plurality Systems

Table 2.1 provides some preliminary information on the electoral systems used for parliamentary elections around the world. One hundred and seventy-eight democracies are grouped according to the four main electoral formulas in use: plurality, majority, proportional, and mixed.[5] Starting with the plurality formula, of the main families of electoral systems dealt

TABLE 2.1 The world of electoral systems: legislative elections in the 2000s

	No. of cases	%	Prominent examples
Plurality formulas			
Single member plurality	36	20.2	United States, United Kingdom, India
Block	11	6.2	Lebanon, Kuwait
Single non-transferable vote	3	1.7	Afghanistan, Jordan
Majority formulas			
Runoff	20	11.2	France, Gabon
Alternative vote	4	2.2	Australia
Proportional formulas			
List	67	37.6	Russia, Spain, South Africa
Single transferable vote	2	1.1	Ireland, Malta
Mixed formulas			
Mixed-member proportional	9	5.1	Germany, New Zealand
Mixed-member majoritarian	26	14.6	South Korea, Japan
Total	178	99.9	

Source: www.sagepub.co.uk.leduc3

with in this chapter, the single member plurality system (SMP, often referred to as "first past the post") predominates in Anglo-Saxon democracies. This was one of the first electoral systems deployed in the emerging democracies of the late nineteenth and early twentieth centuries, and as Table 2.1 reveals, it is still one of the most popular electoral systems in use, with 20% of the world's democracies using it, including some of the largest in the world. Indeed, the case of India, with a population of just over one billion, is singularly responsible for the fact that the plurality system is used by a plurality of the world's voters (Farrell 2001).

A close relative of SMP is the block vote system, in which the plurality electoral formula is applied in multi-member districts. Much more common in the late nineteenth and early twentieth centuries, the block vote system was actually the progenitor of SMP (Carstairs 1980). One of its principal shortcomings is that it produces greater disproportionality than SMP systems (the rule in the case of disproportional systems is that as district magnitude increases so does the disproportionality of election outcomes), and this was one reason for the decision to move to single-member districts, though, today a sizeable number of countries (6%, including Kuwait, Lebanon, and the Philippines) continue to use the block vote system.

One way of reducing the disproportional tendencies of the block vote system while retaining multi-seat constituencies is to reduce the number of votes that a voter can cast.[6] In its generic form this system is known by the name "limited vote" and is used for upper house elections in Spain and also at sub-national level in some US states (Bowler, Donovan, and Brockington

2003). The objective behind the limited vote is simple: allowing the voter fewer votes than the number of seats to be filled reduces the chance of a large party having its full slate of candidates elected (a major problem with the block vote system) and increases the chance for candidates from smaller parties to pick up seats. As the vote becomes more limited (i.e., the number of votes voters have is reduced) the system becomes less disproportional. The limited vote variant in which voters are only able to express one vote in a multi-seat constituency is also referred to as the "single non-transferable vote" system (SNTV), a semi-proportional electoral system that was used in post-war Japan until its replacement by a mixed-member majoritarian system in the 1990s (Grofman et al. 1999). Today SNTV is used in Afghanistan, Jordan, and Vanuatu.

Majority Systems

Majority systems make up the second main set of electoral systems, and are used by 13% of the countries examined (see Table 2.1). Although less popular than the plurality systems, majority systems are used by two leading democracies – Australia and France. As the title suggests, the defining characteristic of these electoral systems is the use of a majority electoral formula in which, to get elected, a candidate needs a majority of the total vote. There are two main forms of majority electoral systems: the runoff systems (which, in turn, can be sub-divided) and the alternative vote. In the first part of the twentieth century a number of countries moved away from SMP to the runoff variant, the principal motivation being that elected politicians would have the support of more than half the electorate in their district. In runoff systems the means by which this is produced entails the holding of a second election, usually one or two weeks after the first. In majority runoff systems (such as those used for the election of the French president) only the candidate winning the most and the candidate winning the second most numbers of votes in the first round are permitted to go forward to the second round, thus ensuring a majority result. A variant of this, known as the runoff-plurality system, as used in French legislative elections, permits more than two candidates in the second round (by setting a vote threshold in the first round that more than two candidates are capable of surpassing) and therefore does not guarantee a majority result, though the very act of reducing the field of candidates in the second round does tend to produce a majority result more often than not. As we shall see, runoff systems are common in many former French colonies such as the Central African Republic or Vietnam; they have also achieved some prominence in former Soviet satellite states such as Turkmenistan and Uzbekistan. Less common than the runoff systems is the alternative vote system (AV) which is characteristic of Antipodean democracies, particularly Australia (for national and most statewide elections) where it goes by the name "preferential voting" (Farrell and McAllister 2006; Reilly 2001).[7] Designed as a "one-shot" variant of runoff, AV operates on the basis of a ballot structure that allows voters to rank order all candidates from all parties (1, 2, 3, etc.). All the number 1 votes are counted and if no candidate achieves an overall majority of the vote (50% +1) then the candidate with the fewest votes is eliminated from the race and their ballots are transferred to the remaining candidates based on the number 2 votes. This process continues until eventually one of the candidates emerges with an overall majority.

List systems

Set against plurality and majority electoral systems are three families of proportional systems: list, single transferable vote, and mixed-member proportional. What all three have in common is a district magnitude greater than 1. District magnitude matters significantly in determining the proportionality of the election result. In countries like the Netherlands, Israel, and Slovakia, where the whole country is treated as a single district, there is very high proportionality.[8] By contrast, elsewhere (for example in Ireland and Spain), the country is divided into a large number of small districts, each of which has low average district magnitudes. As a result we find lower levels of overall proportionality.

It is the combination of district magnitude and electoral formula that plays the greatest role in determining overall proportionality, and these are two of the main sources of variation in the list family of electoral systems. List electoral formulas come in a number of forms, but the basic point of distinction is between one set of formulas that determines seat allocation by subtraction, and another set which does so by division. The former is technically referred to as a "largest remainder" formula (in the US this is sometimes known as the Hamilton method) and operates with the use of an electoral quota. While, theoretically, numerous different quotas are available, the choice tends to boil down to two – Hare or Droop quotas. In largest remainder systems the counting process occurs in two rounds. First, parties with votes exceeding the quota are awarded seats, and the quota is subtracted from the total vote. In the second round, those parties left with the "largest remainder" of votes are awarded the remaining seats in order of vote size.[9] The Hare quota (votes/seats) produces slightly more proportional results than the Droop quota (votes/seats+1) because it uses a larger quota, thus reducing the importance of remainders (cf. Lijphart 1994).

List systems that operate with divisors are referred to technically as "highest average" systems. There are three types of highest average system in use: the d'Hondt method, which is by far the most common, the modified Sainte-Laguë method most associated with Scandinavian democracies (Denmark, Norway, and Sweden), and the pure Sainte-Laguë method (which was adopted by New Zealand for the list element of its new MMP electoral system). A highest average count occurs in a number of stages. First, the votes are sorted into piles for each of the parties. These totals are then divided by the relevant divisors (e.g., the d'Hondt divisors are 1, 2, 3, etc.) until all the seats have been allocated. The seats are awarded to those parties with the "highest averages" in order of vote size. The proportionality of the outcome is influenced by the type of divisors that are used. The d'Hondt divisors tend to produce the least proportional result overall. By contrast, the Sainte-Laguë divisors (1, 3, 5) produce the most proportional outcomes, indeed, so proportional that the Scandinavian countries modified the divisors and used 1.4 instead of 1 as the first, so as to temper some of the proportionality of pure Sainte-Laguë.

The Single Transferable Vote

The second main family of proportional systems – the single transferable vote (STV) – is one of the most unusual and least used. It is unique to Ireland and Malta, although it is also used for upper house elections in Australia as well as in most state elections across Australia (Bowler and Grofman 2000; Farrell and McAllister 2006). STV operates with relatively small multi-member electoral districts, and voters are invited to rank order all the candidates from all the parties that appear on the ballot paper (in Australia in order for the vote to be declared valid voters are required to rank order *all* the candidates). This ballot structure thus gives voters a maximum possible choice. An STV count occurs in a number of stages which means that unless computer counting is used (something that is starting to become more common) the count can take hours or even days to complete. After all the number 1 preference votes have been counted, the officials determine whether any of the candidates have amassed sufficient votes to surpass the Droop quota (which for STV is [votes/seats+1] +1). Any that have attained the quota are deemed elected. Attention then turns to the next stage of the count which either involves the transfer of the surplus votes (i.e., those votes that were over and above the number of votes required to equal the quota) of the winning candidates or – if no candidates were elected in the preceding stage of the count, or the size of the surplus vote of any victorious candidates is too small to make a difference to the result for the remaining candidates – the elimination of the candidates with the fewest votes and the transfer of those votes to those candidates still left in the race. The decision of which actual ballot papers to transfer to remaining candidates is determined by which candidates were ranked next on each ballot paper being transferred. This process of transferring surpluses or transferring the ballots of eliminated candidates continues until all the remaining seats have been filled by victorious candidates.

Mixed-Member Systems

Finally, we have the mixed-member systems, the first of which is unambiguously a proportional system – mixed-member proportional (MMP). Until relatively recently this electoral system was unique to Germany but in the past twenty years or so it has been adopted by seven other countries, including the interesting case of New Zealand which switched to MMP after a referendum process in the mid-1990s. As its title suggests, MMP is a mix of the SMP and list electoral systems, in which the list element of the election is used to balance or correct the disproportional tendencies of the SMP element. While this may sound simple enough in principle, it can actually be quite complex, and can also vary in its details from one country to the next (the most complex variant being that used in Hungary, see Benoit 2005).[10] It is best outlined by summarizing the German variant, which elects 50% of the Bundestag by SMP and the other 50% by list (largest remainder–Hare). The list result is used to correct proportionality imbalances resulting from the SMP result, and to ensure that the larger parties are not unduly rewarded by their ability to win more district seats. It is the mix of single-seat SMP districts electing geographically grounded "constituency politicians" together with multi-seat list districts producing proportional results (thus ensuring that smaller parties win seats) that causes some prominent scholars to question whether this electoral system may be "the best of both worlds" (Shugart and Wattenberg 2001).

The final electoral system to consider bears a large resemblance to the one just dealt with. Referred to as the "parallel" or mixed-member majoritarian (MMM) system, this electoral system (now used in Japan) has one significant difference from its MMP counterpart, as a result of which it is probably most accurately described as a "semi-proportional" electoral system. The key difference is that the proportional element of the system is not used to compensate for the disproportional result in the SMP element: in other words, the two parts of the election are treated as separate, parallel processes. MMM does allow small parties to gain representation but it nonetheless ensures that the larger parties win the lion's share of the seats in parliament and hence stand a greater chance of controlling the executive. MMM is the third most commonly used system around the world, and is far more common than MMP. That said, in both Russia and Ukraine the decision was recently made to drop MMM and move over to list PR.

Multi-tier Districting

MMP and MMM systems share the use of different tiers of representation – a set of single-seat SMP constituencies and a set of multi-seat regions or even one national list. But use of more than one tier of representation is by no means unique to the mixed-member systems. A number of list systems operate with two (in some instances, such as Hungary, even more) tiers of representation. The principal rationale flows from the impact that district magnitude has on proportionality. Using a second tier of representation – in which a certain number of parliamentary seats are determined at the higher tier level – facilitates greater proportionality without having overly large regions: it irons out any discrepancies at the constituency level and produces a result that is more proportional. The basic idea is that any remaining votes not yet used to fill seats at the lower tier are pooled and the distribution of the remaining seats is determined in the second tier. Multi-tier districting is common among largest remainder systems (such as Austria, Belgium, and Greece); it also tends to be used in highest-average modified Sainte-Laguë cases (e.g., Denmark, Norway, and Sweden). Consistent with the fact that the d'Hondt system is the least proportional of the list formulas, most of the countries using it do not bother with a second tier.[11]

Legal Thresholds

Multi-tier districting is not the only means of adding complexity to the process of electoral system design.[12] Electoral engineers can be extremely inventive in finding other ways of influencing proportionality. Prominent among these are legal thresholds, which are now used in the majority of list and mixed-member systems. A legal threshold is a minimum vote that a party is required to achieve before it is awarded parliamentary seats. It can be used to stop small parties from winning any parliamentary seats at all, or to limit the number of seats they do win.[13] Commonly such thresholds are set at about 3–5% of the national vote, though there are some extreme cases, such as Turkey which imposes a 10% threshold and Poland where the threshold is set at 7%. In some instances (as in Belgium and Spain) the threshold may be set at regional rather than national level. Thresholds are also sometimes set for coalitions as well as for individual parties. In the Czech Republic, for example, there is 5% threshold for individual parties, a 10% one for coalitions of two parties, a 15% one for coalitions of three parties, and a 20% one for coalitions of four parties or more.

Electoral System Consequences

Electoral systems have consequences for the political system, as will be demonstrated throughout this volume. The large literature on this (e.g., Cox 1997; Gallagher and Mitchell 2005; Katz 1997; Lijphart 1994; Norris 2004; Taagepera and Shugart 1989) has identified a number of consequences, among them the effects on proportionality, on numbers of parties, and on the representation of women and minorities.[14] In addition to these "systemic" effects, which are all related in some way to the proportionality profiles of electoral systems, there has also been an increasing interest in the "strategic" effects of electoral systems. We deal with each of these in turn.

Proportionality Effects

As electoral systems translate the number of votes won by parties into the number of seats they are awarded in parliament there is always an element of distortion. However, the magnitude of this distortion varies: while some electoral systems translate votes into seats in a relatively proportional fashion, others tend to do this in a disproportional way, with parties ending up with seat shares that are considerably higher or lower than their vote shares. We can examine just how proportional or disproportional different electoral systems are by making use of one of the various indices that have been developed for this very purpose, the most favored of which is the Gallagher index (1991). Table 2.2 focuses on a number of different countries, and (in the first column) reports the average disproportionality scores of national parliamentary elections held since 2000, with high scores indicating a large distortion between parties' vote shares and their seat shares.

It is immediately apparent from Table 2.2 that there is considerable variation in the proportionality profiles of the different systems. We can note, for example, that the average election outcome in the United Kingdom in this period was very disproportional, but that in South Africa there was hardly any distortion between the number of votes parties won and the number of seats they gained in parliament. However, rather than simply pick out individual countries, it is more interesting to see whether different *types* of electoral systems have distinct proportionality profiles, and we can do this by examining the average disproportionality score for each type of system (as reported in italics). This does, indeed, reveal discernible patterns: in general, STV and list PR systems tend to produce more proportional electoral outcomes, whereas the plurality and majority systems and MMM all give rise to less proportional outcomes. There are, however, cases that buck the trend. In Moldova results have been disproportional despite a list system being used. By contrast, in the US outcomes have been proportional in spite of SMP being in operation. These cases (and others) support the general finding that while electoral systems exert a major influence on the proportionality of the electoral outcome, they are not the only factors (e.g., Farrell 2001a; Lijphart 1994).

TABLE 2.2   Electoral system consequences: legislative elections in the 2000s

	Disproportionality	Effective number of parliamentary parties	Women legislators (%)
Single member plurality			
St Kitts & Nevis	**24.07**	1.98	6.7
Gambia	17.79	**1.21**	9.4
United Kingdom	17.25	2.32	19.5
Yemen	13.54	1.68	**0.3**
Canada	10.66	2.93	21.3
Tanzania	9.82	1.48	**30.4**
Ethiopia	7.66	**8.12**	21.9
India	4.53	6.52	11.6
United States	**2.43**	2.00	19.5
Average of all cases	*11.79*	*2.66*	*15.1*
	(N = 26)	*(N = 27)*	*(N = 29)*
Block vote			
Mauritius	**10.25**	1.99	17.1
Philippines	5.11	**3.17**	**20.5**
Mongolia	**2.67**	**1.79**	**6.6**
Average of all cases	*6.01*	*2.32*	*12.5*
	(N = 3)	*(N = 3)*	*(N = 7)*
Runoff			
France	**17.77**	**2.38**	16.7
Haiti	7.60	**8.58**	**4.1**
Kyrgyzstan	**5.69**	4.41	25.6
Average of all cases	*11.88*	*4.84*	*17.1*
	(N = 4)	*(N = 10)*	*(N = 17)*
Alternative vote			
Bhutan	**26.63**	**1.79**	2.7
Australia	9.41	2.39	**26.7**
Papua New Guinea	**7.92**	**16.42**	**0.9**
Average of all cases	*13.90*	*5.78*	*12.1*
	(N= 4)	*(N = 4)*	*(N = 4)*
List PR			
Moldova	**12.74**	2.08	21.8
Morocco	6.30	**9.75**	10.5
Argentina	4.99	6.49	40.0
Indonesia	4.45	7.07	**4.1**
Angola	4.30	**1.31**	15.0
Israel	2.51	7.01	17.3
Sweden	2.27	4.19	**47.0**
South Africa	**0.26**	1.97	33.0
Average of all cases	*4.84*	*3.89*	*21.5*
	(N = 65)	*(N = 66)*	*(N = 66)*

TABLE 2.2   (Continued)

	Disproportionality	Effective number of parliamentary parties	Women legislators (%)
Single transferable vote			
Republic of Ireland	**6.24**	**3.21**	**14.2**
Malta	**1.63**	**2.00**	**9.2**
Average of all cases	*3.94*	*2.61*	*11.7*
	(N = 2)	*(N = 2)*	*(N = 2)*
Mixed-member proportional			
Albania	**19.17**	3.18	**7.1**
Lesotho	8.17	**2.16**	23.5
Mexico	5.93	2.78	23.2
Germany	3.39	**3.72**	10.9
New Zealand	**1.75**	3.37	**33.1**
Average of all cases	*7.10*	*2.93*	*18.1*
	(N = 8)	*(N = 8)*	*(N = 8)*
Mixed-member majoritarian			
Madagascar	**23.07**	2.18	7.9
Singapore	22.22	**1.05**	24.5
Japan	11.88	2.68	**6.4**
Georgia	11.21	3.04	**31.6**
Pakistan	6.31	**5.38**	21.1
Guinea	**0.76**	2.19	19.3
Average of all cases	*10.86*	*2.57*	*15.2*
	(N =19)	*(N = 22)*	*(N = 22)*

Notes: This table shows sample cases only, including those cases that are at one or other extreme of the measures (emboldened). Data on all countries can be found on the *Comparing Democracies 3* website (www.sagepub.co.uk/leduc3). The averages are means calculated from all cases, the number of which varies depending on data availability. The disproportionality measure is calculated using the Gallagher Index and the effective number of parties is calculated using the Laakso–Taagepera Index – see text for details (also: www.tcd.ie/Political_Science/staff/michael_gallagher/ElSystems/index.php). The percentage of women legislators refers to the most recent situation in national parliaments.

Source: www.sagepub.co.uk/leduc3; Farrell (2010)

Party systems

The over- and under-representation of different-sized parties brings us to the relationship that exists between electoral systems and party systems, a subject of much academic discussion and argument for many years. The debate about the precise nature of the link between electoral systems and party systems was set in train most notably by the French political scientist Maurice Duverger, who argued that SMP electoral systems "favored" two-party systems, while proportional electoral systems "favored" multiparty systems (Duverger 1959). And it is easy to see why this might be the case:

by making it more difficult for small parties to win seats in parliament, non-proportional systems (including SMP ones) are bound to result in fewer parties represented in parliament. What is more though, this reductive effect is further exacerbated by the psychological effects that such systems have (Blais and Carty 1991), which come to prominence when voters and elites alter their behavior precisely because they are aware that small parties are likely to be under-represented.

There is broad agreement among analysts of electoral systems that, just as Duverger suggested, certain types of electoral system tend to coincide with certain types of party system: SMP, runoff, and AV systems tend to be used in countries that are characterized by relatively few parties, while proportional electoral systems tend to be found in multiparty systems. And there is evidence to support these arguments in Table 2.2. If we focus on the second column of the table, which reports the "effective number of parliamentary parties" in each country – a figure calculated by an index that counts the number of parties by weighting them according to their seat share (Laasko and Taagepera 1979) – we can discern a number of patterns. More specifically, we can see that in most (but not all) countries that use SMP systems, the effective number of parliamentary parties does indeed tend to be low, whereas it is relatively high in most countries that employ a proportional system – be they list PR, STV, or one of the two forms of mixed-member system. Furthermore, if we move away from considering the type of electoral system, and examine instead the proportionality of the outcome of elections in each country (the first column of Table 2.2), we also detect an association between levels of proportionality and the effective number of parliamentary parties ($r = -0.268$, p (one tailed) <0.01).[15]

That said, as was the case with the proportionality profiles of the different systems, there are some countries that do not conform to our expectations, and where the effective number of parliamentary parties is higher or lower than we would have expected given their electoral system. For instance, the party system of Ethiopia is characterized as an "8.12-party system," even though SMP is in operation, and Papua New Guinea has a staggering 16.42 effective parties, despite AV being used here. By contrast, the effective number of parties in South Africa is low, even though this country uses list PR. These examples therefore suggest the relationship between electoral systems and the number of parties gaining representation in parliament is a *probabilistic* one rather than a deterministic one. That is, while high levels of proportionality *tend* to increase the probability of multipartyism, and low proportionality *tends* to increase the probability that the number of parties in parliament will be low, factors other than the electoral system (most notably the strength and nature of the cleavages of each country) also play an important role in shaping the number of parties that end up being represented in parliament. On top of this (and following Colomer 2005), we should also question the direction of the relationship: can we be sure that multipartyism really is a consequence of proportionality rather than a cause?

Parliament as a "microcosm"?

Our last systemic consequence of electoral systems concerns the representation of women and candidates from ethnic minorities. Advocates of proportional electoral systems argue that proportional systems tend to produce a more socially representative parliament because they allow parties to field more candidates in each district, and so increase the likelihood that both male and female candidates and candidates from different social and ethnic backgrounds will gain parliamentary representation. Much of this depends on the parties themselves, but studies that have focused on this issue (e.g., Norris 1985) have indeed concluded that proportional systems do appear to play a role in promoting greater representation of women. And our own data support this finding too: the last column of Table 2.2 indicates that the percentage of women in parliament is highest in countries that use list PR – the average across all countries that use list PR is 21.5%. What is more, when we correlated the disproportionality of electoral outcomes in each country with the percentage of women represented in parliament, we found a significant, negative relationship ($r = -0.314$, p (one tailed) <0.01). Therefore, although some exceptions exist and other factors may intervene, we can conclude that proportional electoral systems, in general, tend to encourage greater representation of women than non-proportional systems.

Strategic effects

The "maturing" of the field of electoral systems has witnessed a growing interest in what can be referred to as their strategic effects (Shugart 2005b). That is, they influence the behavior of both voters and party elites. We have already pointed to the fact that voters and party elites may act differently if they are aware that, because of the disproportionality of the electoral system, small parties are likely to be under-represented: voters might be prompted to support a large party instead of "wasting" their vote on a smaller contender, or party strategists may decide not to contest certain races. However, the proportionality of electoral systems is not the only factor that has strategic effects. The ballot structure of electoral systems is also likely to exert an influence on the behavior of voters and elites.

In recent years, electoral systems research has been paying growing attention to ballot structure – i.e., to how the ballot paper (or computer screen) that the voter uses to cast a vote has been designed. In our brief discussion of ballot structure at the beginning of this chapter we drew on Rae's classification of electoral systems that distinguished between ballot structures that are "categorical" or "ordinal," but perhaps a more useful and nuanced way of distinguishing between ballot structures is to talk of a spectrum running from "closed" to "open" ballot structures. The point of contention is that there are important differences between those ballot papers that simply allow voters to tick a box for their preferred party (i.e., a "closed" ballot structure) and those that allow voters to express a wide range of options, as in the case of the STV system where voters can rank-order all candidates on the ballot paper (i.e., an example of an "open" ballot structure; more generally, see Farrell and Scully 2007; Shugart 2005b).

This dimension of variation in electoral system design can have important consequences for how politicians behave both with regard to their representative roles (i.e., how they represent their voters) and also in how they campaign at election time. A recent study of the representative activities of Members of the European Parliament (MEPs) shows conclusively a greater emphasis on individual voter contact among those politicians elected under "open" electoral systems than is the case in the more "closed" electoral systems (Farrell and Scully 2007). Similar variations are shown in a study of MEP campaign behavior, which finds a greater concern for individual voter contact in the more "open" cases (Bowler and Farrell 2008).

Design and Reform

One of the core decisions of a new democracy is the design of its electoral system (Colomer 2004; Norris 2004; Sartori 1997). In some instances, this is a matter that is determined by the new political elites themselves. On other occasions the electoral system may be the legacy of a departing colonial power. More often than not the electoral system is the product of a messy process of debate, intrigue, and compromise – a common enough pattern in any process of institutional design (Goodin 1996). A useful way of examining electoral system design over the years is to adopt an historical-institutionalist perspective. We can do this with reference to Huntington's influential (1991) study on the "waves of democratization". According to Huntington, the first wave, from the 1820s to the 1920s, featured the processes of democratization in the US and across much of Europe. The second wave was a phenomenon of post-World War II decolonization and the rebuilding of democracies like the Federal Republic of Germany. The third wave, starting in the 1970s, featured the burgeoning new democracies of Latin America, Central and Eastern Europe, and the former Soviet Union. Reilly and Reynolds (1999) argue persuasively that debates over electoral system adoption vary quite distinctly across these three waves, both in terms of the types of electoral systems selected, and also in terms of the ways in which the electoral systems were chosen.

In the first-wave democracies, the tendency was for electoral systems to emerge gradually, in line with the gradual evolution of the democracies themselves. At least two main patterns are apparent (cf. Carstairs 1980). First, there are the cases of Anglo-American democracies which are characterized by relatively homogeneous societies, a single partisan cleavage, and a simple two-party system (Lijphart 1999). There was a desire by the established elites in many of these countries to retain maximum hold over the system and to constrain the influence of minor groups and parties.

Relatively early on there was a focus on territorial links, tied in with the desire of local elites to hold on to their power bases. Once these countries had settled on SMP systems, there was little desire for change. For the most part, attention was focused on questions regarding constituency boundary divisions and the gradual reform of the administration of elections.

Quite a different pattern occurred in the early continental European democracies, which tended to be characterized by more plural societies, lacking a single dominant group (Lijphart 1999). In these cases, even in the early years, there was recognition of the need to accommodate different groups in the political system. At the turn of the twentieth century, the writings of prominent scholars (like d'Hondt and Sainte-Laguë) influenced a shift towards the adoption of list systems.[16]

In this first wave, therefore, the evidence clearly points to a gradual, evolutionary process in the adoption of an electoral system. In some cases the choice was deliberate, such as Australia's decision to adopt AV in 1918 to try to prevent splits among the parties of the right (Farrell and McAllister 2006). It is also worth drawing attention to the central importance of party politics in influencing the type of electoral system adopted, thus lending support to the argument that Duverger's hypotheses might need to be looked at in reverse (Colomer 2005). Indeed, rational choice perspectives on electoral system design place party interest center-stage (Benoit 2004; Boix 1999). Boix builds on Rokkan's classic (1970) exposition for the move to PR – namely that it was prompted by elite fears over the rise of socialism – to propose a formal model in which parties, as unitary actors, adopted PR systems to reduce the risk of loss of power.[17]

Huntington's second wave is much shorter than the other two: it is focused on the post-war decades which saw the re-establishment of some democracies and the process of decolonization that produced a spate of new democracies. According to Reilly and Reynolds (1999), two central features of electoral system design in this wave were "colonial inheritance" and "external imposition," both of which obviously involved external elites to a significant extent. The influence of historical colonial links is very evident if we glance at countries around the world: over half of the former British colonies use SMP; over a third of the former French colonies use runoff systems and a further 20% use a list system; two-thirds of Spain's former colonies use list PR. As for electoral design by "external imposition," perhaps the best example of this is post-war (West) Germany, where the allied powers played an important role in the adoption of the MMP system. This was designed to avoid the perceived instability of the Weimar period, and also to incorporate some of the supposed "strengths" of the Anglo-American constituency-based system.

The third wave of democratization produced some new patterns of electoral system adoption. A central feature of this wave has been conscious design. Reilly and Reynolds (1999) refer to the cases of democratic transition in Hungary, Bolivia, South Africa, South Korea, Taiwan, and Fiji, among a host of other cases, where there was extensive discussion and debate about the merits of particular electoral systems (on East and Central

Europe more generally, see Birch et al. 2002). This is not to deny the fact, however, that such a process involved close bargaining between competing elites (Nohlen 1997) and that the system which emerged may, indeed, have required some "messy compromise" (Norris 1995; Taagepera 1998). Furthermore, there is also the point that many of these third-wave countries have far from completed the process of democratization (Rose and Chull Shin 1999), and therefore further electoral reforms cannot be ruled out – as we have witnessed with the recent decisions to replace MMM systems in Russia and Ukraine with more proportional list systems.

Electoral Reform

Of course, reform of existing electoral systems is not unique to emergent democracies; we have seen the issue arise in a number of established democracies. However, this is a relatively new phenomenon as, with the exceptions of France and Greece where electoral reforms have been commonplace, the abiding principle had tended to favor the status quo (Katz 2005; Nohlen 1984; Taagepera and Shugart 1989). Yet, quite suddenly in 1993–4, three leading democracies changed their electoral systems to variants of the mixed-member systems: Italy from list, Japan from SNTV, and New Zealand from SMP – providing clear evidence to some that mixed-member systems were now the system of choice (Shugart and Wattenberg 2001).[18]

It is difficult to establish exactly how electoral reform emerged on the political agenda. In one of the first overviews of the phenomenon, Norris (1995: 7) discerns three long-term factors that appear to have played a role in triggering demands for electoral reform: (1) electoral change (and, in particular, the weakening of electoral alignments); (2) "political scandals and/or government failures which rock public confidence in the political system"; and (3) the ability of voters (in Italy and New Zealand) to use referendums to force the hands of politicians. Shugart (2001) makes a useful distinction between inherent and contingent factors, the former creating the pre-conditions for reform, the latter symbolizing the trigger for the process to begin (e.g., a crisis or scandal of some sort, perceived serious problems with the existing system, etc.). Despite such persuasive arguments it remains difficult to theorize about the causes of electoral reform, for the simple reason that, notwithstanding the dramatic developments in New Zealand, Italy, and Japan in the early 1990s (and Italy's subsequent return to a list system in 2005), there have been so few cases, at least at national level. Katz (2005) counts a mere 14 cases of reform in the past half century, and others concur with this low figure (Renwick 2009; Reynolds et al. 2005).

Of course, the national arena is not the only place in which debates over electoral reform can occur, as witnessed for example by the adoption on new electoral systems at sub-national level in the UK in the 1990s (Farrell 2001b) and, more recently, by reforms across a number of Canadian provinces, some of which are still ongoing (Cross 2005). Nor for that matter should we restrict our coverage only to large-scale, fundamental electoral reform (Katz 2005), because there is plenty of evidence of tweaks to existing electoral systems (for instance, changes to electoral formulas, or to the rules relating to legal thresholds) that can have important impacts on election outcomes (cf. Bowler et al. 2003). Finally, there have also been important developments in the process of managing elections, the subject of our final section.

The Management of the Electoral Process

There is a growing interest by governments worldwide in maintaining a smooth, well-run and transparent electoral process. Given the general unwillingness to embrace large-scale reform of the electoral system, it is perhaps understandable that attention would turn instead to the administration of the electoral process itself. This is the area with greatest scope for further development, as shown, for example, by the gradual acceptance that new technologies can have a role to play in making the electoral process more transparent, more efficient, and more cost-effective. We can see this, for instance, in the gradual move away from traditional paper ballots. In recent years, more and more countries have been making use of electronic voting machines. India is moving towards full electronic voting, while in Brazil electronic voting is now the only way for electors to cast their vote. In other countries (such as Belgium and the Netherlands) electronic voting is used alongside traditional manual voting.[19] Estonia enabled online voting in its 2007 parliamentary elections.[20]

But nowhere is reform to the process of election administration more apparent than in the rise of institutions dedicated to the management of the election process itself. Such institutions have assumed responsibility for a number of key functions including determining who is eligible to vote, managing the nominations of parties and/or candidates, conducting the polling, counting the votes, and tabulating the results (Massicotte et al. 2004: ch. 4; Wall et al. 2006: 5). By undertaking such activities, these institutions – known as Election Management Bodies (EMBs)[21] – not only ensure that elections are organized and managed efficiently, but also promote fairness, openness, and transparency, and hence contribute to the legitimacy of democracy and the enhancement of the rule of law. EMBs have played a prominent role in the process of democratic design and consolidation in third-wave democracies (in large part encouraged by foreign NGOs providing appropriate technical assistance).[22]

Despite having a number of common functions, EMBs differ in their structure, and globally, three main types or models of institutions can be identified: independent EMBs, governmental EMBs, and "mixed" EMBs (Wall et al. 2006). Independent EMBs, as their title suggests, are independent of the executive branch of government and have full responsibility for the administration of elections. Often, they also have responsibility for developing policy and making decisions that relate to the electoral process.[23] They are composed of non-aligned experts or of representatives from political parties (or of a mix of both) and are most often accountable to the legislature. Governmental EMBs, on the other hand, are headed by a minister or a civil servant who is accountable to a cabinet minister. In this model, then, elections are organized and managed by the executive branch of government, either through a ministry (such as the Ministry of the Interior) and/or through local authorities. Indeed, in many instances (as in Sweden and Switzerland) a central EMB performs some key functions only, and leaves tasks (especially those that pertain to the election day itself) to local and/or regional bodies. Elsewhere (as in the UK and the US for example), the system is so decentralized that there is no central EMB, and all matters are left to local authorities (Pastor 2006: 273–5). Crucially, and regardless of how decentralized they are, EMBs in the governmental model only have the power to administer the election. They do not have the policy-making powers that independent EMBs have (Wall et al. 2006). Finally, "mixed" EMBs combine elements of the independent and the governmental model. Elections are organized and implemented through a ministry and/or through local authorities, as in the governmental model, but there is a second body, independent of the executive, which assumes responsibility for overseeing and supervising the election, and which, in some instances, has the power to develop a regulatory electoral framework under the law (Wall et al. 2006).

Despite the categorization of EMBs into three types or models, no two EMBs are identical. Rather, the precise structure of each body is a product of the country's history and its political and legal tradition. In many instances the structure has been heavily influenced by former colonial administrations, while in a few cases the slate was "wiped clean" and wholly new EMBs have been established. However, whatever the type chosen, there has been a discernible trend for EMBs to become entrenched as permanent institutions.[24]

Independent EMBs are by far the most common form. Indeed, as Table 2.3 illustrates, of the countries considered in this volume, nearly 65% have an independent EMB. While a number of established democracies such as Australia and Canada have independent EMBs, this type of EMB is most popular in democracies of the second and third wave. A large number of African countries, including many former British colonies, have independent EMBs. Similarly, independent EMBs are favored in South America (only Argentina does not have an independent EMB), in many states that were formerly under Soviet influence, and in many Asian countries. Governmental EMBs, by contrast, are most common in (Western) Europe, North Africa, and in a number of countries in the Middle East. New Zealand and the United States also have governmental EMBs. Mixed EMBs are the least common type of EMB, and are found in France, in a number of former French colonies, in some West European countries (for example the Netherlands, Portugal, and Spain), and in Japan.

The different models of EMBs present both advantages and disadvantages, some of which are quite obvious. For instance, an independent EMB

TABLE 2.3   Election management bodies in the 2000s

	No. of cases	%	Prominent examples
Independent	101	64.7	Australia, Brazil, Canada, India, Israel, Russia, South Africa
Governmental	32	20.5	Germany, Ireland, Italy, New Zealand, United Kingdom, United States
Mixed	23	14.7	Argentina, France, Japan, Netherlands, Spain

Source: Wall et al. (2006)

benefits from being less likely to be subjected to restrictions imposed by the government or to political pressures, and this autonomy, along with its perception of impartiality, increases the chances of it being able to promote electoral legitimacy. This is perhaps why independent EMBs have been so popular among new democracies. Other advantages of independent EMBs are that they may be better able to develop staff professionalism, ensure electoral administration is under unified control, and plan and institutionalize election tasks (Wall et al. 2006: 21). The flip side of this – and hence the advantage of governmental EMBs – is that independent EMBs may lack political influence, which could impede them in carrying out their tasks effectively and acquiring sufficient funding. Furthermore, independent EMBs tend to work at a higher cost since, unlike governmental EMBs, they are not able to draw on a pool of skilled staff and co-opt governmental structures to assist in the administration of elections (López-Pintor 2000).

Of course, it is not only the structure of the EMB which determines how well it performs, and how efficient, open, transparent and impartial it is and is perceived to be. This all depends on the EMB's behavior too. While EMB independence can be legally embedded in the constitution or the electoral law (as in Mexico and Uruguay), this does not mean that impartiality and autonomy from governmental control are impossible in other types of systems. Indeed, many governmental EMBs (such as those in New Zealand and Sweden) are perceived as being fair and impartial despite being governmental ones. The performance of EMBs thus also depends on whether there is political will and commitment to allow the EMB to act freely and impartially, and on how the members of the EMB actually behave (Wall et al. 2006: 11).

Conclusion

The worldwide rise of EMBs is explained, to a large extent, by the dramatic growth in the number of democracies in recent decades and by the desire of these new democracies to pay careful attention to the establishment of transparent electoral processes and institutions. Established democracies have clearly learned appropriate lessons from these developments. As the passing of the Help America Vote Act by Congress in 2002 and the establishment of the UK Electoral Commission in 2000 illustrate, they too have taken steps to strengthen the processes and institutions of electoral administration.

New democracies have also been instrumental in contributing to the diversity of electoral systems used around the world today. While they have not invented new systems *per se*, their enthusiastic adoption of mixed-member electoral systems (especially MMM) has led to these systems becoming more prominent across a range of democracies. In the middle of the twentieth century very few countries made use of mixed-member systems but today they are used in nearly 20% of countries.

With the notable exceptions of New Zealand and Japan (and for a time also Italy), established democracies have been much less keen on adopting mixed-member electoral systems for national level elections. That said, as recent developments in the UK and across the Canadian provinces show, they appear to be growing in popularity at the sub-national level.

If there is some "institutional contagion" between new and old democracies, there are also considerable differences in the motivations behind the reforms and in the enthusiasm that has accompanied them. EMBs were established in new democracies in a bid to promote and protect the rule of law, build and nurture political stability and ensure electoral transparency. As for electoral systems, mixed-member systems have been introduced widely in new democracies because, by their very nature, they appear to offer "something for everyone." In this way then, although not perfect, they perhaps represent the best compromise option for actors with very different interests (cf. Rahat 2008).

In established democracies, by contrast, the lack of any real electoral system reform at the national level, and the trend towards establishing and consolidating institutions of electoral management appear better explained by the desire of governments to try to address the growing dissatisfaction of citizens with the democratic process. Although, in a few instances (notably in the early 1990s), governments did respond to the concerns of citizens with full-scale electoral reform, in the main, full-scale reform has been conspicuous by its absence. Instead governments have chosen to tackle such problems in a variety of other ways, including introducing non-party reforms (such as direct elections of mayors or direct democracy initiatives), implementing reforms at the sub-national level, or institutionalizing a more independent and transparent process for managing elections.

Political elites in new democracies, who have the power to design, shape, and nurture their electoral institutions, therefore face very different demands and pressures and have different priorities than their counterparts in older, more established democracies. This goes a long way to explaining why there is so much variation in the nature of electoral institutions around the world, and why there are very different prospects for the reform of these institutions.

3

Political Parties and Party Systems

Susan E. Scarrow

This chapter examines variations among party systems in contemporary democracies, asking not only why such differences arise, but also how they may affect representation and governance. It begins with a brief discussion of differences between countries' individual parties, and then moves on to consider the origin and impact of party system differences.

Why Do Parties Form?

Today parties play a central role in almost all democratic governments, yet this role was an unanticipated – and in many cases unwanted – feature of popular government. Indeed, well into the early twentieth century some political thinkers portrayed parties and partisanship as threats to public welfare (Scarrow 2002). But neither warnings nor reforms deterred the rise of party-dominated politics. In one country after another, political parties assumed increasingly prominent positions as the franchise broadened and as control of government shifted to elected assemblies (Bartolini 2000). Where parties did not already exist, politicians created them to help with elections and governance; this pattern continues in today's emerging representative democracies. The resulting parties differ widely in the extent of their ideological commitments and the strength of their organizations, and some are very ephemeral creations; some even prefer to call themselves "movements" rather than parties. Despite these differences, organizations with party-like characteristics are found in all representative democracies.

The reason for this common development is that party connections are useful for contesting elections and for conducting legislative business: politicians benefit from creating and sustaining the alliances that become political parties. Such alliances solve coordination problems for politicians, helping them to advance their personal careers and to achieve their wider policy aims (Aldrich 1995; Schlesinger 1994). Within legislatures, political parties forge links across a variety of issues, prioritizing some areas of agreement as the main bond that holds them together. Parties can facilitate action at various stages of the legislative process (committee deliberation, floor debate), something that is particularly crucial as legislative business increases and time becomes a very limited resource (Cox 1987). Legislators have a greater chance of enacting or blocking legislation if they have a reliable group of allies, in other words, a coalition that does not need to be reconstructed ahead of every legislative vote. Legislators who join and stay in such an alliance can more credibly claim to be able to deliver what they promise. Shared party labels, and shared organizational resources that may accrue around these labels, can also more directly help candidates to win elections; as such, they are equally useful to groups that have yet to win any legislative seats. For all these reasons, politicians inside and outside of legislatures are willing to invest resources and political reputations into the creation and maintenance of party institutions (rather than, for instance, building only single issue organizations or purely personal political machines).

These efforts affect the ways that citizens seek to have their interests represented. The emergence of politically meaningful party labels reduces voters' information costs, freeing them from the need to investigate every single candidate's position in order to cast an informed vote. The more that voters come to rely on the cues of party labels, and the more loyal voters become to certain labels, the greater the incentive for politicians to associate themselves with established party "brands" rather than creating new ones, and for politicians to stay within a single party throughout the course of their political career. Such a reinforcing dynamic can help to stabilize existing or emerging party systems. The opposite is also true: in some countries voters may know more about individual politicians than about parties, and their primary loyalties may be to these politicians. In such circumstances, personal mandates give legislators greater latitude to ignore their parties, and office-holders and would-be office-holders have much less incentive to invest in building up a shared party label in order to win elections. In other words, just because parties can be useful does not mean that they are equally useful in all circumstances, or that they will become equally dominant or stable.

These accounts of party emergence highlight the utility of parties as vehicles of representation. They also highlight the interconnectedness of the various facets of party life. Party analysts have traditionally distinguished between parties as electoral organizations (parties as organizations), as groups of loyal voters (parties in the electorate), and as legislative coalitions (parties in government) (Key 1964). These aspects of party activity vary, and parties may be strong in one area and much weaker in another. Yet in large representative democracies, all three facets are clearly intertwined, because parties' legislative opportunities are shaped by their electoral performance, and party organization generally plays a role in achieving electoral success.

What Do Parties Represent? Social Groups, Issues, Personalities

This argument about the utility of parties explains why they seem to be synonymous with representative democracy. It also explains why institutional frameworks shape the parties that emerge, because parties are responsive to the competitive environment. It tells us much less, however, about which parties will form, or the interests that they will represent. To understand this, political scientists generally look to the societies out of which the parties grew, and at the policy conflicts that dominated in these countries in important eras. In countries where democracy gradually evolved alongside a slow expansion of the suffrage, parties often grew out of, and based their appeals on, longstanding social conflicts (Lipset and Rokkan 1967). Support for these cleavage-based parties was reinforced by enduring social structures, creating an electoral base that transcended specific issues and candidates. In the 1960s Kirchheimer and others speculated that political parties in established democracies were moving past a phase of primarily cleavage-based appeals, and were instead trying to increase their electoral success by broadening the coalition to which they appealed, and by de-emphasizing group-building organizational strategies in favor of professional advertising (Epstein 1980; Kirchheimer 1966). Kirchheimer predicted that professionalized parties with catch-all appeals would become the hallmark of parties in large European democracies, though he thought that a variety of niche parties might continue to flourish in smaller democracies. Yet while catch-all appeals have become much more prevalent, in many countries today's Left–Right partisan divisions still have roots in much earlier distributional conflicts, and cleavage-based politics have not disappeared (Bartolini and Mair 1990).

Indeed, social cleavages mark the political party landscape in a variety of democracies. For instance, in India, partisan divisions are now partly structured by caste and religious divides (Chhibber 1999). The Peronists in Argentina and Lula da Silva's Workers' Party in Brazil have identified with, and drawn support from, the working classes and labor unions, though today neither party has an exclusively class-based appeal (Dix 1989; Samuels 2004). Meanwhile in Bolivia, President Evo Morales and his party rose to power in the early twenty-first century by appealing to indigenous, mostly rural, voters (Madrid 2005). Such cleavage-based parties may attract loyal followings whether or not they have well-developed political programs.

Cleavage-based competition is even more pronounced in African democracies, where ethnic and/or religious divisions tend to dominate political conflicts, creating deep-seated partisan preferences. Where there are few cross-cutting cleavages to create alternative claims on voters' loyalties, parties have less need to develop strong organizations or to articulate programs, because mobilizing support within the social cleavage is easy, and winning support outside the cleavage is difficult or impossible. Where cleavage-based politics dominates, a great deal of political competition may take place within the parties that claim to represent each group, as personalized factions struggle for leadership (Mozaffar and Scarritt 2005).

But social cleavages do not always provide the main foundations of political competition. In some countries party competition is based at least as much on personalities and on immediate issues as on deeper social divisions. This may be particularly common in countries where democratic elections emerged relatively suddenly. For instance, newer parties in Central and Eastern Europe had little time to develop links with civil society prior to the first democratic elections. As a result, in many countries voting in the initial rounds seemed to reflect issues and personalities rather than social divisions. In more recent elections, however, social divisions have come to play a larger role in structuring the vote, though issues also remain important (Bakke and Sitter 2005; Evans 2006; Rohrschneider and Whitefield 2009).

In short, historical as well as contemporary social structures can help to explain the ideological contours of contemporary party systems in many established democracies. Where cleavage-based political parties exist, they may bring stability (or even ossification) to a political system, because their claims to voters' loyalty go beyond the issues of any single election. Moreover, the strength of cleavage-based voting can affect the quality of representation, determining whether elections offer voters choices based primarily on appeals to group interests, on leaders' popularity, or on narrow sets of issues. Thus, the strategies and support bases of individual parties affect the choices that voters are offered, as well as the policies that parties-in-government try to implement. But to understand variations in democratic representation, we need to look not just at the individual parties, but also at how they interact with each other. These interactions shape, and are shaped by, the ways that policies are made, the calculations and expectations of individual politicians, and the preferences of voters. Because of this, political scientists have long looked to cross-national differences in party systems to get clues about political dynamics.

Party Systems: Descriptions, Origins and Implications

Three main characteristics of inter-party relations can help to illuminate politically important differences in patterns of party competition: (a) the number of parties; (b) the extent of ideological differences among them;

and (c) the level of party system institutionalization – that is the degree to which patterns of competition are rooted in history and society. The first two factors can be thought of in spatial terms, while the third brings in the element of time. Together these characteristics provide clues about likely coalition patterns, the calculations of would-be office-holders, and the ways that citizens relate to the parties that are supposed to represent them.

Party System Dimensions

Political scientists have long classified countries in terms of the size of their party systems, most often distinguishing between countries with two main parties and those with more. Some of the earliest discussions of party systems viewed the two party system as both the norm and the desideratum, as in Lawrence Lowell's pronouncement that "a division into two parties is not only the normal result of the parliamentary system, but also an essential condition of its success" (Lowell 1897: 72). For Lowell and for others, the stability of the British political system was a prime example of the importance of a two-party system. In the 1950s, the French political scientist Maurice Duverger elaborated on earlier arguments in explaining why the size of the party system mattered. He was not critical of multiparty arrangements *per se*, but he argued that two-party systems were more natural, because "political choice usually takes the form of a choice between two alternatives" (Duverger 1959: 215). Duverger and others viewed two-party systems as more accountable, because their elections produced single-party winners, without a need for post-election coalition negotiations, and because under single-party government citizens could use elections to hold parties responsible for their actions in government (Ranney 1954). Parties in two-party systems were also expected to make more inclusive political appeals, and to be less subject to capture by narrow interests (Neumann 1956, a view that Epstein contested: 1967: 77). The two-party/multiparty distinction is also crucial to Lijphart's distinction between majoritarian and consensual political systems, each of which is said to have distinct political styles and policy outcomes (Lijphart 1999).

While this distinction between two- and multiparty systems is an enduring one with clear implications about the dynamics of competition and lines of accountability, it has several obvious limitations. First, while some democracies with multiparty systems may have collapsed, many more did not, which leads to questions about why some multiparty systems have been more functional than others. Second, and equally important, even under lenient counting rules, there are not that many two-party systems, so this most simple classification system leaves a great deal unexplained. Because of these limits, researchers have suggested other classification rules for distinguishing between systems with more than two parties (for instance, Blondel 1968; Dahl 1966; see also Mair 2002 for details). Probably the most frequently referenced is that devised by Giovanni Sartori, who distinguishes between party systems based on both the number of parties and the ideological distance among them. Sartori divides party systems into one-party, hegemonic-party, predominant-party, two-party, moderate-pluralism, polarized-pluralism, and atomized. Of these, the one-party and hegemonic-party systems are not democracies, because only one party is allowed to win. The former East Germany had a hegemonic party system, in which small parties were allowed to co-exist, but not to compete, with the Communist Party. In contrast, a predominant party system is much more democratic, as long as the dominant party is truly vulnerable to loss in fair elections, even if such a loss is rare (a situation that seems to characterize the long dominance of the Liberal Democrats in Japan after 1955). Sartori described two-party and moderate multiparty systems as the most stable types of systems, whereas extreme multiparty systems are less likely to be stable. Sartori placed the approximate division between moderate and extreme, or polarized, multipartism at five parties, arguing that above this number political competition was likely to push towards the extremes. The exception was in cases where the parties belonged to two distinct and stable ideological sub-blocks, in which case competition would approximate the centrist tendencies of a two-party system (Sartori 1976). In other words, while Sartori used counting rules to distinguish between party systems, he also considered parties' ideological distance to be crucial for determining party interactions.

Explaining Party System Size

To make numerical classification schemes useful, we need good rules for counting parties. When, as here, the focus is on legislative bargaining and voter strategies, the parties of interest are those that win legislative seats. But legislative parties come in many different sizes, and these differences are crucial for understanding the ways that they interact. A country with three parties of equal size will have very different politics than a country with three parties, one of which controls over half the legislative seats. To help capture these differences, researchers have devised a measure of the *effective number of parliamentary parties*, a measure that weights big parties more than small ones (Laakso and Taagepera 1979). The advantage of such a measure can be illustrated by seeing how it captures changes in the German party system between 1980 and 2005. At the beginning of the period, Germany had two large legislative blocs in the lower house of its parliament, each receiving over 45% of the vote, and one smaller party. In other words, there were three party groups, but because one of these parties was relatively small, the effective number of parties was closer to two (2.4). And indeed, German politics in this era functioned much like a two-party system, with alternations of center-left or center-right governments. However, by 2005 the number of party groups in the Bundestag had grown from three to five, with the newer parties taking votes away from both previously dominant large parties. As a result, the effective number of parties rose from 2.4 to 3.5. This change in the effective number of parties correctly indicates a significant shift in German political dynamics, with the larger number of coalition possibilities generating much greater uncertainty about likely election outcomes.[1] As this example suggests, by comparing the effective number of parties within or across countries, we can better understand the context of coalition negotiations, and, if combining this with Sartori's insights about ideological distance, we may get some idea of whether political dynamics are more likely to be centrist or polarizing.

Democracies vary widely in terms of their effective number of legislative parties, as shown elsewere in this volume (Table 2.2). The examples presented in this table include 11 countries with 2.0 or fewer effective parties, including Malta and South Africa, and nine countries with 5.0 or more effective legislative parties, including Argentina, Israel, and Haiti.

As explained more fully in Chapter 2, electoral rules have a big role in explaining these differences. Proportional representation is generally associated with larger party systems than are majoritarian rules, and the more proportional the electoral system (the lower the effective threshold), the greater the number of parties. On the other hand, while most two-party systems use majoritarian rules, these do not guarantee the emergence of a two-party system (Lijphart 1994; Riker 1982a). And party system size is also affected by two other institutional features: the centralization of the state, and the relation between legislative and executive elections. Even in countries with majoritarian electoral systems, federalism may produce varied sets of parties at the provincial level, and this in turn may translate into a greater number of legislative parties at the national level (Chhibber and Murali 2006; Gaines 1999). Indeed, in linguistically divided Belgium, increasingly federal arrangements have facilitated the emergence of two completely separate party systems at the regional level, one where there is no assurance that parties from the same ideological families will work together in a national government. The divergence or overlap of federal and provincial party systems shapes political careers, as well as politicians' decisions about the various party structures in which they should invest (Caramani 2005; Mainwaring and Jones 2003).

Party systems also are shaped by the type of regime, especially by the different competitive circumstances in parliamentary and presidential systems. In parliamentary systems, the executive (prime minister) is selected as the result of the legislative negotiations, and small parties often play an important role in coalition calculations. In contrast, competition for the winner-take-all presidential office may exert pressures towards party consolidation, because small parties have no chance of winning the top office. But this effect seems to be reduced where legislators are elected on different timetables than the president, so that legislators' electoral fates are less closely tied to that of a presidential candidate, popular or otherwise (Jones 1995; Shugart and Carey 1992).

Institutions like those described above may go a long way towards explaining why some countries have more parties than others. But as the previously cited German example suggests, party systems can change even when the basic institutional structures remain fairly stable. In Germany, the changes described were promoted by underlying social changes, including the emergence of a new lifestyle cleavage, the expansion of the electorate in the wake of unification, and weakening overall party attachments. These developments encouraged voters as well as politicians to shift their support away from established parties and to pursue their interests by backing newer alternatives: past outcomes contributed to new defections. This cross-temporal dynamic is captured by the concept of party system institutionalization.

Party System Institutionalization

Party system institutionalization describes the extent to which politics is rooted in competition between a particular set of political parties. Strongly institutionalized party systems have stable party alternatives, a stability that is reinforced by voters' strong attachments to particular parties, and by the perceived legitimacy of party-based democracy. In such systems, the stability of political alternatives encourages politicians to make careers within the existing party structures and discourages the rise of challenger parties; it also enables voters to use elections to hold governments accountable. In strongly institutionalized party systems, parties that win elections tend to be cohesive enough to play an important role in the governing process, because their elected members need to work together to win re-election under a shared label: as a result, new party creation is rare, as are party defections. In contrast, where party system institutionalization is weak, political alternatives are in flux. Where most parties are short-lived, voters cannot use elections to hold governing parties accountable, nor do they have much information about the likely performance of new parties; as a result, this instability weakens representative processes. Weak institutionalization also weakens the cohesion of legislative parties, thus reducing their ability to deliver on electoral promises. In short, the degree of party system institutionalization tells us about the predictability of politics within a country, describing how today's political parties have interacted in the past, and by extension, giving clues about the likelihood that the same parties will continue to interact in the future. As with financial investments, "past performance is no guarantee of future returns," but past patterns matter because they provide voters and politicians with important information about how best to advance their interests through electoral politics.

Party system institutionalization was originally described in terms of four components: the regularity of patterns of party competition, the extent to which parties have stable roots in society, the extent to which parties are viewed as the main and legitimate means of determining who governs, and the solidity of party organizations (Mainwaring and Scully 1995). Subsequent researchers have adopted variations of this definition, and some have simplified this into two components: the regularity of the political framework within which parties compete (structural factors) and the ways that citizens view political parties and party competition (attitudinal factors) (Randall and Svåsand 2002). Party organization is left out of this simpler definition, because the strength of individual party organizations is viewed as a potential contributor to, not a facet of, party system institutionalization. This understanding will guide the comparisons that follow.

However it is defined, party system institutionalization tends to be low in new democracies, not least because voters in such countries rarely have a strong loyalty to parties that have just formed. On the other hand, party system institutionalization does not necessarily increase as democracies age (Mainwaring and Zoco 2007), nor do all new democracies start at the same place on this measure. In some third-wave democracies, particularly those in Latin America, new parties inherited names and/or traditions of parties from earlier democratic eras, and inherited shared histories of party-based governance; this contrasted with the experience of most African democracies, which had much shorter post-colonial histories (Kuenzi and Lambright 2001). In some (but not all) European post-communist countries, former communist parties – and those who opposed them – played a big role in defining and regularizing clear patterns of electoral competition, particularly when former ruling parties re-invented themselves as moderate oppositions (Gryzymala-Busse 2006). The continuation of pre-existing organizations and conflicts into the democratic era may help party systems to institutionalize relatively quickly in some new democracies, providing predictable patterns of competition that help to clarify political choices. But such a development is by no means inevitable, and in some countries party systems remain weakly institutionalized over long periods.

Levels of party system institutionalization can also reflect the electoral system, and the type of regime. As explained in Chapter 2, electoral systems with low effective thresholds make it easier for new parties to win entrance into the legislature, which is likely to reduce party system stability. Presidential regimes also may reduce some aspects of party system institutionalization by encouraging voters to form attachments to particular candidates rather than to party labels (Shugart and Carey 1992).

So far most researchers who have examined party system institutionalization have been concerned with the effects of under-institutionalization on democratic stability and performance (for instance, Hicken 2006; Kuenzi and Lambright 2001; O'Dwyer and Kovalčik 2007). But the other end of the spectrum may also hold threats to representative processes. In very strongly institutionalized party systems, the continuity of party alternatives could be so high that new alternatives would be frozen out, leaving unhappy citizens with limited options for representation. Such a development could even lead to the decoupling of the attitudinal and structural elements of party system institutionalization, with extreme structural institutionalization – the freezing of competition – undermining attitudinal support for the competitors, and for the system of party competition. And indeed, in recent years many established democracies have apparently witnessed such a change, with citizens becoming less supportive of parties in general, and with voters expressing weakened attachments to particular parties (Dalton 2000; Dalton and Weldon 2006). In many of these same countries, the legal institutionalization of parties has increased as countries introduce public subsidies for parties. Some argue that these diverging trends are directly linked (Katz and Mair 1995; van Biezen and Kopecký 2007). The connection between various aspects of party system institutionalization will be examined in more detail below.

Comparing Indicators of Party System Institutionalization

Party system institutionalization is thus a concept that tells us a great deal about the environment and expectations that shape political competition, and it is one that may be useful for comparing established and new democracies alike. How much do contemporary democracies vary in the extent of their party system institutionalization, and to what extent do national political structures or histories explain these variations? We can get some answers to these questions by comparing indicators of party system institutionalization for a broad group of democracies from around the world.

The picture presented here looks at both the structural and attitudinal aspects of party system institutionalization. The attitudinal measures come from two major cross-national surveys, the World Values Survey (WVS) and the Comparative Study of Electoral Systems (CSES). The structural data come from several other cross-national data collections, as detailed below. The countries to be examined are ones that received Freedom House ratings of free or partly free in 2006, which had populations of more than one million, and, importantly, were ones for which data were available on at least one of the two attitudinal measures. This last criterion in particular limited the sample size to a small but diverse sample of 39 democracies. A majority of them are European, of which slightly more than half are more established Western European democracies, while the rest are newer democracies from East Central Europe. Twenty of the countries in the set have been continuously democratic since at least 1980; 19 are newer democracies.[2]

Structural Indicators

The structural side of party system institutionalization describes the relationship between parties and the state, and the stability of party competition. To measure the first part of structural institutionalization, the strength of the party-state relationship, we can look at three indicators of the legal treatment of political parties: (1) whether the state provides monetary subsidies for political parties; (2) whether parties have a legal right to free media access (an indirect subsidy); (3) whether parties are legally recognized and defined, either by statutes or in the constitution (following Randall and Svåsand 2002). Information on all three features is presented in Table 3.1, and this is used to construct a legal status score for all 39 countries, presented in Table 3.1 and in the first column of Table 3.2. This score shows that most of our democracies do offer strong legal support for party competition: almost all give some sort of subsidies to their political parties, and over half (24) grant legal recognition to political parties. (For a more detailed discussion of differences in party finance systems and a listing of other types of regulations, see Chapter 4.) Newer democracies are more likely to give parties special legal status than are the more established democracies. Indeed, this is probably no accident, because institutional designers in new democracies often deliberately create structures to bolster fledgling parties. However, when this aspect of party system institutionalization is used to distinguish among new and established democracies, and not just to compare new democracies, it has the somewhat odd effect of coding established democracies lower on this measure.

The stability of party competition is the second main structural feature of party system institutionalization. Stability (or instability) structures current competition by affecting the expectations of both voters and politicians. Here, stability is measured by looking at the long-term performance of specific parties, and at fluctuations over time in the distribution of votes among the parties.

The first stability measure assesses the continuity of the main party alternatives, the ones that are most likely to play a big role in coalition negotiations. The measure compares the share of seats in the lower house of the national legislature held by significant parties in the first democratic election held after 1978, compared with their seat share after the last national election held in 2006 or before (following Payne 2007).[3] "Significant" parties are defined as those winning at least 10% of the seats. Scores of 100 indicate complete continuity in the share of seats held by the bigger parties. Much lower scores indicate that initially dominant parties have been sidelined by new, or newly important, competitors (including by new offshoots of older parties). Scores of over 100 indicate a growth in the seat share of the initially large parties, generally because the initially larger parties displaced smaller parties.[4]

Countries show great variation on this measure, even over the relatively short timespan studied here. In a few countries, some initially important parties had almost entirely disappeared by the end of the period (as, for instance, Israel) (see Table 3.2). Not surprisingly, the turnover of alternatives was higher in new democracies; eight of the 12 countries with continuity scores under 50 came from this group. Among the established democracies, the countries with the lowest continuity included Belgium, where a one-time

TABLE 3.1 Structural institutionalization of party systems: legal status

Country	Established democracy (pre-1980)	Regime type	Region	Public subsidy to political parties	Free media for political parties	Recognized legal status	Summary: legal status score
Argentina	No	Presidential	Latin America	Yes	Yes	Yes	3
Australia	Yes	Parliamentary	Asia/Pacific	Yes	No	No	1
Belgium	Yes	Parliamentary	W Europe	Yes	Yes	No	2
Brazil	No	Presidential	Latin America	Yes	Yes	Yes	3
Bulgaria	No	Parl./Pres.	E Europe	Yes	No	Yes	2
Canada	Yes	Parliamentary	North America	Yes	Yes	No	2
Chile	No	Presidential	Latin America	No	Yes	No	1
Czech Republic	No	Parl./Pres.	E Europe	Yes	Yes	Yes	3
Denmark	Yes	Parliamentary	W Europe	Yes	Yes	No	2
El Salvador	No	Presidential	Latin America	Yes	Yes	Yes	3
Estonia	No	Parl./Pres.	E Europe	Yes	Yes	Yes	3
Finland	Yes	Parl./Pres.	W Europe	Yes	No	Yes	2
France	Yes	Parl./Pres.	W Europe	Yes	Yes	Yes	3
Germany	Yes	Parl./Pres.	W Europe	Yes	Yes	Yes	3
Hungary	No	Parl./Pres.	E Europe	Yes	Yes	Yes	3
India	Yes	Parl./Pres.	Asia/Pacific	No	Yes	No	1
Israel	Yes	Parl./Pres.	Middle East	Yes	Yes	Yes	3
Italy	Yes	Parliamentary	W Europe	Yes	Yes	Yes	3
Japan	Yes	Parliamentary	Asia/Pacific	Yes	Yes	No	2
Korea, Republic of	No	Parl./Pres.	Asia/Pacific	Yes	Yes	Yes	

TABLE 3.1 (Continued)

Country	Established democracy (pre-1980)	Regime type	Region	Public subsidy to political parties	Free media for political parties	Recognized legal status	Summary: legal status score
Latvia	No	Parl./Pres.	E Europe	No	Yes	No	1
Lithuania	No	Parl./Pres.	E Europe	Yes	Yes	Yes	3
Mexico	No	Presidential	Latin America	Yes	Yes	Yes	3
Netherlands	Yes	Parliamentary	W Europe	Yes	Yes	No	2
New Zealand	Yes	Parliamentary	Asia/Pacific	No	Yes	No	1
Norway	Yes	Parliamentary	W Europe	Yes	Yes	No	2
Peru	No	Parl./Pres.	Latin America	No	Yes	Yes	2
Poland	No	Parl./Pres.	E Europe	Yes	Yes	Yes	3
Portugal	Yes	Parl./Pres.	W Europe	Yes	Yes	Yes	3
Romania	No	Parl./Pres.	E Europe	Yes	Yes	Yes	3
Slovakia	No	Parl./Pres.	E Europe	Yes	Yes	Yes	3
Slovenia	No	Parl./Pres.	E Europe	Yes	Yes	No	
South Africa	No	Presidential	Africa	Yes	Yes	Yes	3
Spain	Yes	Parliamentary	W Europe	Yes	Yes	Yes	3
Sweden	Yes	Parliamentary	W Europe	Yes	Yes	No	2
Switzerland	Yes	Parliamentary	W Europe	Yes	No	Yes	2
Ukraine	No	Parl./Pres.	E Europe	No	Yes	Yes	2
United Kingdom	Yes	Parliamentary	W Europe	Yes	Yes	No	2
United States	Yes	Presidential	North America	No	No	No	0

Sources and coding: See Appendix 3.1.

breakup of national parties into their federal constituents accounts for most of the change, Italy, which experienced a collapse of its party system as well as several electoral reforms, and Israel, where a very low electoral threshold and an influx of immigrants both helped to support the formation of new parties.

Variations in the continuity of large parties help to capture one aspect of variations in political dynamics, but it is also useful to examine variation on an election-by-election basis. Average electoral volatility provides such a measure, summarizing the total change in all parties' vote shares from one election to the next. A volatility score of 20 indicates that 20% of the vote was distributed differently than in the last election.[5] Low electoral volatility means there is a great deal of continuity in the distribution of support between parties. If volatility is low over a long period, it means that that there is high predictability about likely contenders, and likely coalition possibilities. In contrast, high electoral volatility reflects either the emergence of successful new parties, and/or vote shifts between established alternatives. In practice, both phenomena may go together, because where voting patterns are fluid over a series of elections, political challengers and voters have more reason to take a chance on new parties.

Previous research on electoral volatility has found that the age of democracy is the best predictor of this type of stability (Mainwaring and Zoco 2007), and the cases in this sample conform to this finding (see Table 3.2). Only three of the established democracies had average volatility scores of more than 20 (India, Israel, and Italy). In contrast, only two of the newer democracies (Chile and South Africa) had average scores below this. Among the newer democracies, the parliamentary democracies of East Central Europe display much more volatility than the mainly presidential democracies in Latin America.

Attitudinal Indicators

The structural aspects of party system institutionalization described above tell us about the institutional and historical settings of party competition. Attitudinal aspects describe the extent to which citizens think about politics in party terms. Party systems are more weakly institutionalized where citizens are more concerned about personalities than party labels, or where they lack strong attachments to particular parties. In a weakly institutionalized party system, citizens may even reject the idea that parties are necessary for – or capable of – good government. In countries where citizens hold negative attitudes towards political parties, important aspects of political competition are more likely to take place outside party realms. Moreover, in such circumstances those parties that do form may take non-party names, calling themselves "movements" or "popular fronts," and eschewing organizational features commonly associated with political parties.

The attitudinal dimension of party system institutionalization is assessed here using two direct measures of public opinion: the extent to

TABLE 3.2 Party system institutionalization: structure and attitudes

Country	Region	Established democracy	Regime	Legal status score	Party continuity	Average electoral volatility	Party confidence %	Party closeness %
Argentina	Latin America	No	Presidential	3	9.4	24.9	49.8	
Australia	Asia/Pacific	Yes	Parliamentary	1	103.6	6.4	82.5	81.5
Belgium	W Europe	Yes	Parliamentary	2	16.5	11.5		34.9
Brazil	Latin America	No	Presidential	3	39.2	24.1	52.9	48.4
Bulgaria	E Europe	No	Parl./Pres.	2	56.7	36.8	66.9	42.7
Canada	North America	Yes	Parliamentary	2	85.0	16.8	80.4	37.3
Chile	Latin America	No	Presidential	1	101.7	16.7	61.4	34.1
Czech Republic	E Europe	No	Parl./Pres.	3	30.8	25.7	71.3	57.9
Denmark	W Europe	Yes	Parliamentary	2	102.8	12.2		46.7
El Salvador	Latin America	No	Presidential	3	70.5	27.1	46.1	
Estonia	E Europe	No	Parl./Pres.	3	112.6	42.4	69.0	
Finland	W Europe	Yes	Parl./Pres.	2	98.5	10.4	78.3	45.7
France	W Europe	Yes	Parl./Pres.	3	42.2	17.5		55.2
Germany	W Europe	Yes	Parl./Pres.	3	83.6	8.7	82.0	37.6
Hungary	E Europe	No	Parl./Pres.	3	30.7	25.1	65.4	52.2
India	Asia/Pacific	Yes	Parl./Pres.	1	92.4	25.0	77.6	
Israel	Middle East	Yes	Parl./Pres.	3	15.0	34.4		60.4
Italy	W Europe	Yes	Parliamentary	3	26.5	22.1		35.2
Japan	Asia/Pacific	Yes	Parliamentary	2	87.5	18.6	76.7	52.1
Korea, Republic of	Asia/Pacific	No	Parl./Pres.		43.8	24.6	76.7	34.1
Latvia	E Europe	No	Parl./Pres.	1	46.0	58.2	57.2	
Lithuania	E Europe	No	Parl./Pres.	3	49.7	49.2	86.4	
Mexico	Latin America	No	Presidential	3	62.4	22.7	63.6	51.2
Netherlands	W Europe	Yes	Parliamentary	2	78.0	16.6		39.2
New Zealand	Asia/Pacific	Yes	Parliamentary	1	92.8	19.7	66.4	53.1

TABLE 3.2 (Continued)

Country	Region	Established democracy	Regime	Legal status score	Party continuity	Average electoral volatility	Party confidence %	Party closeness %
Norway	W Europe	Yes	Parliamentary	2	72.9	14.1	92.8	40.6
Peru	Latin America	No	Parl./Pres.	2	76.7	51.9	58.3	38.9
Poland	E Europe	No	Parl./Pres.	3	60.3	46.6	61.1	37.6
Portugal	W Europe	Yes	Parl./Pres.	3	61.0	14.1		51.7
Romania	E Europe	No	Parl./Pres.	3	95.4	53.0	59.5	38.1
Slovakia	E Europe	No	Parl./Pres.	3	47.4	38.0	76.6	
Slovenia	E Europe	No	Parl./Pres.		75.6	38.2	66.2	19.7
South Africa	Africa	No	Presidential	3	84.3	5.3	81.8	
Spain	W Europe	Yes	Parliamentary	3	114.2	16.5	78.5	59.1
Sweden	W Europe	Yes	Parliamentary	2	87.1	13.5	90.5	48.2
Switzerland	W Europe	Yes	Parliamentary	2	101.0	9.4	83.6	44.4
Ukraine	E Europe	No	Parl./Pres.	2	93.8	59.2	63.6	
United Kingdom	W Europe	Yes	Parliamentary	2	90.0	8.2		35.1
United States	North America	Yes	Presidential	0	100.2	3.2	83.4	56.6

Sources and coding: See Appendix 3.1

which citizens express confidence in political parties in general, and the extent to which they express attachment to particular parties. The measure of confidence sets a low threshold, looking at the extent to which citizens express any confidence in political parties. While in most countries more than half the population endorsed parties in at least a half-hearted way, the extent of the endorsement varied widely, ranging from 46.1% (El Salvador) to a resounding 92.8% in Norway. Put differently, however, many countries had a large minority of citizens who said they had absolutely no confidence in parties. Such widespread distrust is not a comforting figure for representative democracies in which parties play such central roles.

Citizens were less likely to express attachment to specific parties than to express confidence in parties in general. In Norway, for example, fewer than half as many respondents (40.6%) expressed closeness to a particular party than expressed confidence in parties in general. For most countries, the share of those expressing some party attachment ranged between 33% and 66%. The lower the figure, the greater the likelihood of major shifts in the political landscape, whether by new party emergence, or by swings in the votes of existing parties.

Dimensions of Party System Institutionalization

How do these various indicators of party system institutionalization fit together, and do they cluster into distinct patterns of political competition? Is it possible to draw any conclusions about factors that are associated with higher or lower levels of party system institutionalization? Performing factor analysis on the component measures of party system institutionalization can help us to answer these questions. Exploratory factor analysis is a data reduction technique that looks for underlying structure within a set of variables, finding common patterns that explain their associations. Using the party system institutional variables described above, for example, we can explore how different countries' party systems relate to each other.[6]

The results of the analysis are presented in Figure 3.1 and in Appendix 3.2. These results show that the first and most important dimension classifies countries on important regime features, such as whether it is a new or established democracy, how the executive is selected (presidential, mixed, parliamentary), and the confidence voters have in their parties. This dimension, which we might call *Regime Age*, shows that confidence in parties is generally much higher, and electoral volatility is much lower, in the more established democracies.

A second significant dimension classifies countries on *Party Continuity* features, such as the continuity the party labels offered to voters and the prevalence of party attachments. These two features are mutually reinforcing, with citizens' attachments being stronger when the same menu of parties contest and win elections, and with parties more likely to

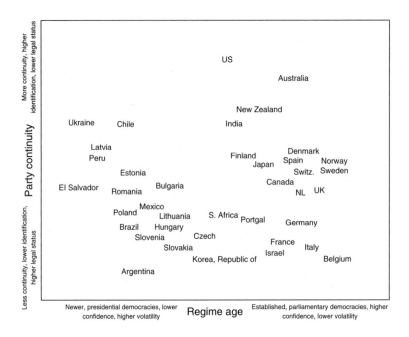

Figure 3.1   Elements of party system institutionalization

persist because citizen attachments block the rise of challengers. Importantly, this second dimension is independent of regime type and age, showing that patterns of political competition vary within these groups, not just across them. Thus, longer experience with representative democracy may reduce the most extreme skepticism about parties – citizens are less likely to reject parties altogether – but it does not necessarily lead to high levels of identification with specific parties. Similarly, no particular regime type seems to undermine or bolster the continuity of party alternatives, or to reduce support for particular parties: both presidential and parliamentary regimes are distributed across this dimension.

Party Systems and Patterns of Political Competition

Over sixty years ago the American political scientist E.E. Schattschneider wrote his oft-quoted pronouncement that "modern democracy is unthinkable save in terms of party" (1942: 1). While this general assessment seems to be as true today as it was when he wrote it, such a common understanding still leaves much to be said about how these modern party democracies work, because political parties assume such different forms and play such varied roles within them. The challenge for analysts is to understand how these differences affect the dynamics of political life within each country. This chapter has shown how aspects of party systems can provide clues about cross-national differences in patterns of political competition. Knowing the number of parties and their ideological types tells us about the likely direction of political competition, and about the types of political appeals that are most likely to succeed, be that catch-all and centrist, polarizing, or fragmenting appeals to social sub-groups. Party system institutionalization, a newer measure for analyzing party systems, adds social and temporal information to these quantitative descriptions. It helps to describe the partisan context in which voters and politicians make their choices. As such, it helps us to predict whether existing parties are likely to play central roles in future political conflicts, or whether new issues and new personalities are more likely to result in new party alternatives. With party system numbers, as with party system institutionalization, we cannot distinguish specific levels above or below which stable democratic competition is impossible. However, countries that register on the extremes on any of these measures are likely to be those where the legitimacy and smooth operation of partisan government face the greatest challenges. Because of this, those looking for insights into cross-national differences in patterns of politics do well to pay attention to the inter-relation of parties within party systems, and not merely to the fortunes of individual parties.

Appendix 3.1   Variable Description and Sources for Tables 3.1 and 3.2

Established democracy   Continuous democracy since 1979 or before.

Regime type; Religion   Taken from the common data set for all countries on the *Comparing Democracies 3* website (www.sagepub.co.uk/leduc3).

Public subsidy to political parties   Direct payments. From: Austin and Tjernström (2003). IDEA Database on Political Finance: www.idea.int/partiesfinance/db/

Free media for political parties   Sources same as for public subsidies.

Recognized legal status   Are parties distinguished from other associations in constitutional or ordinary law? From Janda (2005).

Legal status score   Additive score based on presence of public subsidies, free media for political parties, and recognized legal status.

Party continuity   Change between first and last election in combined share of legislative seats held by parties winning at least 10% of seats in first election, subtracted from 100. The elections are the first and last democratic elections in the 1978–2006 time period. High scores indicate low change. Where not continuously democratic, first election is same as Mainwaring and Torcal (2006) for average electoral volatility.

Average electoral volatility For all democratic elections 1978–2003. From Mainwaring and Torcal (2006) except Canada, El Salvador, Finland, Israel, New Zealand, Slovakia, South Africa, calculated by author.

Party confidence Percent expressing "a great deal," "quite a lot" or "not very much" confidence in political parties, as opposed to the alternative, "none at all." World Values Surveys 1995–2006; average where multiple values are available for a country. World Values Survey Association, 2008. *World Values Survey 2005 Official Data File v.20081015.* (www.world valuessurvey.org).

Party closeness Percent saying they feel close to a specific party. Comparative Study of Electoral Systems Module II, 2001–06. www.umich. edu/~cses/

Appendix 3.2   Factor Analysis

Factor analysis with rotated (varimax) scores for the 39 countries listed in Tables 3.1 and 3.2 using the variables established democracy, regime type, party continuity, legal institutionalization, average electoral volatility, party confidence, and party closeness. Coding for all variables is described in Appendix 3.1. Missing values estimated using multivariate imputation by chain equations (MICE) in R 2.7.

Rotated component matrix

	Component	
	1	2
Established democracy	0.888	0.280
Legal institutionalization	−0.170	−0.828
Regime type	−0.738	−0.129
Party continuity	0.120	0.760
Average volatility	−0.714	−0.133
Party confidence	0.876	0.092
Party closeness	0.085	0.426

Extraction method: principal component analysis.
Rotation method: varimax with Kaiser normalization.

4

Campaign and
Party Finance

Ingrid van Biezen

"Trying to take money out of politics," suggested former United States Senator and retired NBA basketball player Bill Bradley, "is like trying to take jumping out of basketball." Although money should be seen as a normal and necessary element of the democratic process, its relationship with politics is blemished by its frequent association with practices of fraud, bribery, and corruption. Whether in old or new democracies, the financing of parties and candidates is perhaps the most obscure of all political activity. The place of money on, and often beyond, the edges of what is legally and morally permissible is fostered by the spate of financial scandals that are afflicting democratic governments today. The pervasiveness of political finance scandals means that this constitutes a very real problem for contemporary democracies, with evidence suggesting that it undermines the legitimacy of political parties, politicians, and potentially the democratic process itself: as parties and politicians are increasingly seen as office-seekers driven primarily by their material self-interests, and are regarded by the public as highly susceptible to corruption, they have become the least trusted among democratic institutions and actors (e.g., Dalton and Weldon 2005).

As the levels of popular disengagement, disaffection, and cynicism are rising and as party leaders are increasingly perceived as incompetent, dishonest, and corrupt, the concern for the impact of money on good governance has acquired an increased importance and attention in recent years. As Casas-Zamora (2005: 1) notes, "the growing awareness of the risks posed by corruption to the viability of democratic institutions have moved the funding of political activity to the centre of public debates all over the world." As a result, a host of international governmental institutions and non-governmental organizations are now independently investigating the funding practices of political parties and election campaigns, and are analyzing the possible ways in which illicit modes of party financing might be curtailed. These include organizations such as the African Union

(AU), the South African Development Community (SADC), the Council of Europe (CoE), the Organization of American States (OAS), the International Institute for Democracy and Electoral Assistance (IDEA), Transparency International (TI), and the World Bank. Indeed, the problems with party finance are affecting both the older advanced industrial democracies and the transitional and consolidating democracies.

National governments have also begun to pay more attention to the question of how the problems with campaign and party financing can be best addressed. One of the most tangible products of these concerns has been the enactment of a flurry of new political finance regulations. In the UK, for example, the Political Parties, Elections and Referendums Act adopted in 2000 radically reformed the environment of party and campaign finance by establishing a regulatory framework for party finance at the national level and by creating a new monitoring agency for its enforcement (Grant 2005). In the US, campaign finance was substantially reformed by the Bipartisan Campaign Reform Act of 2002, also widely known as McCain–Feingold, at the heart of which was the aim to reduce the role of political party "soft money" (Briffault 2006). In Canada, Bill C-24 was passed in 2003, which restricted private contributions by limiting corporate and individual donations while at the same time providing for a much more generous framework of public funding (Young 2004).

These are but a few examples of the abundance of recent regulatory changes, which have occurred in both the established and the consolidating democracies. As a result, the need for more comparative frameworks that may help us understand the paths taken by a variety of countries has become ever more pressing (Fisher and Eisenstadt 2004: 623). Although academic scholarship has long had an interest in the question of how parties and campaigns are financed and regulated, the field of political finance has long been populated predominantly by empirical case studies with little emphasis on efforts to establish cross-national explanations. As Scarrow (2007) has recently reiterated, the study of political finance suffers from a lack of theoretical foundations and comparative scholarship. Overall, therefore, there continues to be relatively little understanding of the various contexts and implications of funding sources, campaign expenditures and regulatory systems (Alexander 2001: 197).

This chapter addresses some of the gaps in the contemporary study of campaign and party finance by systematically exploring the variation in existing regulatory frameworks in light of potential explanatory factors. It provides a three-dimensional typology of financing regimes, which focuses on the control of income and expenditures, the transparency of donations and expenditures, and the availability of direct and indirect public funding. It examines several possible structural and institutional explanations for existing patterns of party regulation, including the pervasiveness of corruption, the level of economic development, the newness of democracy, and the type of electoral system. However, few of these factors seem to provide a satisfactory explanation, with the possible exception of the electoral system. In addition, the type of party regulation and party funding also appears to vary to some extent among regions.

Variation in Finance Regimes

The regulation of political finance can be directed at political parties, candidates, individuals, and groups, and focus on income and expenditure controls, transparency or state support in a variety of combinations, such that regulatory frameworks across the globe have taken a myriad of forms. Despite the large variety of financing regimes across the globe, one common development shared by many countries is a tendency towards conceding a greater responsibility to the state in the organization and regulation of political finance. As a consequence of recent finance scandals, or indeed as a general response to the perceived failings of parties and politicians, in many countries the state has now assumed a considerable, and increasingly legitimate, role in regulating parties and candidates, and in overseeing campaign and party financial activities in particular (van Biezen 2008).

The regulation of political finance involves several aspects, including the provision of public support to political parties and candidates, the regulation of donations and expenditures, as well as the transparency of the financing process. The table in Appendix 4.1, which is based on IDEA's comprehensive handbook of political funding (Austin and Tjernström 2003), summarizes the main characteristics of these financial regulations in 53 of the world's contemporary democracies where information was available.[1] The majority of these democracies appear to have established some form of regulatory framework for the financing of political parties, candidates, and election campaigns, with few significant differences between the older advanced industrial democracies and the more recently established ones. The variation in financing regimes as well as the distribution along three key dimensions is shown in Figure 4.1, which schematically represents the political financing regimes in democratic regimes across the globe. The first dimension ("regulation") refers to the regulation of donations to, and expenditures by, political parties and candidates, which includes limitations or prohibitions on specific kinds or total amounts of expenditure or sources of income. The second dimension ("transparency") indicates the presence of rules for reporting, disclosure, monitoring, and enforcement, which aim to increase the transparency of the financing process and thereby enhance the accountability of political actors. The third dimension ("subsidization") refers to the availability of various forms of direct and indirect public funding.

To an important extent, the mass party model of funding has become increasingly unsustainable in the established West European democracies, in part due to a rapid decline in membership over the past two decades (Mair and van Biezen 2001). Because of the relatively lower levels of economic development and the lack of a democratic participatory culture, the mass

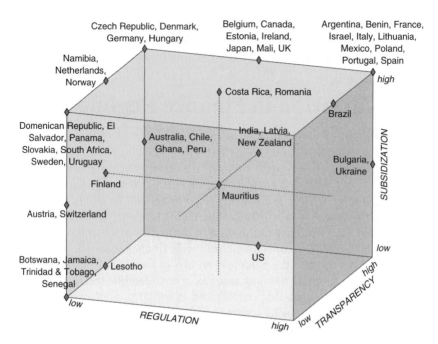

Figure 4.1   Typology of financing regimes

Note: "Regulation" refers to the degree of control over income and expenditure, ranging from "low" (no ceilings on contributions or expenditures) to "high" (ceilings on both contributions and expenditures). "Transparency" represents disclosure requirements, whereby "low" signals the absence of provisions for disclosure of income or expenditures, and "high" the requirement that both income and expenditures are disclosed. "Subsidization" refers to the availability of state subventions, ranging from "low" (no access direct or indirect subsidies) to "high" (the availability of both direct and indirect subsidies).

party has always been of limited relevance as a model of party organization in the more recently established democracies elsewhere in the world. The waning of the mass party model of funding leaves various alternative models of political finance (Hopkin 2004). In the absence of bottom-up financing from the grass roots, some parties will give more prominence to the role of private money, while for others the resources of the state will acquire more significance. Externally financed elite parties come to rely on private donations from individuals or private business to fund their increasingly capital-intensive campaigns, while the self-financing of wealthy candidates such as Ross Perot, Silvio Berlusconi or Thaksin Shinawatra might equally become an increasingly prevalent phenomenon in modern democracies. Cartel parties, on the other hand, come to depend primarily on the subsidies provided by the state (see Katz and Mair 1995). These alternatives have implied a greater involvement of the state in political finance, either in the form of increased access to direct state subventions or the need for greater public control over private donations to parties and candidates.

We might thus expect that the nature of political finance regimes is contingent upon various structural and institutional factors such as the levels of democratization and economic development, the prevalence of political scandals and corruption cases, or the types of party organization and the electoral system. In more recently established democracies, for example, the state may have assumed a greater role in political finance in order to support the relatively weakly institutionalized party organizations. Public regulation of political finance may also have been enacted as a response to high levels of corruption, aiming to control the amounts of political donations or seeking to improve the openness of the financial transactions of parties and candidates.

The relevance of these possible explanatory factors has been examined for our sample of 53 democracies. The first observation to be made is that they actually explain relatively little of the existing variation in the patterns of finance regulation. Table 4.1, for example, shows the variation in finance regimes by age of democracy, whereby all countries that democratized after 1974 have been considered as new democracies. As can be seen from

TABLE 4.1   Variation in finance regimes by level of democratization

			Age of democracy		
			Old democracies (before 1974)	New democracies (after 1974)	Total
Income/ expenditure limits[a]	Low	N	13	14	27
		%	52.0%	50.0%	50.9%
	Medium	N	9	4	13
		%	36.0%	14.3%	24.5%
	High	N	3	10	13
		%	12.0%	35.7%	24.5%
Disclosure rules[b]	Low	N	6	7	13
		%	24.0%	25.0%	24.5%
	Medium	N	5	4	9
		%	20.0%	14.3%	17.0%
	High	N	14	17	31
		%	56.0%	70.4%	58.5%
(In)direct public funding[c]	Low	N	3	3	6
		%	12.0%	10.7%	11.3%
	Medium	N	7	6	13
		%	28.0%	21.4%	24.5%
	High	N	15	19	34
		%	60.0%	67.9%	64.2%

[a] Income/expenditure limits: Is there a ceiling on contributions to political parties and/or on party expenditures?

[b] Disclosure rules: Are there provisions for disclosure of contributions to political parties and/ or party expenditures?

[c] (In)direct public funding: Do political parties receive direct and/or indirect subsidies from the state?

TABLE 4.2 Variation in finance regimes by levels of corruption

			Corruption			
			High	Medium	Low	Total
Income/expenditure	Low	N	10	8	9	27
limits		%	45.5%	44.4%	69.2%	50.9%
	Medium	N	4	5	4	13
		%	18.2%	27.8%	30.8%	24.5%
	High	N	8	5	0	13
		%	36.4%	27.8%	.0%	24.5%
Disclosure rules	Low	N	6	4	3	13
		%	27.3%	22.2%	23.1%	24.5%
	Medium	N	5	1	3	9
		%	22.7%	5.6%	23.1%	17.0%
	High	N	11	13	7	31
		%	50.0%	72.2%	53.8%	58.5%
(In)direct public funding	Low	N	4	2	0	6
		%	18.2%	11.1%	.0%	11.3%
	Medium	N	6	2	5	13
		%	27.3%	11.1%	38.5%	24.5%
	High	N	12	14	8	34
		%	54.5%	77.8%	61.5%	64.2%

this table, the newer democracies show a slightly higher, but statistically insignificant, propensity to regulate income and expenditures, but there is no correlation between the availability of (in)direct state subsidies to political parties or transparency rules and the newness of democracy. In the same vein, there appears to be little to no relationship between the type of finance regime and the level of economic development, except that the level of subsidization is moderately higher in high income economies (table not shown).

The prevalence of political corruption and the seemingly increasing frequency of finance scandals are often assumed to have contributed to the enactment of political finance legislation. Table 4.2, however, using the Kaufmann–Kraay (World Bank) index of corruption, reveals that the level of corruption has only a limited potential as an explanation for the nature of the political finance regime. Although there appears to be a positive correlation, albeit statistically insignificant, between the levels of corruption and the existence of income and expenditure limits, there is no clear relationship between the existence of disclosure rules or the availability of public funding and the level of corruption. This suggests that countries with higher levels of corruption may be more likely to establish legal norms to control political donations and expenditures, but are not necessarily more inclined to introduce transparency legislation or to concede a greater role to the state in the funding of political actors.

TABLE 4.3   Variation in finance regimes by electoral system

			Electoral System			
			Majoritarian	Combined	Proportional	Total
Income/expenditure	Low	N	6	5	16	27
limits		%	50.0%	45.5%	53.3%	50.9%
	Medium	N	5	2	6	13
		%	41.7%	18.2%	20.0%	24.5%
	High	N	1	4	8	13
		%	8.3%	36.4%	26.7%	24.5%
Disclosure rules	Low	N	3	2	8	13
		%	25.0%	18.2%	26.7%	24.5%
	Medium	N	1	1	7	9
		%	8.3%	9.1%	23.3%	17.0%
	High	N	8	8	15	31
		%	66.7%	72.7%	50.0%	58.5%
(In)direct public	Low	N	4	2	0	6
funding		%	33.3%	18.2%	.0%	11.3%
	Medium	N	4	2	7	13
		%	33.3%	18.2%	23.3%	24.5%
	High	N	4	7	23	34
		%	33.3%	63.6%	76.7%	64.2%

Instead of structural conditions such as the levels of economic development, democratization, or corruption, one institutional factor that appears to be important for explaining the patterns of political finance is the electoral system (see Table 4.3): there is a strong and positive correlation ($r = 0.455$**) between systems of proportional representation and the use of direct or indirect state funding. More than three-quarters of the countries with PR use both direct and indirect funding, against only about one-third of the majoritarian systems, with the mixed systems falling somewhere in between. The pattern is similar when direct and indirect funding are considered separately. A possible explanation for this finding is that it is related to the nature of the party system and the number of competing parties. Highly fragmented systems, with more and smaller parties, might be more inclined to introduce public subsidies with a view to the fairness of political competition. Alternatively, following the lines of the cartel party thesis, established parties in a highly competitive electoral context may use public subsidies to better protect themselves against outsider challengers. Which of these two interpretations holds true depends in large part on the allocation mechanisms of state support and its distribution between small and large parties. It is also possible, however, that the observed relationship is simply a spurious one, due to the fact that the IDEA database includes only public subsidies to political parties but not to individual candidates, which are likely to be more prevalent in candidate-oriented systems.

Finally, there seems to be a certain amount of regional variation between finance regimes. Table 4.4 shows, for example, that income and expenditure controls are relatively infrequent in Africa and South America, while they are more prominent in Central and Eastern Europe. Similarly, disclosure rules are prevalent in Central and Eastern Europe, as well as in Western Europe and North America, but less so in Africa and South America. The established democracies in Western European, the newer democracies in Central and Eastern Europe as well as South American democracies show a somewhat higher incidence of state support for political parties than is the case in Africa. In the following sections, this variation in financing regimes is discussed in more detail, focusing on both the existing patterns across the globe and the underlying principles of regulation, transparency and public support.

Controlling Contributions and Expenditures

While contribution limits aim to prevent the perversion of elections by quid pro quo exchanges, expenditure limits are essentially aimed at preventing candidates and parties from buying elections. Expenditure limits, which are somewhat less common than contribution limits, can either restrict the total amount a party or candidate may spend, or limit the amount spent in particular ways and on particular activities, including the possibility that some forms of spending may be banned altogether (Katz 1996: 125). These limits may consist of an absolute sum per candidate or party (such as in the UK), a certain amount relative to a statutory yardstick such as the minimum wage (as in Portugal), or a maximum sum depending on the number of inhabitants in the constituency (such as in Spain).

Expenditure limits exist in just over one-third of the democratic polities in our sample. They are particularly rare in Latin America, where they only exist in Argentina, Brazil, and Mexico, and in Africa, where they are in place only in Benin and Mauritius. One of the main reasons why expenditure limits are seen as controversial is that they necessarily impose restrictions on the freedom of speech, or on the freedom to disseminate speech. The desire to curtail moneyed interests in elections thus implies a fine balancing act with other key democratic principles. The United States is known for having privileged the freedom of speech and represents a particularly permissive tradition with regard to campaign expenditure, as spending by candidates is not limited (with the exception of presidential candidates who voluntarily accept spending limits in exchange for public subsidies). In fact, the US Supreme Court ruled in 1976 in *Buckley v. Valeo* that expenditure ceilings impose direct and substantial restraints on the quantity of political speech (Katz 1996: 124), thus deeming expenditure limits unconstitutional and in violation of the First Amendment.

TABLE 4.4 Variation in finance regimes by region

			Africa	Asia–Pacific	C&E Europe	Middle East	N America	S America	W Europe	Total
Income/ expenditure limits	Low	N	6	1	3	0	1	8	8	27
		%	66.7%	25.0%	30.0%	.0%	33.3%	72.7%	53.3%	50.9%
	Medium	N	2	3	3	0	1	1	3	13
		%	22.1%	75.0%	30.0%	.0%	33.3%	9.1%	20.0%	24.5%
	High	N	1	0	4	1	1	2	4	13
		%	11.1%	.0%	40.0%	100.0%	33.3%	18.2.0%	26.7%	24.5%
	Total	N	9	4	10	1	3	11	15	53
		%	100.0%	100.0%	100.0%	100.0%	100.0%	100.0%	100.0%	100.0%
Disclosure rules	Low	N	3	0	1	0	0	6	3	13
		%	33.3%	.0%	10.0%	.0%	.0%	54.5%	20.0%	24.5%
	Medium	N	3	0	1	0	0	2	3	9
		%	33.3%	.0%	10.0%	.0%	.0%	18.2%	20.0%	17.0%
	High	N	3	4	8	1	3	3	9	31
		%	33.3%	100.0%	80.0%	100.0%	100.0%	27.3%	60.0%	58.5%
	Total	N	9	4	10	1	3	11	15	53
		%	100.0%	100.0%	100.0%	100.0%	100.0%	100.0%	100.0%	100.0%
(In)direct public funding	Low	N	3	0	0	0	1	2	0	6
		%	33.3%	.0%	.0%	.0%	33.3%	18.2%	.0%	11.3%
	Medium	N	2	3	3	0	0	2	3	13
		%	22.2%	75.0%	30.0%	.0%	.0%	18.2%	20.0%	24.5%
	High	N	4	1	7	1	2	7	12	34
		%	44.4%	25.0%	70.0%	100.0%	66.7%	63.6%	80.0%	64.2%
	Total	N	9	4	10	1	3	11	15	53
		%	100.0%	100.0%	100.0%	100.0%	100.0%	100.0%	100.0%	100.0%

European democracies have tended to adopt a different approach to party and campaign finance, moving instead towards much more restrictive regulations. The European approach has been to justify restrictions on campaign expenditures as a means to control the potentially disruptive role of money in politics. Restrictions to campaign expenditure are accepted on the grounds that unrestricted spending gives an unfair advantage to interests with privileged access to financial resources, and might make elected officials dependent on their economic contributors at the expense of the general interest and the population at large (Alexander and Shiratori 1994). Similarly, the Canadian Supreme Court ruled in 2004 in *Harper v. Canada* that spending limits are justified with a view to preventing the most affluent citizens from monopolizing the electoral discourse (Feasby 2006). In contrast with the "libertarian" paradigm that prevails in the US, therefore, Europe and Canada can be seen to represent a rather more "egalitarian" approach to political finance (Griner and Zovatto 2005).

Contribution limits are more common than expenditure limits. They are often motivated by a desire to prevent that economic inequality should translate directly into political inequality. If no contribution limits are in place, financial disparities between parties might become exacerbated. A second concern with private donations is that financial exchange relationships between parties and candidates and private individuals or groups open up the potential for a conflict of interest. As private contributions may tempt the recipient to privilege the interests of its donors over those of the general public, there is a danger that certain private interests rather than the general public interest will guide the conduct of parties and elected officials. Private donations can thus generate suspicions of vote buying and trading influence. Although some scholars have argued that such fears are often exaggerated (e.g., Lösche 1993), others argue that the extent to which those in public office exploit their decision-making capacity to the benefit of private contributors should not be underestimated. The problems of vote buying appear to be particularly profound in many of the transitional and consolidating democracies, where the political process more broadly tends to be dominated by particularistic exchanges. Even in the US, where the Supreme Court ruled that expenditure limits place severe restrictions on constitutionally protected expression, it did not rule out contribution limits, which it deemed justified in the interest of preventing corruption or the appearance thereof.

Contribution limits may apply to parties or candidates, or both. They are especially common in the younger democracies in Southern and Eastern Europe, but relatively rare in Latin America and Africa. Such provisions may involve restrictions on the acceptable amounts of contributions, either in the form of a maximum on the amount of money that can be accepted from a particular source (whereby different ceilings may apply to different types of donors) or a limit on the total sum of acceptable private contributions. They may also involve prohibitions of certain types of donors and donations, such as anonymous donations or public and semi-public organizations, the latter with a view to avoiding a concealed form of state funding.

Restrictions commonly apply to corporate donations. Although private business remains an important source of finance, some countries have moved towards more stringent legislative frameworks on corporate donations in an attempt to limit the influence of plutocratic financing on democratic politics. Some countries, such as Belgium, France, Israel, Mexico or Poland, have imposed a complete ban on donations from corporate entities. In others, such as Brazil and Japan, a partial ban on corporate donations exists. Many of such decisions were taken as a response to the eruption of corruption cases. Japan, for example, tightened the rules on political donations in the 1970s and again in 2000, in the wake of a series of financial scandals. Similarly, illicit financial deals and corruption scandals in France in the 1990s encouraged the enactment of new legislation, which made it illegal for private business to donate money to political parties and candidates. As a consequence, political activity is now financed – at least formally – primarily from public funds.

Some countries prohibit or restrict contributions from trade unions. In Europe, the links between the economic and political branches of the labor movement have traditionally been very strong, whereby trade union funding has often been essential for labor parties to compete with the much larger funds available to middle-class parties from corporations and wealthy individuals. However, the channeling of political donations through interest associations may generate suspicions of undue political influence, especially if an exchange relationship appears to exist between the contributions and certain public policy decisions. Moreover, donations from interest associations do not necessarily reflect the views of the entire membership. This is the reason why trade union contributions are prohibited in North America, where unions have been banned from making political contributions in Canada since 1920 and in the United States since 1943. Another, and less extreme, solution is provided by the UK and Denmark, where trade unions are allowed to contribute to parties and campaigns provided that any member must be offered the possibility to opt out of the scheme (e.g., Ewing 2002).

Parties may furthermore be banned from accepting money from foreign entities, governments or individuals, usually with a view to safeguard a country's domestic autonomy and sovereignty, or, more pragmatically, with reference to the difficulty of ensuring the accountability of the donor. Foreign donations, however, do not always have subversive intentions and may in fact be a welcome contribution to efforts of democracy promotion and assistance. The role of the German parties and their associated research institutes in the democratization processes in Southern and Eastern Europe, for example, is relatively well known and documented (e.g., Mair 2000). More generally, financial support to political parties has acquired an increasingly important and legitimate role in the overall domain of international democracy assistance, alongside the promotion of free and fair elections, the development of a vibrant civil society, and an effective rule of law (e.g., Burnell 2005). For Southern Africa, Southall (2006) has argued that party aid is in fact of critical importance for transitional societies, in particular because it supports the existence of a viable opposition in a context of patronage-dominated politics.

Transparency and Enforcement

Just as contribution and expenditure controls seek to prevent the role of money from perverting the democratic process, transparency requirements seek to enhance political accountability by providing insight into the actual levels of income and expenditure. Indeed, although factor analysis confirms that both types of regulation co-vary, they are underpinned by very different logics. This is most clearly illustrated by the United States, which can be seen to represent a financing paradigm that pivots more on full transparency in order to limit the potential contamination of the democratic process by private money than on income and expenditure control; hence its particular location in Figure 4.1. The threshold of disclosure in the US is set at a relatively low limit, the law requires full details of the donor to be made public, and candidates are subject to strict reporting rules.

Transparency is increasingly seen as a key safeguard against the illegitimacy of political finance. Moreover, because secrecy about private contributions is feared to breed suspicion and thus to undermine democratic legitimacy, transparency is often advanced as a necessary condition for public confidence and trust in the democratic system. To this effect, political finance regimes have resorted to increasingly strict requirements for the disclosure of financial accounts and their monitoring by a specially designated body. In addition, an effective system of enforcement demands that these requirements are embedded in a context of legal sanctions that impose penalties on violations of the law. As Casas-Zamora (2005: 23) observes, "a copious comparative experience suggests that a demanding set of requisites must be met if political finance disclosure is to be enforced." But, he continues, "the presence of such requisites is by no means guaranteed." No matter how detailed the regulations on income and expenditure or how strict the requirements for disclosure and transparency, a lack of authoritative enforcement mechanism or the absence of meaningful sanctions will render parts of the system effectively inoperative.

While transparency rules are a critical component of political finance regulations in many countries, they are also associated with several practical and normative dilemmas. First of all, political parties, candidates, and enforcement agencies incur considerable costs in providing, auditing, and processing the necessary information (Nassmacher 2003: 143). Secondly, it is not certain to what extent transparency can reduce corrupt practices, which can be illustrated by the persistence of political finance scandals across the globe in spite of increasingly strict requirements for disclosure. Besides, full publicity appears to have a limited capacity to diminish the influential role of private money more generally. As West (2000) has recently argued for the United States, politics is increasingly dominated by more or less transparent financial exchanges between private donors and elected politicians, to the point that the system can be best described as a "checkbook democracy" in which policies can effectively be bought and sold. Finally, and perhaps paradoxically, transparency may actually have an adverse effect on democratic legitimacy, as the availability of more information might effectively breed more suspicion. Openness may thus enhance rather than diminish the levels of perceived corruption, and thus further contribute to the erosion of public confidence in parties and politicians, regardless of whether these suspicions are well grounded (Fisher and Eisenstadt 2004). It remains an open question whether these scandalizing effects outweigh the positive benefits of regulation (Scarrow 2007: 201).

From a normative perspective, moreover, a trade-off exists between transparency and privacy. Disclosure requirements reflect the notion that "the collective benefits of disclosing sources of financial support of political actors outweigh the donors' right to privacy" (Casas-Zamora 2005: 23). Disclosure of political donations makes it easier to detect (and thus perhaps to avoid) political corruption because it may expose the connection between large donations and certain government decisions to the public and the media. To the extent that disclosure enhances transparency, it may therefore prevent or limit improper financing. More generally, voters may claim to have a right to know who are the financial supporters of the different political parties and candidates running for office, as this could influence their electoral choice.

On the other hand, however, donors may have a legitimate desire to preserve the privacy of their political preferences. Disclosure requirements may constitute an unjustified infringement on both individual privacy and the autonomy of political parties as private associations. In some of the consolidated democracies, such as Sweden and Switzerland, for example, the notion of political parties as voluntary associations of civil society and a concern with their internal autonomy lie beneath the absence of a statutory control of party financing (Nassmacher 2003: 141). Private donations to political parties can be seen as a form of political participation and an expression of political support tantamount to the act of voting. Just as a democracy would safeguard the secrecy of the ballot, donors should not be required to declare their political allegiances. This argument may carry additional relevance for public officials, such as judges, civil servants, members of the armed forces, and so on, who are expected to maintain a stance of political neutrality, or for representatives of business organizations who fear that they might be discriminated against when government contracts are awarded if they are known to have supported a particular political party or candidate. In transitional and newly consolidating democracies, moreover, disclosure rules may inhibit contributions to opposition parties and candidates, in particular in countries with a dominant ruling party, thus creating a strong bias in the system in favor of the incumbent party.

Consider the case of South Africa, for example, where over the past few years a number of financing scandals have drawn the attention of the media and the broader public. South Africa has a limited level of regulation of non-state party funding, which has encouraged civil society organizations to advocate a greater need for transparency. For this reason, the Institute for Democracy and South Africa (IDASA) embarked upon a court action in 2004, filing petitions against the main political parties requesting access to their funding records. However, Sarakinsky (2007) has argued that, although secret donations appear at odds with the values of democratic governance and accountability, there has been no empirical evidence that supports the allegation of a connection between the secrecy of funding and the presence of corruption. In addition to the question of whether a causal link exists between the lack of disclosure and the existence of corruption, Sarakinsky contends that the disclosure of the donor's identity prejudices smaller opposition parties and thus skews the competitive playing field. The argument about the fairness of political competition has a broader relevance for countries with predominant party systems, a weakly institutionalized opposition and a general lack of alternation in power (cf. Saffu 2003). Here, the anonymity of political donations may help opposition parties raise funds by protecting the identity of their donors. In general, however, the notion that full publicity has the potential to play a powerful cleansing role in politics continues to be the reigning paradigm.[2]

Disclosure requirements nearly always exist if parties or candidates are entitled to direct funding from the state. In fact, many of the rules were first introduced or were substantially extended in the wake of the introduction of public funding for parties, as the provision of state subventions inevitably demanded a more codified system of party registration and control. Conversely, in many countries where parties are not entitled to direct state subsidies, disclosure regulations are weak or absent (e.g., Botswana, Jamaica, Lesotho, Senegal, Switzerland, Trinidad & Tobago). In these systems, the involvement of the state in the financing and management of political parties and election campaigns is thus relatively limited. In political practice, however, this particular model increasingly constitutes an exception to the norm, as the state has assumed an increased importance both in terms of the subsidization of political parties and the regulation of their activities (see also van Biezen and Kopecký 2007). Even the established liberal democracies of Western Europe, where a historical conception of political parties as private associations has long prevailed and respect for the internal autonomy of parties has traditionally outweighed the case for public control, have moved towards progressively more regulation, and indeed more direct public subsidies. The UK, where the financing of parties had previously been largely unregulated and unmonitored, codified new party finance regulations in the 2000 Political Parties, Elections and Referendums Act. In the same vein, the Netherlands adopted the Law on State Subvention to Political Parties in 1999, which not only transformed existing practices into a statutory law but also gave a legal basis to the provision of direct public subsidies (Gidlund and Koole 2001). We will turn to the issue of public funding in the next section.

Public Funding

The third key dimension of underlying the finance regimes in our typology is the availability of state subsidies for political parties, candidates, and election campaigns. This has become increasingly important in recent years, although the practice of direct state funding goes as far back as its introduction in Uruguay as early as 1928. The phenomenon gained momentum in the 1950s in Latin America, with Costa Rica adopting state subsidies in 1954, and Argentina in 1955, both preceding West Germany, the first European country to introduce public subsidies for party organizations in 1959 (Posada-Carbó 2008). In many of the recently established democracies in southern Europe and post-communist Eastern Europe, state support for parties was often introduced on a relatively wide scale during or immediately after the transition to democracy (van Biezen 2003). Public subsidies have now become such a widespread phenomenon across the globe, in both the consolidated and the recently created democracies, that political parties in nearly three-quarters of the modern liberal democracies have access to direct public funding (see Appendix 4.1).

One important motivation for the introduction of public subsidies concerns the rising cost of politics. As modern politics has become increasingly professionalized and cost-intensive, while the reservoirs of volunteers appear to have become depleted, the state in many democracies has intervened by providing direct financial support to parties and candidates in order to support the continuation of party democracy. According to Katz and Mair (1995: 15), the growth in state subvention "has come to represent one of the most significant changes to the environment in which parties act." This environmental change is of course not exogenous to the parties, as parties are ultimately the actors "responsible for both the rules regarding state subventions as well as for the amounts of money and resources that are made available." The increasing relevance of state subventions as a principal resource for modern parties underlines the progressively strong interdependence between parties and the state and the consequent emergence of the cartel party, with colluding parties having become agents of the state and depending on public resources, such as subsidies and state-regulated media access, for their own survival.

Because party activity is carried out in a variety of arenas, including parliamentary work, election campaigning, and routine operational activities, states may provide support for some or all of these types of activity. Direct state funding consequently tends to rest on three pillars: subsidies for the routine operational cost of parties, subsidies for campaigning activity, and subsidies to parliamentary party groups. In addition to direct subventions to support operational activities, electoral campaigns, and parliamentary group work, parties may also receive various forms of in-kind subsidies and indirect funding, such as free radio and television broadcasting, reduced postal rates, or various types of tax exemptions (see Appendix 4.2). The funding regime is closely related to institutional structures such as the type of government and the electoral system. In the presidential systems in North and Latin America, financing electoral campaigns is more customary than subsidizing party organizations (Casas-Zamora 2005: 33). In the parliamentary regimes in Europe, on the other hand, public funding tends to be oriented primarily towards political parties. However, in countries with more candidate-oriented electoral systems, such as Hungary, where a proportion of the parliamentary representatives are elected in single-member constituencies, public reimbursement of election expenses is also available for individual candidates. As Zovatto (2003) argues for the Latin American context, presidential systems of government also have a direct impact on the personalization of politics, as these encourage donors to channel their contributions directly to the candidates for executive office. This tends to undermine the institutionalization of party organizations, a tendency that is further reinforced by a cultural tradition of personalism and *caudillismo*.

The increased availability of public subsidies can be interpreted as an indication of the increasing financial dependence of parties on the state, although comprehensive cross-national data to establish precisely how dependent parties are on state subsidies are not available. Existing studies suggest that significant differences exist between countries, or between parties within a single country. In a comparative analysis of several European democracies, Pierre et al. (2000) found that state support ranged from just over 20% (Denmark) to almost 85% (Finland) of total party income. Many parties in the Southern European democracies of Spain and Portugal are virtually entirely dependent on the state for their income (van Biezen 2003). In some Central and Eastern European countries, such as the Czech Republic, Slovenia, Hungary, and Estonia, the relative importance of state money is similarly large while in others, such as Bulgaria or Ukraine, public funding is merely symbolic in comparison to the resources parties obtain from private and corporate donations (Kopecký 2006). Among the established democracies, parties in Germany, France, and Israel benefit from significant amounts of subsidies, while the UK, on the other hand, provides only token amounts of public support (Pinto-Duschinsky 2002). At the very least however, the introduction of state support for parties appears to have encouraged a dependence on public money that is critical for a lot of parties and non-trivial for many others (Katz 2002).

The one continent to stand in sharp contrast to this trend is Africa, which is the only region where state funding for parties is available in only a minority of democratic states (i.e. Benin, Mali, Namibia, and South Africa). What is more, the absence of direct state subventions in Africa is often accompanied by a relative lack of control on party income and expenditures, such as in Botswana, Lesotho, Mauritius, and Senegal. With the exception of Ghana, this tends to be coupled with limited or no transparency of party financing. The state thus plays a limited role in the regulation and financing of political parties, suggesting that the particular type of party–state linkage which is prevalent in Africa is an informal one, whereby the benefits that parties amass from the state are almost solely derived from the informal practices of patronage, clientelism, corruption (e.g., Kopecký and Mair 2003; van de Walle 2003). As a consequence, as rent-seeking is the key route for parties and politicians to obtain benefits from the state, public resources are distributed highly unevenly among political actors, and incumbents enjoy huge material advantages over the opposition. In many African countries, this form of party–state linkage provides the underpinning of predominant party systems in which there is little or no turnover of executive power.

In one of the oldest democracies on the African continent, Botswana, for example, the Botswana Democratic Party has prevailed in every election since independence in 1966. Opposition parties are small and fragmented and wield little influence. The persistence of the predominant party system is encouraged by a majoritarian electoral system of first past the post. The incumbent BDP enjoys major advantages by virtue of being in power, which enables the party to take advantage of state resources by monopolizing the government-controlled media rewarding party activists and supporters through political patronage (Molomo and Sebudubudu 2005). The lack of resource capacity presents opposition parties in Botswana with difficulties in finding and resourcing viable candidates for public office, and is one of the main factors responsible for their failure to provide the electorate with a meaningful alternative to the BDP (Selolwane 2002: 68). As the absence of state financing for political parties helps to maintain an imbalance between government and opposition in terms of the available resources, opposition parties and civil society have consistently pushed for the introduction of public funding, arguing that it would go a long way in addressing the uneven competitive playing field (Somolekae 2005: 25–6).

The Botswana example, as well as the African experience more generally, underline a second key argument frequently advanced in favor of public funding: state subsidies may provide an important contribution to democracy by contributing to the equality and fairness of political competition. On this view, the fact that not all parties are equally well resourced should not necessarily be to the disadvantage of those that cannot successfully tap into the funds of private contributors. This is relevant primarily for smaller parties, newly established parties, parties whose political program is unlikely to appeal to wealthy or established interests, parties that lack any linkages with affiliated interest organizations, or opposition parties in predominant party systems. Such considerations prevailed also in the early stage of post-communist democratization, where the introduction of state support was motivated by the need to relieve opposition parties from the competitive disadvantages *vis-à-vis* the financially secure Communist Parties. State subsidies can thus create a more level playing field by enabling new, small, and less prosperous parties to compete on a more equitable basis with the dominant and financially more privileged ones. From this perspective, the interest of the state is to facilitate an effective political market and thus to contribute to the creation of a context that provides for adequate party competition. In this sense, state subsidies serve to correct market failures and to prevent possible monopolistic partisan practices, which in some cases might be the only alternative available in party systems where only the governing party benefits from access to state resources through patronage and corruption (van Biezen and Kopecký 2007).

As Katz and Mair (1995) have pointed out, however, public funding may also have the exact opposite effect and contribute to the cartelization of party systems by perpetuating the status quo and actually making it more difficult for newcomers to challenge the incumbent parties. The extent to which the system of state funding discriminates against small and new parties largely depends on two key factors: the threshold for eligibility, with higher thresholds more likely to contribute to the entrenchment of the larger and existing parties, and the mechanism for allocation, whereby a principle of equality, by which each party or candidate receives an equal sum of money or lump sum, will tend to produce a less skewed distribution of money in favor of the larger parties than a principle of proportionality, which allocates public subsidies in relation to the levels of electoral strength or parliamentary size. The more the method of allocation for public subsidies intensifies the disproportional tendencies inherent in the electoral system, the more it penalizes smaller parties and contributes to the cartelization of the party system, as is the case in Spain for example (Gillespie 1998: 81–4). For a summary of the interval and basis of allocation for public subsidies in contemporary democracies, see Appendix 4.2.

In addition to the rising cost of politics or the desire to level the playing field, a third oft-cited argument in favor of public funding is related to attempts to restrict the influence of private money and to counteract the potential for corruption. Japan provides an obvious example in this regard. The fundamental reform of the funding regime which was carried out in 1994, when public subsidies for political parties were first introduced, had little to do with a need for the state to address a shortage of resources, as political parties, and the governing LDP in particular, had strong established links with private business (Ferdinand 1998). Parties and Diet members generated the bulk of their revenues through corporate donations. A series of finance scandals in the early 1990s, however, drove the incumbent LDP to address the issue of the role of money politics, leading to the introduction of public subsidies as well as stricter transparency requirements (Ferdinand 1998: 199; see also Ejima 2006). It appears doubtful, however, that the supply of public funding has eliminated the search of Japanese parties for additional funds from private sources (Blechinger and Nassmacher 2001: 180).

The Japanese case illustrates that the underlying rationale for the introduction of public funding is often premised on the assumption that state subsidization relieves parties from the need to satisfy their financial supporters and will therefore have a diminishing effect on the contaminating influence of private money. This argument has gained an increasingly wide acceptance. However, there is little empirical evidence to support the expectation. This absence of an unequivocally positive impact of direct state funding on the prevention of unlawful exchanges between parties and donors is supported by Casas-Zamora's in-depth case study of political finance in Costa Rica and Uruguay: public subsidies "are not necessarily an antidote to financial dependence on private sources of funding, and, even less, to unsavoury fundraising practices" (Casas-Zamora 2005: 39). Indeed, systems of public funding often supplement rather than substitute clientelistic and corrupt forms of financing (Zovatto 2003: 99). As the excessive dependence on public funds facilitates access to the resources of the state, it may also make it easier and more tempting for parties to turn to the state for resources other than the official subsidies (Katz and Mair 1995). One of the unintended consequences of the extension of public subsidies, therefore, is that it may encourage the unauthorized use of state resources and actually exacerbate rather than reduce the potential for corruption (cf. Gambetta 2002).

Conclusion

This chapter has focused on the various ways in which democratic states regulate the financing of political parties and election campaigns. Concentrating on the regulation of income and expenditures, transparency requirements, and the provision of public funding, it has proposed a typology of financing regimes, suggesting that funding regimes can be modeled along three key dimensions, each of which is underpinned by different logics. It has also proposed various structural and institutional explanations in order to understand the seemingly immeasurable variety of finance regimes in existing democracies. While it appears difficult to identify any regional models, a few patterns can be teased out. African countries tend to be relatively unregulated, for example. Even where the state has assumed some responsibility for leveling the playing field, there is virtually a complete absence of rules for the use of private donations or the disclosure of sources (Pottie 2003: 5). In contrast, parties in Europe and Latin America are relatively highly subsidized and regulated, with the main purpose of regulatory systems and public funding aimed at combating corruption, controlling the power of big donors, and leveling the playing field of electoral politics (Posada-Carbó 2008: 24).

An exploration of several potential explanations suggests that institutional factors such as the type of electoral system may account for some of the variation in finance regimes, with PR systems seemingly more likely to use public funding for political parties. The relevance of structural factors such as the levels of democratization, economic development or corruption, however, appears to be minimal. The nature of the finance regime appears to be scarcely correlated with the levels of corruption, suggesting that political finance regulations might not necessarily be a product of a perceived increase in political scandals. The available evidence also indicates that the potential of public regulation or state funding as effective anti-corruption devices is marginal at best. According to some scholars, this near-exclusive emphasis on corruption prevention is misguided at any rate, and the political finance agenda should instead concentrate on how to enhance democratic principles such as electoral competition and political equality (Malbin 2008). Indeed, what has remained underemphasized in the scholarly literature thus far is that political finance systems are underpinned by different philosophies, and the extent to which these may account for an existing variation between countries.

More fundamentally, rather than a simple trade-off between different democratic values, such as political equality and freedom of speech, debates over political finance are essentially based on competing conceptions of democracy, and are thus ultimately rooted in fundamental disagreements about the nature of democracy itself (Dawood 2006: 271). Although these different visions of democracy might never be mutually reconcilable, one of the key challenges for both scholars of political finance and policymakers and advisors in charge of improving seemingly malfunctioning financing regimes lies in the elucidation of the implicit normative assumptions on which their perspectives are premised. While much empirical work in the field of political finance still remains to be done, it is only with reference to the underlying theoretical and normative foundations of existing approaches that the impact of finance reforms on the quality of democracy can be meaningfully assessed.

Appendix 4.1 Systems of party finance

Country	Donations			Expenditures		Public funding	
	Is there a ceiling on contributions to political parties?	Is there a ban on certain types of donations to political parties?	Are there provisions for the disclosure of contributions to political parties?	Is there a ceiling on party election expenditures?	Are there provisions for the disclosure of expenditures by political parties?	Do political parties receive direct public funding?	Do political parties receive indirect public funding?
Africa							
Benin	Yes	Yes	Yes	Yes	Yes	Yes	Yes
Botswana	No	No	No	No	No	No	No
Ghana	No	No	Yes	No	Yes	No	Yes
Lesotho	No	No	Yes	No	No	No	No
Mali	Yes	Yes	Yes	No	Yes	Yes	Yes
Mauritius	No	No	No	Yes	Yes	No	Yes
Namibia	No	Yes	Yes	No	No	Yes	Yes
Senegal	No	Yes	No	No	No	No	No
South Africa	No	No	No	No	No	Yes	Yes
Asia–Pacific							
Australia	No	Yes	Yes	No	Yes	Yes	No
India	No	No	Yes	Yes	Yes	No	Yes

(Continued)

Country	Donations			Expenditures		Public funding	
	Is there a ceiling on contributions to political parties?	Is there a ban on certain types of donations to political parties?	Are there provisions for the disclosure of contributions to political parties?	Is there a ceiling on party election expenditures?	Are there provisions for the disclosure of expenditures by political parties?	Do political parties receive direct public funding?	Do political parties receive indirect public funding?
Japan	Yes	Yes	Yes	No	Yes	Yes	Yes
New Zealand	No	No	Yes	Yes	Yes	No	Yes
C&E Europe							
Bulgaria	Yes	Yes	Yes	Yes	Yes	Yes	No
Czech Republic	No	Yes	Yes	No	Yes	Yes	Yes
Estonia	Yes	Yes	Yes	No	Yes	Yes	Yes
Hungary	No	Yes	Yes	No	Yes	Yes	Yes
Latvia	Yes	Yes	Yes	No	Yes	No	Yes
Lithuania	Yes	Yes	Yes	Yes	Yes	Yes	Yes
Poland	Yes	Yes	Yes	Yes	Yes	Yes	Yes
Romania	Yes	Yes	Yes	No	No	Yes	Yes
Slovakia	No	No	No	No	No	Yes	Yes
Ukraine	Yes	Yes	Yes	Yes	Yes	No	Yes

Country	Donations			Expenditures		Public funding	
	Is there a ceiling on contributions to political parties?	Is there a ban on certain types of donations to political parties?	Are there provisions for the disclosure of contributions to political parties?	Is there a ceiling on party election expenditures?	Are there provisions for the disclosure of expenditures by political parties?	Do political parties receive direct public funding?	Do political parties receive indirect public funding?
Middle East							
Israel	Yes	Yes	Yes	Yes	Yes	Yes	Yes
North America							
Canada	No	Yes	Yes	Yes	Yes	Yes	Yes
Mexico	Yes	Yes	Yes	Yes	Yes	Yes	Yes
United States	Yes	Yes	Yes	No	Yes	No	No
South America							
Argentina	Yes	Yes	Yes	Yes	Yes	Yes	Yes
Brazil	Yes	Yes	Yes	Yes	No	Yes	Yes
Chile	No	Yes	Yes	No	Yes	No	Yes
Costa Rica	Yes	Yes	Yes	No	No	Yes	Yes
Dominican Rep.	No	Yes	No	No	No	Yes	Yes
El Salvador	No	No	No	No	No	Yes	Yes

(Continued)

Country	Donations			Expenditures		Public funding	
	Is there a ceiling on contributions to political parties?	Is there a ban on certain types of donations to political parties?	Are there provisions for the disclosure of contributions to political parties?	Is there a ceiling on party election expenditures?	Are there provisions for the disclosure of expenditures by political parties?	Do political parties receive direct public funding?	Do political parties receive indirect public funding?
Jamaica	No	No	No	No	No	No	No
Panama	No	No	No	No	No	Yes	Yes
Peru	No	No	Yes	No	Yes	No	Yes
Trinidad & Tobago	No	No	No	No	No	No	No
Uruguay	No	No	No	No	No	Yes	Yes
Western Europe							
Austria	No	No	No	No	No	Yes	No
Belgium	Yes	Yes	Yes	No	Yes	Yes	Yes
Denmark	No	No	Yes	No	Yes	Yes	Yes
Finland	No	No	No	No	Yes	Yes	No
France	Yes	Yes	Yes	Yes	Yes	Yes	Yes
Germany	No	Yes	Yes	No	Yes	Yes	Yes
Ireland	Yes	Yes	Yes	No	Yes	Yes	Yes

Country	Donations			Expenditures		Public funding	
	Is there a ceiling on contributions to political parties?	Is there a ban on certain types of donations to political parties?	Are there provisions for the disclosure of contributions to political parties?	Is there a ceiling on party election expenditures?	Are there provisions for the disclosure of expenditures by political parties?	Do political parties receive direct public funding?	Do political parties receive indirect public funding?
Italy	Yes	Yes	Yes	Yes	Yes	Yes	Yes
Netherlands	No	Yes	Yes	No	No	Yes	Yes
Norway	No	No	Yes	No	No	Yes	Yes
Portugal	Yes	Yes	Yes	Yes	Yes	Yes	Yes
Spain	Yes	Yes	Yes	Yes	Yes	Yes	Yes
Sweden	No	No	No	No	No	Yes	Yes
Switzerland	No	No	No	No	No	No	Yes
United Kingdom	No	Yes	Yes	Yes	Yes	Yes	Yes
Yes:	22 (41.5%)	33 (62.3%)	38 (71.7%)	18 (34.0%)	33 (62.3%)	38 (71.7%)	43 (81.1%)
No:	31 (58.5%)	20 (37.7%)	15 (28.3%)	35 (66.0%)	20 (37.7%)	15 (28.3%)	10 (18.9%)

Note: The main focus of the data in this table is on the financing of political parties, as opposed to individual candidates or parliamentary groups. The countries selected for this table are those included in the IDEA database that were classified as "Free" by the Freedom House in 2007, with the exception of smaller states with a population under 1,000,000.

Source: Austin and Tjernström (2003)

Appendix 4.2 Public subsidies to political parties

	Direct subsidies			Indirect subsidies	
	Allocation interval	Allocation basis	Purpose	Allocation basis for free broadcasting	Tax relief
Argentina	• Election period • Between elections	• Equal funding • Performance at previous election	• General party administration • Election campaign activities	• Equal time	• Tax exemptions for parties • Tax deductions for donors
Australia	• Election period • Between elections	• Performance at previous election	• Non-earmarked	N/A	• Tax deductions for donors
Austria	• Election period • Between elections	• Current representation in the legislature	• General party administration • Election campaign activities	N/A	N/A
Belgium	• Election period • Between elections	• Equal funding • Current representation in the legislature	• Non-earmarked	• Current representation in the legislature	N/A
Benin	• Election period • Between elections	• Current representation in the legislature	• Election campaign activities	• Equal time	• Tax exemptions for parties
Botswana	N/A	N/A	N/A	N/A	N/A
Brazil	• Ad hoc	• Performance at previous election	• General party administration • Election campaign activities	• Equal time • Current representation in the legislature	• Tax exemptions for parties

	Direct subsidies			Indirect subsidies	
	Allocation interval	Allocation basis	Purpose	Allocation basis for free broadcasting	Tax relief
Bulgaria	• Election period • Between elections	• Current representation in the legislature	• General party administration • Election campaign activities	N/A	N/A
Canada	• Election period	• Performance at current election • Number of candidates put forward in present election	• General party administration • Election campaign activities	Other	• Tax credits for donors
Chile	N/A	N/A	N/A	• Performance at previous election	• Tax exemptions for parties • Tax credits for donors
Costa Rica	• Election period	• Performance at current election	• Election campaign activities	N/A	• Tax exemptions for parties
Czech Republic	• Between elections	• Performance at current election • Current representation in the legislature	• Election campaign activities • Non-earmarked	• Number of candidates put forward in present election	• Tax exemptions for parties • Tax deductions for donors
Denmark	• Between elections	• Performance at previous election	• General party administration • Election campaign activities • Non-earmarked	• Equal time	N/A

(Continued)

	Direct subsidies			Indirect subsidies	
	Allocation interval	Allocation basis	Purpose	Allocation basis for free broadcasting	Tax relief
Dominican Republic	• Election period • Between elections	• Performance at current election	• Non-earmarked	• Other	N/A
El Salvador	• Election period	• Performance at current election	• Election campaign activities	• Equal time	N/A
Estonia	• Election period • Between elections	• Performance at previous election	• Non-earmarked	• Equal time • Number of candidates put forward in present election	N/A
Finland	• Between elections	• Current representation in the legislature	• General party administration • Non-earmarked	N/A	N/A
France	• Election period • Between elections	• Performance at current election • Number of candidates put forward in present election	• General party administration • Election campaign activities	• Current representation in the legislature	• Tax deductions for donors
Germany	• Election period • Between elections	• Performance at previous election	• Non-earmarked	• Equal time • Performance at previous election • Current representation in the legislature	• Tax exemptions for parties • Tax credits for donors • Tax deductions for donors
Ghana	N/A	N/A	N/A	• Equal time	N/A

	Direct subsidies			Indirect subsidies	
	Allocation interval	*Allocation basis*	*Purpose*	*Allocation basis for free broadcasting*	*Tax relief*
Hungary	• Election period • Between elections	• Performance at previous election • Current representation in the legislature	• Non-earmarked	• Equal time	• Tax exemptions for parties
India	N/A	N/A	N/A	• Equal time • Other	N/A
Ireland	• Between elections	• Performance at previous election	• General party administration	N/A	N/A
Israel	• Election period • Between elections	• Current representation in the legislature	• General party administration • Election campaign activities	• Equal time • Current representation in the legislature	• Tax exemptions for parties • Tax credits for donors
Italy	• Election period • Between elections	• Performance at current election	• Election campaign activities	• Equal time	• Tax exemptions for parties • Tax deductions for donors
Jamaica	N/A	N/A	N/A	N/A	N/A
Japan	• Election period • Between elections	• Performance at current election • Current representation in the legislature	• Non-earmarked	• Number of candidates put forward in present election	• Tax exemptions for parties • Tax deductions for donors

(Continued)

	Direct subsidies			Indirect subsidies	
	Allocation interval	Allocation basis	Purpose	Allocation basis for free broadcasting	Tax relief
Latvia	N/A	N/A	N/A	• Equal time	N/A
Lesotho	N/A	N/A	N/A	N/A	N/A
Lithuania	• Between elections	• Performance at previous election	• General party administration • Election campaign activities	• Equal time	• Tax exemptions for parties
Mali	• Election period	N/A	• Election campaign activities	• Equal time	• Tax exemptions for parties
Mauritius	N/A	N/A	N/A	• Number of candidates put forward in present election	N/A
Mexico	• Election period • Between elections	• Equal funding • Performance at previous election	• General party administration • Election campaign activities • Education, training, research, publishing	• Equal time • Performance at previous election	• Tax exemptions for parties • Tax deductions for donors
Namibia	• Election period • Between elections	• Performance at previous election	• General party administration • Election campaign activities	• Equal time • Performance at previous election	• Tax exemptions for parties

	Direct subsidies			Indirect subsidies	
	Allocation interval	Allocation basis	Purpose	Allocation basis for free broadcasting	Tax relief
Netherlands	• Election period • Between elections	• Current representation in the legislature	• Education, research, information, promotion of youth participation	• Current representation in the legislature	• Tax deductions for donors
New Zealand	N/A	N/A	N/A	• Equal time • Performance at previous election • Current representation in the legislature • Other	N/A
Norway	• Election period • Between elections	• Performance at previous election • Current representation in the legislature	• General party administration • Non-earmarked	• Performance at previous election • Current representation in the legislature	N/A
Panama	• Election period • Between elections	• Equal funding • Performance at previous election	• General party administration • Election campaign activities • Training	• Equal time	• Tax exemptions for parties • Tax deductions for donors
Peru	N/A	N/A	N/A	• Equal time	N/A
Poland	• Election period • Between elections	• Performance at current election • Performance at previous election	• General party administration • Election campaign activities	• Equal time • Number of candidates put forward in present election	N/A

(Continued)

	Direct subsidies			Indirect subsidies	
	Allocation interval	Allocation basis	Purpose	Allocation basis for free broadcasting	Tax relief
Portugal	• Election period • Between elections	• Performance at current election • Current representation in the legislature	• General party administration • Election campaign activities	• Equal time	• Tax exemptions for parties • Tax deductions for donors
Romania	• Election period • Between elections	• Performance at previous election • Current representation in the legislature	• General party administration • Election campaign activities	• Equal time • Current representation in the legislature • Number of candidates put forward in present election	• Tax exemptions for parties
Senegal	N/A	N/A	N/A	N/A	N/A
Slovakia	• Election period	• Performance at current election	• Non-earmarked	• Equal time	N/A
South Africa	• Election period • Between elections	• Equal funding • Current representation in the legislature	• General party administration • Election campaign activities • Education, training, research	• Equal time	N/A
Spain	• Election period • Between elections	• Performance at current election	• General party administration • Election campaign activities	• Current representation in the legislature	• Tax exemptions for parties

	Direct subsidies			Indirect subsidies	
	Allocation interval	Allocation basis	Purpose	Allocation basis for free broadcasting	Tax relief
Sweden	• Election period • Between elections	• Performance at previous election • Current representation in the legislature	• General party administration • Non-earmarked	• Equal time	N/A
Switzerland	N/A	N/A	N/A	N/A	• Tax deductions for donors
Trinidad & Tobago	N/A	N/A	N/A	N/A	N/A
Ukraine	N/A	N/A	N/A	• Equal time	N/A
United Kingdom	• Election period • Between elections	• Current representation in the legislature	• General party administration • Policy development	• Number of candidates put forward in present election	N/A
United States	N/A	N/A	N/A	N/A	N/A
Uruguay	• Election period	• Performance at current election	• Election campaign activities	• Equal time	N/A

N/A = not applicable

Source: Austin and Tjernström (2003)

5

Election Campaigns

Christopher Wlezien

If elections are the defining characteristic of democracies, then election campaigns are important to understand. But are they themselves important? That is, do they matter? In what ways?

Election campaigns can have many different effects. They can engage our interest in politics, causing us to pay more attention than we do in periods between elections. After all, the campaigns themselves are interesting, the stuff of much political activity and mass media coverage. In fact, many campaigns take it as an objective to pique our interest – or at least to attract our attention. The more we pay attention, of course, the more we may take stock of the government and its policies. We may reconsider our issue positions and possibly adopt new ones. We may even revisit our attachments to political actors, such as political parties or the broader political system itself.[1] We may be more (or less) likely to vote. These all are important consequences, and there are others as well.

Above all else those of us who study elections want to know the extent to which campaigns influence who gets elected. The potential for influence of this sort partly reflects some of the things noted above, as issue positions, party attachment, and turnout obviously matter on election day. Campaigns can influence the outcome in other ways. What is the net effect of these different things? There actually are a number of possibilities. It may be that campaigns completely determine election outcomes. From this perspective, the election outcome is the sum of pretty much everything that happens during the course of the campaign. It alternatively may be that election day outcomes are shaped by forces beyond the control of candidates and parties and their campaigns, for instance, the economy or other conditions. Here, campaigns may not matter at all or else matter only to steer the vote toward its proper equilibrium, which even may be foreseeable in advance. Of course, it might be that campaigns matter in both ways – that they have effects on election day that are unpredictable and predictable.

This chapter assesses how election campaigns influence election outcomes, focusing especially on the national level.[2] It begins with a consideration of what constitutes an election campaign – pretty clearly a campaign aims to win an election, but the characteristics differ across countries. It also considers how campaigns have changed over time. Then the chapter examines the extent to which and how campaigns matter on election day. We will see that campaigns do matter but that it varies somewhat across contexts. We also will see that the effects generally are more limited and subtle than one might expect given the attention they receive.

The Election Campaign

In all democracies, parties and candidates regularly are focused on the next election and doing things to improve their chances of winning. What distinguishes an election campaign is the intensity of the political competition, when political actors are focused almost *exclusively* on winning the election. This obviously happens in the period leading up to an election.

The timing of campaigns differs quite a lot across countries and even within countries over time. In all countries there is an election schedule. In presidential systems, the schedule dictates when elections happen. In Mexico, for example, the president is elected to a six-year term; legislative elections are every three years. In most parliamentary systems, the schedule only stipulates the period within which an election must take place. In the Netherlands, an election must be held within four years after a parliament has been seated. As the end of the period nears, the prime minister must call an election.

In most parliamentary systems, of course, an election can be held well before the mandated date if the legislature is dissolved.[3] One recent study showed that over 40% of elections in parliamentary democracies happened early, specifically, before the final six months of the scheduled inter-election period (Stevenson and Vavreck 2000). An election can be held early because a government falls, say, due to a vote of no confidence or the defection of a coalition party. It also can happen because the government chooses to hold an election for tactical reasons. That is, it may be that government popularity is particularly high and party leaders exploit this opportunity to hold elections while the going is good (Kayser 2006). They also might anticipate declining political fortunes and hold an election before the going gets bad (Smith 2004). Regardless of the specifics, the timing of elections can vary quite a lot.

This timing of elections influences when campaigns begin (Stevenson and Vavreck 2000). In presidential systems and parliamentary systems where the government's term is approaching its end, parties and candidates can anticipate the election and organize their campaigns and actually begin campaigning months in advance of election day.[4] In most presidential systems there is no "official" campaign. The campaign begins when it begins. For US presidential elections, the end of the party nominating conventions traditionally signals the beginning of the general election campaign, but activities by the parties and candidates already are well under way before the parties convene, and increasingly so (see Stanley and Niemi 2008: 71–2).

In parliamentary systems the official campaign begins once the election is called. When nearing the scheduled end of the parliament, of course, parties and candidates have a head start. When elections are unscheduled – especially where they cannot be anticipated – the official campaign period is more meaningful. That is, the election surprises people, possibly even those in government, and so parties and candidates begin campaigning only after the election is called. In effect, the campaign suddenly is on. This can temper its influence on voters. Keep in mind that, in systems where government coalitions are fragile or in systems (typically majoritarian ones) where parties readily call elections for tactical reasons, there is reason to suppose that parties are more prepared for an election throughout the parliamentary term. They may be looking out for a likely coalition breakdown or for when conditions are ripe for the government to call a snap election. Here the "long campaign" that predates the official campaign may be of special importance.

Governments in most parliamentary democracies can not only determine when the campaign begins, they can also determine how long it lasts. Laws can stipulate a minimum length, e.g., 36 days in Canada.[5] There is no explicit maximum length in Canada or most other countries. This may partly reflect the limited effect of such regulations, given that governments cannot effectively control what parties and candidates do in the unofficial pre-campaign period. Even where there are no legal limits on length, there are practical limits – e.g., the need to sit a parliament within a particular period of time, say, every 12 months. Stevenson and Vavreck (2000) show that there are also general tendencies in each country: in the UK the time from announcement to election day has averaged about 30 days in recent years; in Italy the average is 60 days; in the Netherlands and Germany the numbers are over 100 days.

Within countries the length still can vary quite a lot. In the UK the two 1974 campaigns lasted only 21 and 22 days whereas the 1997 campaign stretched out to 44 days. The length varies in other countries too, sometimes quite wildly. Germany has had a campaign as short as 58 days and another as long as 170 days (Stevenson and Vavreck 2000). This is important because the length of the campaign can influence what happens on election day. For instance, a short campaign limits the time for the opposition party(ies) to make a case for change, and this is one motivation for a government to call a quick election in the first place. A long campaign meanwhile can strain the resources of parties relying on limited funding, causing them to spread out monies very thinly.

How the Conduct of Campaigns Differs Across Countries

How campaigns are organized and run differs across countries in many ways. Electoral systems and government institutions are important structuring factors.

The Electoral System and Campaigns

The most important factor is the electoral system itself. In countries where legislators are elected using proportional representation, political parties are the predominant political actors. That is, voters choose parties, not candidates. Candidates are selected from the party lists based on the success of each party at the ballot box. If a party wins 20% of the vote and the legislature consists of 150 members, for example, then the top 30 or so candidates on the party's list will take office (see also Chapter 2). This is the most common approach, especially in Europe, and particularly in the Western parts but also throughout Latin America. In these systems, parties control the main material of the campaign – manifestos, the campaign staff and organization, the use of media, campaign events, and voter targeting and mobilization. Things there are highly centralized.[6]

Parties are less dominant in systems where voters choose directly among candidates and not parties *per se*. Most common is the use of single-member districts (SMDs), where one legislator is elected to represent each particular geographic area. This is standard in Westminster systems and is also used in the US. In these district-based systems things are more decentralized, as the candidates control much of the campaign. Parties are still important in such systems and sometimes more important than the candidates themselves, particularly at the local level (Denver and Hands 1997). National parties are also important, and increasingly so, at least in some countries (Fisher et al. 2005). The role partly depends on campaign finance – where parties control the money, they can more easily control what candidates do. It also depends on the type of government institutions, as we will see.

As noted in Chapter 2, some countries have a mixed electoral system. Here a portion of legislators are elected using proportional, party-based methods and the rest are elected from competing candidates to represent different districts (Shugart and Wattenberg 2001). In these countries, campaigns tend to fall in between what we see in pure proportional and district-based systems – i.e., parties and candidates are both players in election campaigns. This is especially true in countries that use the single transferable vote, such as Ireland and Malta, where candidates are very important (again, see Chapter 2).

Government Institutions and Campaigns

Government institutions also matter for campaigns. Of special significance is the difference between presidential and parliamentary systems.[7] In presidential systems voters choose a president from among different candidates. The campaign for that office thus tends to be candidate-centric. The same is not necessarily true for legislative races in presidential systems, of course, as the electoral system plays an important role. In many presidential systems, especially in Latin America, the legislature is elected using proportional representation. Campaigns for offices there can be party-centric, particularly when elections are not concurrent. In other presidential systems, including the US and the Philippines, legislators are elected directly.[8] There candidates tend to dominate both executive and legislative elections.

Things are different in parliamentary systems. There, only the legislature is elected. In the classic Westminster model, SMDs are used, and so candidates play a role, though national parties are still central. This is partly because of plurality election rules, which *tend* to produce two major parties and majoritarian government, as per Duverger's Law (1959).[9] It provides the basis for "responsible party government," where voters can readily reward or punish the party in power based on their performance. Not surprisingly, national parties matter a lot in election campaigns in Westminster systems. They matter even more in parliamentary systems with proportional representation, the predominant combination throughout Western Europe.[10]

Table 5.1 represents the general effects of the electoral system and executive–legislative division on the campaign. Things are much more complex than the table suggests, of course. Campaign finance is one important variable, as noted above. In SMD systems where legislative candidates can raise a lot of money for their own campaigns, as in the US, they have tended to control campaigns. Where candidates cannot raise as much, as in Westminster systems, parties dominate. This is highly intuitive.

TABLE 5.1 Electoral systems, government institutions, and the control of campaigns

	Electoral system	
Executive-legislative form	*Single-member districts*	*Proportional representation*
Parliamentary	Parties tend to dominate but candidates matter	Parties dominate
Presidential	Candidates dominate	Candidates dominate presidential campaign; parties dominate legislative campaign[a]

[a] The influence in legislative elections depends on whether executive and legislative control is unified and elections are concurrent.

There are numerous semi-presidential systems, the number of which has grown substantially in recent years. These are systems that have both a president and a parliament, and where executive power is shared (Duverger 1980; Schleiter and Morgan-Jones n.d.).[11] The consequences for election campaigns are conditional. Following Lijphart (1994), the president is expected to dominate the campaign when the parliament is controlled by the same party.[12] This is not to say that parties do not matter; rather, it is to say that the president is the leader of the party in government. As such, (s)he has substantial control over the campaign, though particularly when executive and legislative elections are concurrent (Mainwaring and Shugart 1997). In such circumstances, both executive and legislative elections often center on the president and his/her performance. This is less true when elections are staggered. When the presidency and parliament are controlled by different parties, meanwhile, the president and parliamentary executive play a prominent role during the campaign. In semi-presidential systems, while the president and opposing presidential candidates can tend to dominate elections, parties remain important political actors, particularly when proportional representation is used and elections are not concurrent.

To say that campaigns are party-centered is not to say that individual politicians do not matter, of course. We have already considered the importance of presidents in semi-presidential systems. Party leaders are important even in pure parliamentary democracies, however. This has always been true but may be especially so in the modern day, with the rise of mass media. Some argue that party leaders are now the preeminent actors, as parliamentary systems have become "presidentialized" (Mughan 2000). This seemingly is the result of changes in the conduct of campaigns, as we will see.

How Campaigns Have Changed Over Time

Election campaigns have changed in many ways. They once were highly labor-intensive enterprises, where candidates and party workers and volunteers did most of the work. Indeed, campaigning largely involved direct interactions between campaigners and voters. Now, campaigns are much more capital-intensive, where professionals manage things and communication with voters is highly mediated.

Butler and Ranney (1992: 5–6) nicely summarize the old style of campaigning: circulating written documents, door-to-door canvassing by party volunteers, holding public meetings at which candidates and leaders will speak, using billboards, posters, and newspaper advertisements to reinforce the party appeal, door-knocking on election day to get known supporters to the polling booth. These "old style" methods have been around for a long time and are still in active use, particularly in local elections. In some countries, such as Peru, they remain fairly common even in national campaigns (Boas 2008). President Barack Obama's very well-funded election campaign in 2008 actually relied heavily on these methods, particularly in key swing states.

The Rise of Broadcast Television

Campaigning has changed substantially beginning in the 1960s. The spread of broadcast television has been a critical driving force. It had already become a dominant source of news for voters.[13] Getting on the news thus became an effective way to reach many people all at once, but there were others. Early on, free air time was given to parties and candidates in many countries; by the end of the twentieth century this was true in virtually all democracies.[14] By the 1970s paid televised advertising was also being used, at least in a handful of countries – namely Australia, Canada, Japan, and the US. The number of countries with paid political ads expanded in the 1980s and 1990s and into the twenty-first century, though it is still not permitted in a good number, especially in Western Europe and Africa. Table 5.2 summarizes the basic data. Where paid advertising is legal, it is typically limited in various ways, including the number of spots. Even where advertising is not limited, spending often is, which has much the same effect given the high cost of television time.

Successfully using the new medium required new training for candidates and party leaders. It also required expertise in public relations and marketing (Bowler and Farrell 1992; Newman 1999) as well as polling. To appeal to the broader "mass" public, as opposed to the party base *per se*, campaigns needed to identify the issues that the average voter considered to be important and then craft policy positions to address those issues. Doing so is not easy, as one first needs to predict who is going to vote on election day, which is a highly imperfect science (see, e.g., Erikson et al. 2004). Then one needs to discover what voters want. The process actually was (and is) dynamic, as parties and candidates will pay close attention to public opinion when taking positions and then adjust those positions based on the public's response. By the 1980s the daily tracking polls (see Asher 1998) necessary to do this were a regular feature of election campaigns in the US and some Western European countries, and their use was spreading to other countries.

Not only had the practice of campaigning changed, the organization had too. Parties and candidates were now being managed, and party leaders were playing a larger role. This was true both behind the scenes and on the campaign trail itself, i.e., campaigns had become more centralized and "presidentialized" (Dalton and Wattenberg, 2000; Farrell and Schmitt-Beck 2002;

TABLE 5.2   Countries where paid advertising is allowed

Africa	Americas	Europe	Asia and Oceania
Mozambique	Argentina	Armenia	Australia
	Canada	Azerbaijan	Japan
	Columbia	Bulgaria	New Zealand
	Costa Rica	Czech Republic[a]	Philippines
	Dominican Republic	Denmark	Singapore
	Ecuador	Finland	South Korea
	El Salvador	Georgia	Taiwan
	Guatemala	Germany	Thailand
	Honduras	Greece	
	Mexico	Hungary	
	Nicaragua	Italy	
	Panama	Lithuania	
	Paraguay	Malta	
	Peru	Mongolia	
	Uruguay	Montenegro	
	United States	Netherlands	
	Venezuela	Poland	
		Serbia	
		Slovakia	
		Spain	
		Sweden[b]	
		Ukraine	

[a] Only on public television stations.
[b] Only on satellite television.

Sources: Kaid and Holtz-Bacha (2006); Plasser and Plasser (2002)

LeDuc et al. 1996; Schmitt-Beck 2007; Semetko 1996; Mughan 2000). As leaders became more important in the campaign, moreover, they may also have become more important on election day. Whether this is true is the subject of debate – see Barisione's (forthcoming) review. It is also consequential, as the extent to which leaders impact the vote influences the roles they play in governance itself (see Poguntke and Webb 2005).

Post-Broadcast Evolution

The selling of parties and candidates has evolved further in more recent decades. The focus has shifted from a mass, broadcast campaign to a more segmented, targeted campaign. There were hints of this tendency with the advent of direct mail approaches in the early 1980s, where campaigns sent campaign literature and fundraising appeals to particular lists of people. The widespread use of cable and satellite television programming through the 1980s and into 1990s was a significant catalyst for more powerful changes. The proliferation of computers and the

Internet was too. With this technology it became possible to reach specific audiences at home. Election campaigns could advertise on particular cable or satellite television channels for instance. This is important because audiences for different channels differ substantially (Hagen and Kolodny, 2008). It is increasingly possible to advertise to particular geographic areas, even different neighborhoods. The Internet also allows more particular targeting, based on the websites people visit and to which they subscribe.

The availability of micro-targeting permits campaigns not only to communicate with particular voters, it also allows them to tailor messages. What was once a largely homogeneous mass campaign cast very broadly across a country is now much more heterogeneous. In their campaigns, parties and candidates can effectively represent parties and candidates differently to different people. There are still limits to doing so, however.

First, the technology only takes us so far. There are differences in viewing audiences across channels but these are not that wide (Pew Research Center 2006). Consider US cable channels. On the news side, 49% of Fox News viewers are conservative, but 14% are self-described liberals and 31% are moderates; MSNBC is the most liberal but 24% of MSNBC viewers are conservatives and 37% are moderates. CNN is somewhere in between, with 31% of viewers conservative and 28% liberal.[15] Internet access does permit more differentiation, as "audiences" for different websites differ more dramatically, though candidates and parties are only beginning to use it for advertising (Kaid and Holtz-Bacha 2006).

Second, in most countries people receive information from multiple sources (Norris 1999). They watch different television channels (and rely on different Internet sites) with different types of audiences that tend to average out any partisan leanings. Many of the channels people watch are broadcast and so are more likely to target the center of the population's distribution on political matters. Individuals also rely on radio and newspapers and more informal sources, such as family, friends, and co-workers. It is just hard for parties and candidates in most countries to control what information people receive with the available technology. There are exceptions, however. In some democracies, such as Botswana, Pakistan, Turkey, and Venezuela, the mass media are substantially controlled by the state authorities (Plasser and Plasser 2002). Freedom House (2008b) shows that media independence is limited in other democracies, including many in Latin America, Africa, and Asia. This can have serious implications for election campaigns in the modern day, in ways that clearly advantage incumbent politicians.

On the Spread of the "Modern" Election Campaign

The evolution from traditional campaigning to targeted high technology happened in a matter of decades. The changes have not happened equally in all countries, however. They have been most pronounced in those countries with high levels of media penetration (and consumption) where there also are few limits on campaign spending and advertising. While other factors are important, the intensity of modern campaigning to a large extent reflects these three variables: the media environment, the regulation of advertising, and the availability of campaign money .

First, the media environment is of obvious importance. For technology to be effective, citizens must have access to it. One classic indicator is television ownership – see the online table for Chapter 8. For televised information to reach people, however, they do not have to own televisions; they simply need to be able to access them. More importantly, people must actually watch on a fairly regular basis. Though it is difficult to measure, there seems to be a good amount of variance in consumption across countries (see, e.g., Plasser and Plasser 2002). Access and use are obviously even more critical for the effectiveness of targeted strategies, which rely on more exclusive technologies, namely, cable or satellite television, and computers and the Internet.

Second, the regulation of advertising is also important. As we have discussed, most countries grant free television time to parties and candidates on public television, which allows them to advertise effectively – see also Chapter 4. Parties and candidates in these countries cannot advertise as much as they would want, of course. They may also not get any time on private television. As we saw in Table 5.2, most countries now allow paid political advertising, which opens up other opportunities, though many of these countries limit the number of political spots on private television. Unlimited paid advertising is allowed in only a fraction of countries, most notably the US and Taiwan, but also several Latin American countries and Australia. In a good number of countries, particularly in Western Europe, paid television advertising by parties and candidates is prohibited. Here it is difficult to target voters via television and political actors have increasingly used the Internet, as access is very high – over 50%.[16] Internet-oriented campaigning is also big and growing in other countries where penetration is especially high, particularly North America and parts of Asia and Oceania (Ward et al. 2008).[17]

Third, to use paid advertising election campaigns need money. As mentioned earlier, this is especially true for television, because air time is expensive. As with technology and advertising access, campaign spending varies a lot across countries. The differences to a large extent reflect funding regulations.[18] As shown in Chapter 6, most countries provide public funding for parliamentary and presidential elections. It was also shown that the type of public funding differs quite a lot across countries. Regardless of the approach used, the level of funding differs across countries as well (International IDEA 2000). Public funding is very large in the leading Asian democracies while it is much lower throughout much of Latin America.

Parties and candidates are able to raise and spend additional funds in most countries. Indeed, few governments impose limits on the level of

TABLE 5.3   Parameters of "modern" election campaigning, selected countries

Advertising regulation	Campaign spending limits	
	Weak	*Strong*
Where TV consumption is high (% of TV households >80)		
Low	United States, Australia, Taiwan	Argentina, Bulgaria, Poland
High	Austria, Denmark, Norway, Switzerland, Turkey	Chile, Israel, New Zealand, Spain, United Kingdom
Where TV consumption is low (% of TV households <80)		
Low	Peru, Panama	—
High	Jamaica, Senegal, South Africa	Benin, India, Mali

Sources: Austin and Tjernström (2003); International Telecommunications Union, World Development Telecommunications Report (2003); Plasser and Plasser (2002)

campaign spending, though some do, particularly for candidates (Plasser and Plasser 2002). These limits are often not followed, however. This is true even where public funding is large, including in Japan, South Korea, and Taiwan. In the US Barack Obama forwent $84 million in public funding for the last two months of his presidential election campaign and raised and spent over $500 million instead – US election law requires presidential candidates to choose between public and private funding. It has simply proven difficult to control spending in campaigns across the globe and so there is a lot of upward pressure on fundraising in democracies, including Western Europe.[19]

The three variables – mass media use, advertising restrictions, and the flow of money – to a large extent determine the intensity of "modern" campaigning. Indeed, in one sense each is a necessary condition of sorts for the intensive use of high technology. Table 5.3 provides a very general classification of countries using the three variables. The US is at the top of the list. The use of television (and, indeed, of media of all varieties) is high, restrictions on advertising very low, and the flow of money virtually unbounded. Things in Australia and Taiwan are quite similar. Here, in the upper left-hand corner of Table 5.3, campaigns are highly media-intensive. Other countries are not far behind, including some European countries that have few limits on spending and advertising – particularly Finland and Slovakia.

Few countries are at the very opposite end of the spectrum, partly because mass media consumption has expanded tremendously across the globe. Television consumption still does vary of course, and in Table 5.3 we can see that there are some countries where less than 80% of households have televisions, especially Benin, India, Mali, and Senegal, where the numbers are less than 40%.[20] More important is the variation in the freedom to advertise and the flow of money. We have already noted that many countries severely limit advertising, particularly in Europe, Africa, and Latin America. In the bottom row of Table 5.3 we can see that this is true even among countries where television's reach is modest; while some countries here do not seriously restrict spending, most do control advertising. Limitations on advertising clearly preclude media-intensive campaigning. Of course, election campaigns in countries with such regulation still use the media to the extent allowed, and the campaigns are the focus of news attention.

The experience in other countries is somewhere in between the more restrictive countries and what we observe in the US. In Ireland and Poland, for example, there are effective limits on spending but fewer controls on advertising. Here campaign advertising is constrained mostly by spending, and we tend to find that campaigns do advertise but that it is much less common than in the US.

The Effects of Election Campaigns

Election campaigns have clearly become more visible over time. Money flows more freely. Parties and campaigns rely more and more on pollsters to engineer and reengineer tactics and strategies. The use of advertising has exploded. Internet fundraising and communications have done the same. What is the effect of all this spending and activity? And to what extent do campaigns matter to voters?

The study of voters and elections has shed considerable light on people's vote choices and election outcomes (see, for example, Abramson et al. 2007; Budge and Farlie 1983; Campbell et al. 1960; Campbell and Garand 2000; Clarke et al. 2004; van der Brug et al. 2007; van der Eijk and Franklin 1996). Yet electoral scholars are only beginning to understand the evolution of electoral sentiment over time. How does the outcome come into focus over the electoral cycle? Do voters' preferences evolve in a patterned and understandable way? What role does the election campaign play?

Consider the timeline of election campaigns (Wlezien and Erikson 2002). We can start the timeline at the beginning of the "official" campaign or, for a longer view, with the previous election. We can end the timeline on election day. Many campaign events occur over this timeline. We want to know whether these events have effects. Do we observe changes in preferences? We also want to know whether the effects last. Do they persist to affect the outcome on election day? Answers to these questions tell us whether campaigns are important. Getting answers is not that easy, however.

On Assessing Campaign Effects

We know that campaigns influence voter preferences. The difficulty is in characterizing these effects in much detail. There are two main problems.

First, the effects of most campaign events are very small. To be sure, there are some very big events, such as presidential nominating conventions in the US, that typically have "big" effects, shifting the preferences of up to 5–6% of the voters (Holbrook 1996). Debates between presidential candidates or party leaders can also have relatively big effects, on the order of 1–2% in the US (Shaw 1999) but occasionally larger in other countries, e.g., Canada (Blais et al. 2003; Johnston et al. 1992). These events are rare, however. Most things that happen during the campaign have much less dramatic effects. Consider advertisements and speeches and political endorsements, the stuff of the modern daily campaign in most countries. While highly salient to voters, the effects of particular advertisements and even speeches and endorsements are apparently tiny, a fraction of a percent at best. We do not expect a big swing in preferences when the National Party in New Zealand runs a prime time ad in Christchurch, for example. A *flight* of ads may have a larger impact of course (see, e.g., Johnston et al. 1992; Kaid 1999; Scammell and Semetko 1995). A web campaign might do so as well (Gibson and McAllister 2006). Making these determinations may require us to detect the effects in the first place, which may be problematic, as we will now see,

Second, our ability to detect campaign effects is limited. We must rely on polls and we need these at frequent intervals. And even if we have these, which typically is not the case, polls are not perfect. That is, all polls contain survey errors, the most basic of which is sampling error. When the division of preferences between parties is constant and unchanging, for instance, we will observe changes from poll to poll. This is well known. The implications for the study of campaign effects are less obvious but quite powerful, even when sample sizes are large (say, greater than 1000). With random samples of 1000 voters at regular, fairly short intervals, we are about 90% certain to detect effects of five percentage points or more. As the size of effects declines, however, our power to find them drops precipitously. With effects of one to two points, our confidence in detecting them falls to 25%; with effects of 0.5 of a point, confidence is less than 10%.[21] Keep in mind that seemingly most campaign effects are smaller than 0.5 of a percentage point.

Not surprisingly, the effects of almost all campaign activities elude political scientists and practitioners alike, though developments in Internet polling, which make it easier and cheaper to poll large numbers of people, may improve things (Clarke et al. 2008).[22] Very recent work in the experimental tradition is also suggestive about some campaign effects (Green et al. 2008).[23]

Do Campaigns Matter? The Case of the US

Although we have learned little about the effects of specific campaign events, we have learned a good amount about what *generally* happens to voter preferences over the course of campaigns. Much of this work has concentrated on the US, especially on the race for the White House, for which polling data have been plentiful for many years (Campbell 2000; Wlezien and Erikson 2002). From this research we know that the intense and highly salient general election campaign after the party conventions matters surprisingly little for the result. During this period, which in the recent past has lasted about 60 days, the maximum range of voter preferences is plus-or-minus three percentage points in the typical election. The day-to-day activities of US presidential election campaigns just do not have much effect on voter preferences.

These analyses tend to understate campaign effects, however. First, they register the net effect of many different campaign activities, which can cancel out on a daily basis. For instance, one candidate's campaign may shift preferences by 0.5% on a particular day but another campaign may shift preferences by 0.3 in the opposite direction. Thus, while the total effect of the two campaigns is 0.8%, the net effect is only 0.2%. Second, the net effects of campaigns on different days can cancel out. One candidate may gain 0.2% on a particular day but lose 0.1% the following day. Here the total effect for the two days is 0.3% but the net effect is only 0.1%.

Even small changes can make a difference on election day, particularly if the race is close to begin with and if campaign effects accumulate in one direction or the other. The question then is whether the shocks from campaign events take the form of temporary "bounces" or permanent "bumps" (Wlezien and Erikson 2002). Simply put, do the effects decay or last? If campaign effects are bounces, they dissipate over time. In this scenario, preferences revert to an "equilibrium" that is set in each particular election year (also see Gelman and King 1993). The final outcome is the equilibrium plus the effects of any very late events that do not fully dissipate before election day. If campaign effects are bumps, conversely, they last to affect the outcome. The election outcome is the sum of all the bumps – mainly small in size individually – that happen during the campaign, keeping in mind that they can go in both directions and so cancel out. Of course, it may be that campaign events produce both bounces and bumps: some effects may dissipate and others last, or a portion of effects may dissipate and the rest last. The bumps and not the bounces are what matter in the long run. They cumulate over time. Figure 5.1 illustrates the different types of campaign effects – the bump, the bounce, and the hybrid effect.

The evidence of permanent bumps is the fact that presidential election polls are increasingly accurate over the fall, general election campaign. While much of the change that we observe is short-lived, a *substantial portion clearly carries forward to impact the result.*[24] In some years, this has been consequential, including 2008, when Obama regained and then expanded his lead over the last 45 days of the campaign. The 2000 US presidential election campaign is famous for its dynamics (see Johnston et al. 2004). Preference change mattered a lot in other years, as in 1948, when Truman came back from 15 points behind to surprise Dewey. In 1968 Humphrey gained almost ten percentage points against Nixon through the

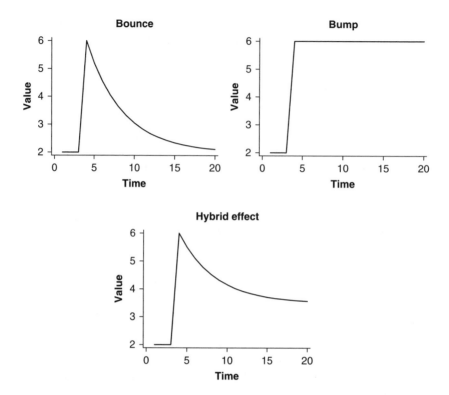

Figure 5.1   Different types of campaign effects

fall campaign, only to fall just short at the end. In legislative elections, of course, such changes, if across the board, would be hugely consequential, causing large swings in the number of seats parties hold.

Although voter preferences typically vary in a narrow range during the general election campaign for president in the US, they change much more dramatically over the long campaign.[25] The electorate's presidential preferences are most volatile during the summer, when change is four times what we see during the heat of the fall campaign. This partly reflects the impact of the national conventions, which stimulate voters' attention. Interestingly, much of the change during the summer does not last, but decays well before election day – this includes the very large convention effects, which mostly are bounces. The pattern of preference change may be surprising if we assume that voters become increasingly attentive as the campaign progresses. That is, the more they pay attention heading into (and through) the fall, general election campaign, the less they change their minds. As preferences become more stable, they also tend to converge toward 50–50, i.e., leads shrink. A lead of ten points at the beginning of the general election campaign, for example, is typically halved by election day (Wlezien and Erikson 2002).[26]

There exists an explanation for the pattern: the more people pay attention, the more their preferences harden. We can imagine that at the campaign's start, voters are sufficiently malleable so that minor campaign events affect voter choice. Then, as the campaign progresses, voters become more set in their choices, making it difficult for events to change many minds. From this perspective, there is a diminishing marginal effect of additional information, at least as regards shifts in their support for either of the two candidates. Regardless of its particular underpinnings, the increasing intensity of underlying preferences over the campaign also produces a predictable decline in poll margins (for details see Wlezien and Erikson 2001).

A Comparative Perspective

The patterns described above are not unique to the US. Indeed, research has revealed similar trends during election campaigns in countries with parliamentary systems. During the official election campaign in the UK, for instance, preferences tend to vary in a narrow range (Norris and Wlezien 2005). Leads also tend to shrink during the period, though this is not always true – witness the 2005 campaign, when Labour slightly expanded its lead over the Conservatives.[27] Much like the US, then, the change in preferences that occurs from election to election in the UK mostly plays out over longer stretches of time, before the official campaign begins. Canada reveals a similar pattern, though possibly slightly greater dynamics during the official campaign period (Blais et al. 2003; Johnston et al. 1992). That is, preferences in recent elections seem to have churned more than in the US and UK, especially in 2006, when the Conservatives came back from ten points behind to beat the Liberals (Pickup and Johnston 2007).

The similarities across the US, UK, and Canada may be surprising. We might have hypothesized, for instance, that parliamentary campaigns have smaller effects on preferences than presidential ones. The logic ultimately boils down to the fact that in presidential elections voters select an *individual* to represent the country whereas in parliamentary elections they select a *legislature*. This seems obvious when we are choosing among parties but should be true even where single-member districts are used – while our preferences among individual candidates may reflect a variety of considerations, when we aggregate they should cancel out.[28] Then again, as noted earlier, elections are harder to anticipate in parliamentary systems, as most governments are able to select the time of the next election. Thus, we might expect more – not less – change in these systems, as the official campaign there does not begin until the election is called.

Both effects may be at work. That is, preferences for presidential candidates may tend to vary more and yet change in voter preferences in parliamentary systems may be much more concentrated in the period of the official campaign. Although there is always some uncertainty until the election date is announced in parliamentary systems, parties and voters effectively may be able to anticipate elections, sometimes because the government wants the date to be known in advance. If parties have anticipated the election and begun their pre-campaign campaigns and voters have begun to think about the election, the official campaign may be less consequential; if the election is a surprise, conversely, the campaign may matter more. The element of surprise might help explain why there was more real change in preferences during the 2006 Canadian election, which was the result of a no confidence vote.[29] Regardless of whether the election surprises parties and voters, the length of the campaign may be important, as the effects of events and deliberation can have a greater cumulative effect.

Electoral systems may also have consequences. Specifically, as hinted at earlier, we might hypothesize that campaigns cause less change in preferences where proportional representation is used as opposed to single-member districts. The intuition is fairly straightforward: voters choose among parties and not candidates, and so preferences may tend to be more stable during campaigns. Of course this depends on the level of voter alignments with parties (van der Brug et al. 2007). Where party alignments are weak, after all, we expect more "undecideds," later decision-making, and greater susceptibility to campaign effects (see Fournier et al. 2004). The basis for party alignments is also important (Clarke et al. 2004). The stability of party coalitions, as well as change in the coalition (or likely governing coalition), can cause voter preferences to change (Strom 1997). The strategic environment can change, too, and with meaningful consequences for preferences (Johnston and Vowles 2006).

Just as there are elements of instability in proportional systems, there are elements of stability in candidate-centered ones: parties matter there too and so does incumbency, which can seriously limit the effects of campaigns (Abramowitz 1988, 1991; Cain et al. 1984).[30] There are yet other possibilities, but there has been little research even on the ones we have outlined. A lot of work clearly remains on the effects of election campaigns across contexts. What we can tell is that the pattern we observe in the US, UK and Canada applies to most national elections (see Farrell and Schmitt-Beck 2002).[31]

While campaigns typically have small to modest effects on *net* voter preferences in national elections, they have had very large effects in a number of cases. The Russian presidential election of 1996 is a particularly noteworthy example. Figure 5.2 displays the results of polls conducted by VCIOM (All-Russia Institute of Public Opinion Research) between January and June of the election year, along with the results of the June 16 first-round election. Here we can see that the eventual winner, Boris Yeltsin, began the election year well behind in the polls and tied for 5th place (out of a field of six candidates) with 8% of the poll share at the end of January, less than five months before election day. Thereafter his poll share climbed steadily: by February he was in third place with 11%; by March he was in second place with 18%.

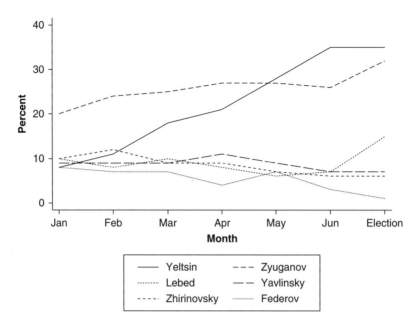

Figure 5.2   Election polls during the 1996 Russian presidential election (first round)

Note: The number of cases per survey is approximately 1600.

Source: VCIOM (All-Russia Institute of Public Opinion Research)

By mid-May he had pulled into a tie, with some 28% of the polls, and then surged into the lead by the end of the month. On election day he won over 35% of the vote to Gennady Zyuganov's 32%. In the runoff election on July 3, Yeltsin won with 54% of the vote to Zyuganov's 40% (5% voted "against all") – the runoff was necessary because Russian law requires that the winner receive a majority of votes and no candidate did so in the first round.

The 1996 Russian presidential election seems pretty exceptional. So what explains it? We do know that it is exactly what we would expect in a new democracy, where partisan preferences are weak (van der Eijk and Franklin 2009). Preferences for the different candidates thus may have been less anchored and more readily influenced by short-term forces (see also Brader and Tucker 2001). It was also a presidential election where we expect more dynamics, as discussed above. There are other explanations. The campaign played out for more than four months, a fairly long time by comparison with most countries. There are also advantages to incumbency, and Yeltsin appeared to use them to good effect (Brudny 1997; McFaul 1997). Incumbency may have mattered in the 2000 and 2004 presidential elections as well, where acting-President Vladimir Putin won the former with a majority in the first round and then was re-elected in 2004 with an even larger first-round majority. The 2008 election was a different circumstance, as Putin was not running, and it showed substantial dynamics, partly due to the incumbent himself.[32]

There are other instances of big campaign effects from more traditional democracies, including parliamentary ones. We have already noted the 2006 Canadian election. The 2002 German general election campaign is another case. Entering the final 60 days of the campaign, the prospects for the incumbent Chancellor Gerhard Schröder and the Social Democratic Party (SPD) did not look good. They faced 10% unemployment rates and trailed the Christian Democratic Union (CDU) by five percentage points in the Politbarometer polls. Thereafter the SPD began a long steady climb that continued through election day, when they outpolled the CDU by a full nine percentage points. This was a striking reversal of fortune. Many credited Schröder's strong stance against a war with Iraq and also his handling of the catastrophic Elbe flood (Paterson and Sloam 2005). This is precisely what we would expect where party leaders really matter in election campaigns and the vote, as we have discussed.

Conclusion: What Do Campaigns Really Do?

We know that campaigns produce change in preferences, sometimes quite substantial, and that the outcome comes into focus over time – while much of the change in preferences decays, a meaningful portion lasts to impact the outcome. We also know that election outcomes in many countries are predictable in advance. Despite all the media attention paid to the many events during the course of political campaigns, there are certain things that powerfully structure the vote in national elections. At the individual level, party identification is of great importance on election day (Holmberg 2007), although that could be declining in many countries, as noted in Chapter 7 (see also Dalton and Wattenberg 2000; Mair and van Biezen 2001).[33] Early on in an election campaign, particularly when selecting among candidates, some partisan voters may in effect "flirt" with candidates from other parties but most of these people will end up supporting the candidate of the party they most prefer. Other factors also matter at the individual level, including class and other cleavages (Knutsen 2007; see Chapter 7). On election day, voters tend to line up as expected.

How people vote changes from election to election, however. It's not that everyone changes or even that most do, as the bulk of partisans vote for their parties or candidates of their parties year in and year out. The ones that change tend to be those who are least attached to particular parties. These "floating voters" are more likely to reflect short-term considerations, such as the state of the economy or the more general performance of the incumbent party(ies) (Zaller 2004). The role of short-term forces actually may have increased with the apparent decline in party identification (Kayser and Wlezien 2006). The same may be true for party leaders and their characteristics too (Clarke et al. 2004; Evans and Andersen 2005).

Taken to an extreme, one can imagine an electorate lined up based on partisanship, and the line in effect shifts slightly from one election to the next based on the performance of the sitting government. This is most straightforward in a two-party parliamentary system. Voters have varying degrees of attachments to the two parties. As the performance of the incumbent changes for the better, support for the incumbent party goes up for all of the voters. Only a small percentage of voters actually crosses the threshold of support and switches from voting for the out-party to voting for the in-party. Then in the next election things go even better and more voters switch to the in-party. In the subsequent election, things turn bad and so the voters switch back to the out-party. The world of course does not work this neatly, but the so-called fundamentals of elections do tell much of the story (see, e.g., Campbell and Garand 2000; Erikson and Wlezien 2008; Lewis-Beck 2005; Lewis-Beck and Stegmaier 2000; Sanders 1996).

To some scholars, the function of election campaigns is to "enlighten" voters about their interests and government performance (Gelman and King 1993). From this point of view, campaigns deliver the fundamentals. They help people sort themselves by party and take stock of performance (Arceneaux 2005). Stevenson and Vavreck (2000) show that this is more likely to happen the longer the campaign. Other research shows that big campaign events, like conventions and debates in the US, help "correct" preferences, bringing them in line with the fundamentals (Holbrook 1996). In one sense, them, campaigns help voters learn about or re-learn the positions of the parties and candidates and government performance, though it is more complex than this.

To begin with, election outcomes don't always play out as we might expect, e.g., the German federal election of 2002. Even when they do, campaigns matter. This obviously is true when party support is balanced and the economy and other aspects of government performance are middling. Under such conditions, everything matters. More typically, some party(ies) and/or candidate(s) have a meaningful advantage in party identification and the economy, and they realize it on election day. This does not happen magically, simply with the passage of time. Parties and candidates compete, and compete fiercely, for our votes. Politicians want to be elected and they want to control government. They attempt to persuade us of their positions and to prime issues on which they have an advantage. Through this competition party identification and the economy become important to voters.[34] The competition itself is critical. Elections are not equally competitive in all countries, at all times, of course. This matters on election day. So do the campaigns that parties and candidates wage.

6

Campaign Communication and Media

Claes H. De Vreese

Campaign communications involve candidates, political parties, organizations, interest groups, news media, and citizens. The flows of communication include elite to media, media to citizens, and elite to citizens – and, to a lesser extent, the reverse flows. This chapter first outlines the *actors* involved in studying and understanding campaign communication (mainly political parties, media, and citizens). Second, it provides an overview of the *developments in campaign communication*: campaigns have professionalized and media markets have changed. The chapter focuses thirdly on the *regulatory framework* within which campaign communication takes place. It considers system characteristics and regulations around political balance in the news, the role of advertising, and the publication of opinion polls.

The chapter fourthly addresses *how* the three main groups of actors communicate: how do parties communicate within, to the media, and to (potential) voters? What kind of news dominates campaign coverage? And how do voters communicate to parties, media, and each other? The chapter finally reviews our knowledge about the *effects* of campaign communications on issue salience, campaign engagement, learning, turnout, and vote choice and the conditionality of these effects.

Actors in Campaign Communication

The most important actors when studying campaign communication are political parties, the mass media, and citizens. Though campaign communication is mostly thought of as communication during elections (which is also the major focus of this chapter), it is a larger phenomenon and other actors such as interest organizations, NGOs, lobbyists, regulators, spin-doctors and campaign professionals also define the "space" in which campaign communication takes place. In the area of public communication campaigns, health communication campaigns (e.g., anti-AIDS, anti-smoking, anti-drinking), environmental campaigns (e.g., pro-recycling, pro-environmental behavior, anti-driving), and public relations campaigns are well known (see Rice and Atkin 2001 for a comprehensive overview). Political communication campaigns are focused on influencing the process of governance (be it in terms of public opinion or electoral behavior), while public communication campaigns are focused on influencing citizen information levels, awareness, and behavior in the social realm (see also Norris 2002). Political campaign communications involves the key actors laid out in Figure 6.1.

Political parties (including candidates and communication professionals), interest groups, and social movements all form **campaign organizations**. These organizations try to achieve strategic goals (mostly maximizing the vote) through *direct and controlled* channels of communication (e.g., political advertisements, meetings, pamphlets, direct (e) mailing, speeches, websites, manifestos, party broadcasts) as well as through *indirect and mediated* channels of communication (e.g., media performances; any type of communication where journalists and (news) editors intervene).

The largest share of campaign communication happens through the **media**. Only a minority of most electorates directly interacts with candidates during a campaign, though new techniques and technologies increase the possibility for personalized contact. In the 2008 US presidential elections, for example, Pew (2008) reported that 76% of registered voters in the battleground states received mail, 23% were visited at home, and 36% received a personal call. A precondition for being informed about a campaign is access to different media, including mass media such as television and newspapers, but also importantly telephones (landline and mobile) and Internet access. There is widespread access to radio, television, and some form of telephony in most Western democracies, while (broadband) Internet and newspaper readership is more unevenly distributed; for example, Internet access figures (2005) varied from almost 0% of the population in some countries to above 90% in others (see online table at www.itu. net for documentation and Norris (2002) on the so-called digital divide). Moreover, access to the mass media is often far more limited in many poorer democracies, such as in sub-Saharan Africa and South East Asia.

The relationship between the political parties and the media is ideally symbiotic (they both need each other). Extant research, discussed in more detail later, suggests that the balance of power in this relationship has moved from the parties towards the media, adhering to a so-called "media logic" rather than a "party logic" (Mazzoleni 1987). In this shift the media are regarded as more autonomous *vis-à-vis* the political parties, not merely passively reflecting but also shaping the process of electioneering. This influence extends beyond campaign periods and also includes the impact

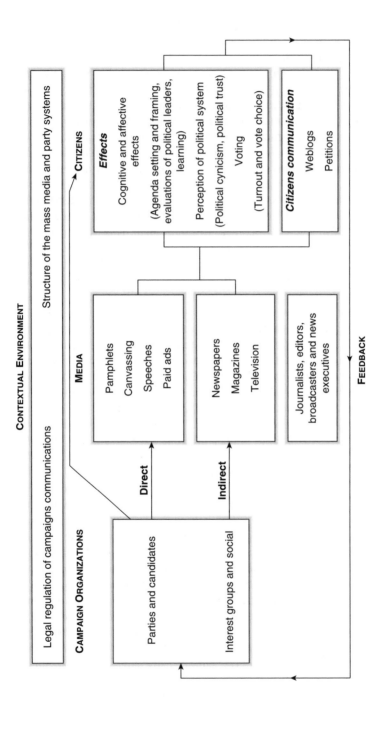

CONTEXTUAL ENVIRONMENT

Legal regulation of campaigns communications

Structure of the mass media and party systems

CAMPAIGN ORGANIZATIONS

Parties and candidates

Interest groups and social

MEDIA

Direct

Indirect

Pamphlets
Canvassing
Speeches
Paid ads

Newspapers
Magazines
Television

Journalists, editors, broadcasters and news executives

FEEDBACK

CITIZENS

Effects

Cognitive and affective effects

(Agenda setting and framing, evaluations of political leaders, learning)

Perception of political system

(Political cynicism, political trust)

Voting

(Turnout and vote choice)

Citizens communication

Weblogs
Petitions

Figure 6.1   Environment of campaign communications

on the policy agenda and the legislative and policy-making process in government. The concept of "the media" has, however, changed and diversified tremendously. While many countries were dominated by a partisan press, the wide availability of radio and later television changed campaign communications. Today, "the media" extend beyond the mass media and also include the Internet and various forms of personalized media consumption.

Citizens form the last group of primary actors. Early research pointed out that most citizens are not easily swayed in voting choice during an election campaign. The studies of the US elections after World War II fuelled an image of campaigns as being of marginal importance in determining citizens' vote (e.g., Lazersfeld et al. 1944). The wisdom was cemented in Klapper's (1960) minimal effects model. These studies debunked the "stimulus–response" model which assumed that media messages had the direct power to change the attitudes and opinions of the mass public. Instead, it was argued, the power of the mass media to *alter* deep-rooted political attitudes and values was limited. The limited effects paradigm has, however, become challenged and in the past 30 years, more sophisticated multimethod research designs have helped to identify and capture both modest and considerable campaign and media effects. During the same period of time, party loyalties have weakened in many countries and voters shift more readily among different political choices (Dalton 2002; see also Chapter 7 in this volume) and rely more on candidates and political leaders as cues. This has also increased the "potential" for campaign and media effects.

Developments in Campaign Communications

In democratic theory, an election campaign functions as an empowerment of the electorate in which knowledge levels increase, engagement is sparked, and voters are mobilized to vote. The process to achieve these civic goals has changed with the media, rather than the political party, as the most important intermediary connecting voters and candidates. Campaigns no longer belong to the party domain, with its local party organizations and volunteers. As press–party loyalties have declined and the outlets for electronic news have diversified, politicians are challenged to operate in and respond to a more complex communications environment. On their part, professionalization of campaigning can be found in the increase of campaign personnel, more sophisticated targeting of key voters, increased expenditure on publicity, and growing use of campaign techniques on the campaign trail and in government.

Extant research from national political contexts suggests that the *professionalization of politics* has increased. In short, a transition has taken place in many Western democracies from campaigns being short, decentralized and dependent on volunteers to a stage of permanent campaigning in which campaign professionals such as pollsters, marketing consultants, and spin-doctors play key roles. Norris (1997, 2000) and Farrell and Webb (2000) developed a typology of the evolution of campaigning and defined three dominating phases. The first phase covers the period from the late 1800s to the 1950s and is characterized by a strong party organization with many decentralized and locally organized campaigns. Volunteers engage in the campaign by distributing pamphlets, canvassing, and organizing local party meetings. This first phase is most effectively distinguished from phase two by the arrival of television (see also Plasser and Plasser 2002). In the second phase, preparations for campaigns are lengthier and more extensive and campaign planning is centrally organized and controlled. The party system undergoes a professionalization transition, electoral research is introduced, and press conferences, staged media events, and political style become important. This phase covers the period from the 1950s up until late 1980s/early 1990s.

The third phase, which according to the literature is still emerging, is characterized by increased use of new information and communication technologies, more sophisticated targeting of key voters, increased expenditure on publicity and growing use of campaign techniques in government. These are implemented internally in the party organizations as well as a means of external communication with party members and potential voters. The time horizon of campaigning is redefined towards some level of *permanent campaigning*. Campaign professionals become increasingly important and the electorate is conceived of as existing of segments of consumers that can be targeted individually.

Elements of the post-modern campaigns are mostly seen in contests such as the general elections in Britain or the presidential elections in the US, where the winner takes all. In such cases it can particularly pay to have a specialized, targeted campaign. A prime example of this is the fall campaign for the US presidency in battleground states: here, spin-doctors and political consultants, widespread use of capital-intensive TV ads in the right media markets, and target usage of the Internet are characteristics. The 2008 Obama presidential campaign serves as the benchmark featuring different campaign techniques. In contrast, premodern campaigning continues to characterize many other types of contest, such as most local elections which are second-order, low-salience contests where "the major parties rely primarily upon volunteer grassroots members, activists and candidates in each community to canvass voters and mobilize partisan support, there is minimal national coverage on television or in newspapers, the chief means of publicity remains a matter of handbill displays and printed pamphlets, and financial resources are restricted" (Norris 2002: 137). It is important to note that the tripartite framework should be seen as supplementary rather than strictly successive, so that campaigners today rather mix techniques from the three prototypical phases (Norris 2000).

In this vein, elections for the European Parliament fall in between the two examples and these campaigns show elements of both postmodern *and* premodern campaigning (de Vreese 2009a).

The developments in political campaigning have taken place in a process of reciprocal influence with changes in the media landscape. The media industry has become one of the world's leading and largest areas of business and increased liberalization and competition have led to a multiplication of media and outlets. These broad changes are mostly discussed in literature based on the US example or theoretical contributions about the (assumed) negative effects of the "Americanization" of campaigns and the relationship between politics and the media. Most of the existing examples are based on national accounts, primarily from the UK, France, Germany, Italy, and Spain (e.g., Esser et al. 2000; Gunther and Mughan 2000; Swanson and Mancini 1996). That said, the developments – *ceteris paribus* – apply to campaigns in Western democracies, though relatively more to North America and Western Europe compared to Central and Eastern European countries or Latin and South America (Strömbäck and Kaid 2008b).

Regulations of Campaign Communications

The regulatory framework of campaign communication touches on the relationship between politics and institutions. Based on characteristics of the media system and the politics system, Hallin and Mancini (2004) identified three different models of media and politics among Western democracies: a Liberal Model, a Democratic Corporatist Model, and a Polarized Pluralism Model. "The Liberal Model is characterized by a relative dominance of market mechanisms and of commercial media; the Democratic Corporatist Model by a historical coexistence of commercial media and media tied to organized social and political actors, and by a relatively active but legally limited role of the state; and the Polarized Pluralist Model by integration of the media into party politics, weaker historical development of commercial media, and a strong role of the state" (Hallin and Mancini 2004: 11).

Within the *political system* several key aspects define the regulatory regime: (1) the political history, in particular patterns of conflict and consensus; (2) consensus or majoritarian government; (3) individual or organized pluralism; (4) the role of the state and state intervention in society; and (5) the development of rational legal authority as opposed to clientelism (Hallin and Mancini 2004). In addition, the *type* of election (including the frequency of elections, the type of office, such as presidential or parliamentary, and whether sub-national, national or supra-national levels) and the structure, organization, membership, and funding of parties (such as whether elite-led, mass-branch, "catch-all," or cartel) are of importance (Norris 2001).

In the *media system* Hallin and Mancini (2004) emphasize four dimensions: (1) the development of media markets, especially with regard to the development of a mass circulation press; (2) political parallelism (the degree and nature of the links between the media and political parties); (3) the development of journalistic professionalism; and (4) the degree and nature of state intervention in the media system. Important media system characteristics also include the level of development of the *political communication industry* (including the availability of professional market researchers, opinion pollsters, advertisers, and campaign managers) and the scope of non-public campaign finance (Norris 2001).

Media systems vary greatly and some countries still know strong alliances between political parties and the press (e.g., Spain) while others have weakened ties. These relationships are not stable and change when countries move, such as in the case of Mexico, from an autocracy to an emerging democracy. In some countries broadsheet newspaper reading is substantial and the audience share of public broadcasters high (e.g., Denmark and Norway), while in other countries television and in particular commercial television dominates (e.g., Greece and the US) (Hallin and Mancini 2004).

Within the media system the most important regulations with regard to campaign communication concern television. This has historical reasons, such as the fear of the power and impact of television when it was introduced on a mass scale in the post-World War II period. The key parameters of regulation refer to the availability to purchase commercial advertisements, the allocation and contents of free party political broadcasts, and rules governing political balance in campaign debates, news coverage, and current affairs (see also Chapter 4).

Table 6.1 shows that three-quarters of OECD countries make available free political airtime to parties on public and/or commercial television. Paid advertisement is allowed in 14 of the 24 countries, but huge cross-national differences exist: in the US television advertising is the single most important part of the campaign budget, whereas in countries such as the Netherlands and Germany it is hardly used. The centrality of candidates and advertising in the US is also reflected in the fact that it is only in the US (and to some extent in Italy) that political candidates are the sponsors of ads. In most countries the sponsor is the political party.

Most countries have fair balance rules (see also Table 6.1). Bias regulations pertain to different elements of the coverage. D'Alessio and Allen (2000), reviewing some 60 studies of bias in the coverage of American presidential election campaigns, concluded that there was no proof of a systematic bias favoring either Democratic or Republican candidates. They propose a threefold typology when considering news bias: *gatekeeping bias*, which refers to the uneven selection of all the events that could potentially be news; *coverage bias*, dealing with an uneven or biased amount of attention within an outlet (measured in, for example, number of words, time, size of articles or photographs); and *statement bias*, which refers to the tone of the

TABLE 6.1 Campaign communication regulations, around 2000

Country	Availability of free political ads on public/commercial TV	Possibility to purchase time on public/commercial TV for political ads	Ad sponsor during parliamentary elections	Fair balance rules	Leader debate last election	Ban on publication of opinion polls prior to elections
Australia	Public only	Commercial only	Parties	Yes	Yes	n/a
Austria	None	Commercial only	Parties	Yes	n/a	No
Belgium	Public and commercial	None	Parties	Yes	Yes	No
Canada	Public and commercial	Public and commercial	Parties	Yes	Yes	n/a
Denmark	Public and/or commercial[a]	None[a]	n/a	n/a	Yes	No
Finland	None	Commercial only	Parties	Yes	Yes	No
France	Public only	None	Parties	Yes	Yes	Yes
Germany	Public only	Commercial only	Parties	Yes	Yes	No
Greece	Public only	Commercial only	Parties	n/a	n/a	No
Ireland	Public and/or commercial[a]	None[a]	n/a	Yes	Yes	No
Italy	Commercial only	Commercial only	Candidates and parties	Yes	n/a	Yes
Japan	None	Commercial only	Parties	Yes	Yes	n/a
Mexico	None	Commercial only	Parties	n/a	Yes	n/a
Netherlands	Public only	Commercial only	Parties	Yes	Yes	No
New Zealand	Public and/or commercial[a]	Public and/or commercial[a]	n/a	n/a	Yes	n/a
Norway	Public and/or commercial[a]	None[a]	n/a	Yes	Yes	No
Poland	Public only	Public and commercial	Parties	n/a	n/a	n/a
Portugal	Public and commercial	None	Parties	n/a	Yes	Yes
Spain	Public only	None	Parties	Yes	Yes	Yes
Sweden	Public and/or commercial[a]	Public and/or commercial[a]	Parties	Yes	Yes	No
Switzerland	None	None[a]	n/a	Yes	n/a	Yes
Turkey	Public and/or commercial[a]	None[a]	n/a	Yes	Yes	n/a
United Kingdom	Commercial only	None	Parties	Yes	No	No
United States	None	Commercial only	Candidates	Yes	Yes	No
OECD Total	18/24	14/24	18/18	18/18	18/19	5/17[b]
Source	Kaid and Holtz-Bacha (2006) [a]Based on Norris (2000)	Kaid and Holtz-Bacha (2006) [a]Based on Norris (2000)	Kaid and Holtz-Bacha (2006)	Norris (2000)	Norris (2000) (extended)	Norris (2000) ([b]corrected)

coverage measured in terms of the favorability towards a candidate. In most countries, some set of more or less explicit regulations exist with regard to the fairness and balance of the news. However, these attempts take many forms. Some countries (for example, Canada, Italy, and Japan) merely state in their constitutions or other regulatory edicts that coverage of candidates and parties should be fair, balanced, equal, or impartial. In France, however, there is a much more explicit approach, requiring a precise balance in print and broadcast media coverage. Elaborate monitoring activities measure and report the coverage allocation among parties. Spain requires neutral coverage of all parties and mandates that reporting on parties be in proportion to their vote in the previous election, but does not engage in meticulous monitoring of these requirements (Strömback and Kaid 2008a).

Another aspect of regulation of news coverage relates to the coverage of opinion polls. Again, there is substantial variation among countries. Many democracies have no restrictions at all on the release of opinion polls in the media (e.g., the US). However, many other countries (still) impose restrictions on the publication of polling results. France and Greece require no poll reporting one week before the election, while Spain, for example, prohibits publication five days before election.

On a concluding note, it can be observed that many countries have moved towards more liberalization, less regulation, and fewer restrictions. Today most media markets are either fully fledged commercial markets or dual systems with both publicly funded and commercial operators competing in the same market. In the same vein, Hallin and Mancini (2004) conclude that among the three media system models there is a gradual convergence towards the Liberal model. In terms of regulations this means that many countries have opened up more to advertising and televised party leader debates and have become less strict in the implementation and monitoring of balance rules. That said, most countries still enforce some level of regulations and in transitional regimes and newer democracies there has been a regulation of campaign communications and party funding while at the same time deregulating media industries. However, even in established democracies each election cycle inevitably brings some accusations of partisan media bias and a plea for restrictions on the publication of opinion polls, most notably from the losers of an election.

Modes and Contents of Campaign Communications

This section addresses how the three main groups of actors are involved in campaign communication: how parties communicate within, to the media, and to (potential) voters; how the media cover elections; and how voters communicate to parties, the media, and each other.

Campaigns and Political Parties

Political parties, interest groups, and movements that participate in a campaign are affected institutionally, both from a short-term and in a long-term perspective. Parties are confronted with the need to raise money for the campaign and to raise the party profile. Over the past decades, political campaigning has become increasingly professionalized and political parties are challenged to respond to the strategies of competitors as well as increasingly professional and critical journalists.

In planning a campaign, political parties are faced internally with strategic choices about candidate recruitment and who will be visible in the campaign (see also Chapter 3). In multiparty systems, political parties are faced with how to campaign against the potential strategic alliances and later potential coalition partners. A continuing source of uncertainty is the lack of knowledge about what opposing parties are doing. In national politics, parties have been described as "owning" certain issues, and although this may change over time there is a predictability in liberals arguing for tax reduction, privatization, and liberation, Greens emphasizing the environment, and Social Democrats often campaigning more on social security. Issue ownership however is blurring and complex. Political parties are also challenged to position themselves strategically in relation to the long-term framing of the issues related to the election. An election is not the end of the road for the debate about policy on this and related issues. The parties on the winning side have a strategic opportunity to control the framing of the issue in the future.

Political parties have three main targets of their communication in a campaign: the party members, the media, and potential voters. Political parties have to communicate *internally* with members and to mobilize volunteers. Party organizations and local party branches form the basic network that most parties rely on. In recent years, party communication tools have expanded from congresses, local meetings, and mailings to include email, e-newsletters, and intranets offering online information for selected groups. The organization and information dissemination strategies of parties have become more electronically based to inform, organize, and mobilize (Gibson, Nixon, and Ward 2003; Rommele 2003). There is some evidence to suggest that internal party communication is also affecting the political parties themselves, many of them suffering from declining membership. It is as of yet unclear if new communication technologies will empower party members or the party elite or leave party politics unchanged (Pedersen and Saglie 2005). Membership empowerment suggests that by new means of bottom-up communication members are better able to communicate with party elites and influence is facilitated. Elite empowerment suggests that ICT provides the party top with additional means of top-down communication resources. Finally, politics-as-usual implies that ICT may not change much, as the large share of passive members will not change their habits due to the introduction of ICT.

Party communication *to the media* includes press releases, press conferences, and staged events and photo opts. As described earlier these elements of campaign communication developed mostly during the second phase of election campaigning and were part of the professionalization transition in which television became a dominant campaign medium. Party communication *via the media* (i.e., direct and paid communication) primarily takes place through resource-intensive advertising. A key question posed to political candidates and parties in a campaign is their advertising message strategy. In particular, choices between the framing of their "own" issues and candidates' versus the opposition's issues are pertinent. Conventional wisdom among political consultants and candidates is that negative campaigning works. In early research on the effects of negative campaigning there was little evidence to suggest that it indeed did. A recent meta-analytic assessment of the effects of negative political campaigns (Lau et al. 2007: 1176) systematically reviewed the by now burgeoning body of research. It reaffirmed the conclusion that negative campaigning seems to have only marginal effects: "All told, the research literature does not bear out the idea that negative campaigning is an effective means of winning votes." That said, there is an emerging consensus (e.g., Geer 1998) that negative campaigning does seem to be more memorable and in fact stimulates knowledge about the campaign. This latter point is corroborated in an elegant study in which detailed advertising data were coupled with survey data and showed that exposure to negative advertisement "produces citizens who are more interesting in the election, have more to say about the candidates, are more familiar with who is running, and ultimately are more likely to vote" (Freedman et al. 2004).

Party communication to *citizens* and prospective voters has developed from being mostly about distributing pamphlets, canvassing, and organizing local party meetings to be (more) focused on online presence and interaction. Research shows that political parties make extensive use of websites. Norris (2003) analyzed party website content in Western Europe and showed how communication and information functions (emailing to party officials, information on party history, organization, and press releases) are part of the online presence. She found that information about both mainstream and fringe parties is widely available across Europe. Websites are not simply top-down but encourage participation and ultimately have the potential to strengthen bonds between voters and parties. Gibson, Margolis et al. (2003) reported that at least in the early stages parties use the Web for providing the same functionality as offline sources and do not use any new approaches, i.e., participation is less of a priority and a top down approach is focused. More recent findings (William and Tedesco 2006) and popular evidence from the 2008 US presidential elections show how the Internet can be used for issue and image promotion, fund raising, and voter mobilization. In fact, in the 2008 cycle, candidates launched their campaign and announced their candidacy on YouTube and the notion of "viral campaigning" (i.e., campaigning that uses online networks to spread messages) gained momentum. Optimists emphasize that the Web's potential in these field is enormous and has acted as a bypass to standard media gatekeepers.

In sum, political parties address three actors in their campaign communication: the party members, the media, and the general public, i.e., potential voters. Political campaigning has evolved and in many places present campaign strategies involve elements from all three phases of campaigning as outlined above. The biggest change in recent years has been the centrality of online communication, used both in the internal party communication and in the communication with citizens.

Campaigns and the Media

An election campaign forces media organizations to prepare. Logistically, campaign coverage is the result of internal cooperation in a news organization, most often between members of the central headquarters-based newsroom and the political unit. In the UK, for example, this means that central newsrooms of the press and broadcasting cooperate with their Westminster Unit (Blumler and Gurevitch 2000). Prior to a campaign, news organizations typically prepare using background research that results in canned items for television and feature articles in the press. These preparations are made in anticipation of certain issues that are likely to appear in the campaign and when they do, background information for a story as well as potential interviewees and key facts are already on file to make it possible to report in a timely manner (De Vreese 2001). During campaigns, news programs and newspapers make use of format alterations. Newspapers typically devote specific pages or sections of the paper to follow the campaign. In television news, a frequently used "tool" in the past was the use of a political editor to chair campaign segments. This type of additional anchor often takes the form of an analysis of the day's events on the campaign trail.

Looking at the media during campaigns, research has provided plenty of national accounts, but little in terms of longitudinal or cross-nationally comparative analyses. Taking a step back to look at the journalists and news organizations, research suggests that journalists may fulfill different roles (Patterson 1998). This also applies to the election period, where Blumler and Gurevitch (1995) distinguish between a "sacerdotal" and a "pragmatic" journalistic approach to elections. In a sacerdotal approach, elections are perceived as the fundamental element of democracy, and campaigns are considered newsworthy *per se*. The attitude towards politicians is respectful, cautious, and reactive. In a pragmatic approach campaign news is evaluated against conventional news selection criteria and is not automatically given special attention. The pragmatic orientation implies that the "amount of time or space allocated to [political events] will be determined by strict considerations of news values, in competition with the newsworthiness of other stories" (Semetko et al. 1991: 6).

While US broadcasters have long tended to adhere to the pragmatic approach (Blumler and Gurevitch 2000), previous research suggested that European public broadcasters have been cautious, respectful towards politicians, and reactive towards the political party agendas (Asp 1983; Gurevitch and Blumler 1993). This situation has changed over time. The change in the basic principle for election coverage was formulated by a news executive in the Netherlands: "We are reporting *about* the campaign, rather than reporting the campaign" (de Vreese 2001). Indeed, many broadcasters have abandoned the daily campaign segment. Election news was to be evaluated according to conventional news values and not be artificially inflated by the fact that it was election time.

In terms of the news *content*, a striking feature of the coverage of elections has been the reduction in the prominence of politicians. Studies of election news in the US (Hallin 1992) have shown this effectively and similar trends have been found in the BBC's coverage of UK general elections in the 1990s (Blumler and Gurevitch 1998) and continuing in 2001 and beyond (Scammell and Semetko 2008). Similarly, an analysis of the airtime devoted to politicians in the news on the Dutch public networks during the 1994 and 1998 national elections suggested that the proportion of time reserved for politicians decreased by 40% (van Praag and Brants 1999).

In general terms issue coverage is said to decrease. Altheide and Snow (1979) and Mazzoleni (1987) identified the emergence of "media logic" in which the content of the news is decided by the media and where political actors adapt their performance to the needs of the media. The literature suggests that election coverage can be focused on issues or more on the polls and the horse race (Patterson 1993), politicians' motives and strategies (Cappella and Jamieson 1997), or on the role of the media in the campaign (for which the phrase "meta-coverage" has been coined) (Esser and d'Angelo 2006). Strategic news emphasizes who is ahead and behind and the strategies, performance, style, and tactics of campaigning necessary to position a candidate to obtain and remain in a lead position (Jamieson 1992; Patterson 1993).

Especially the US case has been flagged as an example of the prominence of game and strategic news reporting at the expense of substantial issues (Cappella and Jamieson 1997). In lieu of longitudinal comparable data cross-nationally, we can review a number of single countries and find evidence of a similar trend in many democracies, albeit at very different levels. In Israel, for example, there has been a relatively stable proportion of issue and game coverage, but a much stronger focus on candidates at the expense of the political party and a high increase in the coverage of opinion polls (Shaefer et al. 2008). In Germany several trends have been observed in election news coverage: increased personalization, a dominance of the strategy frame, and growing negativity (Esser and Hemmer 2008). In the UK too there has been an increase in the game aspects of the news coverage and this development has happened simultaneously with an overall *decrease* in the amount of time that is devoted to elections at the BBC and ITV news (Scammell and Semetko 2008). In France scholars concluded that, since the early 1980s, the political game aspect constitutes about three-quarters of the political information on television news (Darras 2008). In Mexico, Lawson (2008) concluded that most television news was descriptive and focused on candidates on the campaign trail while newspapers and radio talk shows were more interpretative and focused on the electoral competition.

In Spain, part of the polarized pluralist model (Hallin and Mancini 2004), the situation is somewhat different. This had led scholars to conclude that a model of "entrenched" journalism has emerged, implying a journalism that clearly takes sides, with the media playing an advocate role while at the same time more attention is also devoted to the electoral tactics (Lopez-Escobar et al. 2008). In Russia election coverage in the transition period since the early 1990s is unbalanced, with an "undue amount of coverage, much of it positive, to pro-government parties and candidates" (Oates 2008: 360).

In conclusion, some level of horse race and strategic news coverage has been adapted in most countries. Identified several decades ago as a feature of US news, the tendency to focus on who is ahead and who is behind, on poll results, and on the campaign itself, rather than on substantive issues, is applicable in most places. As pointed out above, the fact that this has become more common does not imply that the tendency is unequivocal, and in some cases this development has led to a focus more on the campaign, polls, and strategies whereas in other cases the focus is more on candidates and their personalities (Strömback and Kaid 2008b).

A key feature of campaign communication is that today it not only applies to *national* elections (though we know more about these than most other elections). All members in the European Union, for example, participate in elections for the European Parliament. Research on the EU and European elections in the news is burgeoning. By and large, European affairs in the news tend to be *marginal, cyclical, domestic*, and slightly *negative*. Coverage of European affairs is cyclical in nature, with coverage of the EU virtually absent from the news agenda and then peaking around important EU events only to vanish off the agenda again (De Vreese et al. 2001; Norris 2000). EU actors (such as candidates for the EP and members of EU institutions) tend to be only marginally represented in the news. In fact, most European issues are discussed by national political actors (De Vreese 2002; De Vreese et al. 2006a). Finally, news about European issues is largely neutral, but when it contains evaluations, these tend to be negative (De Vreese et al. 2006a). However, there is huge variation to this pattern. While television news in, for example, Denmark devoted more than 20%

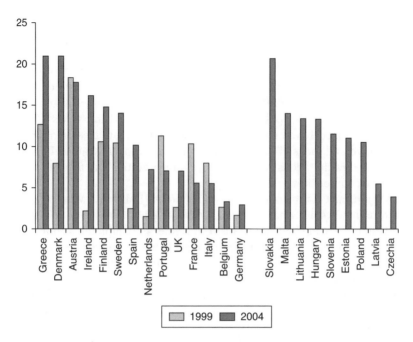

Figure 6.2   Visibility of EU news in television newscasts 1999 and 2004

Note: Values are length-based percentages within the countries and election periods. All stories in television newscasts were included. Values display the proportion of news stories about the EP election and about other EU news. 1999 N=4781; 2004 N=9339.

Source: De Vreese et al. (2006a)

of the news leading up to the 1999 and 2004 European elections to these elections, news in the Netherlands devoted between 2% and 8% of the time to the elections. Figure 6.2 shows this cross-national variation in coverage of the *same* elections and also cautions us to be careful when making too sweeping generalizations about the media's coverage of elections.

Campaigns and Citizens

Citizens are mostly perceived to be on the *receiving end* in a campaign. They are addressed directly by the political parties as potential voters and by the media as audiences. Citizen communication is often seen primarily as interpersonal communication in which the messages of political elites and the media are discussed between family members, friends or co-workers. This form of citizen communication is primarily *between* citizens. Communication *from* citizens to the political elites or the media is much rarer and has traditionally centered around, for example, Letters to the Editor. These letters are generally seen as an empowerment of citizens to express opinions and concerns in a democracy, but research has questioned how news organizations deal with these forms of communication and the representativeness of the opinion voiced (Wahl-Jorgensen 2002).

However, technology has fuelled citizen communication and lowered the barriers for communication both from and between citizens. Citizens are no longer merely *consumers* but also *producers* of political communication. One of the most obvious extensions of user-generated content is the growth of political blogging. Political blogging has opened up an array of questions such as who is blogging, what is being blogged about, for whom, and with what effects. The research literature in this emergent field is much scarcer than the anecdotal evidence. Research suggests that citizen blogging in the realm of politics and public affairs is concentrated around four activities: informing readers, checking the media, engaging in political advocacy, and gathering money (McKenna and Pole 2008). Bloggers inform about other blogs, mainstream media or other sources of information that can be found on the Internet. Political agitation is also common in blogs, as bloggers encourage readers to engage in some sort of political action. Furthermore, many see themselves as media checkers by questioning reports by mainstream media. This has raised the question of whether citizen blogging is dependent on mainstream media or not.

The *effect* of political blogging is an area in which research is only emerging. Early results suggest that weblogs occasionally have an impact on the public opinion, though readership is generally low and the structure of the blogosphere is unorganized. Some US figures suggest that only 7% of the American population read blogs, but that 43% of journalists use blogs weekly (Farrell and Drezner 2008). Thereby stories might be taken over from the blogosphere to the mainstream media (Farrell and Drezner 2008), though Wallsten (2007) finds that the contents of political blogs are independent from mainstream media agendas. An open question is the value attached to citizen blogs, by other citizens, as a source of political information. It is suggested that blogs are rated as highly credible for depth of information, but weaker on fairness of information, and that citizens are well aware of the differences between journalistic products and citizen blogs (Johnson et al. 2007).

Effects of Campaign Communications

This section reviews various types of *effects* of campaign communication on issue salience, campaign engagement, turnout, and vote choice and the conditionality of these effects. The notion of effects of campaign communication is rooted in a long-standing tradition of public opinion research and how public opinion can be swayed. While Converse (1964) initially suggested that the belief systems of mass publics were inconsistent and far away from those of political elites, which were more coherent, consistent, and organized, later research suggested that a typical individual's preferences could be located somewhere in the middle of a continuum ranging at one end from policy preferences that may be described as perfectly stable, informed and consistent to preferences that are entirely random and uninformed (Page and Shapiro 1992). The latter further argue that *information* plays an important role in the opinion formation process and note: "if citizens' preferences are dependent upon uncertain beliefs, bolstered by incomplete bits of information – then new information or arguments that bear upon beliefs about policy alternatives can change people's policy preferences" (Page and Shapiro 1992: 15). In the context of electoral contests, the media are key players and providers of this information. In the words of Dalton (2002: 39), "campaigns are now largely media events." This statement is supported if we look at the sources from where citizens claim to get their news about politics. Table 6.2 shows the use of different campaign and news sources and points to the centrality of television news and newspapers as well as interpersonal communication.

An Overview of Campaign Communication Effects

At the individual level, two types of campaign effects may be distinguished: effects of *direct and personal* campaign experiences and effects of *indirect and mediated* campaign experiences. Direct and personal campaign experiences include attending rallies, signing (online) petitions and the extent to which voters engage in (online) discussions with family, friends or colleagues about politics. Indirect and mediated experiences with politics and campaigning are the most common since only a minority of the electorate is directly involved in a campaign. The vast majority of an electorate only hears about politics and election campaigns through the media and this content forms the backdrop against which political leaders, institutions, and issues are evaluated.

Previous research suggests that exposure to news coverage may increase the level of awareness and knowledge about politics and election themes (McLeod et al. 1994). However, national election studies have often either neglected the role of information effects (see Bartels 1996) or provided either weak or mixed empirical support for media exposure and attention effects on turnout and vote choice (Zaller 2002). This, however, is changing and the role of the campaign and the media has become center-stage in electoral research (Brady and Johnston 2006; Hillygus 2005; de Vreese and Semetko 2004). Individual-level effects of the media can be observed on the processing of information, issue salience, attitudes, and opinions, the perception of the political system, and on behavioral intentions and real electoral behavior. Figure 6.3 provides a typology of information and campaign effects.

TABLE 6.2 Frequency of campaign activities and media use, European Parliamentary Elections 2004

	Total	Austria	Belgium	UK	Cyprus	Czech Rep.	Denmark	Estonia	Finland
Watched program on TV	58.9	67.5	68.7	65.9	76.2	68.7	61	68.9	58.8
Read about in newspaper	54.6	79.1	57.1	65.9	59.6	69.4	61	68.9	74
Talk about with friends and family	58.4	80.9	58.4	67.7	79.2	61.2	68.6	67.6	80.1
Attend rally/public meeting	6.4	8.1	6.1	4.2	21.2	10.6	2.9	4.5	8.1
Look into website	8.1	15.1	9.3	9.8	14.8	8.3	12.1	9.8	19.1

	Total	France	Germany	Greece	Hungary	Ireland	Italy	Latvia	Luxemb
Watched program on TV	58.9	60	86.2	73.8	70.3	75.5	68.5	76.5	48.5
Read about in newspaper	54.6	58.3	66.1	52.6	54.3	76.9	65.7	66.8	58.5
Talk about with friends and family	58.4	67.1	73	73.6	63.3	77.8	78.1	74.4	61.9
Attend rally/public meeting	6.4	8.3	10.4	16.8	8.7	6.1	15.8	6.3	3.4
Look into website	8.1	7.7	11.7	11.6	6	5.6	5.7	10.3	7

	Total	Netherlands	N Ireland	Poland	Portugal	Slovakia	Slovenia	Spain
Watched program on TV	58.9	64.8	55.2	67	72.5	60.2	67.2	65.6
Read about in newspaper	54.6	73.9	49.4	41.7	45.8	50.5	57.9	45.4
Talk about with friends and family	58.4	56.6	37.9	62.1	78.2	54.9	65.4	46.5
Attend rally/public meeting	6.4	2.6	7.4	4.2	4.3	6.8	3.9	9
Look into website	8.1	16.6	1.3	4.7	9.5	4.6	8.1	8.2

Source: European Election Study 2004

	Cognitive and affective effects	Perceptions of political system	Political participation
Agenda-setting and framing	x		
Evaluations of political leaders	x		
Learning	x		
Political cynicism		x	
Political efficacy		x	
Engagement and communication			x
Turnout/mobilization			x
Vote choice			x

Figure 6.3   Typology of information and campaign effects

Source: Extended from de Vreese and Semetko (2004)

Cognitive and affective effects. One of the most influential ideas about campaign effects deals with the media's ability to influence the public salience of issues, referred to as the agenda-setting function of the media. Agenda-setting is a heterogeneous field of research originating in Lippmann's (1922) notion of how the media shape our pictures of the world. Trenaman and McQuail (1961: 178) concluded that "the evidence strongly suggests that people think *about* what they are told." McCombs and Shaw (1972) coined the term agenda-setting in their seminal study of the 1968 US presidential election campaign where they found a strong similarity between the most prominent issues in the news and undecided voters' ranking of the most important political issues. Countless studies of agenda-setting have since been conducted in the context of general election campaigns (e.g., McCombs 2004; Weaver et al. 1981) and the evidence is mixed. In the UK it was found that television had relatively little impact on the public agenda (Miller 1991), while Norris et al. (1999) found that television raised the saliency of "unobtrusive" issues but had no agenda-setting impact on issues that were already high priority. In Israel significant media agenda-setting effects were found (Sheafer and Weimann 2005) after controlling for the effects of real world security and economic variables. In Spain agenda-setting effects were also demonstrated and this research extended to suggest that frequent presentations of certain attributes of a candidate led the public to think about those attributes as more important (McCombs et al. 2000). Suffice to say that the agenda-setting function of the media is an important one, also during elections, and that the effects can either be diminished or enlarged depending on the characteristics of the election, the issues, and individuals.

Framing research is concerned with the media's highlighting of certain aspects of an issue (and de facto negligence of other aspects) and how this can affect citizens' understanding of and attitudes towards an issue. Framing research has expanded in recent years (see D'Angelo 2002 and de Vreese 2009a), but the vast majority of this research is carried out in non-election periods. An important line of research is Cappella and Jamieson's (1997) work on strategic news framing during elections (see above) and the consequences such reporting holds for political cynicism and a public engagement in politics.

Priming has the basic premise that new information renders something – an issue or a trait – applicable for use in subsequent evaluations. Priming is the "ability of new information to alter the standards by which the public evaluates political leaders" (Krosnick and Kinder 1990). An often-cited example stems back to the 1992 US election where Clinton won against Bush Snr. Bush's overall approval ratings were high in 1991 but low in 1992. This was attributed to his perceived strong performance on the Gulf War in 1991 but a poor performance on the economy a year later. Priming theory posits that public evaluations of political leaders are made on the basis of how leaders perform on issues that citizens have in mind when formulating the evaluation. This effect may vary according to preexisting levels of knowledge and there is evidence to suggest that priming particularly plays out for politically sophisticated individuals who more frequently update their political evaluations (Miller and Krosnick 2000).

Another important media effect during a campaign concerns *learning*. Knowledge gain from news media use has been long documented, and research has shown positive effects of exposure to news independent of formal education, demographics, attitudinal factors, and cultural differences (Norris 2000). Such knowledge gains can even be linked to the specific news content of different news outlets (de Vreese and Boomgaarden 2006). In addition to news, political debates and media analyses following these debates are sources of issue information (McKinney and Carlin 2004). In studies conducted during the last five US presidential elections, Drew and Weaver (2006) found that attention to television news, televised debates, and Internet news are important predictors of voter learning of, for example, candidate issue positions.

Perception of political system. The media may also affect citizens' perception of the political system. Cappella and Jamieson (1997) showed that strategic news framing invites the attribution of *cynical* motives to political actors and thereby reduces system support. By "reporting about politicians and their policies repeatedly framed as self-interest and seldom in terms of the common good – whether such characterizations are correct or incorrect – the public's experience of their leaders is biased toward attributions that induce mistrust" (Cappella and Jamieson 1997: 142). Other research has shown that attitudes towards the political system, which have often been assumed to be stable attributes, can change over the course of a campaign. Looking at evidence from the United States, the UK and New Zealand, Banducci and Karp (2003) find significant shifts in system support at the individual level that can be partially explained by attention to the media. In the same vein, Miller et al. (1979) long ago demonstrated that attention to negative newspaper reporting can lower levels of *efficacy* i.e., the sense that one's political voice actually makes a difference (internal efficacy) and that the political system is responsive (external efficacy). This is dovetailed by evidence suggesting that watching negative ads can also lower efficacy (Ansolabehere et al. 1999). The findings in this area, however, are not consistent, and Bennett et al. (1999) found (using US data from the 1996 election) that exposure to national television news and/or newspapers was unrelated to levels of *trust* in government. It is clear that conclusions depend on which sort of system perception and evaluation is investigated, where, and the contingencies stemming from both individuals and media messages.

Political participation. Media effects on varying types of political participation are also well known. One of the more classic ideas is that the media provide information that is subsequently *discussed* in interpersonal networks, at home, the office and/or among friends. A crucial form of political participation in a democracy is *turnout* and mobilization to participate in elections. Overall, there is most evidence to suggest that if news media exert any influence on such political engagement, it is a mobilizing influence. Most assessments of the media's demobilizing capacity are based on anecdotal evidence or bivariate relationships. A well designed study using a repeated measures data set of the 2000 US presidential campaign showed that campaign efforts have a substantial influence on turnout intention, even taking initial turnout intention into account (Hillygus 2004).

In terms of *vote choice*, theories of voting behavior generally emphasize the importance of party support or attachment (Budge and Farlie 1983; Campbell et al. 1980), as well as contextual factors such as economic perceptions (Lewis-Beck 1997), perceptions of issues (Nie et al. 1979) and evaluations of leaders or the top candidates (Wattenberg 1994). Following early research from the post-World War II period, it was long assumed that the media and the campaign exerted little influence on the actual vote choice. This stemmed from the idea that the "highly interested voters vote more, and know more about the campaign and read and listen more, and participate more. However, they are also less open to persuasion and less likely to change" (Berelson et al. 1954: 314). More recent evidence, however, provides a more nuanced picture. Hillygus (2005) showed that campaign events can affect vote choice and that this dynamic is conditional on previous preferences, partisan dispositions, and political context. Huber and Arceneaux (2008) found evidence that citizens are persuaded by ads that affect their vote choice and De Vreese and Semetko (2004) showed how exposure to news affected vote choice in a national referendum.

It is clear that the effects on vote choice are not huge, but can be significant. However, much of the actual effect on political behavior is indirect, by affecting the public agenda, the level of campaign engagement, by framing issues in the news, and by affecting perceptions of the political system.

Conclusion

Campaign communication and the central actors (parties, media, and citizens) are involved in a process of constant development and mutual influence. The importance of understanding campaign communication for the way democracy works originates from the simple fact that people rely mainly on the media for information that might help them decide if and how to vote. The media can thus exert considerable power with regard to which issues, attributes, and frames people consider important and salient. This makes it imperative to study the communication of parties (to the media and prospective voters) and the media (to [news] consumers). In addition, scholars need to pay (more) attention to reverse information and communication flows during elections, with citizens being increasingly able to produce mediated messages. This chapter took stock of our current knowledge of campaign communications and a number of key points emerged.

The **media market** has become a liberalized, competitive, and partially global market, constituting one of the most significant parts of the world economy. News is more readily available than ever before, with the proliferation of television stations, Internet websites, and the emergence of free daily newspapers. Whether the increase in availability has been accompanied by an increase in the use of news and in the diversity of information presented in the news remains an unanswered question. Concentration in ownership structures and international collaboration and mergers in the media sector on the one hand, and increased competition for advertising revenue on the other, are developments that do not *per se* bode well for the diversity of political news. These developments take place against the backdrop of changes in **political parties**. These face dropping membership and increased costs stemming from professionalized modes of campaigning. Today's political campaigns are a mix of classic techniques such as canvassing and attempts to mobilize personal networks through online media. At the same time, alternative political organizations compete for the attention and commitment of citizens.

The contents of the **political news** and the coverage of campaigns and elections show a shift over time: there is an increase in the focus on the electoral *process* and less room for substance. But this is not happening to the same extent everywhere. And it remains an open question as to whether it is only worrisome that process and strategy have become part of the news story. Suffice to say that strategy and process *are* important aspects of politics. **Citizens** are potentially more empowered, especially the technological and "digital haves." They possess the financial and technological resources and the cognitive capacity to voice their opinion through, for example, political blogs, but these new possibilities for user-generated political content may also exacerbate the division between those politically active and those not. The extent to which citizens are affected by professionalized political campaigns and the media coverage of politics has become a question of the different sorts of effects and the conditionality of those effects, i.e., that they depend on individual and contextual factors. Indeed some contexts seem to be more prone for media effects than others: in places where general mass media appealing to a broad audience are still in existence and where an increasing share of the electorate are changing their vote between elections, the potential for media effects is substantial. In contexts such as the US, where media markets are highly fragmented and political news consumption is primarily a self-selecting process, this is entirely different, and the role of the media is perhaps better seen as preaching to the already converted and catering to the well-defined segments in the market.

PART II

PUBLIC OPINION
AND VOTING

7

Ideology, Partisanship, and Democratic Development

Russell J. Dalton

Electoral politics provides a means for society to make collective judgments about the past policies of government and the direction a future government should follow. Often elections will represent a competition between groups and their contending interests within a nation. Of course, these divisions can take many forms. For a large part of the twentieth century the economic competition between social classes seemed to dominate politics in many Western democracies. In other nations, religious, regional, or other social cleavages define the issues of electoral politics and public policy. The issues and personalities of campaigns are often derived from these competing social interests, or at least this is the presumption of many election campaigns.

At a deeper level, democracy should be a competition between different worldviews or ideologies that address societal needs. Social Democrats, if elected, approach public policy with a different framework than Christian Democrats. Liberals have a different *Weltanschauung* than Green parties. And often the reporting on elections stresses the competition between liberal views and conservative views, Left versus Right, or other ideological frameworks.

This chapter examines the roots of such political division. How does social modernization and democratization transform the ideological basis of citizens' political orientations? Furthermore, how does modernization affect partisan attitudes and voter choice?

We begin by discussing the theoretical debates about how socio-political development shapes citizens' broad political orientations. We map the distribution of these orientations – measured by Left–Right identities – for citizens in a set of contemporary democracies surveyed by the Comparative Study of Electoral Systems (CSES). Because the survey focuses on democratic elections, the CSES nations tend to be more affluent and established democracies. This under-represents the poorest democracies, although several of these nations are included in the CSES. The next section describes the correlates of these Left–Right orientations to illustrate their varied content. We also describe how these same developmental processes affect party attachments. Finally, we examine the extent to which Left–Right orientations are linked to party choices – the extent to which voting is ideologically based. These results allow us to describe how social and political modernization broadly affects electoral behavior.

Modernization and Political Division

Research on development and electoral politics is framed by two debates about the nature of political cleavages in democratic nations. One debate involves Daniel Bell's provocative (1970) claim that socio-economic development moderates political differences in a nation, leading to an "End of Ideology." Affluence, the growth of the welfare state, expanding employment in the tertiary sector, and increasing geographic and social mobility all contribute to the blurring of traditional political divisions based on an economic cleavage. For instance, the widely acknowledged decline in class voting in Western democracies demonstrates the moderation of the historic economic cleavage underlying a Marxist view of human development (Knutsen 2006; Nieuwbeerta and De Graaf 1999). Bell also argued that modern societies were steadily becoming more secular, which lessens the moral content of political debate (also see Norris and Inglehart 2004).

At the same time, Bell held that deep ideological divisions are still a powerful political force in developing nations. He emphasized the importance of nationalism, ethnicity, pan-Arabism, and other ideological conflicts in the developing world. In a recent update to his book, Bell (2000) stressed the role of ethnicity and nationalism as sources of division in developing nations.

In summary, the **End of Ideology Thesis** claims that political cleavages, and thus political conflict, will lessen as societies modernize. In part, socio-economic progress provides the resources to address the economic needs that stimulate many group conflicts. In addition, the increasing diversity and complexity of modern societies produce cross-cutting interests that blur existing lines of division. In practical terms, this implies that citizens and political parties start to converge to moderate centrist positions (e.g., Kirchheimer 1966). The most definitive study of voting behavior in advanced industrial democracies found that social divisions in voting choice were weakening, which the authors attributed to the resolution of long-standing social cleavages through the democratic process (Franklin et al. 1992: ch. 15). In short, modernization produces centripetal forces that moderate political polarization and ideological conflict.

Other evidence supported Bell's claim of the continuing potency of ethnic divisions and other social cleavages in many new democracies (e.g., Bratton et al. 2004; Horowitz 2000). The struggles over economic well-being and individual rights are still very contentious in the developing world. Thus, politics will be more polarized in developing democracies because of the centrifugal forces of divisive lines of cleavage.

A second research debate involves the content of political competition. The **Postindustrial Thesis** maintains that the extent of political division does not systematically decline because of the modernization process, but the content of political competition changes. While there might be a withering away of Marxian economic conflicts in advanced industrial democracies, this produces new political controversies over lifestyle issues, quality of life, and self-expression issues (Inglehart 1990: ch. 9). Especially among the young, postmaterial or libertarian issues provide a new basis of political orientation. Alternatively, modernization may stimulate dormant cleavages such as regional identities, or create new bases of political competition, such as gender-based politics or ethnic/racial divisions (Deegan-Krause 2007). Thus, social modernization does not end ideological competition, but it changes the bases of electoral politics to new issues and forms of division.

Our analyses first ask whether citizens have broad political orientations that they use to orient themselves to politics, and does social and political modernization lessen polarization in such broad orientations? Then, if such orientations exist, are there systematic and predictable differences in the content of these orientations?

Citizen Political Orientations

Our first empirical challenge is to compare the broad political orientations of citizens in very diverse political settings – ranging from new democracies to well-established democracies, from poor to affluent societies. The nature of political issues, and even political discourse, can vary widely across these nations, so it is impossible to meaningfully examine the End of Ideology Thesis based on a single issue or a subset of issues.

If we look beyond the specific issues of the day, some political framework or core political identity organizes political discourse in a nation and citizens' individual belief systems. Sometimes these identities are linked to a specific party, broad views of the appropriate role of government, or a political philosophy. To facilitate our cross-national comparisons, we focus on the Left–Right framework as a way to summarize individuals' political orientations and meaningfully compare the level of political polarization in a nation (Fuchs and Klingemann 1989; Knutsen 1995).

Left–Right terminology is common in elite discourse; it is frequently heard in press descriptions of parties and candidates. Electoral scholars routinely interpret shifts in party vote shares as reflecting this dynamic (McDonald and Budge 2005). In media and academic electoral analyses the Left–Right dimension provides a framework for discussing issues, party positions, and the dynamics of electoral choice.

There is a considerable academic debate on whether citizens conceptualize politics in ideological terms as implied by the Left–Right labels.[1] We have a less philosophical view of the meaning of Left–Right orientations (Fuchs and Klingemann 1989; Inglehart and Klingemann 1976). We accept that most citizens do not have a sophisticated philosophical understanding of ideological concepts such as socialism or liberalism that are often implied by the terms Left and Right. Instead, the Left–Right framework provides a source of *political identity* that helps orient the individual to politics. This identity provides a shorthand for summarizing the enduring issues of political debate – whether it is a poor developing nation or an affluent advanced industrial democracy. Ronald Inglehart has shown that most people can locate themselves on a Left–Right scale in most nations. He describes the scale as a super-issue that represents "whatever major conflicts are present in the political system" (Inglehart 1990: 273; see also Fuchs and Klingemann 1989; Knutsen 1995). This sponge-like characteristic of Left–Right allows us to meaningfully compare citizen orientations across nations.

The Comparative Study of Electoral Systems asked respondents to position along a Left–Right scale using the following question:[2]

> In politics people sometimes talk of left and right. Where would you place yourself on a scale from 0 to 10, where 0 means the left and 10 means the right?

Despite past questions about the existence of Left–Right orientations among mass publics, almost 90% of the public in this diverse set of nations have a Left–Right position (Figure 7.1). This high level of Left–Right orientations also transcends old and new democracies, and nations of quite different political heritages. For instance, more than 90% of the Albanians, Czechs, Bulgarians, and Hungarians have a Left–Right self-location. The nations with low levels of Left–Right identities are also relatively mixed. For example, only 73% of the British public express a Left–Right position, and the percentage drops below two-thirds only in Ukraine, Slovenia, Kyrgyzstan, and Taiwan. Furthermore, the generally high levels of Left–Right self-placements in the CSES are consistent with results from the World Values Survey (WVS) that asked the same question in many of these same nations (Dalton 2006a).[3]

The End of Ideology Thesis

The End of Ideology Thesis focuses on the extent of political polarization within a society. It implies that citizens in less developed nations are more likely to be highly polarized because of intense political divisions among

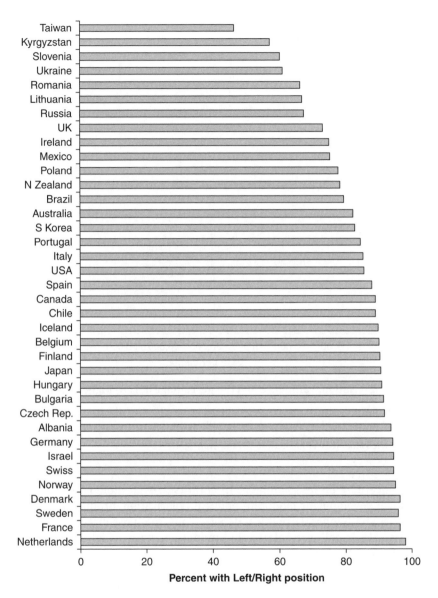

Figure 7.1 The percentage of the public who can position themselves on the Left–Right scale

Note: The figure displays the percentage of the public in each nation that can position themselves on the Left–Right scale.

Source: CSES Module II; Lithuania and Ukraine from Module I

competing interests. Politics may be more divisive in these nations because the political stakes are greater and the norms of reciprocity and political

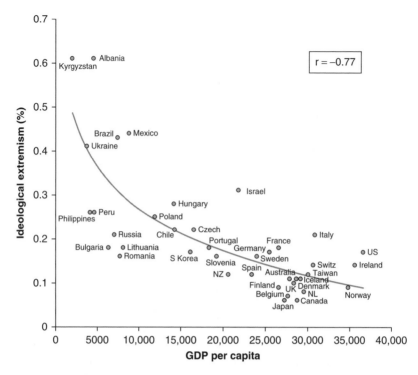

Figure 7.2 National affluence and the percentage of Left–Right extremists

Note: The figure displays the percentage of the public in each nation who position themselves at the extremes of the Left–Right scale by the GDP/capita (ppp) of each nation.

Source: CSES Module II; Lithuania and Ukraine from Module I

tolerance may be less common. In contrast, social modernization and political development moderate political polarization, producing a more centrist and temperate political debate. Thus, the most direct test of the thesis asks if political polarization moderates with social and political development.

The sources of political polarization obviously vary cross-nationally, but this is why a summary measure such as Left–Right orientations provides a way to compare the level of polarization across nations. We calculated the percentage of the public in each nation that scored at either of the two poles of the Left–Right scale (based on those who positioned themselves on the scale). Figure 7.2 presents the relationship between national affluence (GDP per capita) and ideological extremism. The trendline shows a strong negative curvilinear relationship between extremism and affluence (r = –0.77). Extremism is highest in less affluent nations, reaching over 60% of the public in Albania and Kyrgyzstan, with high levels in many other developing nations. Ideological extremism averages only about

10% of the public in the most affluent societies. The 1999–2002 World Values Survey shows similar results for an even more diverse set of nations (r = −0.64) (Dalton 2006a: 8–10).[4] Thus, independent of the content of political controversy, citizens in lower income nations are more likely to divide themselves into sharply opposing political camps.[5]

A nation's political development is also related to the level of political extremism among the citizenry. Using the Freedom House scores of democracy, there is a strong negative curvilinear relationship (R = −0.71) with the total percentage of Left and Right extremists.[6] This relationship, and the correlation with economic development, might be partially reciprocal. That is, sharp polarization may also hinder economic growth and democratization for less developed nations. High levels of polarization are thus a cause and a consequence of national circumstances. However, the end product is that development and polarization display a strong negative relationship.

Our findings thus broadly affirm Bell's thesis of the decline in political polarization with socio-political development. In other words, less affluent and less democratic nations have a public that is often sharply polarized on the dominant political divisions of the nation. The centrifugal forces created by such polarization likely make elections more contentious and party cooperation after the election more difficult. This polarization can also generate strains in governing, which may lessen the performance of the government and even weaken the stability of the regime (Dalton 2006a).

Conversely, political polarization is more moderate in advanced industrial democracies. Far fewer individuals place themselves at the extreme positions on the Left–Right scale in these nations. This suggests that political competition will be more manageable in these nations, because a large moderate center provides a middle ground for political discourse and cooperation. Even when elite debates may become intense between the ideological extremes, the lack of a highly polarized public moderates these controversies. Thus, while the centrifugal forces of polarization create political strains in many developing nations, a large moderate center exerts centripetal forces in most advanced industrial democracies.

Political Cleavages and Left–Right Orientations

Social modernization also might change the sources of political division in a nation. Historically, two factors have defined the major lines of political conflict in Western democracies: economic and religious cleavages (Lipset and Rokkan 1967). In European political systems, economic conflicts were typically expressed in Marxian class-based issues such as the nationalization of industry, redistribution of income, and the government's role in the economy. Religion defined a cleavage between different denominations or between religious and secular values. The religious cleavage generated issues such as state support for church schools, adherence to traditional lifestyles, and an endorsement of family values.

The End of Ideology Thesis claims that the salience of these cleavages has decreased in advanced industrial democracies. Economic growth resolved the most pressing issues of living standards and economic security that shaped the class cleavage, and secularization has gradually lessened the impact of the religious cleavage. Other social trends attenuated regional, urban/rural, and other social divisions.

The Postindustrial Thesis, in contrast, holds that as these traditional sources of political division decrease in importance, public and eventually government attention shifts toward a new set of political needs. Issues such as environmental protection, social equality, self-expression, and lifestyle choices typify this new issue agenda. Inglehart demonstrated that the Left–Right identities of Western Europeans were a mix of traditional economic issues and postmaterial issues (Inglehart 1990: ch. 9; also Knutsen 1995). In comparison, class, religious, and other social divisions are presumably more important bases of political cleavage in less developed nations. Region and ethnicity also may be stronger sources of cleavage in developing nations, tapping conflicts over national identity and contrasting value sets that established democracies have presumably addressed.

Comparing the content of Left–Right identities cross-nationally is difficult because the specific issues vary from election to election depending on current social conditions and the strategies of parties. In addition, the CSES does not include a battery of issue questions. Therefore, to map the sources of ideological cleavage, we compare how major social groups differ in their Left–Right positions.

We first examine the extent to which social class determines Left–Right identities, and thus the bases of political division in a nation. Social scientists have probably devoted more attention to the class cleavage than to any other demographic influence on political behavior. The class cleavage represents the economic and material problems of societies: providing for the economic security of all citizens and ensuring a just distribution of economic rewards. Issues such as unemployment, inflation, social services, tax policies, and government management of the economy reinforce class divisions. The tendency for leftist parties to derive the bulk of their support from the working class, and rightist parties to draw support from the middle class, is widely replicated in electoral research (Knutsen 2006; Lipset and Rokkan 1967).

The first two data columns of Table 7.1 describe the relationship of social class and union membership with Left–Right orientations (also see Norris 2004: ch. 5).[7] The strongest class correlations occur in Northern European party systems (Sweden and Finland), where class politics has a long political history. In Sweden, for example, 55% of workers hold a Leftist orientation, compared to only 16% among self-employed/professionals. Class still matters in structuring Swedes' political orientations, which should translate into positions on class-based issues and voting for parties on class terms.

However, social class is only weakly related to Left–Right identities in most established democracies. Even union membership, which is a clearer measure of attachment to a working class milieu, is weakly related to Leftist orientations. Social class as a political cleavage has gradually eroded as a political cleavage in most established democracies as Bell described (Knutsen 2006; Nieuwbeerta and De Graaf 1999). Social modernization has addressed many pressing economic issues, and life changes and social relations are less bound to class position.

Social class has even weaker correlations with political orientations in post-communist societies. Most East European party systems experienced limited class voting differences immediately after the democratic transition; and in some instances the cleavage ran in the opposite direction to the West (workers holding Rightist identities). The dramatic economic changes wrought by the transition, the ambiguous position of occupation groups in the new economic system, and the fluid nature of contemporary politics blur the political meaning of social class (Kitschelt et al. 1999; Lawson et al. 1999). This does not mean that economic issues are unimportant, only that economic concerns do not have a class basis that shapes broad political identities. Most Eastern European parties are gradually integrating social class interests into their political identities, but social class and union membership do not clearly define the Left–Right orientations of most post-communist citizens.

Similar weak class relationships exist in the new Asian democracies of Taiwan and South Korea, and in Japan. This reflects both the weakness of the working class movement in these nations and the lack of a strong social democratic political tradition, as well as each nation's unique political history (McAllister 2008; Norris 2004: ch. 5). Class also has weak relationships with Left–Right identities for the two Latin American nations in Table 7.1, and there is supporting evidence from the Latinobarometer for a larger group of Latin American nations.[8]

The other main social group alignment discussed in the cleavage literature is religion. Measuring the effect of religion on political identities is more complicated than analyzing the class cleavage, especially across the wide range of CSES nations. The class composition of most industrial nations is similar, but their religious composition is quite varied. Some nations are predominantly Protestant; Mediterranean Europe and Latin America are predominantly Catholic; other nations are characterized by religious diversity; and Asian democracies have non-Western religious traditions. The political tendencies of religious denominations also vary cross-nationally (Esmer and Petterson 2007; Lipset and Rokkan 1967). In some nations Catholics lean toward the Right; in other nations they are part of a Left alliance. This means that religious affiliation may produce different Left–Right orientations across nations.

TABLE 7.1 The relationship between Left–Right orientations and class and religion

	Class	Union member	Religious denomination	Religiosity
Established democracies				
Australia	0.03	0.18	0.25	—
Belgium	0.03	0.08	0.18	—
Canada	0.01	0.07	0.26	0.08
Denmark	0.07	0.07	—	0.15
Finland	0.25	0.04	0.23	0.23
France	0.12	0.11	0.26	—
Germany	0.03	0.16	0.21	0.09
Iceland	0.06	0.04	—	—
Italy	0.05	0.15	0.04	0.16
Japan	−0.03	0.15	0.10	0.08
Netherlands	−0.03	0.03	0.26	—
New Zealand	0.09	0.14	0.20	0.10
Norway	0.08	0.10	—	—
Portugal	0.05	0.14	0.14	0.20
Spain	0.17	0.11	0.20	0.35
Sweden	0.30	0.19	—	0.12
Switzerland	—	0.15	0.16	—
United Kingdom	0.00	0.15	0.25	0.08
United States	0.06	0.12	0.32	0.25
Average	*0.08*	*0.12*	*0.22*	*0.17*
Post-communist countries				
Albania	−0.06	0.05	0.08	0.22
Bulgaria	—	0.00	0.07	—
Czech Republic	0.19	0.04	0.16	0.16
Hungary	−0.06	−0.03	0.09	0.11
Kyrgyzstan	0.00	—	0.14	—
Poland	0.03	0.00	0.10	0.17
Romania	—	−0.04	0.06	0.02
Russia	—	−0.04	0.09	0.02
Average	*0.02*	*0.00*	*0.10*	*0.12*
Other countries				
Brazil	0.00	0.07	0.17	0.08
Chile	—	—	0.11	—
Israel	−0.05	0.05	0.33	0.26
Mexico	−0.02	0.03	0.09	0.06
South Korea	0.08	0.03	—	0.07
Taiwan	−0.04	−0.04	0.19	—

Note: Entries are Pearson correlations, exception for religious denomination, which are eta correlations. Dashes indicate the question was not asked in this survey.

Source: CSES Module II

The third column in Table 7.1 describes the relationship between religious denomination and Left–Right orientations.[9] The continuing relevance of the religious cleavage within the established democracies is one striking finding. On average, the impact of religion on Left–Right orientations is nearly triple that of social class. In addition, feelings of religiousness are consistently related to Rightist identities across all the established democracies. Thus, religion remains part of the agenda of politics in most established democracies. It is a core value that still influences broad political identities and eventually party choices.

Overall, religion has a limited impact outside the established Western democracies. Religious differences in Left–Right orientations are modest in most post-communist states, even in Albania and Bulgaria where the population divides along Christian/Muslim lines. Religion is also generally not a basis of political polarization in Asian democracies and the two Latin American nations.[10] Israel is the notable exception to this pattern, with strong relationships for religious denomination and religiosity.

The cross-national pattern of the relationship of class and religion with Left–Right orientations differs from much of the theoretical literature on this topic. The End of Ideology Thesis posits that these two cleavages are weakening in advanced industrial democracies. Yet, the strongest impact of class and religion still occurs in the established Western democracies. Similarly, the World Values Survey asked a battery of economic policy issues, and these issues are most strongly related to Left–Right orientations in Western democracies (Dalton 2006a: 12–14). Feelings of being religious also display some of the strongest correlations with Left–Right among the established democracies. The strength of these relationships in the established democracies reflects long political and partisan histories in which strong class and/or religious groups have articulated their interests and political parties represent these viewpoints.

Other global regions have different developmental courses. East European nations began their current democratic experience with weakly institutionalized social groups, a fluid political environment, and an instantaneous creation of a party system. The issues of democratization also tended to cut across class and religious lines. This limited the impact of class and religion in initially structuring political competition in post-communist nations. The new democracies of East Asia also developed without the strong class and religious polarization of Western Europe. Even the long-established Japanese political system has shown a persistent weakness of the class cleavage (Flanagan et al. 1991). The weak influence of social class on Left–Right identities also applies to the Latin American democracies in CSES. Thus, despite frequent academic claims about the global importance of social class and religion as a basis of citizen identities and political cleavage, this pattern seems most applicable to the Western democracies.

The End of Ideology Thesis also claims that national and ethnic cleavages will be more powerful in developing democracies where these political identities are still in dispute. Regional cleavages often reflect a tension

TABLE 7.2   The relationship between Left–Right orientations and social characteristics

	Region	Race/ Ethnicity	Education	Gender
Established democracies				
Australia	0.10	0.08	−0.13	−0.05
Belgium	0.07	—	0.01	−0.03
Canada	0.17	0.13	−0.05	0.02
Denmark	—	—	−0.02	−0.07
Finland	0.21	0.10	0.15	0.04
France	−0.08	0.10	−0.04	0.04
Germany	−0.08	0.21	—	0.03
Iceland	—	—	−0.10	−0.10
Italy	0.21	—	0.04	0.00
Japan	0.10	—	−0.13	0.05
Netherlands	0.06	—	−0.03	−0.07
New Zealand	0.03	0.11	−0.07	−0.04
Norway	0.14	—	−0.01	−0.07
Portugal	0.13	—	−0.06	0.04
Spain	0.27	—	−0.05	0.04
Sweden	0.20	—	0.13	−0.07
Switzerland	0.16	0.06	−0.07	−0.09
United Kingdom	0.16	0.15	−0.04	−0.02
United States	0.13	0.32	−0.12	−0.06
Average	*0.15*	*0.14*	*−0.04*	*−0.03*
Post-communist countries				
Albania	—	0.08	−0.06	0.04
Bulgaria	0.18	0.18	0.16	0.02
Czech Republic	0.17	—	0.16	−0.05
Hungary	0.17	0.08	−0.04	0.05
Kyrgyzstan	0.18	0.15	0.03	0.03
Poland	0.09	—	0.06	0.00
Romania	0.19	0.05	0.06	0.00
Russia	0.27	0.15	0.02	0.08
Average	*0.18*	*0.12*	*0.04*	*0.02*
Other countries				
Brazil	0.19	0.13	−0.15	0.02
Chile	0.13	—	−0.01	0.02
Israel	—	0.40	−0.12	0.03
Mexico	0.11	0.09	−0.09	0.09
South Korea	0.26	—	−0.07	−0.03
Taiwan	0.15	0.11	−0.06	0.04

Note: Entries for education and gender are Pearson correlations, statistics for region and race/ethnicity are eta correlations. Dashes indicate the question was not asked in this survey.

Source: CSES Module II

between the cultural norms of the nation's political center and the contrasting values in regional peripheries. The first column of Table 7.2 shows that regional cleavages in political orientations now exist in many established and developing democracies. However, on average, regional differences are modest in most established democracies.

Most post-communist nations have larger regional differences in Left–Right orientations than the average for the established democracies.[11] Regional differences in Russia are as large as in any other nation, which might be expected for such a geographically and ethnically diverse nation. The same applies to the other developing democracies. Region is not a strong basis of Left–Right polarization in most new democracies outside of Europe, although it looks more substantial when compared to the class or religious cleavage. Complementary analyses based on the World Values Survey find that feelings of national pride – a more direct measure of nationalist sentiments consistent with Bell's thesis – are more strongly related to Left–Right orientations in Asian, African, and Latin American nations, with weaker relationships for the Western democracies (Dalton 2006a: 15–16).

Another potential social cleavage contrasts the majority population and distinctive racial, ethnic, or linguistic minorities (Horowitz 2000; Saggar 2007). Bell (2000) saw these cleavages as providing a major basis of division in many developing nations, often impeding the development of democracy. Earlier studies of European party systems overlooked this cleavage because most of these nations were relatively homogeneous, although these societies are becoming more ethnically diverse. Moreover, ethnic and racial divisions may influence political orientations because they often involve sharp social differences, institutionalized networks within these communities, and strong feelings of group identity.

The CSES does not include the ethnically fragmented African and Asian nations that might best fit the theoretical pattern (such as Nigeria, or India). However, the CSES does include several new democracies with significant ethnic divisions, such as Albania, Bulgaria, Brazil, and Taiwan. While Table 7.2 shows moderate Left–Right differences by ethnicity or race in several of these nations, the relationships are just as strong in established democracies such as Canada or the United States.[12] (Many nations are so homogeneous that neither race nor ethnicity was included in the questionnaire.) Only Israel displays extremely high levels of ethnic polarization for obvious reasons. Thus, ethnicity or race can be an important basis of political identities in culturally divided nations, and in developing democracies these effects may outweigh cleavages such as class or religion.

The Postindustrial Thesis maintains that new cleavages might tap the emerging divisions of advanced industrial societies. Postmaterial issues draw disproportional support from young, better-educated citizens in advanced industrial societies who support leftist programs such as those advocated by Green and New Left parties (Inglehart 1990). Education can also provide a postindustrial cleavage separating the information-rich, technologically sophisticated voter from the information-poor, unskilled voter. The traditional class alignments would suggest that the better educated will lean toward the Right because of their middle class position. The Postindustrial Thesis argues that the better educated will lean to the Left because of their postmaterial orientations.

The third column of Table 7.2 displays the correlation between education and Left–Right orientations. Even though social class significantly affects Left–Right orientations in many established democracies, the education relationship runs in the opposite direction: the better educated generally lean toward the Left in most established democracies. In fact, the major exceptions are nations where the class cleavage remains so strong that it overpowers educational patterns (e.g., Finland and Sweden). Post-communist parties reflect the "normal" class alignment, with the better educated leaning toward the Right in most nations. Surprisingly, in the other developing democracies the better educated have Leftist orientations. In Israel, Korea, and Taiwan this may reflect the relative affluence of these nations, which encourages postmaterial orientations (Lee 2008).

An even more direct test of the Postindustrial Thesis should be the relationship between postmaterial values and Left–Right identities. However, analyses from the WVS show that this value cleavage has a strong relationship across most global regions (Dalton 2006a). It may be that these issues are more visible in advanced industrial democracies, because in these nations the two sides are relatively balanced. However, where differences in opinion exist in these other regions, it serves as a basis of polarization between traditional and modern values (see also Lee 2008). Taken as a whole, there is some evidence that a new postindustrial value cleavage is emerging in affluent democracies, but this cleavage currently overlaps with other bases of political division.[13]

Gender is another potential new basis of political cleavage (Inglehart and Norris 2003). The feminist movement and the changing social role of women have brought issues of gender equity and family policies onto the agenda of most established democracies. A feminist view presumes that women lean toward leftist parties, and men toward rightist parties.

The rightmost column in Table 7.2 shows that gender differences in Left–Right orientations are fairly modest across virtually all nations. Still, one can see evidence of an emerging cleavage. Historically, women leaned toward the Right in most established democracies because of their religiosity, family values, and security concerns. However, changing social roles in these societies are leading many women to lean toward the Left, which is more supportive of gender equality. In half the established democracies women are more Leftist, especially so among younger women. However, in post-communist and other developing democracies the traditional pattern still emerges, with women leaning toward the Right. There is a potential for a significant gender gap in Left–Right identities, but it does not yet exist in most democracies.[14]

Social Modernization and Partisanship

Another possible cognitive framework for citizens consists of attachments to a political party. In established democracies, long-term psychological predispositions – party identifications – are an important cognitive mechanism for orienting oneself to politics (Campbell et al. 1960; Inglehart and Klingemann 1976). Partisanship serves as a heuristic to organize the complexities of politics, integrate information into a political belief system, and evaluate political phenomena.

Like Left–Right orientations, partisanship typically encapsulates a mix of political values and a sense of how "people like me" normally stand politically. Partisanship also guides the decision to participate in election campaigns and politics in general. A vast literature demonstrates the importance of party attachments as a central element of democratic politics (Dalton and Wattenberg 2000; Green et al. 2002). Thus, Weisberg and Greene (2003: 115) conclude: "Party identification is the linchpin of our modern understanding of electoral democracy, and it is likely to retain that crucial theoretical position."

The development of partisan loyalties may be even more significant for new democracies. Partisanship involves attachment to a key political institution that integrates citizens into the new democratic political order. Research thus treats the growth of partisanship as a sign of developing ties to the new democratic system. This applies to democratizing societies (McDonough et al. 1998; Tóka 1998) and Latin American democracies (Hagopian 1998; Mainwaring 1999). The development of partisanship also can indicate a transformation in mass loyalties from a charismatic leader who created the new political system to more enduring party organizations.

The classic model of partisanship presumes that these attachments strengthen as nations democratize and establish stable party systems (Dalton and Weldon 2007; Norris 2004: ch. 6). However, there is mounting evidence that partisanship is eroding in advanced industrial democracies, which contradicts the classic partisanship model. Dalton and Wattenberg (2000: ch. 2), for example, find that the percentage of party identifiers has decreased in 17 of the 19 advanced industrial democracies for which long-term trends are available. Figure 7.3 illustrates this pattern for four large established democracies. In the United States, for example, about three-quarters of the American public were partisan identifiers in the 1950s and early 1960s, and this decreased by 15–20% by the 2000–04 elections. The UK, France, and Germany follow a similar downward trajectory in the percentage attached to a political party. Indeed, a variety of attitudinal and behavioral measures document a general erosion in partisanship in most advanced industrial democracies (Berglund et al. 2005: 199–201; Clarke and Stewart 1998; cf. Green et al. 2002).

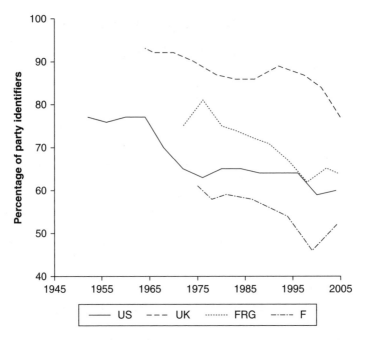

Figure 7.3 The percentage of partisan identifiers in four nations

Sources: United States, 1952–2004: American National Election Studies; UK, 1964–2005: British Election Studies; Germany, 1972–2005: German Election Studies (Western Germany only for 1990–2002); France: Eurobarometer Surveys (1975, 1978, 1981, 1986, 1988), European Election Studies (1994, 1999, and 2004)

One explanation for partisan dealignment is the diminishing value of partisanship in contemporary politics. The mass media fulfill many of the information functions once performed by political parties; citizen groups are active in interest articulation; and parties recruit fewer members. In addition, many better-educated citizens have the political skills to make their own political decisions without a strict reliance on habitual party ties (Dalton 2007a).

The dealignment thesis primarily applies to advanced democracies because their socio-economic development produces the societal and individual conditions that weaken partisanship. But there is some evidence that dealigning forces are also present in developing societies. For instance, Sánchez (2003) assembled an impressive time series of opinion surveys that documents the slow weakening of partisanship in Costa Rica between 1978 and 2002 (also see Hagopian 1998). The time period for post-communist societies is shorter, but the evidence of strengthening party ties is also ambiguous.

It is difficult to precisely compare levels of party identification across nations because linguistic and political differences affect how this concept is interpreted in each nation (Budge et al. 1976). In the United States, for instance, the concept of a partisan independent is widely understood, while this terminology is uncommon in many other democracies. The structure of other electoral systems also affects the nature of party identities. At the same time, most electoral scholars accept that most voters develop such long-term, affective partisan attachments, even if they occasionally vote for another party.

To measure partisanship the Comparative Study of Electoral Systems asked the following question: "Do you usually think of yourself as close to any particular political party? Which party is that? Do you feel very close to this party, somewhat close, or not very close?" This question sacrifices the notion of long-term partisan identity for a feeling of closeness to a party. This should make it easier for respondents to express an attachment; and these attachments may be more directly related to immediate vote preferences because of the phrasing of the question.[15] Still, the question taps affinity to a party separate from vote, and it can be used in systems with diverse party traditions.

Because partisanship is learned from electoral experience, either the individual's experience or experience inherited from one's parents, partisanship should be more common in nations with a longer history of stable party competition (Dalton and Weldon 2007). The question is whether dealignment is now reversing this pattern in long-established democracies.

Figure 7.4 presents the level of party attachments in each CSES nation as a function of the age of the party system to represent the continuity of the nation's electoral experience.[16] A nation has a younger party system age if it is a new democracy or if there has been considerable party turnover that weakens the acquisition of stable party attachments. We find a positive relationship between the age of a party system and the percentage of partisans in the nation ($r = 0.48$).[17] The average percentage of partisans in established democracies (48%) is half again higher than in new democracies (30%).

At the same time, one can see a non-linear pattern in partisan development. The percentage feeling close to any party is limited in many new democracies or systems with unstable party systems, such as several post-communist nations and the new East Asian democracies. Party attachments are more common in middle age party systems. And then partisanship dips among the oldest party systems. Surveys from a single point in time cannot test such a developmental sequence, but the longitudinal trends in Figure 7.3 show that partisanship has declined in advanced industrial democracies.

In summary, the levels of partisanship in established and new democracies are broadly similar, but represent separate political conditions. For most of the established democracies, social modernization has weakened

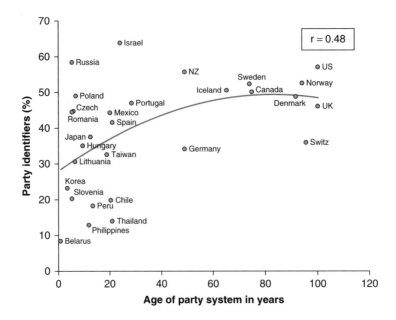

Figure 7.4 Age of party system and strength of partisanship

Note: The figure displays the percentage of the public that expresses a party attachment by the age of the two major parties (see note 16).

Source: CSES Module I

affective party ties in recent years. This may signal the development of a more discerning public that votes based on the issues and candidates of a campaign, rather than inherited partisan loyalties. The weakening of party identities thus increases the potential for political orientations such as Left–Right to have a stronger impact on voting choice.

The creation of stable party systems and routinized electoral processes should slowly develop stronger party identities in new democracies (Dalton and Weldon 2007). Such attachments to parties are an important element in the development of stable and meaningful democratic elections. These party attachments will mobilize citizens to participate in the electoral process, provide a heuristic for judging the issues and candidates in a campaign, and provide the cognitive cues that help citizens orient themselves to the world of democratic electoral politics. Once established, however, these identities may also be eroded by the forces of social modernization – but the initial step for new democracies is to develop party attachments in the first place. Thus, as Almond and Verba (1963: 86) wrote, "Open and moderate partisanship, then, are essential to a stable democracy." Tracking the growth of partisanship in new democracies is an indicator of their democratic development.

Left–Right and Voting Decisions

The ultimate outcome of electoral politics is to make a voting decision. As the impact of long-term partisan predispositions (social group cues or party attachments) on voting decisions weaken in advanced industrial democracies, issue opinions and other campaign factors may exert an increasing influence. In their comparative study of voting behavior, Franklin et al. (1992: 400) conclude: "If all the issues of importance to voters had been measured and given their due weight, then the rise of issue voting would have compensated more or less precisely for the decline in cleavage politics." There is also evidence of a shift towards a more candidate-centered politics (Aarts et al. 2010; Wattenberg 1991). Candidate-centered voting has potentially far-reaching implications for contemporary electoral politics, but it lies outside of this chapter's coverage.

One form of issue voting involves controversies reflecting the long-standing economic or social divisions in a nation, such as concerns about social inequality or economic well-being. For instance, the apparently growing emphasis on economic performance as a basis for voting may illustrate such patterns (Lewis-Beck and Stegmaier 2007). Voters are judging parties on their economic achievements, but these judgments are not as firmly based on class or social group positions as in the past.

Other issues arise from new political controversies, such as the postmaterial concerns of advanced industrial societies, new aspects of identity-politics, or issues linked to democratic transitions and marketization (Dalton et al. 2007; Inglehart 1990; Lawson et al. 1999). These issues expand the boundaries of politics to include topics that were once the prerogative of markets or individual choice. Until recently, politicians and voters did not even know that problems of global warming and ozone depletion existed. Furthermore, new issues can provide a political base for new parties and reorient the voting patterns of the young. The available longitudinal data suggest that postmaterial values gradually have strengthened as a predictor of party preferences in Western democracies (Knutsen 1995).

Faced with a diversity of issues across elections and electoral systems, it is difficult to compare the impact of issues across the large set of nations discussed in this chapter. This, again, is where the inclusive nature of Left–Right orientations facilitates our analyses. We presume that Left–Right attitudes act as a "super issue," summarizing positions on the issues that are most important to each voter. Some voters' Left–Right attitudes reflect positions on traditional economic conflicts; others' Left–Right attitudes reflect postmaterial or foreign policy issues. Specific issue interests may vary across individuals or across nations, but Left–Right orientations provide a way to summarize a citizen's overall political views.

Many factors might affect the degree of issue or Left–Right voting in an election. Our emphasis on the relationship between social modernization

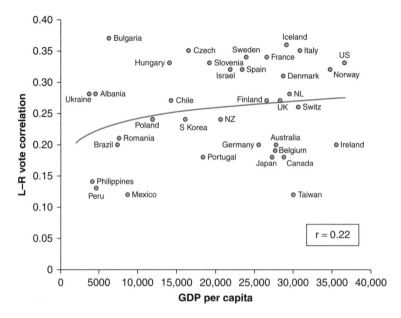

Figure 7.5 National affluence and the correlation between Left–Right orientations and voting

Note: The figure displays the Cramer's V correlation between Left–Right orientations and legislative vote choice on the vertical axis; the horizontal axis is national GDP per capita.

Source: CSES Module II; Ukraine from Module I

and electoral politics leads to the expectation that Left–Right orientations are more likely to influence voting in advanced industrial democracies with established parties that have clear Left–Right identities. These societies also have more sophisticated electorates who are less likely to vote on fixed social cues or party attachments, and more likely to vote on the issues and candidates of a campaign. In contrast, in new democracies the partisan choices are often less clearly defined. Voters are also less likely to have complex and sophisticated issue beliefs because they are learning the democratic electoral process. In short, the level of sociopolitical development should affect the level of Left–Right voting in elections.

Figure 7.5 displays the *correlation* between Left–Right attitudes and voting choice in each nation with a legislative election, with nations arrayed by their level of affluence.[18] In every case, Left–Right orientations are a significant, and often a very strong, predictor of voting choice. In France, for example, a full 96% of self-identified leftists favored a leftist party (Communists, Socialists, or Greens) in the 2002 legislative elections, compared to only 14% among self-identified rightists (Cramer's V = 0. 34). In overall terms, however, the relationship is stronger in more affluent democracies, as shown by the trendline in the figure; and separate analyses display a similar relationship for the Freedom House measure of democratization.

This developmental pattern may initially appear counter-intuitive, because we have previously shown that ideological polarization within the electorate decreases with social and political development. Even though there are fewer ideological extremists in advanced industrial democracies, Figure 7.5 shows that there is greater congruence between the Left–Right position of voters and their party choices in these nations. Or in other words, the public in developing nations may be more polarized in their Left–Right orientations, but these orientations are not as clearly translated into their party choices. The representation of Left–Right orientations in party preferences works better in established democracies, all else being equal.

At the same time, these developmental processes appear secondary to the pattern of party competition in a nation. If parties offer clear Left–Right choices, then voters can more easily transfer their orientations into party choices. Using a measure of party system polarization (Dalton 2008), we found that Left–Right attitudes have the greatest impact where parties offer clear Left–Right options. Even in new, less affluent democracies such as Albania and Bulgaria, Left–Right orientations are very strongly related to vote choice because the parties are highly polarized along Left–Right lines. Similarly, there is considerable variability in the relationship between Left–Right orientations and vote in the established democracies that reflects the degree of political choice offered by the parties. France, Iceland, and Sweden, for example, have highly polarized party systems that facilitate Left–Right voting, while Australia, Belgium, and Canada have party systems with moderate party polarization, which attenuates Left–Right voting.[19]

In summary, this is another example of the development course of electoral politics. Socioeconomic and political development appear to foster issue voting as party systems become established and citizens become more sophisticated voters. Yet, the campaign choices of political parties in offering Left–Right or issue choices have an even greater impact on whether citizens can readily translate their political orientations into party choices.

Social Modernization and Electoral Politics

This chapter has tried to map how social and political development broadly shape citizen orientations and the patterns of electoral behavior in a polity. Central to our conclusions is the relationship between sociopolitical modernization and the extent of Left–Right divisions within the public. There is convincing evidence that the degree of ideological polarization among the citizenry declines with modernization. Like many aspects of political development, this may occur because less polarized nations find it easier to develop and democratize. In addition, there are strong theoretical and empirical reasons for thinking that modernization encourages centripetal forcesthat reinforce democratization. In this sense, development leads to a moderation of ideology if not to an end of ideology.

A nation's social and political conditions also shape the nature of electoral politics. Even though class and religious cleavages in advanced industrial democracies have weakened in recent decades, these cleavages remain more important in shaping citizen Left–Right identities than in other global regions. Western democracies also show signs of developing new cleavages based on education, gender, and possibly ethnic divisions. Yet even though these publics are less polarized politically (in Left–Right terms), voters are more likely to translate their political orientations into their voting choices.

Post-communist nations seem to be gradually developing a system of cleavage-based politics. Rapid democratization created new parties that have gradually established political identities linked to basic societal interests, and thus group-based politics is evolving. Similarly, party attachments in these nations were initially weak – because democratic parties and electoral politics were new experiences – and these attachments are strengthening over time. But the inchoate nature of many of these party systems means that citizen orientations are less strongly related to voting choice.

The other new democracies in the CSES are too few and diverse to broadly represent other developing democracies. Yet, they suggest a pattern that seems common in many developing nations. Class and religion generally have less weight in shaping citizens' Left–Right orientations in these nations, and postmaterial cleavages are not definitive. Instead, citizens appear to draw upon region, ethnic, and national identities to shape their basic Left–Right identities. Yet, despite the fact that these publics are often highly polarized in their Left–Right orientations, this does not translate into citizen voting choices based on their Left–Right positions.

In short, as democracy develops, the nature of the electorates systematically changes in both the level of political division and the sources of division. Moreover, citizens appear better able to use elections as a means of meaningful political choice, which is the ultimate objective of democratic electoral politics.

8

Political Participation

André Blais

In a democracy, every citizen should have the right to express his or her views about what the government should do, should have the right to vote and to have a say about the selection of lawmakers, and should have the right to run as a candidate in elections if he or she so wishes. A democracy is a polity in which citizens are given the opportunity to participate.

Many democratic theorists argue that without substantial citizen participation democracy falls short of its goals (Pateman 1970) and that as a consequence the quality of democracy in a given polity can be ascertained by the degree of citizen involvement. Participation is a "good" thing, and a crucial challenge is to understand why so many people remain "passive" citizens.

A different perspective is offered by rational choice, a theoretical model inspired by an economic perspective according to which individuals make decisions after having considered the expected benefits and costs of the various options (see, especially, Downs 1957; Olson 1965). Rational people realize that their individual participation, by itself, is very unlikely to affect the course of events the expected benefits of getting involved are minimal, they will be inclined to stay home and invest more time and energy in private matters. They will "free ride" and let others participate if they wish to. From such a vantage point, participation appears "irrational" and the challenge is rather to account for the fact that quite a few people do get involved.

The chapter examines the nature, amount, and determinants of political participation. Because of the central place of elections in democracies, I distinguish between electoral and non-electoral participation.

Voter Turnout over Time

Table 8.1 shows mean turnout by decade in democratic legislative elections held since the 1960s. An election is deemed to be democratic when it takes place in a country with a score of 1 or 2 on the Freedom House ratings of political rights the year the election was held. Turnout is measured as a percentage of those registered who cast a vote.[1]

TABLE 8.1   Voter turnout by country and decade

Country	1960	1970	1980	1990	2000
Africa					
Benin				76	57
Botswana		55	68	77	76
Cape Verde				77	54
Mauritius			87	82	81
São Tomé & Príncipe				58	67
South Africa				89	98
Asia					
Israel		79	79	79	65
Japan	72	71	69	61	62
Korea				64	54
Mongolia					78
Europe					
Andorra				81	81
Austria	94	92	87	84	80
Belgium	91	93	94	91	91
Bulgaria				75	61
Croatia					61
Cyprus			95	92	90
Czech Republic				85	61
Denmark	87	88	87	84	86
Estonia				63	60
Finland	85	78	74	67	66
France	77	76	72	68	60
Germany	87	91	87	80	78
Greece		80	83	80	75
Hungary				67	69
Iceland	91	90	89	86	86
Ireland	74	76	73	67	65
Italy	93	92	89	85	82
Latvia				72	66
Liechtenstein				87	87
Lithuania				53	51
Luxembourg	90	90	88	87	92
Malta		95	96	96	95
Monaco				66	78
Netherlands	95	84	83	76	80
Norway	83	82	83	77	76
Poland				48	47
Portugal		85	79	65	64
Romania					62
San Marino				78	73
Slovakia				84	62
Slovenia				80	65

TABLE 8.1 (Continued)

Country	1960	1970	1980	1990	2000
Spain		68	73	78	73
Sweden	87	90	89	85	81
Switzerland	64	52	48	44	47
United Kingdom	77	75	74	75	60
North America					
Antigua & Barbuda					91
Bahamas		90	89	92	91
Barbados		74	74	62	60
Belize			74	82	77
Canada	78	75	73	68	61
Costa Rica	81	81	80	78	67
Dominica			77	66	60
Dominican Republic			70		54
Jamaica	78	82	78		
Mexico					50
Panama				76	76
St Kitts & Nevis			72	67	62
St Lucia			64	64	56
St Vincent & Grenadines		64	81	67	66
Trinidad & Tobago		56	61	65	66
Oceania					
Australia	95	95	94	96	95
Kiribati		81	81		68
Marshall Islands					50
Nauru			91	96	88
New Zealand	89	86	91	86	77
Palau				79	78
Samoa				82	83
Tuvalu		79	85		80
Vanuatu				56	67
South America					
Argentina		86	83	90	72
Bolivia				71	
Brazil			85		83
Chile				89	87
Guyana				88	92
Peru					81
Suriname		78			58
Uruguay			89	92	90
Average	84	80	80	76	71
Net Change		−1	0	−3	−4

Note: The figures for the 2000 decade cover elections from 2000 to 2008 inclusive, except with respect to the 2008 Palau election, about which data were not available when this table was finalized. The figures for net change indicate mean change in turnout compared to the previous decade and are based only on those countries that were democratic in that decade as well as in the previous one.

Source: International Institute for Democracy and Electoral Assistance (www.idea.int/vt/index.cfm)

Mean turnout in legislative elections is now around 70%. Whether this is high or low depends on one's expectations. The bottom line, however, is that in almost all elections, voters outnumber abstainers and that typically between two-thirds and three-fourths of those registered cast a vote.

Table 8.1 shows that turnout has declined in the recent past. Mean turnout from the 1960s through the 1980s was close to 80%. There has been a substantial turnout decline, and the decline can be observed in almost all countries. The only countries where turnout has not gone down since the 1980s are: Botswana, Luxembourg, Bahamas, Belize, Trinidad & Tobago, Australia, and Uruguay. In the opposite direction, mean turnout has declined by more than 10 points in each of the following countries: France, Portugal, the United Kingdom, Barbados, Canada, Costa Rica, Dominica, St Vincent & Grenadines, Kiribati, and Argentina.

A number of studies have shown that the turnout decline is concentrated among the youth (Blais et al. 2004; Clarke et al. 2004: ch. 8; Lyons and Alexander 2000; Miller and Shanks 1996: ch. 5; Wass 2007; Wattenberg 2007: ch. 4). This suggests that the decline is the result of generational replacement. This, of course, raises the question of why recent generations are less prone to vote, a question that we address below. This trend has spurred great concern about how to get more young people to the polls, including some consideration for compulsory voting (see Milner 2002; Wattenberg 2007: ch. 7).

This does not mean that turnout is doomed to be low in all elections and that it is impossible to get young people excited about an election. At the same time, it seems to be the case that turnout in a typical election is not what it used to be.

Why Is Turnout Higher (Lower) in Some Countries?

The literature on cross-national variations in electoral participation has focused mostly on the impact of various institutional variables. Among the variables that have been most extensively studied one finds: the existence of compulsory voting laws, the electoral system, the number of parties, and voting age.

There is consistent evidence that compulsory voting increases turnout, and the magnitude of the estimated impact is around 10–15 points (Blais and Dobrzynska 1998; Franklin 2004; Jackman 1987). We know little, however, about the exact reasons why it is so. We do not know, for instance, how informed or misinformed citizens are about the nature of the sanctions and their degree of enforcement and how these perceptions interact with other attitudes.

There has been strong interest in determining whether proportional representation systems foster a higher turnout. There is overwhelming support for the hypothesis that PR is associated with higher turnout among established democracies (see Blais and Aarts 2006 for a review of the evidence). Things are much more ambiguous in non-established democracies, however (see, especially, Fornos et al. 2004). This suggests that the pattern is not very robust. Furthermore, there is no solid explanation for why PR would contribute to a higher turnout. One reason could be that PR produces more parties and therefore more choice for voters, but there is little support for the assumption that more parties leads to a higher turnout (see below). Another reason could be that elections are more competitive under PR (see Franklin 2004), but it turns out that the relationship between PR and competitiveness is a dubious one (Blais and Lago 2009).

One of the most intriguing sets of findings that the literature has produced concerns the link between number of parties and turnout. The conventional wisdom was that people would be more inclined to vote when there are more parties because they would be more able to find a party that they feel represents their interests or values. It turns out that most studies have reported a negative, not a positive, correlation. This had led scholars to conjecture that having too many parties means complex coalitions and weakens government accountability, which reduces the incentive to vote (Jackman 1987), but direct tests of that interpretation are not conclusive (Blais 2006; Blais and Aarts 2006). So the conclusion must be that it is not at all clear whether turnout increases or decreases when the number of parties increases or whether the relationship is curvilinear.

There is also strong evidence that lowering the voting age from 21 to 18, which has occurred in most democracies (Massicotte et al. 2003), has contributed to the turnout decline (Blais and Dobrzynska 1998; Franklin 2004). The reason is obvious. Young citizens are much less likely to vote. Lowering the voting age amounts to increasing the fraction of the segment of the electorate that is most prone to abstain, and the unequivocal consequence is a lower turnout.

Finally, in a recent study of turnout in Latin America and Eastern Europe, Kostadinova and Power (2007) have highlighted two important findings. They first show that voter turnout drops sharply after founding elections and continues to decline thereafter. It remains to be seen whether the drop is more pronounced, as is the case in established democracies, among younger generations. They also report that, after appropriate controls, turnout in Eastern Europe is consistently higher than in Latin America. The authors speculate that the difference could be imputed to historical legacies and the mode of transition to democracy.

All in all, then, we do not have a very good grasp of why turnout varies so much from one country to another. It is clear that compulsory voting and voting age matter but the evidence concerning other potential factors such as the electoral system and the number of parties is ambiguous.

Why Do People Vote (or Abstain)?

Four major interpretations have been advanced for explaining the decision to vote or not to vote. People decide to vote rather than abstain if and when: (1) they perceive the benefits to outweigh the costs; (2) they adhere to the norm that a "good" citizen ought to vote in every election; (3) they think in group terms; (4) they have a "side" in the election.

The most influential model in the field is the rational choice model, as elaborated initially by Downs (1957) and amended by Riker and Ordeshook (1968; see also Aldrich 1993). The basic idea is that people vote when expected benefits are higher than expected costs and abstain otherwise.

The costs involved are those associated (mostly in time) with going to the polling booth (or casting a mail ballot) and with searching for information in order to decide which party or candidate to vote for. These costs are usually assumed to be relatively small for most individuals.

The benefits are linked to the eventual outcome of the election. In a two-party system, they correspond to the difference it will make whether party A or party B is elected. If voters believe that it will make no difference, they are indifferent and abstain. The stronger one's preference for a party the greater is the propensity to vote.

Expected benefits also depend on the probability that one's vote is *decisive*, that is, it will determine whether one's preferred party is elected. In large electorates, the probability that one's vote will be decisive is extremely small. As a consequence, the expected benefits are supposed to be tiny.

The standard prediction of the rational choice model is that for most citizens the expected benefits are bound to be smaller than expected costs and that most people will decide to abstain. Unfortunately for the theory, more people vote than abstain, which suggests at the very least that the theory is not completely satisfactory. This has spurred a series of refinements to the initial model, some of which are considered below.

Before moving to consider alternative explanations it is appropriate to mention some of the patterns that have been observed and that are consistent with a rational choice model. Many studies have shown that the closer the outcome of an election (and thus the higher the probability of casting a decisive vote), the higher the turnout (Blais 2000; Franklin 2004). Similarly, the stronger one's preference and the lower the cost of voting, the greater is the propensity to vote. The problem is that most of the time these relationships are modest and/or conditional, and so the relative contribution of the rational choice model appears limited.

A good example of the limits of the rational choice approach is provided by Figure 8.1, which shows the relationship between turnout and the closeness of the race in the 2005 British general election. The data confirm that turnout increases with competition, that is, turnout tends to be low when there is a large gap between the winner and the second contender

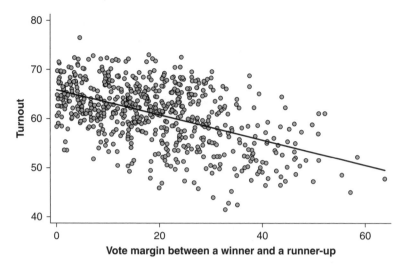

Figure 8.1   Turnout and competitiveness in the UK in the 2005 general election

Source: *The British Parliamentary Constituency Database, 1992–2005*, Release 1.3 compiled by Pippa Norris

(the outcome is a foregone conclusion) and it gets higher when the gap shrinks. Yet the difference in turnout remains modest. As the graph indicates, turnout was about 65% in constituencies with extremely close contests and it remained only about 10 points lower (55%) in contests with a huge 40-point gap between the winner and the runner up. Even when and where there is no race, turnout remains over 50%.

Down's initial model was amended by Riker and Ordeshook (1968). The two authors argue that one needs to incorporate additional benefits to the vote calculus model, that is, consumption benefits. The traditional model includes investment benefits, which hinge on the outcome of the election. But there are also consumption benefits, which derive from the act of voting as such, such as the satisfaction of "complying with the ethic of voting." They call this new term D, corresponding to the sense of civic duty.

Adopting such a perspective, Blais (2000) argues that indeed a substantial fraction of the electorate feels that it is the citizen's duty to vote in an election and that those who think in those terms do not weigh the benefits and costs of voting. Blais contends that "rational" cost–benefit considerations play a role only among those with a weak sense of duty. He concludes that the rational choice model has considerable limitations.

Franklin (2004) proposes another amendment to the rational choice model. There are in fact two amendments. The first amendment is that voters do not care solely about the probability that their own single vote could be decisive. Many of them are socially connected people who think in terms of groups or potential coalitions. As a consequence, "if each vote has a motivating impact on other members of a group, then each vote effectively counts more than once" (Franklin 2004: 51). The second amendment is that after some time people come to a standing decision about the benefits of voting and are thus likely to develop the habit of systematically voting or abstaining. It is only in the first few elections that the calculus of benefits and costs is crucial.

The first amendment boils down to stating that the individual citizen is not as egocentric as the traditional model assumes. In that sense it is similar to interpretations where altruism is deemed to be an important motivation for turnout (Edlin et al. 2007; Fowler 2006; Fowler and Kam 2007). The problem is that the exact nature of the group that the individual identifies with remains ambiguous. If it is a small group of friends and relatives, the probability of being decisive is still very small. If it is a large group, the intensity of attachment to the group is likely to be weaker, and it becomes implausible to think of the group as a homogeneous voting coalition, which unanimously supports a given party or candidate.

The idea that voting may be a habit has been advanced by a number of authors (Denny and Doyle 2009; Gerber et al. 2003; Plutzer 2002). The evidence that has been marshalled to support such a view is still very indirect. It does not suffice, for instance, to show that those who have voted previously are more inclined to vote in future elections, since they may do so for the same (good) reasons. The crucial test would be to show that the decision to vote or not to vote is more strongly correlated with benefits or costs among "new" electors than among "old" ones. As far as we know, no evidence of such a sort has yet been presented.

A more radical proposition is that voting is basically an "expressive" act and that the primary motivation to vote or not to vote is whether the citizen has "something" to express. This is the kind of interpretation that is advanced by Achen and Sinnott (2007). From that perspective, an election is about taking a side among competing teams. Most people come to believe that one party or candidate is "better" than the others and they vote to express their opinion while others fail to form preferences and abstain. This boils down to arguing that everything is in the benefits term, that the cost of voting is uniformly low and that people do not think about the probability of being pivotal. The fact that age and education are powerful predictors of the vote is consistent with such an interpretation. It remains to be demonstrated, however, that the decision to vote is driven almost entirely by the presence or absence of preferences.

Strikingly, the recent literature has used a rational choice interpretation as its starting point (to be amended) or a point of departure, in spite of the fact that the model has yet to offer a compelling explanation of the paradox of voting and in spite of the fact that its potential utility is dubious given that voting is a low-stake action (Barry 1978; Blais 2000).

Strikingly as well, the most influential model for the study of political participation in general, the resource model (see below), has not been a major source of inspiration. The reason is simply that the main proponents of the resource model have themselves recognized the limitations of their perspective in the specific case of voting. Brady et al. (1995: 361) indeed conclude that "what matters most for going to the polls is not the resources at voters' disposal but, rather, their civic orientations, especially their interest in politics."

The conclusion must be that we still do not have a coherent and compelling explanation for why people do or do not vote. It appears relatively clear that both the standard rational choice theory and the resource model are not very satisfactory. Perhaps the most provocative interpretation is that it all depends on whether individuals have relatively strong preferences, though the paucity of empirical research along those lines makes it difficult to appreciate the merits and limits of the approach.

The major debate is between those who favor an economic perspective (rational choice) with a special attention to the political context (Franklin 2004) and those who are more inclined to adopt a sociological approach in which values and norms such as civic duty are the predominant factors (Blais 2000). There has been much less interest in the potential effect of psychological factors such as personality traits (but see Fowler and Smirnov 2007 on the role of patience, and Fowler and Kam 2007 or Edlin et al. 2007 on the role of altruism). The new kid on the block is the genetic explanation (Fowler and Dowes 2008; Fowler et al. 2008), which is bound to spur a lively debate.

Which of these theoretical perspectives best explains the recent turnout decline? The rational choice approach tends to focus on the relative closeness of the race but there is no indication that elections are systematically less competitive than before. Overall turnout decline cannot be accounted for by a general drop in electoral competition.[2]

Younger generations seem to have changed, however, in at least two respects. First, they are less inclined to develop strong party attachments (Dalton 2002). Second, they are less prone to construe voting as a civic duty (Wass 2007; Wattenberg 2007). It would thus appear that the turnout decline reflects a change in political culture as well as in the place that political parties play in society.

Other Forms of Political Participation

Voting is only one form of political participation. There are many other ways in which citizens can get involved in the political process. Once this is recognized, the challenge is to clarify what we mean by political participation, what activities are and are not covered by the concept.

Verba et al. (1995: 38) provide the standard definition of political participation. For them, it refers to "activity that has the intent or effect of influencing government action – either directly by affecting the making or implementation of public policy or indirectly by influencing the selection of people who make those policies." They also specify that they focus on voluntary activity, that is, not obligatory and unpaid.[3] In practice, this amounts to, beyond electoral activity (voting and campaigning), contacting government officials, being active in groups that attempt to influence governments, and being involved in protests and demonstrations.

There have been some attempts to stretch the concept of political participation so as to cover a wider array of activities. Perhaps the most important one is the suggestion to include political consumerism as a new form of political activity. The problem then becomes how to define such a concept and whether or not it is appropriate to consider it as a form of political participation. Stolle and Hooghe (2004: 283) argue that the concept should apply "to those consumer decisions that are taken on the basis of public motivation and awareness as well as taken on a regular basis by the actor." The definition refers to there being "public" motivation, which raises the issue of how public and private motivations are to be distinguished. Because of these conceptual problems, there is still a debate about whether such activities should or should not be included into political participation.

An important challenge is provided by the recent comparative study of citizenship and involvement in 12 European countries (Van Deth et al. 2007). In their definition of political participation, the authors (Teorell et al. 2007: 336) argue that four conditions must be satisfied to call something political participation: that there be an action, that the action be undertaken by individuals, that it be directed by an intention to influence, and that the target be "any decision over the authoritative allocation of values for society." The first three conditions are not controversial, the fourth is. More specifically, the issue is how one draws the line between what is and what is not "authoritative." The dominant approach is to suggest that the clearest distinction that we can make is between governmental and non-governmental targets, but that dominant approach is being challenged more and more.

We have seen above that turnout is declining. Is the same trend going on with respect to non-electoral forms of participation?[4] Putnam (2000: ch. 3) shows declining trends in "civic participation" in the United States, that is, membership in associations, active organizational involvement and club meeting attendance. His critics argue that he is looking at "old" forms of group activity and that new forms of social organization are not taken into account (Dalton 2006b: 48).

Figure 8.2 presents evidence from the World Value Surveys about participation in boycotts, demonstrations, and petitions in 1980 and 2000 in the nine largest democracies (that is, the nine largest countries among those that were democratic both years). The pattern is quite clear. In every country, the percentage of participants is increasing.

This suggests that non-electoral forms of political participation have been going up while electoral activity has been going down. This raises the question of whether there is a correlation between the two patterns, that is, whether new generations are gradually abandoning "conventional" forms of activity in favor of "new" forms.

Two pieces of evidence are consistent with such an interpretation. First, there is the temporal sequence. Turnout is going down precisely at the time when other forms of political participation are going up. Second, we observe that younger citizens are more inclined to abstain in elections

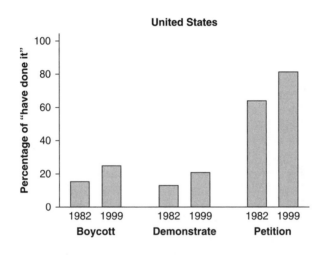

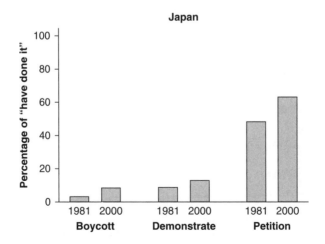

(Continued)

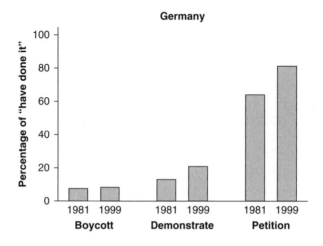

Germany

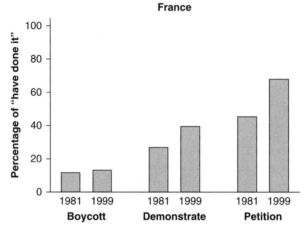

France

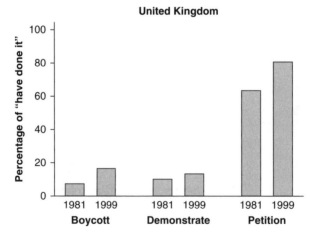

United Kingdom

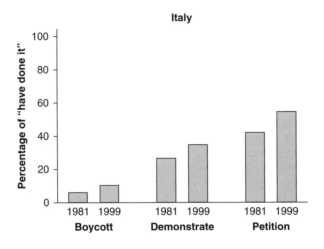

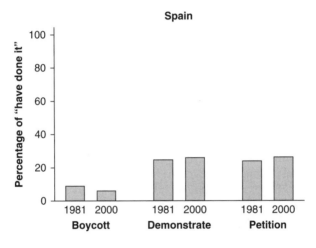

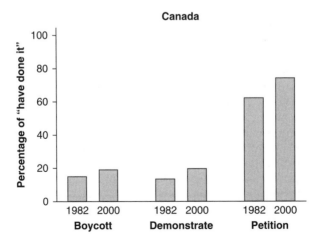

(Continued)

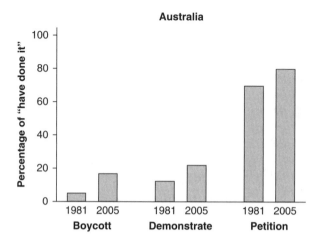

Figure 8.2   Changes in non-electoral forms of political participation

Source: World Values Survey

and also to be involved in protest activity.[5] Two other pieces of evidence, however, are difficult to reconcile with this viewpoint. First, several studies have shown that there is a generalized propensity to be active or inactive, that all forms of participation are positively correlated with each other, that is, someone who votes is also more likely to be engaged in groups, to contact public officials, and even to march in the streets (Milbrath 1965; Parry et al. 1992; Teorell et al. 2007; Verba et al. 1995). It is not clear that people select among forms of activity. Second, the usual contrast is made between so-called "conventional" and "unconventional" types of political activity. But the relevant distinction appears to be between electoral and non-electoral involvement. It seems that "traditional" activities such as membership in associations and contacting government officials are also showing a rise.[6]

The story is thus complex. On the one hand, electoral activities seem to have less appeal than before, especially among the youth, to the benefit of more direct forms of involvement. On the other hand, at the individual level, there remains a strong cleavage between the few who are very active and the more numerous who systematically stay away from politics.

Finally, there remains a relatively stark contrast in the overall level of political participation observed in new democracies, compared to that in more established democracies. Rucht (2007: 714), in particular, shows that all forms of protest activity are less widespread in less developed "southern" countries as well as in East/Central Europe than in Western Europe.

Why Do People Participate?

Many studies have examined the factors that lead people to contact (or not to contact) government officials and to get involved (or not) in groups and in demonstrations. As mentioned before, the factors that seem to account for these other forms of activity appear to be different.

The dominant model is the resource model, and the seminal analysis is *Voice and Equality* (Verba et al. 1995). The key claim is that the decision to participate or not depends first and foremost on whether one is able to, that is, on whether one has the resources to get involved. Verba et al. distinguish three basic resources: money, time, and civic skills. They show that each of these resources has an important impact on the propensity to participate, paying particular attention to the development of civic skills on the job, in organizations, and in churches. They also show that the more advantaged groups in society participate to a much greater extent than their less advantaged counterparts, that education is a central element in the process, and that religious institutions play an important role in the United States in enriching the politically relevant skills of those who are otherwise disadvantaged.

Voice and Equality makes a compelling case for the role of resources in the decision to participate or not to participate in time-consuming political activities. Verba and his co-authors acknowledge that resources are not the whole story; as they put it, people do not become political activists because they can't, because they don't want to, or because nobody asked. Their study focuses on the question of "capacity" (resources), but they devote some attention to the issue of psychological engagement (whether people are interested, whether they want to). They demonstrate that resources matter, even when psychological engagement is taken into account, that is, the effects that they examine are not spurious. There remains, however, the more difficult question of whether resources matter more or less than engagement, which is not really addressed in their book.

Then there is the question of whether resources matter more for some political acts than for others. *Voice and Equality* distinguishes voting and making political contributions from "time-based" acts. But it may well be that resources play a more or less important role for some of these "time-based" acts than for others and/or that different resources are most consequential for different types of activities. Parry et al. (1992) find that resources have the weakest effect on protest activity (direct action). It would appear that resources do not matter that much for both the most conventional (voting) and the most unconventional (protest) political activities.

The resource model tells us that an important part of the story as to why many people do not participate is that they do not have the communication and organization skills that are so useful in the conduct of political activities. The empirical findings clearly establish that resources are important, though perhaps not for the most direct form of political action.

The implication is that there are other factors at play, and the most obvious suspects are those political attitudes that are likely to foster or hinder a willingness to intervene in the political realm. Parry et al. (1992) focus on two such attitudes: political efficacy and political cynicism. They conclude that political efficacy seems to be more important, but their results also indicate that this attitude appears to be unrelated to direct action. Verba et al. (1995), for their part, consider political interest, political information, political efficacy, and partisan strength. Their data suggest that political interest is the only attitude that drives political participation.

The verdict must thus be that the decision to participate in politics depends as much on whether one likes politics or not as on whether one has the relevant skills. Of course, saying that one participates because one is interested is not really a satisfactory answer. We would want to understand how a taste or distaste for politics develops. Unfortunately, the state of knowledge on this crucial question is quite limited, in good part because of limited recent interest in the process of political socialization (for "old" studies see Jennings and Niemi 1981; for an important exception, see Campbell 2006).

The resource model is the dominant model when it comes to explaining non-electoral participation, but there have also been some intriguing attempts to explain protest activity from a rational choice perspective. Since protest is a relatively high-cost engagement (it usually takes more time and there is sometimes the risk of being arrested), one would predict that people are more prone to calculate the benefits and the costs when making up their minds on whether to participate or not.

The most prolific author to study participation in a protest movement from a rational choice perspective is Karl-Dieter Opp (Opp 1986; Opp et al. 1981, 1995; see also Finkel et al. 1989; Muller and Opp 1986). The biggest challenge for a rational choice theorist is to explain why an individual would come to the conclusion that it is in his or her interest to join a protest when it appears extremely unlikely that his or her being involved will make any difference in the protest being successful or not. Because the probability of being pivotal is so small, the temptation to free ride (and do nothing) appears irresistible.

Opp and his collaborators acknowledge that the free rider problem cannot be solved from a strict rational choice model, and so they propose a more "flexible" approach. Their interpretation puts a special emphasis on two types of considerations. First, they argue that perceptions that the protest or movement can be successful and/or general feelings of political efficacy are crucial in the decision to participate. Second, they assert that some people feel that it is their moral duty to get involved when they have strong views on an issue. The empirical analyses show that these perceptions and beliefs are associated with various forms of direct action.

It is not clear, however, how much support this provides to a rational choice interpretation. The fact that social norms such as sense of duty play an important role does not seem consistent with a benefit/cost calculus model. Furthermore, it is interesting to see that people consider the probability of success of the group, but we are not provided with evidence that they pay any attention to whether they could personally be pivotal or not, which is a central element of the rational choice model (see Blais 2000).

Finally, political participation has been associated with social capital. According to Putnam (2000), the decline of political participation in the United States is linked to the general decline in social capital. Putnam's thesis has been hotly debated. Much of the debate has focused on whether social capital has really declined in the United States or whether the decline is confined to the American case (for a review, see Stolle and Hooghe 2005).

Independent of whether social capital is increasing or decreasing, the question of whether the propensity to engage in political activities is enhanced by one's belonging to social networks remains an important one. Indeed, Verba et al. (1995: 389) document the crucial role of membership in social institutions in nurturing political participation. In their view, membership in organizations fosters political activity through two complementary mechanisms: by contributing to the development of civic skills and by acting as a source of requests for political involvement. According to Putnam and others (see, especially, Campbell 2006), however, social capital instils norms of reciprocity and engagement, which then lead to a greater willingness to be politically active.

Individuals who are isolated and who are not integrated into social networks are unlikely to be involved in politics. We still do not know, however, whether informal networks matter more or less than membership in formal groups, and whether the crucial intermediary mechanism is resources, recruitment, or norms.

Conclusion

Most people do not care much about politics and get involved in the political realm only exceptionally and sporadically. The only political activity that is widespread is voting. The typical turnout in contemporary national legislative elections is around 70%.

There has been much debate about whether political engagement is on the decline. There is a clear (but recent) downward trend in electoral participation, the form of political activity about which we have the most reliable longitudinal information. Data about other dimensions are more limited, but there appears to have been an increase in most forms of non-electoral participation, most especially in protest activity.

This has led to the suggestion that some people (especially youth) have shifted away from voting to more direct types of political engagement. There is a kernel of truth in the assertion; electoral activities have lost some of their appeal among young people. We should keep in mind, however, that those who march in the streets are also more inclined to go to the polling booth. The dynamics is more complicated. The two major groups are still those who are systematically passive and those who get minimally involved only at the time of the election. The latter is probably still the largest group, though it has been decreasing over time. Then there are those who are systematically active and those who decide to express their views in the streets without bothering to vote. This last group is probably the smallest, though it is growing.

Partly because of the increasing relevance of non-electoral participation, the recent literature has come to consider new forms of engagement that used to not be considered as mainstream research on the topic. For instance, there is growing interest in deliberative experiments, new social movements, participatory budgeting, online political networking, as well as terrorist acts and hate crimes (see Stolle 2007). This raises the thorny issue of where exactly *political* participation starts and ends. The traditional approach has been to equate politics with government. That approach is being challenged, but the new literature has failed to provide a clear alternative definition.

When we look at the correlates of political participation, one clear and strong pattern emerges in all places and periods. The better educated are much more prone to get involved than the less educated. This enduring inequality is troubling and should be a cause for concern. It is often argued that the role of governments is to help out those who are left behind by market forces. The question then is whether politicians hear these voices if the disadvantaged remain largely outside of the political arena. Age is also a crucial factor but its role seems to be mostly confined to electoral activities. With respect to turnout, politicians may be tempted not to pay too much attention to younger citizens, many of whom do not bother to vote. However, young people are willing to shout about it if and when they disagree with what is going on.

Finally, the two most influential theoretical perspectives when it comes to explaining political participation are the resource model and rational choice. *Voice and Equality* is the seminal book on political participation, and its authors powerfully demonstrate how a lack of resources, most especially civic skills, is a crucial factor in why so many people stay out of politics. Unfortunately, the model is much less fruitful with respect to the simplest form of political activity, voting. Furthermore, it remains to be seen whether resources matter more or less than a simple interest in politics, and we know surprisingly little on how and why an interest or disinterest in politics develops.

As for the rational choice model, paradoxically, the model has been applied most extensively to the study of turnout, where it should be least relevant, because the stakes are lower and the incentive to calculate benefits and costs is weaker. From that perspective, any form of political activity is unlikely to occur, and so other factors have to be invoked to account for the fact that some people do decide to participate. The two most frequent interpretations refer to habit and sense of duty. Both interpretations raise complex methodological issues about how to measure such concepts and about how to sort out possible rationalization effects.

There are finally issues related to the consequences of political participation. Does it matter that turnout is declining? Does a healthy democracy demand a certain degree of citizen participation?

We need to think not only about the causes of participation but also about its consequences. Research on these consequences is rather scarce, and this is clearly one avenue that ought to be pursued more extensively. There have been a good number of studies that have looked at the partisan effects of low turnout, and these studies suggest that such partisan effects are minimal (see the special September 2007 issue of *Electoral Studies*; Lutz and March 2007). But we need to look at other potential effects, such as the perceived legitimacy of the government and democracy.

Perhaps, even more importantly, we need to understand whether, how, and why the fact of voting (or not), contacting government officials (or not), or marching in the streets (or not) does or does not change people's view of society. Supporters of participatory democracy assume that being engaged makes one a "better" citizen. We still do not know whether that claim is (mostly) valid or not (for a sceptical viewpoint, see Hibbing and Theiss-Morse 2002).

9

Elections and
the Economy

Timothy Hellwig

Does the economy matter for elections? Given the amount of material written on the subject, we might expect the answer to be "yes, of course." And for validation we have to look no further than the 2008 elections in the United States. The economy was in free-fall, as vividly shown by the collapse of the US financial industry and subsequent bailouts as well as by falling growth rates and unemployment reaching a 14-year high. Thus, citing the economy as the number one issue, voters dutifully punished the incumbent Republican Party in elections to both the presidency and Congress. In many other electoral contests, however, the economy apparently did not matter – or at least not in the way that we might expect in terms of political incumbents being rewarded at the polls for good economic outcomes and punished for bad ones. We have only to look back eight years previous for a case in point. In 2000 the US economy was strong and unemployment was at a 30-year low. Yet Al Gore, the incumbent Democratic Party's candidate for president, lost (in the Electoral College) to George W. Bush in the race for the presidency. Other recent examples of incumbent defeat during economic good times include the 2000 presidential election in Mexico and the 2004 Spanish election. And many times the opposite is true as incumbents hang on despite economic downturns. Prominent examples of late are the 2002 elections in Germany and the 2007 presidential and legislative vote in France.

These and many other cases give us pause. So does the economy matter or not? And if it moves election outcomes in some cases but not in others, then what explains this? And, further, which actors drive the economy–election connection – voters, politicians, both, or neither? For a variety of reasons, the economy stands out among factors influencing elections. For one, "the economy" is not solely or even primarily designed to serve political ends. It ebbs and flows, and how these fluctuations affect election outcomes is a central issue for those interested in democratic accountability.

Moreover, where electoral rules appear as exogenously determined, students of economic voting assume that politicians have some control of how the economy performs – an assumption made less tenable by the wide reach of the recent international financial crisis.

These issues – and the questions they imply for the economy–election connection – are the focus of this chapter. I begin with the voters, asking why and how citizens incorporate information about the economy into their decision at the ballot box. I first report results of analyses of survey data from 28 established and emerging democracies to show the extent to which the economy matters for individual voting decisions. Here, I focus on four points of debate from recent work on economic voting: how voters judge satisfactory performance, national economic considerations versus pocketbook evaluations, the role of voter perceptions of the real economy, and measurement issues involved in gauging voter choice.[1]

It is one thing to measure the influence of the economy on an individual's preference for one party over another – which in turn affects his/her vote – but what does this mean for election outcomes themselves? Does the economy make any difference? Does it determine who wins and who loses? The second part of the chapter, accordingly, migrates from the micro to the macro. Examination of elections from 77 countries over a 50-year span shows that the effect of the economy on elections is driven by a variety of factors, including political regimes, experience with democratic rule, and the quality of democratic institutions, and all in ways consistent with the incentives different environments provide.

The third section looks at the role of politicians. Issues of political control are of critical importance. If Barack Obama was elected to help fix an ailing US economy, then it must be believed that the American president's policies have an impact on real economic outcomes. Where the first two sections of the chapter emphasize the voter's capacity to use information about the economy when making decisions, this section notes that voters' propensities to connect the economy to their choice at the polls is itself shaped by politicians. Politicians deliver messages designed to increase their chances – or harm their competitors' – in the next election. Some political systems facilitate manipulation by elites while others impede it. Factors considered include the opportunistic timing of elections, elite polarization on the issues, and policies designed to tie policymakers' hands and evade the blame for bad economic times. The conclusion argues that a complete understanding of how the economy matters for work must give greater credence to the role of strategic political elites.

The Economy and Voter Choice

Though "the economy" and "the election" are system-level phenomena, the "economic vote" plays out at the level of the individual. Political scientists usually conceive of the individual's decision as akin to a stock-taking exercise in which the voter asks herself how the economy is doing. Citizens with positive evaluations signal their endorsement of the status quo by supporting the incumbent government at election time. Those who evaluate the economy negatively communicate their dissatisfaction by casting ballots for the opposition. This basic relationship between economic perceptions and voter choice is often referred to as the reward–punishment hypothesis.

Table 9.1 examines this basic connection between perceptions of the economy and voter choice from over 40,000 individuals from 28 countries. The data are from post-election surveys between 1996 and 2002 compiled by the Comparative Study for Electoral Systems project (CSES, Sapiro et al. 2003). Economic perceptions are measured using responses to the survey question, "Would you say that over the past twelve months, the state of the economy in [country] has gotten better, stayed about the same, or gotten worse?" Voter choice is categorized in two ways: whether the individual voted for the party of the incumbent chief executive, as well as whether he or she voted for one of the incumbent government parties.[2]

Regardless of how the vote is measured, the data show that about three out of every four voters who believe the economy has gotten worse vote against the political incumbent. This result confirms, over a large number of individuals, the most widely recognized finding in the economic voting literature: "when economic conditions are bad, citizens vote against the ruling party (coalition)" (Lewis-Beck 1991: 2). Not all of those with negative economic evaluations, however, vote against the incumbent. Moreover, large shares of those who believe that the economy has improved in the past year report voting against the incumbent (59% voted for a party other than that of the chief executive; 49% voted for a party outside the incumbent government).

The picture painted in Table 9.1 is clearly incomplete. Evidently it is not just the economy that matters for the vote. We can use multivariate analysis to control for things other than the economy that belong in the voter's calculus. Accordingly, I use the CSES data to estimate a series of logistic regressions, one per country, in which the dependent variable is scored 1 if the individual cast his or her ballot for the party of the incumbent chief executive (or for any sitting government party) and 0 otherwise. Each regression model includes a series of other variables shown to influence voter decisions. These include ideology, age, gender, religion, sector of the economy, and region.[3]

Table 9.2 displays the results of this analysis, presented in terms of the influence of a uniform change in economic perceptions on the probability that a given individual voted for the incumbent. Following the practice used by Duch and Stevenson (2008), the table reports the expected change in the probability of voting for the incumbent attributable to a change in one's economic perceptions from being of the belief that, over the past

TABLE 9.1 Economic perceptions and voter choice in 28 Countries, 1996–2002

Of those who perceive ...	*Percent who vote incumbent chief executive*		*Percent who vote for party in incumbent government*	
	Yes	*No*	*Yes*	*No*
The economy has gotten better	**41%**	59%	**51%**	49%
The economy has stayed the same	28%	72%	35%	65%
The economy has gotten worse	21%	**79%**	25%	**75%**

Notes: Cells report percent of respondents who reported voting for the incumbent in post-election surveys from 28 countries. Figures in bold correspond to expected outcomes according to the reward–punishment hypothesis. The total number of respondents is 43,705. Non-voters are excluded from the analysis. Elections included are those reported in Table 9.2.

Source: CSES Module 1

12 months, the state of the economy had "stayed about the same" to thinking that it had "gotten worse." This means that the more *negative* the probability swing, the *stronger* the magnitude of the "economic vote" for the political incumbent. Results show perceptions of economic decline generally reduce the probability of voting for an incumbent political party. The "average" size of the economic vote across these 28 elections is 8%.

But grounds for skepticism remain, even after taking account of a battery of voter characteristics. If Table 9.2 results are any indication, the economic vote varies considerably from country to country, from over 15% to virtually no effect or even an unexpected positive effect in some instances.[4] This might give us reason to question Lewis-Beck and Stegmaier's (2000: 183) claim that "although voters do not look exclusively at economic issues," a point supported by Tables 9.1 and 9.2, "they generally weigh those more heavily than any others, regardless of the democracy they vote in."

Skepticism deepens if we consider the many areas of debate in current research on the individual economic vote. Disagreements abound, but can be organized into four areas. The first pertains to the basis for evaluating the economy as "good" or "bad." In order to vote on the basis of the economy, the voter must pick some point against which current economic performance is compared. What is this threshold? In the 1980 US presidential election, Ronald Reagan put this threshold as four years ago, the time of the previous election. In the analysis above we imposed a threshold of just one year into the past. This choice rests on a couple of assumptions about individual behavior. It assumes, for one, that voters are *myopic*, or short-sighted, in that they consider only what has occurred in the immediate past. Second, it assumes that voters are *retrospective*, basing their economic vote on past considerations rather than on future ones. This notion was succinctly summed up by V.O. Key: "Voters may reject what they have

TABLE 9.2   The magnitude of the economic vote in 28 countries, 1996–2002

Country	Election year and type	Economic vote for incumbent chief executive	Economic vote for party in incumbent government
Belarus	2001 Presidential	−0.37	−0.37
Australia	1996 Parliamentary	−0.18	−0.18
United States	1996 Presidential	−0.18	−0.18
Russia	2000 Presidential	−0.14	−0.14
Czech Republic	1996 Parliamentary	−0.11	−0.21
Hungary	1998 Parliamentary	−0.11	−0.14
Spain	2000 Parliamentary	−0.11	−0.11
Denmark	1998 Parliamentary	−0.09	−0.11
New Zealand	1996 Parliamentary	−0.09	−0.09
Germany	1998 Parliamentary	−0.08	−0.11
Netherlands	1998 Parliamentary	−0.07	−0.18
Portugal	2002 Parliamentary	−0.07	−0.07
Canada	1997 Parliamentary	−0.07	−0.07
United Kingdom	1997 Parliamentary	−0.07	−0.07
Romania	1996 Parliamentary	−0.06	−0.06
Iceland	1999 Parliamentary	−0.06	−0.06
Korea	2000 Legislative	−0.05	−0.06
Taiwan	1996 Presidential	−0.05	−0.05
Belgium	1999 Parliamentary	−0.05	−0.04
Sweden	1998 Parliamentary	−0.04	−0.04
Slovenia	1996 Parliamentary	−0.04	−0.04
Norway	1997 Parliamentary	−0.04	−0.04
Poland	1997 Presidential	−0.03	−0.04
Switzerland	1999 Parliamentary	−0.02	−0.09
Mexico	2000 Presidential	−0.02	−0.02
Japan	1996 Parliamentary	−0.01	−0.01
Ukraine	1998 Parliamentary	+0.04	+0.04
Israel	1996 Parliamentary	+0.05	+0.10
Mean		−0.08	−0.09
Median		−0.07	−0.07

Notes: Cells report the predicted change in the probability a given individual votes for the party of the incumbent chief executive (first column) or party in the incumbent government (last column) given a change in retrospective economic perceptions from "the state of the economy in [country] has stayed about the same" to "the state of the economy in [country] has gotten worse." Predicted probability changes reported in all cells are statistically significant at $p < 0.05$ except for both models for Mexico, both for Japan, and both for the Ukraine.

Source: CSES Module 1

known; or they may approve what they have known. They are not likely to be attracted in great numbers by promises of the novel or unknown" (1966: 61; see also Ferejohn 1986; Fiorina 1981).

The assumption of shortsighted retrospective voters has the virtue of setting a low hurdle for rational behavior.[5] A potential problem, however, is that the vote is conceived mainly as a tool for calling a referendum on the current government: if the economy performed well on the government's watch, then the incumbent is deemed a competent economic manager and, thus, should remain in power. There are at least two problems with this logic – one pertaining to the link between (observed) economic performance and (unobserved) government competence, and the other to the environment of political competition. Both these problems ignore questions about the direction of the economy under alternative governments. What is the set of viable alternatives for office? It is one thing to observe a strong economic vote in Belarus, where there has been effectively no viable alternative to President Lukashenko since 1994. The economic vote means something quite different in the United States, where the 2000 and 2004 presidential elections were decided by less than 5 percentage points in the popular vote. Which candidate or political party has the best ideas about solving current and future economic problems? To what extent are competitors' positions on the economy and other issues similar or different from one another? These questions cannot be easily addressed by retrospective models of economic voting, myopic or otherwise.

Questions such as these have led many students of economic voting to assert that expectations about the *future* are what matters most for voters. Some researchers have tackled the question of retrospections/prospections head-on, by comparing aggregated opinion data to government approval ratings (MacKuen et al. 1992; Sanders et al. 1987). Others have argued that prospective evaluations matter, but their salience is conditional on factors such as individual knowledge (Uslaner 1989), gender (Clarke et al. 2004) or certainty about the election outcome (Ladner and Wlezien 2007). Research in this line has very different implications for how elections serve to connect voters to politicians. Where the retrospective model sees elections as referendums on the current government, evidence supporting the prospective orientation implies that the election is about choosing effective policies for the future, or what Fearon (1999) calls "selecting good types."

A second node of debate in the study of economic voting asks just what *is* "the economy" that the voter evaluates. Is it assessments of the national economy as a whole? Is it the voter's own material well-being? Or is it something in between? For example, is an economic voter in Michigan concerned chiefly with the economic vibrancy of the Detroit metropolis? Or even of the auto industry? On the one hand, if the "economic vote" is meant to relate economic perceptions to the vote in national elections, then the rational voter should incorporate information about the national economy in his or her voting decision. Indeed, this expectation has been borne out empirically in many contexts. In an analysis of surveys from six countries, for example, Lewis-Beck (1988) found that evaluations of the national economy, but not individuals' assessments of their own finances, strongly and consistently affected vote choice. However, research on specific countries has since revealed exceptions. Analyses of British and Danish voters, for instance, find evidence that personal financial concerns are politically more salient than national economic considerations (Nannestad and Paldam 1997; Sanders 2000; Sanders et al. 1987).[6] More systematically, Gomez and Wilson (2001, 2006) assert that the voter's level of political sophistication conditions his or her ability to attribute responsibility for the economy to government actors. "High sophisticates" are able to link information across levels of abstraction necessary for connecting the government policy to their own personal financial situation. The implication is that only the more sophisticated voters should engage in "pocketbook" voting; the less sophisticated individuals vote according to national conditions. The authors support their argument with individual-level data from Canada, Hungary, Mexico, Taiwan, and the United States.

Questions of "which economy" are of interest not only academics but policymakers too. If only the national economy matters, then the prescription is for policymakers to use macroeconomic levers (broad tax policy and control of interest rates) to smooth business cycles and create a favorable environment for investment and growth. If personal finances instead are the most salient politically, then governments seeking reelection might be better served by using public revenues to bolster unemployment benefits to alleviate feelings of insecurity or to enact tax cuts for adversely affected constituencies. And recent discussions in the United States and Europe to use tax monies to bail out adversely affected (and politically important) industries, such as automobiles, point to the salience of an intermediary, group-based economy.

A third point of contention characterizing scholarship on economic voting is the relationship between voter perceptions and the actual economy as gauged by leading economic indicators. Perhaps it comes as no surprise that the economic vote appears as strong or stronger when the economy is measured with individual perceptions than with indicators like growth, unemployment, or inflation (Nadeau and Lewis-Beck 2001). The critical question for democratic accountability, however, is whether these perceptions are related to the real economy.[7] If they are not, then a cause for concern is that incumbents are evaluated not as based on actual economic trends (i.e., departures from some performance threshold), but based on some biased view of economic performance. On this point, recent research has uncovered some troubling findings – troubling in that they suggest that evidence of an "economic vote" cannot be taken as proof positive that incumbents are accountable for the economy. Rather, statistical analyses of survey data suggest that individual economic evaluations are endogenous to political ones (Evans and Andersen 2006; Wlezien et al. 1997).[8] For this reason, some studies have refrained from examining economic perceptions altogether, preferring to use aggregate economic indicators in models of individual vote choice (e.g., van der Brug et al. 2007).

The fourth controversy in studies of economic voting involves the voter's choice itself. While studies typically operationalize the individual's choice as one of being for or against the incumbent, the voter, in fact, is rarely faced with such a dichotomous decision. It is more realistic to recognize that the voter can select from many credible alternatives, including the party of the chief executive, a junior partner in government, or an opposition party. This approach has become increasingly commonplace among studies of the economic vote in comparative politics, with Duch and Stevenson's (2008) study of 163 voter preference surveys the most exhaustive to date. We can look back at Table 9.2 to get a sense of the extent to which these distinctions matter for the economic vote. The column on the far right, *Economic vote for party in incumbent government*, is equal to the probability change caused by a worsening economy of voting for *any* of the parties in government, whereas *Economic vote for incumbent chief executive* is simply a vote for the party of the incumbent chief executive. For some elections this distinction matters a great deal. The economic vote is at least twice as great in the Czech, Dutch, and Swiss cases, for example, when all parties in government are considered.

Another approach designed to better match data with the voter's actual decision process has been advanced by van der Brug, van der Eijk, and Franklin (2007). Their approach avoids vote choice altogether. A focus on choice, they argue, is "unable to determine whether the party that was actually voted for was one that a voter was really positive about or whether it was voted for because of the absence of any attractive alternative" (2007: 14). The authors' alternative is to examine the effect of economic performance not on voter's decisions at the polls but on party support propensities.

On each of these four points of debate scholars hold varying opinions. Each may give us reason to be skeptical about whether the economy really does matter for elections. And critically, these conceptual and empirical distinctions have implications for big questions in political science, questions of political accountability, institutional design, and democratic performance.

The Economy and Election Outcomes: When Does the Economy Matter?

If perceptions of the economy affect voter decisions, as Tables 9.1 and 9.2 show, then does the economy itself matter for the outcome of the election? To address this question, let us migrate from the micro-foundations of economic voting to investigate the connection between national economic performance and election outcomes. Data are from every national-level executive and legislative election from the 1950s through 2004 in 77 countries with populations of one million or more that ranked six or better on the Polity IV democracy score.[9]

The dependent variable *Incumbent Vote* is the percentage of votes received by the incumbent head of government's party.[10] Economic performance is measured as the annual percentage change in per capita gross domestic product.[11] If economic good times benefit the incumbent, then the parameter estimate on *Economy* will be positive in magnitude and statistically different from zero. Control variables include the incumbent party's percentage of the vote in the previous election (*Previous Vote*), an indicator for presidents standing for re-election, election type (a dummy equaling 1 for presidential elections), and democratic experience (*Age of Democracy*).[12]

Table 9.3 reports the results of several models.[13] Model 1 is a baseline model encompassing all elections. The coefficient on *Economy* is statistically significant with an estimate of 0.30, meaning that for every 1% increase in per capita growth, the party of the incumbent gains nearly $\frac{1}{3}$ of a percent of the total vote share. The sample mean value for annual per capita growth is 2.2% with standard deviation of 4.0. A 4% increase in *Economy*, therefore, is worth 1.2% gain in incumbent party vote share. This serves as a baseline estimate of the impact of economic performance on the election outcome.

Given the wave of democratization in the past 30 years, one question that bears consideration is the effect of regime type on economic voting. Evolving from single-country studies, many cross-national analyses focus on the (relatively limited) sets of established democracies, nearly all of which have parliamentary forms of government (e.g., Powell and Whitten 1993; Whitten and Palmer 1999). However, of the 78 democracies with a population of greater than one million in 2004, 31 were parliamentary, 26 were presidential, and 21 were semi-presidential. The next three regressions examine incumbent accountability for the economy separately for parliamentary, presidential, and semi-presidential regimes.[14] Results show that the influence of the economy is about twice as strong in presidential as in pure parliamentary regimes – the coefficient on *Economy* is 0.53 in Model 3 but only 0.24 in Model 2. All else equal, incumbent political parties benefit only half as much from an improving economy under parliamentarism as they do in presidential regimes. Model 4 shows that elections in semi-presidential democracies fare the worst when it comes to economic voting. The non-significant effect of the economy is consistent with arguments that having a two-headed executive (a president plus a prime minister) makes it difficult for voters to assign responsibility for policy outcomes while making it easier for politicians to shift blame onto other actors when things go bad (or claim credit when things go well).[15]

Another point of variation across these political systems is their experience with democracy. Does the economy matter more in more established democracies? Since most of what we know about the micro-foundations of the economic vote is restricted to evidence from older democracies, the jury is still out on this question. We might think, however, the answer to be "yes" insomuch as the mechanics of punishment and reward should

TABLE 9.3 Influence of the economy on incumbent vote in 77 democracies, 1950–2004

	Model 1 Baseline	Regime type			Age of democracy		Quality of democracy	
		Model 2 Parliamentary	Model 3 Presidential	Model 4 Semipresidential	Model 5 Young (≤ 10 yr)	Model 6 Old (> 10 yr)	Model 7 Unconsolidated	Model 8 Consolidated
Previous Vote	0.72**	0.80**	0.75**	0.46**	0.67**	0.74**	0.67**	0.77**
	(0.05)	(0.05)	(0.11)	(0.08)	(0.12)	(0.05)	(0.09)	(0.05)
Economy	0.30**	0.24**	0.53**	0.05	0.59**	0.16	0.51**	−0.01
	(0.13)	(0.09)	(0.22)	(0.35)	(0.18)	(0.14)	(0.18)	(0.13)
Re-election	6.37**		9.68**	4.14	9.25*	5.44**	6.07*	7.19*
	(2.16)		(2.37)	(3.11)	(4.69)	(2.32)	(3.08)	(3.02)
Presidential Election	−3.63**		−3.64**	1.54	−3.69	−3.62**	−3.45*	−2.42*
	(1.24)		(1.41)	(2.77)	(2.28)	(1.51)	(1.79)	(1.30)
Age of Democracy	0.21*	0.24	−0.08	0.35	0.66	0.18	0.18	0.17
	(0.11)	(0.17)	(0.18)	(0.36)	(1.64)	(0.14)	(0.24)	(0.13)
Age of Democracy^2	−0.003*	−0.004*	0.003	−0.01	−0.03	−0.003	−0.005	−0.003
	(0.002)	(0.002)	(0.003)	(0.01)	(0.13)	(0.002)	(0.004)	(0.002)
Constant	4.07*	1.92	4.53	11.53**	4.05	4.12	5.79	4.71*
	(2.26)	(2.91)	(4.42)	(5.60)	(6.71)	(2.80)	(4.19)	(2.69)
R^2	0.46	0.64	0.47	0.27	0.37	0.52	0.38	0.60
Model F	46.75**	105.46**	21.13**	11.20**	13.86**	56.05**	11.79**	123.90**
N	695	301	247	147	173	522	300	395

Notes: Cells report OLS parameter estimates with robust standard errors, clustered within countries, in parentheses. The dependent variable is Incumbent Vote. $**p < 0.05$, $*p < 0.10$ (two-tailed test).

Sources: National-level election results as reported in Appendix 9A (www.sagepub.co.uk/leduc3). Economic data from the Penn World Tables v6.2

work with less friction in countries with more consolidated democratic institutions. Likewise, office holders may be more accountable when voters have more experience using elections as sanctioning devices. Model 5 examines cases in which democratic elections have been held for 10 years or less. In these cases we might expect the economy–vote connection to be weak. Yet the results imply just the opposite: the economy has a strong effect in young democracies. But in democracies older than 10 years, shown in Model 6, the impact of the economy is no different from zero. The last pair of regressions in Table 9.3 compare unconsolidated and fully consolidated democracies. Model 7 shows that for unconsolidated regimes (i.e., cases with a Polity IV democracy–authoritarian score less than +10), the effect of economic performance is strong and precisely estimated. For fully consolidated democratic regimes, however, economic performance registers zero effect on incumbent party electoral fortunes (Model 8). All told, results show that the economy–election relationship works for younger and less institutionalized democracies but *not* for older, more consolidated ones.

Shirking Responsibility?
Opportunities for Elite Control

Several results reported in Table 9.3 seem puzzling. Regarding regime types, many observers deride presidentialism for how it connects voters to politicians, deeming it to be inferior in terms of the "quality of democracy and democratic representation" (Lijphart 1999: 303) and suggesting that its "dual democratic legitimacies" confuse voters and impede accountability (Linz 1990). Why, then, do presidential regimes outperform parliamentary regimes? Regarding quality of democracy, why is electoral accountability for the economy non-existent in established democracies, where voters ought to have experience in linking economic messages to their votes, but strong in young democracies, where electorates may still be becoming conversant in the democratic process?

In this section I suggest that these findings stem from a lack of consideration of politicians as protagonists in the economic voting story. Standard tales of economic voting put the voter front and center. It is the *voter* who evaluates the current state of the economy, compares it to some threshold position, and then sanctions or rewards politicians accordingly. In these accounts politicians matter only as members of government or opposition and are evaluated only in terms of how competent they are as economic managers.[16] But politicians are much more than economic managers. First and foremost they seek to obtain and retain office. One recipe for holding onto power certainly is to send credible signals about their competence as economic managers. But incumbents could be evaluated on any number of performance issues. And, aside from performance evaluations, there are many tools at office-holders' disposal.

Politicians, then, have a variety of techniques to use to help them shirk from a responsibility for economic performance. Consider the tools derived from constitutional rules. Table 9.3 showed that the impact of the economy on incumbent support is stronger in presidential systems and weaker in parliamentary ones. One reason for this may be the separation of powers. By institutionalizing conflicts of interest between branches of government, presidentialism facilitates the revealing of information about policy choices in ways parliamentarism does not (Persson et al. 1997). The weakness of electoral accountability for the economy in parliamentary and semi-presidential systems could also stem from the greater power of politicians in these systems to act opportunistically. Under parliamentarism voters do not always have the opportunity to reward or punish the party they empowered at the previous election. Along these lines, the health of the economy has been shown to contribute to election timing: incumbents call elections when times are good and delay them when times are bad (Smith 2004). If the election calendar is endogenous to economic performance, then we should expect economic voting to be affected by the government's ability to face the voters at a time of its own choosing.

Model 9 in Table 9.4 re-examines a subset of assembly elections in pure parliamentary and semi-presidential regimes. Rather than estimating solely the direct effects of economic performance, I specify the influence of *Economy* on *Incumbent Vote* contingent on whether the election was called by the government in advance of the mandatory end of its term in office. Of the 425 elections for which information on election calls was collected, 92 occurred early by governments acting opportunistically.[17] We find that an opportunistic election, on average, pays dividends: incumbents increase their vote share by about 3.7% by calling an election before the end of the mandate. Our main interest, however, is whether governing elites can use opportunistic calls to *avoid being held accountable for economic performance*. To answer this question, we must evaluate the coefficients on *Economy* and the interaction term, *Economy* × *Opportunistic*. When elections are not called early at the government's volition (*Opportunistic* = 0), then per capita growth rates have the expected positive and statistically significant effect on incumbent vote shares (coefficient is 0.32). When elections are called early, however, the effect of the economy is no different from zero.[18] This provides solid evidence that governments can successfully use endogenous elections to evade blame.

A second way in which politicians maintain control over the economy–election connection is through the signals they send to voters. Imagine an election in which all the credible contenders for office held identical prescriptions for the future direction of policy. In such a situation party contenders become nearly indistinguishable from one another. Having little policy-based reason to prefer one party over another, voters must draw

TABLE 9.4   The Economy and incumbent vote: opportunities for elite control

	Model 9 Opportunistic elections	Model 10 Elite polarization	Model 11 Economic liberalization
Previous Vote	0.78**	0.84**	0.72**
	(0.04)	(0.03)	(0.05)
Economy	0.32**	0.39*	1.29**
	(0.11)	(0.20)	(0.39)
Opportunistic Call	3.67**		
	(1.00)		
Economy × Opportunistic	−0.29		
	(0.24)		
Elite Polarization		0.06**	
		(0.03)	
Economy × Elite Polarization		−0.006	
		(0.005)	
Liberalization Index			0.05
			(0.03)
Economy × Liberalization			−0.02**
			(0.01)
Re-election		3.85**	5.86**
		(1.21)	(2.37)
Presidential Election		−4.33	−2.21
		(4.12)	(1.40)
Age of Democracy	0.18	0.42**	0.23
	(0.12)	(0.14)	(0.15)
Age of Democracy ^{2}	−0.003*	−0.007**	−0.003
	(0.002)	(0.002)	(0.002)
Constant	2.05	−3.82	−0.15
	(2.05)	(2.94)	(3.02)
R^2	0.57	0.66	0.46
Model F	100.56**	122.73**	29.73**
N	425	341	453

Notes: Cells report OLS parameter estimates with robust standard errors, clustered within countries, in parentheses. The dependent variable is Incumbent Vote.
**$p < 0.05$, *$p < 0.10$ (two-tailed test).

Sources: National-level election results as reported in Appendix 9A (www.sagepub.co.uk/leduc3). Economic data from the Penn World Tables v6.2. Data on Elite Polarization from the comparative manifestos project (Klingemann et al. 2006). Data on Economic Liberalization from the KOF Index of Globalization

on other criteria for making their decisions. These non-policy criteria – or valence issues, as the voting and parties literature refers to them – include things like charisma, integrity, and competence (e.g., Schofield and Sened 2006). In such an environment, the economy offers a credible signal for voters trying to steer between candidates. In this scenario, challengers seeking office during economic downturns would be well advised to focus on the economy as a valence issue. James Carville's "It's the economy, stu-pid" signposted at Bill Clinton's campaign headquarters in 1992 concisely communicated this message and, many claim, accounted for the latter's successful bid for the US presidency (Alvarez and Nagler 1995). In good economic times, challengers should seek to separate themselves from the incumbent by carving out unique positions on other issues – in essence, making the election about something other than the economy.

The expectation, then, is that purely economic considerations matter less for the election outcome when contending elites offer a wide menu of policy options. To assess this claim, I include a measure of party issue dispersion in the basic regression specification. Following Golder (2006a; see also Alt and Lassen 2006), the measure is the absolute ideological distance between the largest left-wing and right-wing parties in the sys-tem. Ideological positions are produced using party positions on the Left–Right "super dimension" taken from party platforms and coded by the Comparative Manifestos Project (CMP). Using data for elections covered by the CMP (Klingemann et al. 2006), I developed polarization scores for 341 elections. *Polarization* is included in Model 10 as a predictor variable, both directly as well as interactively with *Economy*. The expectation is that the effect of economic performance on election outcomes is moderated when voters face more divergent issue environments.

Figure 9.1 evaluates this expectation using Model 10 estimates to plot the magnitude of the coefficient on *Economy* as it varies across the range of values of *Polarization*.[19] When there is perfect consensus between the two main parties in the system (*Polarization* = 0), then a 1% increase in per capita growth produces a 0.4% vote gain for the incumbent – a mod-est but statistically significant impact. Having little other basis for steer-ing between parties, competence in running the economy should matter in this case. As parties become more polarized on the issues, however, the utility of voting simply according to the incumbent's record as an (in)com-petent economic manager declines and, accordingly, we see less economic voting. When *Polarization* surpasses its median sample value of 25, then the coefficient on *Economy* is no longer statistically significant, according to 90% confidence intervals. The economy "matters," that is, for only half of the elections included in Model 10. While the effect is not overpowering, we can say with some conviction that issue polarization weakens the bond between the economy and elections.

A third way incumbents can improve control over their fortunes is to tie their own hands. If, due to a lack of room to maneuver in the economy, poli-ticians can credibly pass the blame for poor economic performance onto other actors, then the reasons for voters to hold them to account for the economy should decline. There are several ways in which this might be done. For example, Duch and Stevenson (2008: ch. 7) find the economic vote is weaker in countries in which agreements on prices and wages are made outside direct government control, through peak-level bargaining

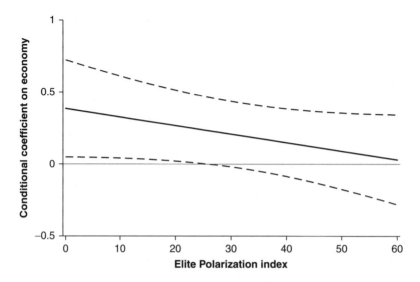

Figure 9.1 The conditional effect of elite polarization on economic voting

Notes: Dashed lines display 90% confidence intervals calculated from Model 10 in Table 9.4. Higher values on the Elite Polarization index denote a greater dispersion of messages between the two largest parties competing in the election.

between unions and producer groups (see also Pacek and Radcliff 1995). They find a similar result for countries where elected officials delegate a great deal of authority to non-elected regulatory agencies.

In addition to these specific constraints on policymaker efficacy, governments have pointed to the growth of the economy beyond national borders as a basis for blame avoidance. Evidence from surveys shows that many voters, in the developed and developing world alike, cite non-elected international actors and market forces as responsible for the state of the economy (Alcañiz and Hellwig forthcoming; Hellwig et al. 2008). Consistent with such evidence, Hellwig and Samuels (2007) use a global sample of elections to show that country exposure to international trade and financial flows means less economic voting. A reason for these findings, the authors suggest, lies in the degree to which politicians communicate that globalization ties their hands as policymakers.

Model 11 in Table 9.4 re-examines the conditional effect of globalization on electoral accountability for the economy. Where Hellwig and Samuels (2007) consider the effect of actual country exposure to global economic activity, here I examine the conditional influence of international economic *policies* on accountability for economic performance. Policies having the effect of tying the hands of domestic policymakers are those pertaining to restrictions on trade and capital movements and include tariffs, non-tariff barriers, and restrictions on capital accounts. To capture these

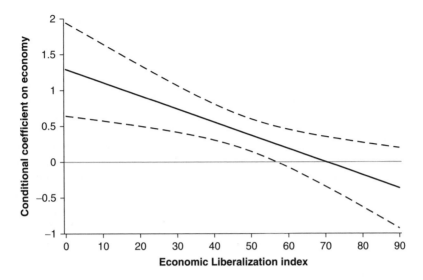

Figure 9.2 **The conditional effect of economic liberalization on economic voting**

Notes: Dashed lines display 90% confidence intervals calculated from Model 11 in Table 9.4. Higher values on the Liberalization index denote fewer restrictions on international trade and capital movements.

restrictions I use an index of economic liberalization that takes the form of an index from 0 to 100 where higher values designate more liberal (less restrictive) policies (Dreher et al. 2008).[20] The measure *Liberalization* is entered into the regression model interacted with *Economy*. As with elite discourse, I plot the effect of retrospective economic performance on election outcomes over a range of values on *Liberalization*. Figure 9.2 shows that in a (hypothetical) autarkic economy closed off to trade and capital flows, national economic performance has a large effect on the election outcome. A 2% drop in per capita growth rates, for example, would translate into a 2.5% decline in vote share for the incumbent. That same 2% drop in performance in an economy with a moderate degree of restriction on flows (*Liberalization* = 50), would cost the incumbent only about 0.8% of the vote. And with economies at or beyond the sample mean on the index (*Liberalization* ≥ 62), such an economic decline is estimated to have zero electoral effect for the sitting government.

The electoral consequences of pro-globalization policies are particularly salient when we consider the rapid increases in market liberalization and economic openness attained by many countries in recent years. Consider, for example, a country like Romania. At the time of the 1996 election Romania scored a 49 on the liberalization index, a value at which we would predict a healthy economic vote. Yet just two election cycles later, in 2004, the county's index score was 62, a value at which the state of the national economy is expected to have no effect on incumbent party fortunes, as shown in Figure 9.2. A similar story could be told for Brazil, where rapid liberalization moved the country from a score of 37 on the globalization index in 1990 to 61 in time for the 2002 elections. These two countries are by no means unique. Liberalization strategies have the effect of reducing the influence of national economic conditions on government fortunes at the polls.

The broader point of this section is that elected officials do not survive in office solely at the beckon of the voter as *homo economicus*. Rather, politicians themselves can shape their own electoral fate, and do so despite the state of the economy. The sources of elite control identified in Table 9.4 bring us closer to accounting for some of the puzzles of non-economic voting revealed in Table 9.3. The election as a mechanism of accountability performs worse during elections in older, more consolidated democracies than in newer, less established ones. It is precisely in these old democracies that competing elites have the most capacity to shirk responsibility by manipulating electoral calendars, by staking out divergent positions on the issues, and by calling on global economic forces as a source of blame avoidance.[21] However, these examples of elite manipulation probably do not take us *all* the way to a full understanding of when and to what extent the economy drives the outcome of democratic elections. For this reason, it is doubtful that we have reached the end of economic voting as a scholarly pursuit (cf. Anderson 2007).

Conclusion

Writing in the first edition of *Comparing Democracies*, Norpoth asserted that although the economy does not account for all the variance in a voter's decision, no other short-term factor does either. Paraphrasing Churchill's view on democracy, he noted that "the economy may be the worst explanation of voting, but it is still better than another one" (Norpoth 1996: 137–8). Fifteen years on, we reach a similar conclusion. Evidence both at the micro and macro levels of analysis provides some grist for those who are convinced that economic voting exists. Yet this evidence is not overpowering – there is much room for other factors to matter as much or more in shaping political outcomes. At the individual level, these factors may be tied into political knowledge, partisan attachments, and/or voter positions on non-economic issues, including the now not-so-new "new politics" dimension of political contestation (see Chapter 7). At the macro level, political institutions and, as shown here, regime types may sharpen or blur the economy–election connection.

Along with highlighting ongoing debates and pointing to the many contingencies involved in the hunt for the economic vote, analyses reported in this chapter emphasize two findings that must play a role in our understanding of the consequences of the economy in twenty-first century elections. First, political manipulation matters. It's not just the voter who has a say. Nor, as much of the cross-national research implies, is it just political and economic contexts that pre-ordain electorates in certain countries to cast an economic vote and prohibit others from doing so. Politicians can use their asymmetric powers of information control, media access, and policymaking to modulate the extent to which an election is decided on economic grounds. An outstanding question, then, is whether still-consolidating cadres of political elites in emerging democracies will take note of this and use economic information selectively toward their advantage (see Zielinski et al. 2005). The second finding of note speaks directly to the theme of this volume, on the challenges of democratic governance new democracies will face in the twenty-first century. Unlike in established democracies, statistical analyses show that the economy matters for incumbent fortunes in countries where democracy has not (yet) taken firm hold. This provides reason for optimism for the capacity of elections even in new democracies to act as mechanisms of political accountability. Future work must ascertain the extent to which growth rates in these regimes are the outcomes of policymaker competence, as the basic reward–punishment story would have it, or whether the economy–election connection is just an unintended effect of the whimsy of market forces – forces that, in reality, may have nothing to do with who's in charge of the government.

10

Women and Elections

Marian Sawer

In the 1990s, the representation of women in public decision-making, and more specifically in legislatures, was put firmly on international and national agendas. For the first time in history, there was widespread agreement that the under-representation of women in legislatures was itself a sign of democratic deficit. It became emblematic of women's unequal citizenship, a rallying point for women's non-government organizations (NGOs), and a priority issue for the 1995 Beijing Platform for Action, adopted by 189 countries. One approach to increasing the parliamentary presence of women, the adoption of electoral quotas, became an international movement that spread swiftly around the globe. A range of multilateral bodies, including the United Nations (UN), the European Union (EU), the Inter-Parliamentary Union (IPU), United Nations Development Fund for Women (UNIFEM), and the International Institute of Democracy and Electoral Assistance (IDEA), furthered the promotion of the presence of women in parliaments, and the IPU performed an invaluable monitoring role to underpin these efforts.

The increased salience of the issue of women's parliamentary presence (or absence) has generated a wealth of research on the factors that facilitate women's legislative recruitment. There is an established body of work on supply and demand variables affecting such recruitment, including socio-economic, cultural and religious constraints, and women's movement mobilizations. Cultural values and gender norms have often confined women to the "private sphere." Where caring responsibilities are allocated exclusively to women, rather than being shared or supported by community services, it remains difficult for women to participate effectively in the public sphere or to enter the occupations from which political candidates are drawn. Where household tasks are more equally shared, parliaments are likely to include more women (Mateo Diaz 2005: 63).

This chapter will provide an overview of how the parliamentary presence of women became a key indicator of democracy. It will discuss some of the barriers to women's entry to parliaments, including aspects of party and electoral systems, and the strategies that have been adopted to overcome these barriers. The chapter will cover some of the debates between those who have used the concept of "critical mass" and those who have used more institutional explanations of what makes women legislators more likely to advocate for other women. Finally, it will examine some of the expectations generated by the campaigns to increase women's parliamentary representation and whether women can "make a difference."

The core argument is that within a certain international conjuncture – the collapse of the Soviet Union and the multiplying of newer democracies – an international women's movement embodied in feminist officials and networks was able to promote an effective means of increasing women's parliamentary representation. Hence women's movement mobilization at the international level, manifested in electoral quotas, became a key driver of increased representation, regardless of the mixed motives involved in their adoption. In the new world of quotas, variables previously of considerable importance for predicting women's representation, such as the difference between Catholic and Protestant countries, faded in significance.

How the Absence of Women from Parliament Became a Democratic Deficit

In the 1980s the second-wave women's movement, and the flow-on effects on political parties, led to significant increases in the number of women in parliaments in Western democracies, as can be seen from the IPU data on the 20 OECD countries that have been continuous democracies since 1949 (Figure 10.1).[1]

At the global level, however, there was no guarantee of this increased presence, and the next decade was to see a significant reverse. At the beginning of the 1990s, the collapse of communism led indirectly to a rapid drop in the proportion of women legislators. While women had constituted 14.8% in 1988, by 1993 the global average had dropped to 10.3% and was still only at 11.3% in mid-1995 (IPU 1997: 83–4). Although the number of countries in the world with competitive elections tripled in the 1990s, women did not appear to be sharing equally in the new democratic freedoms.

The rapid expansion of the number of democracies in the world was accompanied by an equally rapid growth of bodies providing assistance in strengthening democratic governance. Technical assistance and capacity development were linked to assessment, to ensure that progress was being made in institutionalizing transparency and accountability and in preventing corruption. Increasingly, the representation of women was viewed as a readily quantifiable indicator of such democratic progress and was included prominently, for example, in IDEA handbooks on democracy assessment and

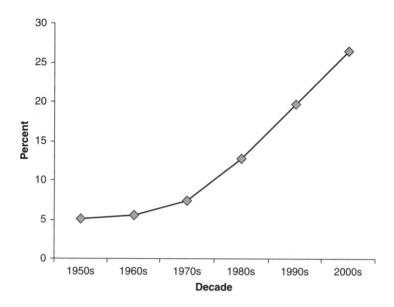

Figure 10.1 Trend in the percentage of parliamentarians who are women

Note: These data are drawn from the 20 OECD countries that have been continuing democracies, with universal suffrage, since 1949.

Source: IPU

as a specific target in the Millennium Development Goals, agreed by the world's governments in 2000. The European Union also viewed the under-representation of women in decision-making as a democratic deficit and as an issue of concern for both member states and candidate members.

The existence of corruption was an influential argument for opening up the political process. In countries such as Armenia, which ranked high on perceptions of corruption and low on representation of women, the entry of women was seen as one way to transform the existing rules of the game. The presence of women had become not just an indicator of the quality of democracy and an antidote to corruption but also a proxy for equal citizen-ship and equal opportunity. Some countries in which women had already achieved a significant presence in parliament and government, such as the Norwegian Agency for Development Cooperation (Norad) in Norway, became prominent bilateral donors to projects in developing democracies to promote and support women's political participation. A good example is the Center for Asia–Pacific Women in Politics established in 1992 in Manila with support from the Netherlands.

In the post-conflict situations discussed later in this chapter, international donors often funded coalition-building among women's NGOs to press for electoral quotas for women in electoral legislation and in new constitu-tions. From the 1990s, the IDEA began to generate research and comparative data directed to enhancing women's political participation. This included handbooks for women in parliaments (Ballington and Karam 2005; Karam 1998) and a world-wide project on gender quotas undertaken with Stockholm University (Dahlerup 2006). Meanwhile, the IPU had begun directing attention to support structures for women newly elected to parliaments, including women's caucuses and parliamentary committees with a gender mandate. Donors (including the IPU) might provide technical and financial assistance for a cross-party women's caucus or a researcher for a parliamentary committee with a gender equality mandate, as in some African countries. Making parliaments more "woman friendly" might also mean establishing a childcare center and changing sitting hours to accommodate family responsibilities.

The close monitoring of women's representation in public decision-making, both by the IPU and through the reporting process under the UN Convention on the Elimination of All Forms of Discrimination against Women (CEDAW), was important in maintaining a focus on initiatives to increase the legislative representation of women. CEDAW was adopted by the UN General Assembly in 1979 and by November 2008 had been ratified by 185 countries. Article 7 covers women's rights to participate in politics and public life on equal terms with men[2] and states parties are required to report on this along with the other provisions of the Convention every four years. The CEDAW Committee, in a General Recommendation concerning Article 7, has made it clear that, in order to make up for centuries of male domination of the public sphere, the removal of formal barriers is not sufficient and temporary special measures such as quotas are required (CEDAW 1997: para. 15).

The major turning point in putting the parliamentary representation of women on the international agenda was the UN's Fourth World Conference on Women in Beijing in 1995. Women's NGOs engaged intensively in the preparatory process, with, for example, 800 NGOs from India being involved in regional meetings (Kabeer 2005: 5). About 20,000 women attended the NGO forum held in conjunction with the Beijing Conference and there were 6000 women present from Japan alone. Donors were again involved, with Australia, for instance, funding one government and one non-government delegate to attend from each Pacific Island country. The full participation of women in public decision-making became a critical area of concern of the Beijing Platform for Action (PFA), Section G of which endorsed targets, special measures, and monitoring mechanisms. This section asked governments to review the impact of electoral systems on the representation of women in elected bodies and to consider, where appropriate, electoral reform (PFA 1995: para. 190).

Regional bodies took up the PFA goals. In 1997, for example, the Southern African Development Community committed its member governments to a target of 30% participation of women in all areas of decision-making by 2005. The PFA goals were given an added boost in post-conflict situations by the adoption in 2000 of UN Security Council Resolution 1325. This historic resolution was initiated by the Namibian Minister for Women's Affairs. It was the first Security Council resolution to deal specifically with the impact of war on women, including issues such as sexual violence. It called on all member states to increase the participation of women in conflict resolution and to mainstream a gender perspective in peacekeeping operations. Also in 2000, the PFA goals were enshrined in the UN Millennium Development Goals. Goal 3 concerned gender equality and the empowerment of women; one of the three indicators for monitoring progress towards this goal was the proportion of women in national parliaments.

The influence of the PFA has owed much to the proposition we shall examine more closely later in this chapter, that:

> women's equal participation in decision-making is not only a demand for justice or democracy but can also be seen as a necessary condition for women's interests to be taken into account. Without the active participation of women and incorporation of women's perspectives at all levels of decision-making, the goals of equality, development and peace cannot be achieved. (PFA 1995: para. 181)

In addition to the arguments for justice and the representation of interests, the PFA reflected arguments about how the presence of women enriches debate through broadening the experience and perspectives articulated within it: "Women ... contribute to redefining political priorities, placing new items on the political agenda that reflect and address women's gender-specific concerns, values and experiences, and providing new perspectives on mainstream political issues" (PFA 1995: para. 182).

The Role of Electoral Systems

As we have seen, the PFA specifically called on governments to review the impact of electoral systems on the representation of women. Much evidence had been produced by political scientists, including Wilma Rule, a pioneer in this area, showing the advantages of proportional representation (PR) in achieving a greater political representation of women and minorities (Rule 1981, 1987). The difference between PR systems and those based on single-member electorates, whether of the plurality (first-past-the-post) or majoritarian variety, lies in the differing incentives they create for candidate selection. While single-member systems favor "lowest common denominator" candidates, PR creates an incentive for parties to present a balanced ticket appealing to all sections of the community. There is also an incentive to appease all sections of the party, including women's sections, and relatively few costs. In 2008 parliaments elected by PR had 50% more women members (21.4%) than those elected from single-member

TABLE 10.1 **Proportion of parliamentarians who are women by type of electoral system**

Electoral family	Average percentage women in lower house, 2008	Number of nations
Proportional	21.4	68
Combined	16.0	35
Majoritarian	13.6	72

Sources: IDEA and IPU

electorates (13.6%), while those with mixed systems produced results in between (Table 10.1).[3]

While PR electoral systems are generally more favorable to women's political representation than single-member systems, some forms of PR are more favorable than others. If we think of the three main families of PR as the closed party list system, the open party list system, and the single transferable vote (STV), we find that it is the closed party list that is the most positive for the representation of women (but see Matland 2006). Where there are open party lists, voters may be attracted by the best-known candidates, who are usually male. In the Hare–Clark version of STV, where party lists are both open and rotated on the ballot paper, women may lack the resources required to compete effectively against party colleagues.

Another significant factor concern is district magnitude: women and minorities usually do better where there are more seats to be filled per constituency, whether in a party list or STV system.[4] Larger district magnitude facilitates the representation of smaller and newer parties, such as the Greens, in which women play a major role. A larger number of seats may also, however, facilitate the representation of small parties of the religious or populist Right, which tend to be male-dominated. For this and other reasons, large district magnitude has not been associated with a significant representation of women in countries such as Israel or Italy.

In the 1990s there was increased interest in another type of electoral system – the mixed-member proportional system (MMP), in which electors vote both for a constituency member and for a party list, with the party lists used to ensure each party receives an overall number of seats proportional to its total vote. In a country such as New Zealand, which moved from a single-member electorate system to a mixed-member system in the 1990s, there was an expectation that women and minorities would benefit from the PR element of MMP. The ethnic diversity of the New Zealand parliament has indeed increased significantly but the effects for women have been more mixed. While women have generally done better from the party lists than from the constituencies, this has not always been the case. The increase in women's representation in New Zealand has owed more to the success of left-wing or progressive parties than to the electoral system (Curtin 2008a).

The Role of Political Parties

In most democracies, political parties effectively control parliamentary recruitment and hence are the gatekeepers for the political representation of women (Lovenduski and Norris 1993). Party ideology is a significant factor in determining attitudes towards women candidates and it is parties of the Left, particularly those with a centralized process of candidate selection, that have been more likely to nominate women (Stevens 2007: 84). The women's wing of the Socialist International has helped promote quotas among social democratic parties, with dramatic effects on parties such as the Spanish Socialist Workers' Party (PSOE). The adoption of quotas in party rules is now one of the factors taken into consideration when new parties apply to join the Socialist International.

Parties on the Left that have been formed since the arrival of the "second wave" of the women's movement are even more likely to nominate women. Generally, Green parties, with their links to community-based environmental movements and participatory organizational philosophies, field a higher proportion of women candidates than older parties of the Left with their industrial traditions and historical links to male-dominated trade-union movements. "Post-materialist" parties are also less likely to be dominated by the "machine" politics and patronage networks found in older parties and are more likely to have open procedures through which women can make their claims.

While parties of the Left, and particularly new parties of the Left, are more likely than conservative parties to nominate women, it has been suggested that the fielding of women candidates may have a "contagion effect" (Matland and Studlar 1996). Once one party, often a new party, has begun putting forth more women candidates, the imperative of electoral competition is likely to cause other parties to increase the number of their women candidates as well. In Germany, for example, after the Greens adopted quotas in 1987 the Social Democrats followed closely in 1988, in an effort to win back women's votes. While such contagion effects may operate up to a certain point on the political spectrum, as right-wing parties move further to the right they are less inclined to field women candidates, particularly those who identify with feminism or women's rights issues (see for example, Carroll 2002).

In general, conservative parties have eschewed special measures such as electoral quotas on the grounds that they are "patronizing to women." If they try to emulate the positive measures taken by other parties this is more likely to be in the form of mentoring and candidate training than electoral quotas. So-called "family values" or conservative attitudes towards gender roles may also militate against the nomination of women candidates, who may be asked by selectors about their childbearing intentions or how they will manage family responsibilities. In the UK, as in many other countries, politics was regarded as a two-person career and the Conservative Party traditionally expected to get a husband and wife team when they selected a male candidate. The presenting of a male spouse, however, might be construed as challenging traditional gender relations (Lovenduski 2005: 70).

Another kind of "contagion effect" is evidenced by the short-lived women's parties that appeared in many countries at the height of women's mobilizations during the first and second "waves." The most successful of these was the Iceland Women's List, a feminist party that first won seats in the national parliament (the Althing) in 1983 and at the next election peaked with six seats (10%). One of the Women's List MPs, Ingibjörg Sólrún Gísladóttir, became Mayor of Reykjavik (1994–2003).[5] An important function of women's parties may be to galvanize other political parties into running more women candidates in order to diminish their appeal. In the long run, however, other identities have proved more enduring in party politics than those based on gender.

Quotas

Worldwide there has been a dramatic increase in the use of quotas to increase women's parliamentary representation. While only about 20 countries had some form of electoral quota prior to the 1990s, this had increased to over 100 countries by 2008 (Krook 2008). Quotas are of three main types: they may be inscribed in constitutions, in ordinary statute law, or in the internal rules of political parties. They may also apply to different stages of the electoral process, whether to the pool of candidates for party nomination, the candidates actually nominated by parties, or to seats reserved within the legislature, whether elected or appointed. Different types of quota systems are more common in different parts of the world. For example, legal candidate quotas are widespread in Latin America and the Balkans, while in the Arab region, in South Asia and some parts of Africa, reserved seats are preferred (Dahlerup 2006: 294). Constitution-making in post-conflict situations and international influences on this process may result in quotas being constitutionally guaranteed, as in Afghanistan, Iraq, and Rwanda. Famously, however, quotas were rejected in Timor Leste, due to opposition from the head of the UN's Electoral Assistance Division, despite support from other UN agencies (Ballington and Dahlerup 2006: 252).

The practice of reserving seats for a range of minorities is an element of the British colonial inheritance in parts of Africa and in South Asia. When parliamentary seats were set aside for women after independence they were usually elected indirectly rather than by popular vote. However, when quotas were introduced at the local government level in India, Pakistan, and Bangladesh in the 1990s, the seats were directly elected. In India over one million women were swept into local government. The verdict on these quotas was mixed, with some Indian studies suggesting that the reserved seats were being filled with women who had no real power of their own and merely acted as proxies for male politicians (Rai et al. 2006). In any event, as with the women swept into African parliaments in post-conflict situations, training to compensate for lack of political experience was of great importance.

When "quota fever" arrived in Latin America in the 1990s, beginning with Argentina, it was in the form of legislation to enact candidate quotas.[6] This was also the form taken by the parity legislation introduced in France in 2000 and in Belgium in 2002, requiring half the candidates nominated by parties to be women. In both France and Belgium the legislation lacked any placement requirement and the electoral system was an important variable in determining the success of the quotas. Belgium, with its party list system, had twice the proportion of women in its national parliament in 2008 than did France, where a two-round majoritarian system is used for the National Assembly.[7] In the Balkans, where women's representation had plummeted with the collapse of communism, Bosnia–Herzegovina was the first country to introduce legislated quotas (in 1998) but was soon followed by Macedonia, Serbia, and Kosovo. One characteristic of quota legislation is that it applies to all parties, unlike party quotas, which are adopted voluntarily and usually only by Left parties. Quota legislation may also be accompanied by financial sanctions, such as the loss of campaign subsidies by non-complying parties, although these sanctions are not always effective.

In Scandinavia women already made up between 20% and 30% of parliamentarians when they started persuading parties to introduce party quotas. By 1983 the Norwegian Labour Party had adopted a rule that neither women nor men should make up less than 40% of its candidates. Ten years later, the Swedish Social Democratic Party moved on to the principle of "every second on the list a woman," soon known as "zipping." The zipping principle can easily be applied in party list systems of PR or in the party list element of MMP and, at the urging of women, has now been adopted by other parties around the world. Placement requirements of this kind (sometimes called "double quotas") may also be found in quota legislation and help forestall the filling of quotas by placing women at the bottom of party lists (or fielding them in unwinnable seats in single-member systems).

In general, as in the example of zipping, it is much easier to apply quotas within PR systems, particularly centrally determined party-list systems, than in systems based on single-member electorates (Caul 2001). This is particularly the case where the selection of candidates is a decentralized process largely controlled by local party members. In this context, the introduction of quotas may be seen as a stalking horse for increasing the power of central bodies over local party branches. This is a specific example of a more general proposition, that political powerholders will be likely to have mixed motives for adopting electoral quotas for women.

The difficulty of introducing quotas where they are viewed as overriding local democracy is illustrated by the United Kingdom, where a policy of all-women short-lists for target seats was adopted by the Labour Party and used in the run-up to the 1997 general election. After women had been selected for 35 such seats, however, the process was successfully challenged under the UK Sex Discrimination Act, although the strategy and the Labour landslide still contributed towards a doubling in the proportion of women elected to Westminster in the 1997 general election.

One example of the successful introduction of constitutionally guaranteed reserved seats into a single non-transferable vote system for multi-member electorates is that of Taiwan. The provision requires that for each electorate with more than four members a woman must be elected. If no woman has been elected among the first four candidates then the next seat will go to the woman with the highest number of votes, not the candidate with the highest number of votes. This has given all parties an incentive to promote women candidates rather than lose a seat to a rival party and the number elected has far exceeded the guaranteed 10% of seats (Matland 2006: 288–9).

Patterns of Women's Representation

As a result of all the special measures outlined in this chapter, by October 2008 the global representation of women in parliaments had risen to 18.4% (IPU 2008a). The Nordic region retained its lead, with women averaging 41.4% of members of national parliaments. However, the introduction of quotas, particularly in post-conflict situations, has led to a rapid increase in the proportion of women parliamentarians in other parts of the world. For this reason quotas have been labelled the "fast track to gender balance in politics" (Dahlerup 2006: 3). Rwanda, for example, led the IPU league table, with women constituting 56.3% of its parliament (Table 10.2), and Mozambique, Angola, and South Africa were also among the top 20 countries. Between 1990 and 2008 the proportion of women in sub-Saharan parliaments had more than doubled (from 7.2% to 17.3%).

It is not only in post-conflict situations that new regimes can result in significant increases in the representation of women. Party quotas in new legislatures created by devolution can also have this effect. For example, women were 40% of those elected to the new Welsh Assembly in 1999 and 50% in 2003. In other words, the "fast-track" mechanism of quotas, particularly in new regimes without existing political incumbents, has proved remarkably effective in increasing the presence of women in parliaments. It has been supported by women parliamentarians themselves, with an IPU survey finding that 80% of respondents supported quotas of at least 30% (Waring 2000: 67).

While Norway might have slipped (at least temporarily) out of the top ten for parliamentary representation, it compensated in other areas of

TABLE 10.2   Women in national parliaments, 2008

Rank	Country	Last election	% women (lower or single house)
1	Rwanda	Sept 2008	56.3
2	Sweden	Sept 2006	47.0
3	Cuba	Jan 2008	43.2
4	Finland	March 2007	41.5
5	Argentina	Oct 2007	40.0
6	Netherlands	Nov 2006	39.3
7	Denmark	Nov 2007	38.0
8	Angola	Sept 2008	37.3
9	Costa Rica	Feb 2006	36.8
10	Spain	March 2008	36.3
11	Norway	Sept 2005	36.1
12	Belgium	June 2007	35.3
13	Mozambique	Dec 2004	34.8
14	Iceland	May 2007	33.3
15	Nepal	April 2008	33.2
16	New Zealand	Sept 2005	33.1
17	South Africa	April 2004	33.0
18	Belarus	Sept 2008	31.8
19	Macedonia	June 2008	31.7
20	Germany	Sept 2005	31.6

Source: IPU, Women in National Parliaments, October 31, 2008. The full IPU ranking of 145 countries is available at www.ipu.org/wmn-e/classif.htm

public decision-making. Women have held a stable minimum of 40% of positions on public sector boards in Norway, thanks to a legislative require-ment introduced in 1988. More recently, Norway has again led the world, this time in relation to the private sector, introducing legislation requiring companies listed on the stock exchange to have no fewer than 40% women on their boards by 2008.

The "rising tide" brought about by education and the paid employ-ment of women, by secularization and, more recently, by quotas, has not yet brought women into public decision-making in all parts of the world. Women are least well represented in Oceania where the representation of women actually fell between 2000 and 2008. Elsewhere, conservative Islamic traditions or fundamentalist Islamist movements are also proving to be powerful barriers to gender equality (Inglehart and Norris 2003: ch. 3). In both Oceania and in the Arab states there were still parliaments in 2008 with no women members.

Women in Executive Government

The same agenda-setting over women in public decision-making that has brought electoral quotas to much of the world has also brought about

TABLE 10.3   Women in national cabinets, 2007

Rank	Country	% women in cabinet	IPU rank for women in parliament
1	Finland	55.0	3
2	Chile	47.6	73
3	Norway	47.4	5
4	Spain	47.0	8
5	France	46.7	86
6	Switzerland	42.9	31
7	Nicaragua	41.7	58
8	Sweden	40.9	2
9	South Africa	40.7	12
10	Burundi	40.0	16
10	Germany	40.0	15
11	Ecuador	38.9	31
12	Austria	35.7	13
13	Iceland	33.3	14
13	São Tomé and Principe	33.3	111
13	Grenada	33.0	26
14	Malawi	31.8	79
15	Denmark	31.6	6
15	Lesotho	31.6	36
16	Peru	31.2	19
17	Panama	30.8	67
18	Liberia	30.0	84
19	Costa Rica	29.4	4
19	Netherlands	29.4	7

Source: Women's Environment and Development Organization, *Getting the Balance Right in National Cabinets*: www.wedo.org/files/50/50_CabinetsFactsheet02.pdf

rapid increases in the representation of women in some national cabinets, whether as a result of formal quotas or a commitment on the part of a prime minister or president. Once again Norway led the way, with Prime Minister Gro Harlem Brundtland appointing a cabinet in 1986 of which almost half the members were women. Between 1999 and 2007 the percentage of women in cabinets worldwide rose from 8.7% to 15.2% (Women's Environment and Development Organization 2007: 1). In 2007 there was one country (Finland) where women were over 50% of national cabinet members, five where they were over 45%, and 22 where they were 30% or more. In some countries it proved much easier to put women into cabinet than into parliament, so there is a wide gap between rankings on these two measures in countries such as Chile, France, Switzerland, and Nicaragua (see Table 10.3). "Critical mass" in one domain did not necessarily translate into critical mass in the other.

Another significant feature of women's cabinet representation is that it has almost always begun with "sociocultural" portfolios like education or welfare, and 45% of women ministers still held such portfolios in 2007, far more than held economic, infrastructure or "basic" (foreign affairs, defense, internal affairs, justice) portfolios (WEDO 2007: 4). However, countries with a high proportion of women in cabinet were beginning to break out of these stereotyped portfolio allocations, and in 2008, for example, the new Spanish cabinet included a pregnant defense minister. Women in political leadership positions may be constrained in terms of explicit advocacy for women but their view of the national interest may be informed by different priorities (Curtin 2008b).

Making a Difference?

As already noted, international human rights instruments include the principle that participation by women in public life on equal terms with men is a matter of justice. Although the justice argument does not require women to make a difference to public life, this normative claim is often closely linked to the suggestion that they will. Indeed, it is this assumption that has fuelled the worldwide movement for quotas. It is often taken as self-evident that because men and women are allocated different roles in society, the presence of women is required for these differing life experiences to be reflected in decision-making. The one major exception to this argument is the French concept of *parité*. When parity legislation was introduced in France, after long philosophical debate, it was couched in "republican" terms of the equal right to represent the interests of the nation rather than representing social differences or women's interests. Parity was seen as a permanent guarantee of equal citizenship, rather than a temporary measure to facilitate women's entry to male domains.

In examining the question of whether women make a difference to public life, either in terms of content or process, it is important to distinguish carefully between the presence of women and "acting for" women. Hannah Pitkin was the first political scientist to make the distinction between descriptive and substantive representation in this way (Pitkin 1967). Women politicians will not necessarily identify politically with other women or wish to advocate on their behalf. However the acting for or agency argument is only one of a number of arguments that can and have been put for increasing women's political presence.

Arguments for women's increased representation have been of five main kinds (summarized in Table 10.4). The justice or human rights argument simply asserts the right of women to participate in public life on an equal basis with men and requires barriers to this goal to be removed, whether institutional or attitudinal. This is also a democratic argument, as political equality is a fundamental democratic principle. But to persuade power holders of the priority of this goal, a number of utility arguments may be advanced, ranging from reducing corruption and increasing the national talent pool to providing partisan advantage. Partisan advantage may include

TABLE 10.4   Arguments for increasing women's political representation

Equal right to represent (justice arguments)	Right to participate in public decision-making
	Right not to be discriminated against by the structure of public life
Utilitarianism (utility arguments)	Increase the pool of talent
	Reduce corruption
	Partisan advantage
Improving deliberation (deliberative democracy arguments)	Debate needs to be enriched by women's perspectives or collectively mediated experiences
	Civilizing effect on debate
Representativeness (symbolic argument)	Effects on the status of the group
	Effects on aspirations
	Legitimacy of the institution
	Widening cultural choices
Protection of interests (agency arguments)	Women have different interests and/or values from men and these need protection

Source: Sawer et al. (2006: 19)

winning women's votes or providing a "clean" image for parties beset by scandal or a more "caring" image for parties associated with harsh economic policies.

Another argument is associated with the recent surge in the influence of ideas about "deliberative democracy." Theorists such as Iris Marion Young (2000), Anne Phillips (1995), and Jane Mansbridge (2003) have written of the need for women and minorities to be present to ensure that public debate is enriched by their diverse life experiences and perspectives. For example, women have been more affected than men by the collision between work and family and the experience of violence at the hands of intimate partners. The parliamentary presence of women may be necessary to bring such issues out of the "private sphere" to which they were previously consigned. Linked to the quality of public deliberation and respectful listening to others is the idea that the presence of women will "civilize" debate, by bringing a more consensus-seeking approach derived from gender socialization and family roles. This may, however, be an unrealistic expectation where norms of adversarial behavior are entrenched in parliamentary culture and political party traditions.

Different again from the justice, utility or deliberative democracy arguments are symbolic arguments for the presence of women in public life. These arguments point to three main symbolic effects: raising the status of women as a group, raising women's aspirations, and strengthening the legitimacy of parliaments. While the first women in parliaments are characteristically mistaken for secretaries, because of the expectation that women will be in subordinate rather than leadership roles, the normalizing of women's presence changes such expectations. It also helps raise women's aspirations: the "girls can do anything" effect, which some regard as the most important argument for increasing women's presence.

The demonstration effect of women in public office may also extend the range of cultural choices available to women, showing that female identity does not need to be bound up with domesticity. In some countries, however, there is significant pressure on women in public life to advertise domestic virtues such as making "cookies," as Hillary Clinton found in the United States. A final symbolic argument is that the legitimacy of parliament is strengthened when it is a "mirror" of the community – a sign that no section of the community is locked out of decision-making. One related effect is that having women as MPs may increase women's interest in and engagement with politics and even boost their turnout as voters (Norris et al. 2004).

The most difficult argument for increasing the representation of women in public decision-making is also one of the most common – the argument that women have different interests from men and that the presence of women is required to protect those interests. There is much theoretical debate over whether women can be said to have collective interests, such as interests arising from their reproductive role (Sapiro 1981). In the 1990s there was greater emphasis on the contingent nature of collective identities, on diversity and "intersectionality." Intersecting identities were seen as cutting across any "totalizing" gender identity and as complicating any collective interest in contesting gender subordination or promoting greater autonomy for women. Political ideology and affiliation, religiosity, class, race or ethnicity might be better predictors of political attitudes than gender. Even where gender is almost always significant, as on questions of equal opportunity for women, different generations may have different views (Erickson 1997).

As mentioned above the protection of interests is commonly described as "substantive representation," in contrast with descriptive or symbolic representation. Substantive representation requires not only presence but also commitment and action. What kind of action signifies that women are being substantively represented is an important question, as is the nature of the constituency. A number of strategies have been adopted to avoid essentialism in defining the constituency. Some link the substantive representation of women to the gender differences in policy priorities found in public opinion research – substantive representation occurs if the priorities of women representatives reflect those of women in the population as a whole, as measured by survey research (Campbell et al. 2007). Others link substantive representation to representation of the priorities and discourses crystallized within organized women's movements; this is a more deliberative approach (Vickers 2006). In other words, the constituency consists of those who have mobilized around the identity "woman" and are making claims in that name. For these researchers, substantive representation occurs when legislators introduce women's movement discourses, for example on domestic violence or childcare, and seek corresponding policy solutions and budgetary allocations (Mackay 2006). Yet another approach avoids the constituency problem altogether and simply measures substantive representation in terms of interventions to increase gender equality (Waylen 2008).

Regardless of how substantive representation is conceptualized, in practice it is likely to involve co-operative action by women across party lines, in partnership with women's NGOs and, perhaps, with women's policy agencies in government. A recent study examines a case in Australia, where women senators from four parties (both in government and in opposition) co-sponsored a Bill to make the abortion drug RU486 available (Sawer 2007). The study concluded that among the factors enabling this historic and successful cross-party initiative were *critical actors*, who had learned to trust each other across party lines, *critical mass* (35.5% of senators being women, almost all of whom supported the Bill unlike the male senators), a *critical juncture* in the electoral cycle and the *role of NGOs*, including one with a presence inside Parliament House.

Survey research finds that women politicians often believe they have a special responsibility to represent the interests of women and that they are more likely than their male colleagues to pursue these interests (Wängnerud 2000). But even where women politicians have such commitments, cross-cutting pressures such as party loyalties and constituency demands may prevent their acting on them or pose considerable constraints (Swers 2002). Furthermore, not all women parliamentarians are committed to pursuing women's interests, due to party ideology or a rejection of the idea that collective disadvantage arises from the gender order. We might find that men from a political party committed to women's rights are more likely to support such demands than are conservative women. One of the dangers of the agency argument, and of tying the substantive representation of women too closely to the physical presence of women, is that it may absolve male legislators from a responsibility for representing women's interests or from considering the gender implications of policy.

The Concept of "Critical Mass"

One answer to observations that the arrival of women does not necessarily change politics is the concept of "critical mass." The idea is that while women are only present in token numbers, there are exceptional pressures on them to demonstrate their loyalty to the values and norms of the dominant group. This theory was first set out by Rosabeth Moss Kanter in her classic (1977) work *Men and Women of the Corporation*. Kanter explored the effects of relative proportions on group behavior and found enormous pressures imposed on those in a small minority to overcome the distrust associated with being visibly "different"; they were often desperate to be accepted as part of the larger group. Kanter suggested such constraints lessened as minorities grew larger and that by the time they reached around 30% they were able to exercise greater influence on the organization.

Danish political scientist Drude Dahlerup was the first to explore the relevance of Kanter's work to women in politics. She concluded by querying the relevance of the critical mass concept, taken from physics, to the social sciences and suggesting that the willingness and ability of members of minority groups to engage in critical acts were perhaps more important than critical mass (Dahlerup 1988). As one respondent to the 1999 IPU survey of women politicians said: "Just one courageous woman can be a vehicle for profound change where 30% may be of little effect" (Waring 2000: 68). Others have emphasized the contextual nature of gender identity and how gendered norms and expectations are reshaped over time and place, regardless of relative numbers (Mackay 2004; Towns 2003). Shifts in dominant discourses, the strength of the women's movement and the nature of the political opportunity structure are also influential. The ability of women in parliaments to "make a difference" has been increasingly constrained by the rise of neoliberal discourses hostile to the public provision associated with the woman-friendly state.

A number of studies have been undertaken to test the propositions of critical mass, and in particular as to whether changes occur when numbers reach around 30%; for example, an acceleration of women's candidacies, the civilizing of debate or parliamentary advocacy on behalf of women (Grey 2002; Studlar and McAllister 2002; Trimble 1997). In general, an increasing number of studies have demonstrated that there is no simple relationship between an increase in the numbers of women and the passage of legislation beneficial to women. Some researchers have even suggested that when women are no longer in a small minority, they might feel less responsibility to advocate for women, because there are others to do so, and feel more free to pursue other policy goals (Childs and Krook 2006).

Despite these scholarly caveats and the difficulty of finding supporting evidence, the concept of critical mass swept the world. The argument was seized upon by women's activists and NGOs, by women's party organizations pressing for quotas, by politicians and multilateral institutions. In 1997 it was reflected in the CEDAW Committee's General Recommendation on Article 7 of the Convention:

> Research demonstrates that if women's participation reaches 30 to 35 percent (generally termed a "critical mass"), there is a real impact on political style and the content of decisions, and political life is revitalized. (CEDAW 1997: para. 16)

The rhetorical claim of critical mass has exercised real power in terms of mobilizing support for quotas at both the international and the local level. It reflects disillusionment with the "old" politics and the hope that women will change the nature of political institutions, as long as there are enough of them.

Institutional Supports for Substantive Representation

One alternative to relying on relative numbers (critical mass) to achieve substantive representation is to create institutional support for interventions to promote gender equality. A mobilized women's movement and strong women's organizations have traditionally provided a political base for gendered claims-making. Exposure to organized feminist advocacy, whether through membership of organizations or being lobbied by them, continues to be important in encouraging women MPs to advocate on behalf of women (Tremblay 1998). Women's NGOs characteristically seek out women MPs, in the expectation that they will have more empathy with the experiences and concerns of women. The IPU has found that the overwhelming majority of women MPs feel they have a special responsibility to represent women and that women's NGOs are an important source of information and support (Waring 2000: 133–41). These results are confirmed by other surveys, which have found that women MPs are much more likely than their male colleagues to nominate promoting the interests and views of women as an important representational task and to seek information from women's NGOs (see for example, Mackay 2006: 177; Wängnerud 2000: 75). Of course, the kind of prompts included in surveys on representative roles will affect answers and self-reported claims need to be checked against actual parliamentary interventions or other forms of political action.

Aside from women's movement organizations, there are a number of more recent sources of institutional support for feminist advocacy. These range from women's policy machinery inside government to structures within parliament itself. For example, the IPU has supported the establishment of parliamentary committees on gender issues and the creation of gender documentation centers. In 2006, when the IPU brought together chairs of parliamentary committees on gender equality from all over the world, the discussion included the role of parliamentarians in the oversight of gender budgeting and CEDAW implementation as well as the role of NGO partners. The president of the European Women's Lobby discussed its campaigns to defend the Committee on Women's Rights of the European Parliament (IPU 2007: 95). Such committees were important in many countries, but nowhere more so than in post-conflict situations such as in Angola, Cambodia, El Salvador, Ethiopia, Guatemala, Lebanon, South Africa, and Uganda. In 2008 the IPU found that there were 93 such committees in 80 countries (IPU 2008b: 65).

The IPU has also provided financial and technical support for cross-party caucuses of women MPs, to enhance their capacity to develop women-centered policy perspectives and to act on specific gender issues such as domestic violence. Such cross-party caucuses are more common outside Europe and where party discipline is weak, including in Rwanda, Burundi, and Indonesia. Elsewhere women's caucuses within single parties have been more important, as in the labour parties of Australia and New Zealand, in the Liberal Party in Canada and in the African National Congress (ANC) in South Africa. Both parliamentary and party bodies with a gender mandate serve as what may be called an alternative reference group for women politicians, validating a different set of norms as well as providing policy leverage and personal support networks (Githens 2003: 43). Research has been conducted on the role of such separate institutional space within electoral and parliamentary politics in countries such as South Africa (Goetz and Hassim 2002), Australia (Sawer 2006), Canada (Trimble 2006), and New Zealand (Curtin 2008b).

Conclusion

The barriers to the election of women to parliaments have by no means disappeared. Basic issues such as illiteracy among women or practices such as purdah continue to be important in many parts of the developing world. For women in all parts of the world the impact of political careers on family responsibilities remains a major issue, and one that may dampen political ambition. Apart from lacking time, women may find it difficult to mobilize the financial or patronage resources needed for effective campaigns, particularly in candidate-centered systems. In party-centered systems, however, women face the barriers of entrenched party elites and unwelcoming political cultures. Nevertheless, in an outstanding example of global agenda-setting, the issue of women's presence in public decision-making became a critical concern for many international institutions in the 1990s. The absence of women from decision-making became a sign of democratic deficit and a matter of concern to donor agencies.

The establishment of these new international norms for the representation of women is linked to a policy transfer of the mechanisms for achieving it. The speedy dissemination of electoral quotas as an appropriate special measure for achieving gender equality is a remarkable story in itself. It was facilitated in post-conflict and in transitional regimes by a reliance on international donors and by the absence of entrenched incumbents. It also benefited from a critical juncture – the appearance of many new democracies at a time when there was an international mobilization of women's NGOs and feminist officials around the time of the Fourth World Conference on Women. But it was also energetically taken up in many older democracies, despite the increased sway of neo-liberal discourses. For the cynical, it might seem there was a displacement of energies from achieving women-friendly policies to securing the parliamentary presence of women.

All in all, the agenda-setting on the parliamentary representation of women had many parallels with the international agenda-setting on women's suffrage almost a century earlier. Key differences were that by the end of the twentieth century there were far more democracies involved and the dissemination of policy innovation took place much faster. This time, far more feminists were involved in key positions in international institutions, not just in international NGOs, and while institutional processes remained slow, the transfer of the latest models of best practice took place at lightning speed, thanks to new information and communication technologies. Despite all the counter trends, such as the spread of religious fundamentalism, women continue to increase their presence in public decision-making. It remains to be seen, however, whether this will truly change the world.

PART III
CONCLUSION

11

Consequences of Elections

G. Bingham Powell, Jr.

Many of the chapters in this book discuss elections. In a book about comparing democracies this is understandable. Competitive elections in which citizens choose their policymakers play a critical role in contemporary democracy. Democracy means government by the people. The election of representative policymakers is the essential institution that systematically induces policymakers to take account of what the people want in national policymaking. If a country has no elections, such as Saudi Arabia or Myanmar, or no elections at the national level, as in China, we do not consider the country to be a democracy, however important it may be or whatever other virtues it may have. Moreover, to qualify as democratic, the election must be competitive and take place in a context of political rights and civil liberties. Most of the discussions in previous chapters assume such a competitive context.

In this chapter I want to be consistent with these discussions and with our usual understanding of democracy by considering some of the main consequences of citizens choosing one party or candidate instead of another. These choices affect what happens to incumbents, to representation, to policy directions, and to executive stability. These outcomes depend on the context in which citizens choose. They depend on what policymaking positions are subject to election, on the choices that have been offered by the party system (or candidate configuration), on the rules that convert votes into victories, on the various institutional and substantive constraints that shape government policies. Many of these contextual factors have already been mentioned in previous chapters. Here I want to pull them together in a single overview of consequences.

Elections can have consequences even if democratic conditions are not fully realized. Indeed, almost all real elections fall short of the democratic ideal. They may fall short in apparently small matters of administration, such as equal ballot access or error-free voting machines. An extremely close national election, such as the American presidential election in 2000, usually reveals a variety of flaws that can make a difference in a tight contest. Or, they may fall short in larger and more systematic ways, such as the exclusion of certain types of candidates or issues from the competitive arena or a continuing bias in campaign coverage. If the flaws are large and glaring enough, observers may rightly decide that the election should be considered "authoritarian," rather than democratic. Yet, even these elections may have important consequences. We shall begin by briefly discussing these non-democratic elections before turning to the main consequences of (somewhat idealized) democratic elections.

Elections without Democracy

Many countries hold elections under non-democratic conditions. A recent literature has emerged investigating the consequences of elections without democracy. This literature has begun to explore the conditions under which elections that fall short of democracy can nonetheless serve to move countries in a more democratic direction, or at least serve to limit government abuses and repression.

One point seems to emerge consistently in this literature: some degree of competition between parties or candidates is necessary for elections to encourage liberalization (Davenport 2007; Richards 1999). Elections without competition are merely a means to draw citizens into symbolic support activities, as in the Soviet Union and the states it dominated in Eastern Europe, which regularly claimed 99% voter turnout. The evidence suggests that in these "hegemonic authoritarian" systems elections support the antidemocratic forces domestically and provide them some degree of cover internationally. Incumbents regularly "win" by huge margins over non-existent or purely symbolic opposition and their repressive tendencies are unabated.

On the other hand, in the interesting category of "electoral autocracies" (see Chapter 1), elections can play a more positive role, although they need not do so (Richards 1999). This type of political system allows some degree of competition under various forms of manipulation of elections by the incumbents. Andreas Schedler (2002) discusses seven types of manipulation, any one of which can break the chain of citizen control, thus rendering the system undemocratic. Typical forms of manipulation are fraud in vote counting, unfair denial of media access to the opposition, restriction of political and civil rights, coercion or intimidation of opposition party organizers, and so forth. When these types of manipulation occur the country remains more authoritarian than democratic. The election may even help sustain the authoritarian government in such instances (see Brownlee 2007 on Egypt and Malaysia).

Yet, there is evidence that under some circumstances these highly flawed elections can help restrain government repression, giving a voice to dissent, encouraging the flow of information, providing coordination points and symbols to opponents. If the opponents can work together, forming a coalition against the government, they can raise the hope (and threat) of a possible opposition victory, push policy in a more liberal direction, even occasionally win a surprise victory against heavy odds (see Brownlee 2007 on the Philippines and Iran; Davenport 2007; Huntington 1991: 174ff.). In Howard and Roessler's (2006) study of 50 elections in 31 countries under electoral authoritarianism they found that in nearly a third of the cases the elections served to push the country in a liberal direction. Among these cases were the surprise opposition victory in Ghana in 1996 and the liberalizing elections in Indonesia in 1999 and Kenya in 2002 (2006: 370). Moreover, while liberalization may not follow or be sustained, sometimes highly flawed, non-democratic elections can nonetheless provide a pathway from open civil war towards an authoritarian accommodation of government and opposition that is less disastrous for the beleaguered citizenry (as in the Congo in 2006, or Mexico, an electoral autocracy throughout most of the twentieth century).

As competition becomes a more serious threat and manipulation is less extensive, we consider the country to be moving from an authoritarian to a democratic, if still very imperfect, regime. In these electoral democracies the media may still be imbalanced and political rights more constrained than in liberal democracies. Yet, with more electoral competition governments are increasingly constrained in their abuse of human rights (e.g., Davenport 2007; Poe et al. 1999; although Richards and Gelleny 2007 only find such constraint following competitive legislative elections). Huff (2003) also shows that the probability of mass genocide is greatly inhibited by democratic regimes. Having competitive elections does make a difference for the net welfare of democratic citizens.[1]

Having competitive elections is no guarantee of peaceful government. Under some circumstances, especially in ethnically divided societies, electoral competition may stimulate or be an occasion for manipulated political violence. (In general see Snyder 2000; on induced violence in India, see Wilkinson 2004.) But the balance seems to favor democratic competition as a constraint on government-initiated violence and abuse.

The Fate of the Incumbents

Perhaps the most powerful consequences of election choices concern the fate of the incumbents, the candidates or party members that are currently holding office. If citizens are content with their performance, they can return them for another term. If they are unhappy, they can, in the classic phrase, "throw the rascals out."

For some theorists of democracy this possibility of evicting the incumbents from office is the essence of democracy itself. As thoughtful a scholar as William Riker (1982b), deeply aware of the flaws even in this incumbent rejection as a reflection of voter preference, sees it as the most that democracy can offer its citizens. It is the fundamental mechanism of the "liberal" democracy that he supports. Most students of democracy probably agree that if an election does not make it possible to evict incumbent policymakers and bring another set of individuals to power, we would be reluctant to characterize the election as democratic. One of the best-known empirical studies of democracy uses election-based turnover in policymaking officeholders as an essential criterion of a democratic regime (Przeworski et al. 2000). Democracy may fail to exist because the true policymakers, such as members of a military council or royal family, do not subject themselves to the trials of the vote. Or because they manipulate the election process in such a way as to guarantee their own re-election (Schedler 2002: 200). But in either case the political regime is fundamentally flawed as a democracy.

The other side of the coin is that the annals of democracies are filled with instances of shocking blows delivered to confident incumbents by insurgent, even ungrateful, electorates. In a democracy the voters retain the right to use the electoral weapon to replace previously dominant rulers. They may be showing their disapproval of incumbent performance, a rejection of proposed policies, or merely a desire to change the subject.[2]

The eviction of incumbents can have consequences well beyond the specific replacement of one incumbent with another, with whatever alteration in competence or policy commitments that implies. The more important consequence may be to remind present and future incumbents of the need to pay attention to the preferences of the voters. It is fair to say that for better and worse democratic politicians are almost always looking ahead to the next election. This anticipation may occasionally make them short-sighted, or even myopic about the larger national interest. But it also serves as a check on personal tendencies towards abuse, corruption, personal obsession, and a forgetfulness of promises. It is part of the democratic faith that by creating a systematic need to pay attention to citizens, who are themselves paying attention to their own self-defined interests, democracy in the long run ties its policies to what its citizens want (Dahl 1989: 95). The ability to evict the incumbents plays an indispensable part in that linkage.

The context of the democratic election shapes the usability of that powerful, blunt, retrospective weapon. Among the important elements in the electoral context are the decision rules of the democratic regime: parliamentary or presidential, unicameral or bicameral, federal or unitary, and so forth. There may be a few parliamentary systems with simple and centralized institutions, but these are rare. More typically policymaking power is diffused across multiple democratic institutions, requiring citizen, or, more typically, elite party coordination if elections are to provide a coherent check on the policymakers (see, e.g., Lijphart 1999: chs 10–13).

Similarly, the election rules, as we know from Carter and Farrell (see Chapter 2), can provide different kinds of correspondences between

TABLE 11.1 Government change by outcomes in SMD and PR parliamentary systems

Type of electoral system	Incumbent loss or gain	No change in party government	Some parties change	All new parties in government	Total
Single-member district	−5% or more	53%	0	46%	99% (15)
	−4.9 to −.1	56%	0	44%	100% (18)
	Even or Gain	100%	0	0%	100% (7)
	All SMD	63%	0	37%	100% (40)
Proportional representation	−5% or more	27%	27%	47%	101% (30)
	−4.9 to -.1	47%	42%	11%	100% (45)
	Even or Gain	63%	25%	13%	101% (32)
	All PR	46%	33%	21%	100% (107)

Note: Single-member district systems are Australia, Canada, France, New Zealand, United Kingdom (40 elections). PR systems are Austria, Belgium, Denmark, Finland, France 1986, Germany, Greece, Ireland, Italy, Japan, Netherlands, Norway, Spain, Sweden, Switzerland (107 elections). Time period: 1969–94.

Source: See Powell (2000: ch. 3)

votes and legislative or presidential outcomes, depending on their interactions with party systems and voter choices. The combination of policymaking rules and election rules does much to magnify or disperse the effect of voter choices in incumbent eviction. Table 11.1 shows in parliamentary systems the consequences of "single-member district" and "proportional representation" election rules for the retention or change in government following varying levels of incumbent vote losses (or gains) in 147 elections in 20 established democracies.

On the one hand, elections do make a difference for incumbent retention or eviction in both types of systems. We see that in about half of the elections where the governing parties lost 5% or more of the total vote, the incumbents were completely replaced with new parties; this complete change happened only 10% of the time where the incumbents did not (collectively) lose votes. Conversely, in only a third of the cases where the incumbents lost 5% were they unambiguously retained in office, as compared to 69% of the cases where they were not vote-losers. Elections matter in democracies.

On the other hand, we see notable differences between the consequences under single-member district and PR election rules. In the five parliamentary SMD countries the incumbents were retained in office after 63% of the elections and evicted after 37%. In such countries the outcomes are almost always clear-cut retention or eviction. We see a sharp break in retention–eviction right around the point where incumbents go from being vote-losers to vote-gainers. The fit is far from perfect because of varying incumbent margins as well as the vagaries of vote–seat conversion. In the

UK elections of 2001 and 2005, for example, the incumbent Labour Party lost 2% in the first election and 6% in the second (from 41% to 35%), yet still remained the largest party and received an absolute parliamentary majority. Although few parties are coming into or leaving incumbency because they have won voting majorities (even in "majoritarian" systems with SMD rules), the exaggerated distributions of legislative seats to large (usually plurality) parties usually create clear majority governments for single parties or pre-election coalitions.

In the parliamentary systems with PR election rules, operating with multiparty competition, a very different pattern appears: a third of the time some parties stayed in office while others left. Governments were completely replaced only 21% of the time, completely retained 46% of the time. While there is a significant, visible, important relationship between vote losses and retention, there is no simple break-point, rather a gradual slope, with eviction declining as votes are gained. This notable proportional, rather than all-or-nothing, effect of the election outcome is shaped by post-election negotiation between multiple parties in legislatures without single-party majorities. That absence of legislative majorities follows from both the accurate reflections of votes into seats and the somewhat larger number of electoral parties (as we would expect from Chapters 2 and 3). In Sweden in 2002 and 2006, for example, no party was close to a majority of either votes or seats. A three-party governing coalition was retained in office after gaining a single seat in 2002, but evicted by a four-party opposition Alliance after collectively losing over 6% of the vote in 2006. In Germany in 2005 the incumbent coalition of the Social Democrats (SPD) and the Greens lost nearly 5%. In this case the coalition split up and the incumbents were partially replaced. The SPD joined their former rivals the Christian Democrats (CDU/CSU) in a new government headed by the latter, while the Greens went into opposition.

In presidential systems the fact of a single president gives something of an all-or-nothing flavor to the treatment of incumbents. As in the SMD parliamentary cases, the relationship is uneven, as incumbents elected by large margins may lose substantial numbers of votes and still be re-elected. Moreover, in multicandidate contexts the ways the votes are split across candidates may result in surprising outcomes. The fate of incumbents in presidential elections is also affected by term limits, which are common in presidential systems and almost never found in parliamentary ones. Presidential incumbents are often prohibited from serving more than two consecutive terms, so the voters frequently face elections without an incumbent. Cheibub and Przeworski (1999: 231) report that 80% of the cases where a change in presidential incumbent was associated with an election involved term limits. However, they also note that in elections in which individual incumbents did run for a second term, they lost over 40% of the time (1999: 235). (Two of their cases were in the US, in 1976 and 1980, as also happened in 1992, and two in the Philippines; others appeared in Latin

America.) The extent to which a new candidate of the same party as the current office holder should count as an "incumbent" is debatable. Still, there is no doubt that presidential systems give voters the opportunity directly to evict unpopular incumbents or to penalize their party, as happened to Republican candidate John McCain in the US presidential election in 2008.

Which of these patterns of chastising the incumbents – all-or-nothing replacement or proportional rebalancing – is more desirable depends on the orientation of the analysts. To majoritarian and presidential theorists gradualist rebalancing is a sad deficiency of proportional election rules and parliamentary negotiation, removing direct control from the hands of the voters, or at least making it necessary for them to take more extreme actions to use their ultimate weapon.

Moreover, this disconcerting replacement of direct, mechanical vote–incumbent conversion by inter-party elite negotiation is compounded by the difficulty created for the individual voter in determining proper accountability in parliamentary PR contexts. This has been most persuasively demonstrated in the studies of economic voting, where the connection between negative economic performance and anti-incumbent voting is weakened in complex conditions of shared responsibility between parties, which is a feature of the minority or coalition governments typically emerging in proportional systems (see Chapter 9). We presume that it also applies to voter desires to hold incumbents responsible for incompetence or corruption.

To proportionally oriented analysts, on the other hand, the irregular and exaggerated outcomes of SMD legislative elections (and plurality presidential elections), providing unchecked control to mere plurality vote-winners (and occasionally to plurality vote-losers), are too blunt and unreliable a weapon to be worth the satisfactions of unambiguous treatment of the incumbents. Major-party politicians, at least, will receive enough electoral reward and punishment in the prime minister's position to keep their narrow interests in check. After all, the plurality party winds up in government 80% of the time (Laver and Schofield 1990: 113) and usually holds the prime ministership. Loss or conferral of plurality status is a powerful sanction, which is reliably in the hands of the voters in PR systems. The frequent presence of pre-election coalitions, to which voters can respond in a nuanced as well as accurate way, enhances voters' control (Golder 2006b; Powell 2000: ch. 3).

But whichever approach the analyst or the citizen prefers, there is no doubt that the general power of elections to keep incumbents in check is evident within a variety of democratic contexts – and that the context shapes that application of the voters' ultimate weapon.

Representing Citizens: Advocacy

Punishing the incumbents envisions citizens acting retrospectively in response to incumbent behavior. Advocacy envisions citizens looking ahead to their representatives providing them a voice on issues that may arise after the election. Legislatures are the elected institutions that are especially expected to provide these voices in the policymaking process.

Election rules, policymaking institutions, and party systems all play a part in shaping the representation of citizens' voices. An assumption widely shared in the literature is that such correspondence should be proportionate to the votes that parties receive in elections. In this way the parties will provide an advocacy voice to the degree that they receive voter support. Various measures of vote–seat proportionality have been designed to capture this proportional correspondence (Gallagher 1991; Lijphart 1999).

A large literature has shown that PR election rules are in general more effective than the main alternatives, such as single-member district plurality and majority rules, in generating proportional representation in a legislature. They are explicitly designed for that purpose. Larger district magnitudes (more representatives per district) and low thresholds (the minimum vote required for representation) also encourage more accurate representation. The explicit formulae for distributing seats make a small, but significant, difference (Lijphart 1994; Rae 1971; Taagepera and Shugart 1989). However, the number of political parties and the geographic distribution of party preferences also play a role, especially in the case of low magnitude rules, where the number of parties may easily overload the "carrying capacity" of the election rules (see Chapter 2; also Cox 1997; Powell 2004).

More diverse advocacy may also be generated by involving multiple policymaking institutions in the policymaking process, especially if elected by different rules and/or at different times. Different rules and non-concurrent elections may often result in different institutions, such as lower and upper houses of the legislature, or executive and legislature in presidential systems, or national and regional governments in federal systems, being controlled by different parties. (This division is typically called "divided government," a term referring to somewhat different institutions in different countries.) Or, at least, the different institutions may represent different balances of partisan strength (see Colomer 2001; Lijphart 1999). So far as I know, however, there are no single advocacy measures that are designed to capture the diversity of advocacy across the full range of policy-making institutions.

Although the legislative vote–seat disproportionality measures tell us a great deal about the consequences of elections for party advocacy under various rules and institutions, they also have some fundamental limitations. These measures typically assume a great deal about the political parties in the election in question. On the one hand they assume that a "party" vote means the same thing to voters in different parts of the country. This assumption is essential to any measurement procedure that allows the unrepresented party losers in one district to be compensated by over-represented party winners in another district. If the same party label means something different in the two districts (as in the case of liberal and conservative Democrats in different regions of the United States), then the results of compensating across districts will be misleading. Some real party groups may in fact be severely underrepresented and others over-represented. Parties that are merely coalitions of diverse local notables or regional patrons, or that contain contentious policy factions, may fit the fundamental assumption of party homogeneity across districts rather badly. This will particularly be a problem in low magnitude districts, such as under SMD plurality rules.

Another problem with party vote–seat proportionality as a measure of fair advocacy is the assumption that each party, in both voter group and corresponding legislative group, is a unique categorical entity. Purely vote-based approaches do not discriminate between parties on any other basis than votes received. In fact, some parties may be much more similar in the policies they advocate than others. If a plurality vote-winner (or even a second-place finisher) gains a legislative majority because two other parties have split the vote, we have no idea whether the winner is sub-stantively far from positions favored by the other parties, compounding the vote–seat party disproportionality, or substantively close to them, in which case party disproportionality seems less of a problem.

An alternative approach to analyzing the advocacy consequences of elec-tions is to investigate citizens' preferences and their representation in the policymaking institutions, rather than using party vote as the citizen base-line. The research in this line was inspired by Miller and Stokes's classic (1963) study of constituency influence in Congress, which compared citizens' opinions reported in survey research with issue positions taken by their congressional representatives. A variety of interesting studies in other countries followed, usually focusing on multiple issue correspondences between party voters and their party representatives, rather than on district constituents and their legislative office holders (e.g., Irwin and Thomassen 1975 in the Netherlands; Barnes 1977 in Italy; Dalton 1985 in the European Parliament; Converse and Pierce 1986 in France; Granberg and Holmberg 1988 in Sweden; McAllister 1991 in Australia; Norris 1995 in the UK; Matthews and Valen 1999 in Norway). More recently, some explicitly cross-national works have appeared, such as Miller et al. 1999; Schmitt and Thomassen 1999; Kitschelt et al., 1999; and Holmberg 2000. (See the review in Powell 2004.)

Because these issue studies typically involve only one or a handful of elections, it is difficult to discern the systematic effects of contextual factors such as election rules and party systems on issue correspondence. However, the advocacy advantage seems to rest with proportional representation rules and multiparty systems (see especially Dalton 1985). (However, Ezrow 2007 finds advocacy responsiveness greater in less proportional systems.) This is also the conclusion reached by Golder and Stramski's interesting and original (2007) analysis comparing the cumulative fre-quency distributions of voters and legislative party representatives on a unidimensional Left–Right scale, rather than multiple issues. They find a better match of the cumulative frequency distributions of Left–Right attitudes under PR election rules and, more generally and significantly, where vote–seat disproportionality is less.

A final approach to advocacy consequences focuses on the representation of demographic groups, rather than partisan or issue groups. This approach is sometimes called "descriptive" representation (Pitkin 1967: ch. 4). Scholars working on descriptive representation have been particularly interested in the representation of women and minorities in legislative bodies. As shown by Sawer's discussion in Chapter 9, this work has now gone beyond demographic analysis to a consideration of the attention to women's issues in legislative discourse and other consequences. The representation of women in legislative bodies has been increasing impressively in recent years, but this phenomenon is much more advanced in some countries than others. Analytically, PR election rules, especially when linked to explicit quotas, usually within closed party lists, have been shown to be strongly associated with the greater representation of women (e.g., Tremblay 2008).

Setting Policy Directions

According to Gary Cox's thoughtful analysis, "the nature of the representational problem is quite different when one talks of enacted rather than advocated policy" (1997: 227). While policymakers may consider a variety of policy alternatives, in the end they must settle on one of them. These policy choices anticipate and interact with environmental conditions as they attempt to shape policy outcomes. In this role elections contribute to setting general policy directions, although the details and impacts must still play out.

This setting of general policy directions is an important consequence of democratic elections. As a mechanism or instrument of democracy the election's normative role is to connect the preferences of the citizens to the policy choices of the government. Retrospective sanctioning of incompetent or unfaithful governments can play a role by encouraging parties in government to keep their promises. Representation of voices in advocacy can play a role by seeing that the distribution of preferences in the electorate is reflected in the alternatives being considered. But the most direct role of elections in setting policy directions appears when citizens deliberately use the election to give a dominating role to a party committed to a particular policy direction. Most parties do make policy promises, generally called "manifestos," during election campaigns. The (limited) evidence on the topic suggests that they usually keep most of these promises, if they can ("Has Labour kept its promises?" 2002; Klingemann et al. 1994; Royed 1996; Thomson 2001).

The literature on election consequences setting policy directions contains several important ambiguities. One corresponds to the proportional or all-or-nothing distributions that we encountered in discussing incumbent eviction. Do we expect policy directions to change gradually as voters shift support from 48% backing the left-wing party to 52% backing that party? Or do we expect a sudden policy break as voters cross the 50%+1 threshold? European and American analysts are typically divided on just this definition of ideal "responsiveness" to election outcomes. Europeans tend to expect a proportional ideal, whereas Americans define responsiveness as a sharp break at the point where voting majorities change (Gelman and King 1994; Powell 2000: ch. 6). Katz (1997) considers proportionality and "responsiveness" in representation as contending democratic virtues in his analysis of vote–seat connections – and finds them inversely related to each other.

Another ambiguity concerns whether to infer citizen policy preferences from categorical party vote distributions or from some kind of substantive estimate. The former compares changing vote distributions to government party distributions. Research based on this approach suggests that PR and SMD election rules each produce the kind of party vote–government responsiveness (proportional or majoritarian) that we might associate with the respective rules (Powell 2000: ch. 6). However, in the SMD systems absolute voter majorities are rarely achieved, so their "responsiveness" places complete control of government in the hands of plurality winners. For example, parties winning 40% or less of the vote won absolute legislative majorities in Australia in 1996, the UK in 2005, Canada in 1997, France in 2007, and New Zealand in 1993.

The more substantive approach estimates citizen preferences, especially the position of the median voter, from survey research or some combination of voter choices and party commitments (as in Kim and Fording 1998, 2002). The median voter position is the primary focus of attention because it has the normatively appealing property of being able to defeat any other position in a straight majority vote. The legislative or government directions are estimated from party commitments (as attributed by expert surveys, such as Castles and Mair 1984 or Benoit and Laver 2006, or from party manifestos, as in Budge et al. 2001 and Klingemann et al. 2006, or by citizens). Although these substantive comparisons could be based on specific issues, the largest body of research has focused on Left–Right "ideological" correspondence between the median voter and the median legislator or government (Huber and Powell 1994; McDonald and Budge 2005; McDonald et al. 2004; Powell 2000; Powell and Vanberg 2000).

The first studies of voter–government ideological correspondence suggested that PR election rules generated, on average, governments closer to the median voter. This finding was challenged by Blais and Bodet (2006) and Golder and Stramski (2007), in studies based on new party position estimates (based on citizen perceptions) from the CSES project and

TABLE 11.2 Ideological correspondence with the median voter by party polarization in SMD and PR parliamentary systems

Type of electoral system	Party polarization level	Ideological distance from median voter legislature	Government	Total cases
Single-member district	Low	5.3	5.6	42
	Moderate	12.5	15.2	22
	High	19.1	20.4	20
	All SMD	10.5	11.6	(84)
Proportional representation	Low	3.0	4.5	91
	Moderate	3.6	9.1	69
	High	6.2	14.2	83
	All PR	4.3	9.1	(243)

Note: Single-member district systems are Australia, Canada, France, New Zealand, United Kingdom. PR systems are Austria, Belgium, Denmark, Finland, France 1986, Germany, Greece, Ireland, Italy, Japan, Netherlands, New Zealand 1996–2002, Norway, Spain, Sweden, Switzerland. Time period: 1947–2003.

Source: Based on party manifesto and election data. See Kim et al. (forthcoming)

recent elections. Powell (2009) and Kim, Powell and Fording (forthcoming) suggest that this difference is time-dependent and that the effects of election rules are shaped by the polarization of the party system.

This effect of the party system is illustrated in Table 11.2. In contexts of low party polarization, especially characterized by the large parties converging towards the center, either type of election rule will generate governments and legislative medians close to the median voter (as in the UK in 2005). Where higher polarization exists, PR systems produce governments and legislative medians closer to the median voter than SMD systems. The SMD elections typically create single-party (or pre-election coalition) majorities for the largest party, which is quite distant from the median voter in higher polarization situations (as in the UK in 1983). The PR elections generally involve multiparty bargaining after the election, in which the powerful role of the median legislative party helps counter-balance the more distant plurality vote winner. As higher polarization situations are more common, appearing about half of the time even in the SMD systems, the average advantage over the 50 year timespan in Table 11.2 favors the PR systems in creating closer correspondence, especially of legislative medians, but also of governments, as we see in the "All SMD" and "All PR" lines.

Presidential systems provide a similar set of issues in linking voter preferences and presidential commitments. The presidency is usually a winner-take-all office that can have a powerful influence on policymaking, depending on the specific presidential powers, as well as on the partisan configuration. The two most common rules for directly electing strong presidents are plurality and majority runoff. In the former the candidate with the most votes is the winner; in the latter, an absolute majority of votes is required to win on the first round, with a runoff election between leading candidates if no candidate wins a majority. (There are also a number of variations, such as qualified plurality winners, in which some threshold short of a majority is sufficient to avoid a runoff.)

In a straight two-candidate competition the presidential situation is simple. Both plurality and majority rules yield the same result, a majority victory. Substantively, if policy can be reduced to a single dimension, and citizens vote their policy preference, the candidate with the backing of the median voter will win the election. However, most presidential races do not feature only two candidates; in this situation, there may be no majority winner and outcomes may vary widely, especially under plurality rules. In terms of votes, the winner may have captured little more than a third of the votes, or less. In Venezuela in 1993, for example, the vote was split rather evenly among four presidential candidates, with former president Caldera winning with only 30.5% of the vote.

More disturbing, even elections where the voters' policy preferences can be expressed in a single dimension may produce winners who could be defeated by one or more of the other candidates in a straight competition between them. (Multiple dimensions, including such features as a candidate's personal attractiveness, compound the uncertainty.) The candidate backed by the median voter could always win such a runoff (he or she is the "Condorcet winner," in technical social choice language). Colomer (2001: 107) estimates that in plurality rule elections in Latin America (1945–2000) there was a majority winner only 30% of the time and the candidate backed by the median voter won only 59% of the time. In the other 41% of the cases candidates on one side of the political spectrum split the vote, depriving either of them of victory. (Also see Cox 1997, who calls this a "coordination failure.")

Although such failures of the candidate backed by the median voter to win the election are more common under plurality rules, they can also happen with majority runoff rules if many candidates compete. The French presidential election in 1995 provides a classic example, for which we have particularly good evidence of voter preferences. The vote was split among eight candidates. The candidate apparently backed by the median voter was Prime Minister Edouard Balladur, who, according to opinion poll simulations, could have defeated any other single candidate and was the expected winner. However, Balladur was the victim of votes split among many other contenders. He finished third on the first round and with 19.6% failed to make the second round runoff against Lionel Jospin, who had received 23.3% of the vote in the first round. The runoff was won by Jacques Chirac, who had captured only 20.8% on the first round and who, according to survey results, would have been easily defeated by Balladur, if the latter had made the runoff (Colmer 2006: 96–8). According to Colmer, this kind of outcome happened in 15% of the Latin American elections under majority runoff or qualified plurality rules (2006: 107).

It is, of course, also likely that decision rules that disperse policymaking roles across different institutions, such as bicameral legislatures, strong presidents and assemblies, and federalism, will affect the connections between voter choices and policy directions. The greater inclusiveness demanded by these rules may either weaken a clear policy direction provided by voters in the popular chamber or presidential election, or compensate for a distortion in one of these. These institutional variations have yet to be explored in empirical research. (However, Colmer 2006: ch. 4 provides a useful beginning.)

Promoting Stable Executives

In democratic elections the citizens' election choices shape the selection of the chief executive, directly or indirectly. We have already touched on this consequence from the points of view of retrospective and prospective control. Another dimension that is often valued is the stability of the executive: does the president or prime minister serve a complete term, or is he or she forced prematurely from office?

In presidential systems the executive is ordinarily directly elected, but after that election he or she is insulated from the consequences of voters' choices. Presidents can be prematurely removed from office only by some elaborate impeachment or recall procedure or by an overthrow of the democratic regime itself. Presidential systems are less durable as democratic regimes than parliamentary systems, even taking account of the level of economic development and the region of the world; they are more often replaced by military or executive coups. But the configuration established by the election has not been conclusively demonstrated to contribute to that instability (Przeworski et al. 2000: 128–36). If the democratic regime can be sustained, executive stability is likely to follow the presidential election.

In parliamentary systems, on the other hand, the government formed after the election is always subject to legislative confidence votes that can remove it immediately. In some countries and circumstances such a confidence failure can trigger a new general election; in others it may lead to negotiations for a new government. Whether the parliamentary government is likely to suffer such instability is a product of continuing events in the political world, such as scandals and economic shocks, which may change the salience of the political issues being debated, or alter the perceived chances of one of the coalition partners if an election were called. Governments in most parliamentary democracies may also call early elections themselves, if they can see a political advantage in doing so, although the manipulation of election timing somewhat in advance of a scheduled election deadline is not usually considered government "instability."

In addition to unpredictable events and strategic election timing, there is a connection between the election outcome and the subsequent parliamentary government's stability or instability. It lies in the legislative party configuration that the election creates (see Laver 2003; Warwick 1994). Most important, does the election result in a voted majority for a single political party, which then gains a majority in the legislature? If this happens, the majority winner almost always forms a parliamentary government by itself, with the party leader becoming prime minister and appointing party colleagues to the various cabinet positions. (The major exception to this rule is found in conditions of national emergency, as in wartime, when it is considered vital to rally all the forces of the country to respond to the emergency.) When this happens, the subsequent government is very likely to be stable and continue until the next election. However, voted majorities for single parties are unusual in parliamentary systems.

Equally important, does the election result in a "manufactured" legislative majority for a single political party, even though that party did not win a vote majority? If so, the party will almost always behave in parliamentary government just as though it had won a voter majority: proceeding to form a stable, single-party government commanding a legislative majority, carrying out policies, and enduring until the next election. Such legislative majorities result from the interaction of voter choices and the election rules. While any set of election rules can result in such manufactured majorities, they are particularly likely under SMD election rules or PR election rules with high thresholds. The typical outcome of a British national election is a manufactured single-party legislative majority, which generally proves quite durable despite its slim vote base (under 35% in 2005).

Of course, this single-party stability depends on the cohesion of the political party itself. In the established parliamentary democracies of Western Europe it is unusual for a party not to display high levels of party cohesion, especially on votes, such as confidence votes, that could deprive it of executive office (see Bowler et al. 1999; Laver and Schofield 1990: ch. 2 and App. A). The Italian Christian Democrats were a rare exception here, partially because of the nature of the election laws in their environment. However, in the much newer democracies of Eastern Europe a lack of party cohesion and the associated government instability have been more of a problem, compounded by the loose nature of "party" organizations themselves. These have often been more similar to linked coalitions than unified parties. Under conditions where parties cannot count on their members to provide unified support, they may bring additional parties into the government to ensure their majority. (In elections where the party's victory is dependent on a pre-election coalition, it may also honor that coalition by bringing its partner into the government, even though winning a majority alone, as happened in France in 1981.)

Third, does the election result in a polarized legislature or, similarly, one with a strong representation of extremist political parties? Although there is substantial dispute about the theoretical linkages involved, there is also good empirical evidence (King et al. 1990; Powell 1982; Warwick 1994) that parliamentary governments formed in these multiparty polarized environments are less durable that those formed in less polarized settings. Polarization or the strength of extremist parties depends in part on the choices offered by the party system to the voters. But it also depends crucially on voter choices. Voters in troubled times can simply ignore the temptation to support extremist parties – or they can enhance them from minor gadflies to major legislative players.

If extremist parties become major legislative players, then the government formation must either include them, and create likely-unstable governments of great internal diversity, or pointedly exclude them and have to build also diverse and potentially unstable governments from the remaining parties. The fate of the short-lived Dutch government after 2002 that included members of the Fortuyn List illustrates the first option. The short-lived Italian governments in the 1960s and 1970s illustrate the second. In either case when elections create polarized parliamentary environments, government instability is a likely consequence. When the elections result in multiparty legislatures of relatively centrist parties, stable coalitions can usually be negotiated without difficulty.

Thus, stable parliamentary governments can result from the voters electing single-party voted majorities, or from the election laws (especially SMD or high threshold PR) converting voting pluralities into legislative majorities, or from the party system and voters electing depolarized, multiparty legislatures that can negotiate stable executive coalitions.

Concluding Comments

Competitive elections enable citizens to shape policymaking in the societies in which they live. Even unfair, authoritarian elections may enable citizens to push their societies in a more liberal direction if some competition is allowed. Competitive elections provide a variety of types of opportunities. Elections give citizens the opportunity to evict incumbent policymakers, penalizing perceived incompetence or unfaithfulness. They allow voters to choose representatives to voice the diversity of their preferences in policymaking. They connect citizen choices to the broad patterns of prospective policy directions. These consequences of elections make citizens' voting choices meaningful to government policymaking, thus implementing the promise of representative democracy to embody indirectly government by the people. Moreover, competitive elections constrain the temptations of governments to abuse or constrain their citizens in pursuit of self-interest.

These connections of representative democracy take many forms. Patterns of eviction, voice, and responsiveness may be directly mechanical or indirectly negotiated. They may exaggerate the influence of the strong in pursuit of stability and majority or emphasize values of proportionality.

They may consolidate the weight of the mainstream or give purchase to its challengers. These variations are shaped by the institutional settings in which elections are held: the multiplicity of institutions involved in policymaking, the rules for electing legislatures and chief executives, the number and diversity of party choices. These institutional combinations, themselves the outcome of complex political bargains and normative predispositions, have interactive, not merely additive, effects, with each other and with the strategies of political leaders. Moreover, they shape as well as aggregate individual citizen's choices.

Thus, while particular analysts have strong preferences for different patterns of electoral institutions, the strength of comparative analyses of democratic elections is to illuminate the diversity of consequences within the democratic family.

Notes

Chapter 1   Introduction

1   This label was offered by former US Secretary of State Condoleeza Rice.
2   The Freedom House scores for 193 countries may be found at www.freedomhouse.org
3   OSCE/ODIHR. September 28, 2008. *OSCE/ODIHR Belarus Parliamentary Elections Election Observation Mission Final Report.* www.osce.org/documents/odihr/2008/11/35145_en.pdf
4   See, for example, reports by Amnesty International, www.amnestyusa.org/annualreport.php?id=ar&yr=2008&c=BLR
5   EU Election Observation Mission. December 9, 2008. *Ghana Presidential and Parliamentary Elections, 2008*, p. 1. http://www.eueomghana.org/EN/PDF/Press/EU%20EOM%20Ghana%20Statement%20Final.pdf
6   www.freedomhouse.org
7   UNDP (2008). Human Development Indices 2008. http://hdr.undp.org/en/statistics/data/
8   For a review of this literature, see Geddes (1999) or Bunce (2003). On more recent trends, see Diamond (2008).
9   The lower house of the legislature must be elected; the chief executive must be elected (directly in presidential systems and indirectly by members of the elected legislature in parliamentary systems); there must be more than one party; if, after passing the previous rules, the incumbent party held, but never lost an election, such regimes are regarded by default as authoritarian.
10   The notion of several distinct "waves" of democratization was highlighted by Huntington (1991).
11   Qatar has promised to hold parliamentary elections but these have not yet been scheduled.
12   Bangladesh, Madagascar, Malawi, Nepal, Pakistan, Russia, Thailand, Venezuela.

Chapter 2   Electoral Systems and Election Management

We are grateful to Hein Heuvelman and Joanna Rozanska for gathering the data used in Table 2.2, and to our editors for their advice and feedback. The usual disclaimer applies.

1   This chapter deals only with national-level electoral systems. Clearly, another interesting dimension of variation is the large range of different electoral systems at sub-national level, such as in the US (Bowler, Donovan

and Brockington 2003), the UK (Farrell 2001b), and Australia (Farrell and McAllister 2006).

2   The primary emphasis of the standard electoral system classifications is on proportionality variations, which in large part explains our decision to focus on these three components. Clearly there are other dimensions of variation in electoral system design such as: assembly size, electoral threshold (in essence the mirror image of M) and legal thresholds. For more discussion, see Blais and Massicotte (2002); Farrell (2001a). Other features of variation – that significantly affect gender and ethnic minority representation – include gender quotas and reserved seats (cf. Norris 2004).

3   After district magnitude, the electoral formula also has a significant effect on proportionality. A third characteristic, which has come to prominence quite recently (Lijphart 1994; Taagepera 2007) is assembly size, i.e., the number of seats in the parliament. Technically assembly size is not actually part of the electoral system (and hence is not covered in this chapter) but, in combination with district magnitude, it does have a profound effect on the proportionality of the election result.

4   More sophisticated classifications are available which give equal attention to all three components of electoral systems (Blais 1988; Taylor and Johnston 1979), but while these may produce more theoretically appropriate typologies they also tend to be somewhat unwieldy.

5   Note that throughout this chapter (as, indeed, throughout this volume) the number of cases varies depending on data access. This chapter focuses on electoral systems for legislative elections. Inevitably things are much simpler when it comes to presidential elections for the simple reason that just one office holder is being elected, thus by definition ruling out any proportional electoral systems. Here, with very few exceptions (such as Ireland's president who is elected using the alternative vote system), the choice boils down to a single member plurality system or a majority runoff one. About two-thirds of cases use the majority runoff system (cf. Blais and Massicotte 2002).

6   Another way of reducing the disproportional tendencies of the block vote system is to allow voters to express more than one vote for a candidate. This is known as the cumulative vote, which is now used by a number of states in the US (Bowler, Donovan and Brockington 2003).

7   In the US this is sometimes referred to as the instant runoff vote (IRV). It is used in San Francisco city elections and is being pushed by the Fairvote group (www.fairvote.org).

8   See data for all countries on the *Comparing Democracies 3* website (www.sagepub.co.uk/leduc3)

9   For illustrations of how this works in practice, see Blais and Massicotte (2002); Farrell (2001a).

10 For more on how mixed-member systems can vary, see Farrell (2001a) and Shugart and Wattenberg (2001).

11 For more details, see Blais and Massicotte (2002), and Farrell (2001a).

12 On the problems of introducing too much complexity into electoral system design – a feature becoming ever more common in recent times – see Taagepera (2007).

13 The number of seats a party might win can be limited by imposing a legal threshold on one or more of the tiers of representation.

14 In itself this is a large and complex area, to which we cannot do full justice in the space we have. As we shall touch on below (and is also developed by other

chapters in this volume), there are questions to be asked about the direction of causality, and also about the effects of other institutional and cultural features on some of these relationships. There are also many other potential electoral system consequences that do not feature in our analysis, perhaps most prominent among these being the role of electoral systems (as part of the process of institutional design) in facilitating conflict-reduction and peace-building (e.g., Reilly 2001; Reynolds 1999, 2002).

15 Clearly the relationship is weaker than shown in earlier studies (e.g., Lijphart 1994). In large part, this is due the large number, and more particularly the range, of countries included in our sample, lending support to Baldini and Pappalardo's (2009) argument in favor of a smaller, less diverse, number of cases in the analysis of electoral system consequences.

16 As Carstairs (1980) shows, in many cases this shift from SMP to list was via a two-round majoritarian system.

17 For important critiques, see especially Blais et al. (2004), who find no evidence to support the "socialist threat" thesis. See also Katz (2005) and Rahat (2004) who dispute the simplistic assumptions that underlie these rational choice perspectives.

18 These were not the only electoral reforms at that time, though they were certainly the most notable. Another democracy to change its electoral system was Israel, which introduced a system for directly electing the country's prime minister (judged as a variant of MMP – see Hazan 2001). This ill-conceived reform was repealed in 2001 (Rahat and Hazan 2005).

19 More generally, see: http://aceproject.org/epic-en/vo#VO11

20 http://www.guardian.co.uk/technology/2007/mar/03/news.international news (last accessed 07.04.2009).

21 Election Management Bodies have a number of different titles. For instance, the body responsible for the management and administration of federal elections in Australia is known as the Australian Electoral Commission, while the EMB in charge of national elections in Canada is known as Elections Canada.

22 For a discussion on when EMBs fail in their mandate, see Wall et al. (2006: 297).

23 In some countries, such as Jamaica and Romania, the tasks of implementation and policy making are in fact split between two separate independent bodies (http://aceproject.org/ace-en/topics/em/ema/ema02).

24 That said some countries do have temporary EMBs that exist during election periods only. For instance, in mixed systems, the governmental component of the EMB is sometimes temporary as civil servants are redeployed to their "home" ministry or department outside of election periods (Wall et al. 2006: 17).

Chapter 3   Political Parties and Party Systems

1 The formula for calculating the Effective Number of Parties (seats) is $1/(\Sigma \text{seats}^2)$.

2 The author gratefully acknowledges David Llanos-Paez and Anna Mikulska for their help in assembling the data for this section, and Ernesto Calvo for advice on data interpretation.

3 These terminus data coincide with the most recent of the attitudinal measures.
4 Such growth could also result from a decline in the number of independent deputies.
5 Electoral volatility is measured by comparing the sum of the absolute difference between vote percentages for each party between two elections, divided by two.
6 Details of the factor analysis are reported in Appendix 2. Missing values have been imputed using MICE in R 2.7 and factor analysis was estimated in SPSS 13. Only the first two dimensions were saved, which explained approximately 60% of the variance in the data.

Chapter 4   Campaign and Party Finance

1 Broadly speaking, political finance involves the public and private funding of both political parties and individual candidates, and includes routine operational costs as well as the cost of election campaigns. This chapter focuses primarily on the financing of political parties, including the rules that govern both their organizational and their electoral activities. For a useful overview of the funding of election campaigns in particular see the UDNP handbook *Getting to the Core: A Global Survey on the Cost of Registration and Elections*, available at www.undp.org/governance/docs/Elections-Pub-Core.pdf
2 See Ackerman and Ayres (2002) for a compelling but unconventional argument that a system of decentralization and anonymity – whereby the recipients are fully unaware of the identity of their contributors – is a much better solution for the problems with political finance than regulation and control, full information or bureaucratic subsidies.

Chapter 5   Election Campaigns

I am most grateful to Shaun Bowler David Farrell, Mark Franklin, Michael Hagen, Richard Johnston, Larry LeDuc, Richard Niemi, and Pippa Norris for very helpful advice and comments.

1 See, for instance, Banducci and Karp's interesting (2003) comparative examination.
2 Sub-national elections are interesting and important of course, and much of what is discussed here applies there, though perhaps to a differing degree. The same is true for supra-national elections, such as those in the European Union (EU). At these levels referenda have become more important (see LeDuc 2003). For an interesting examination of EU campaigns, see Hobolt (2005).
3 Sweden is one exception. Here early dissolution of the legislature is prohibited by the constitution. Parties simply have to find some way of forming a government.
4 There are prohibitions on election campaigning in some countries. In Italy, for instance, explicit campaigning activities cannot start until 45 days in advance of an election.

5   Canada Elections Act (www.parl.gc.ca/common/bills_ls.asp?lang=E&ls=C2&Parl=36&Ses=2).

6   In the many countries that use an "open party list," where voters select candidates to determine the votes for the parties and order of candidates on the party lists, the candidates do matter to some degree.

7   Federalism also is important, as it influences the degree of decentralization of campaigns (Farrell, 1996).

8   The specifics of direct elections can differ quite a lot. In the US, senators and House members are both elected from particular geographic areas, while in the Philippines senators are elected at-large and House members are elected from districts.

9   Where this does not hold, it can be due to differential party support across regions or provinces itself, as in Canada and India (Rae 1971; Riker 1982a; Chhibber and Kollman 2004). Multipartyism at the local level also is important in Canada (Johnston 2008).

10 While parties tend to play a big role in all parliamentary systems, the tone of campaigns tends to differ a lot depending on the electoral system/number of parties. That is, proportional representation, in increasing the number of parties and the need for coalition government, encourages parties to be less explicitly negative toward potential coalition allies (Powell 2000). This is not the case in majoritarian systems, where the winner takes all.

11 See also Shugart (2005a).

12 One interesting exception at present may be Russia, where former President Putin looks to control almost all of the country's politics as Prime Minister.

13 The nature of news coverage differs across countries in important ways – see de Vreese et al.'s interesting (2006) examination of the 2004 European parliamentary elections.

14 Exceptions include Honduras, Switzerland, and the US. See also Chapter 4.

15 A similar pattern holds on the entertainment side. For instance, while more than 70% of the ESPN audience is male, nearly 30% is female. The figures are much the same, in reverse, for the Lifetime Network.

16 See Internet World Stats at www.internetworldstats.com

17 Note that there are legal restrictions on Internet usage during election campaigns in Japan, though (predictably) these have proved difficult to enforce.

18 To a lesser extent, they reflect the wealth of countries – the more wealth there is, the more there is to spend.

19 Although the party or candidate spending the most money does not always win, a certain amount of money is necessary for a candidate to be competitive. Speaking with his tongue partly in his cheek, one American political observer noted, specifically in regard to high-level statewide races in Texas, that even if "you don't have to raise $10 million, you have to raise $8 million." The observer is Jim Hightower, former Texas Agricultural Commissioner and current political columnist in "The Senate Can Wait," from an interview in *The Texas Observer*, January 27, 1989, p. 6.

20 There is also tremendous variation in Internet consumption, as usage has exploded in some countries and only just begun in many others (Internet World Stats: www.internetworldstats.com). As of 2009, in North America nearly 75% had Internet access and in Europe almost 50% did; in Latin America the number was less than 25%, in Asia 15%, and in Africa only 5%.

The role of the Internet in election campaigns necessarily differs widely across continents, and also across the countries on each continent – see Chapter 6.

21 These are conservative estimates, as there are other sources of survey error that further complicate things (Wlezien and Erikson 2001). For difficulties in establishing the effects of political communications across individuals, see Zaller (2002).

22 Even if we had perfect polls – no survey error – at regular intervals over time, it would not be easy to isolate the effects of campaign activities. That is, we could not be sure that the change in the polls we observe is due to a particular event and not the many other things that happen on a daily basis during campaigns, some of which are exogenous, i.e., from outside the campaigns *per se*.

23 See also Huber and Arceneaux (2007). There is a lot of experimental research on voter mobilization, much of which has been conducted by Alan Gerber and Donald Green, and is summarized in their 2004 book. One interesting and important finding is that traditional door-to-door canvassing matters much more than more modern approaches, such as telephone calls and direct mail.

24 In the language of political psychologists, voters are, at least to some extent, "online processors" (see Lodge et al. 1995). That is, they update their preferences based on new information about the parties and candidates.

25 Campaigns also have a much greater effect during the primaries, when the two major parties choose the candidates to run in the general election (Bartels 1988).

26 A similar pattern holds in US congressional elections (see Erikson and Sigelman 1996).

27 The small change also appeared to alter the balance of power in meaningful ways, costing the Conservatives 38 seats, 23 of which went to Labour and 14 of which went to the Liberal Democrats (Norris and Wlezien, 2005).

28 The logic applies equally well to legislative elections in presidential systems, and is precisely what we observe in US House elections: poll variation over time is about half that for presidential candidates, even in presidential election years (Erikson and Sigelman 1996).

29 The unfolding of events also appears to have mattered greatly (Clarke et al. 2009).

30 The "personal vote" also can matter in proportional systems that use open lists (see Shugart et al. 2005). The causal effect of incumbency is debatable – see Fenno 1978; Zaller 1998.

31 The pattern in referendum elections is very different indeed – see LeDuc (2003).

32 Based on data from Levada Center in Moscow, Dmitry Medvedev held a 33–25% lead over Sergei Ivanov in the polls at the beginning of 2007 and then fell behind (34–30%) during the summer before regaining it through the fall, in a more crowded field, with Viktor Zubkov in third with 17% and Zyuganov and Vladimir Zhironovsky at 11%. This hinted at an intense campaign leading up to the March 2, 2008, election. Then, in December 2007, Putin endorsed Medvedev, and Ivanov and Zubkov did not stand for election. Medvedev pulled away, winning in the first round with 71% of the vote.

33 The opposite may be true in the US, where the level and effect of party identification have been on the rise (Bartels 2000).

34 The extent to which this is true, especially as regards the latter, varies considerably across elections and countries in understandable ways (see Nadeau et al. 2002). See Chapter 9 for more on economic voting.

Chapter 7   Ideology, Partisanship, and Democratic Development

1   Many public opinion researchers have questioned whether ordinary citizens can understand and utilize abstract political concepts like "Left" and "Right." For a discussion of this topic in advanced industrial democracies see Converse (1964), Lewis-Beck et al. (2008: ch. 9), and Fuchs and Klingemann (1989). See Mainwaring (1999) for a discussion on developing democracies.

2   The data in this chapter are drawn from the Comparative Study of Electoral Systems. The first module of CSES was conducted between 1996 and 2001 and the second module was done between 2001 and 2006. These data and documentation are available for free download at www.cses.org. We supplemented this with the original data for France that included the prospective vote in the 2002 legislative election, the Chilean survey with a corrected Left–Right variable, and the 1998 Philippines survey. The nations in each figure/table vary because some variables are not available in all surveys.

3   On average, 89% of the public in the CSES nations positioned themselves on the Left–Right scale, and 84% in the 1999–2002 WVS nations that overlap with CSES II. In the WVS, 97% of the Taiwanese respondents place themselves on the Left–Right scale.

4   The five WVS nations with the highest percentage of Left–Right extremists were: Uganda (50%), Mexico (47%), Morocco (43%), the Dominican Republic (43%), and El Salvador (41%).

5   The same pattern emerges for the United Nations Human Development Index ($r = -0.78$) in the CSES nations (logarithmic curve). Furthermore, people are not polarized toward the Left in one nation, and the Right in another; the percentage of both extremists in a nation is positively related ($r = 0.51$). National affluence is also negatively related to both the percentage of Leftist extremists ($r = -0.56$) and Rightist extremists (-0.74).

6   Freedom House codes nations on both political rights and civil liberties. We combined the two scores to measure democratic development. The overall index was recoded so that higher values are more democratic. These data and documentation are available from www.freedomhouse.org. There is a very strong relationship between national affluence and democracy ($r = 0.70$), which makes it difficult to separate empirically the distinct effects of these two national characteristics.

7   To fit the Marxian framework, we code social class as (1) working class; (2) white collar middle class; and (3) self-employed and professionals. Union membership is a three-point scale in most nations: (1) respondent is a member of a union; (2) someone in household belongs to a union; and (3) no union member in household. In some nations the family membership question was not asked, so here we use only a question on the respondent's union membership.

8   The 2003 Latinobarometer surveyed 17 Latin American nations (www. latinobarometro.org). We used a measure of interviewer perceptions of the respondent's social status because an occupation or union question comparable to the CSES was not available. The average correlation (Pearson r) between social status and Left–Right identities was 0.07, and only one nation had a correlation about 0.10.

9   The CSES coded approximately two dozen religious denominations and those with no religious affiliation. The largest single group was Roman Catholics, followed by Protestants, and then Eastern Orthodox, Muslims, and Buddhists. The religiosity question asked: Would you say you: (1) have no religious beliefs; (2) are not very religious; (3) are somewhat religious, or (4) are very religious? See the study documentation at www.cses.org

10   We replicated the religiosity and Left–Right analyses with the 2003 Latinobarometer for 17 Latin American nations. The average Pearson r correlation was only 0.06.

11   Regional differences are often strengthened when they find formal representation in the party system, such as in the UK (Scottish National Party and Plaid Cymru), Canada (Bloc Québécois), Germany (the PDS.Linke), and Spain (EAJ/PNV and CiU).

12   Comparing distinctive populations across nations is complicated because the primary division can be based on race, ethnicity, or language. Table 7.2 uses ethnicity as the most general measure, but in some nations only race was available and this is substituted for ethnic differences.

13   For instance, education and social class effects are cross-cutting as we have noted. In addition, gender equality and religious values also tap traditional/modern value differences, so the interpretation of these issues can be ambiguous (Dalton 2006a; Inglehart and Norris 2003).

14   However, the WVS finds that attitudes toward gender equality are often strongly related to Left–Right orientations in less developed nations where the status of women was severely restricted and there are new international pressures to reform gender policies. This is another example of where traditional/modern values may have differential patterns in developing nations and advanced industrial democracies (Dalton 2006; Inglehart and Norris 2003).

15   Barnes et al. (1988) compared the traditional American party identification question and a party closeness question. They found high correlations between both measures at two timepoints and a general consistency in the correlates of both questions.

16   The source for the age of the party system is Bargsted (2007). We capped the age of the party system at 100 years, figuring that by this time (or before) party attachments should have reached an equilibrium point. In addition, we adjusted the age of the party system in a few nations because there was an extensive period of a non-democratic regime that would have disrupted partisanship. For instance, the CSES gives the Czech party system an age of 67.5 years in 2002, but the democratic transition was only 12 years earlier.

17   We replicated the analyses with the CSES Module II nations, which show virtually no relationship between the age of the party system and levels of partisanship (r = 0.03). We suspect this is because the CSES partisanship question is susceptible to short-term electoral effects. For instance, several nations increased partisanship by 20% or more between the two modules; real party identifications would not change so rapidly.

18   A fully defined model would include social characteristics in predicting the vote. As noted above in the case of region, we expect that when political parties explicitly emphasize social identities, this may increase the influence of social characteristics on voting behavior beyond their relationship with citizens'

Left–Right identities. This contrasting pattern of correlations is apparent in some nations in our analyses, but not in others.

19 We combined GDP/capita and a measure of the ideological polarization of the party system derived from Dalton (2008) in a multiple regression analysis to predict the strength of Left–Right voting in a nation; ideological polarization has a much stronger impact on the degree of Left–Right voting in a nation ($ß = 0.72$), while national affluence has a more modest impact ($ß = 0.23$).

Chapter 8   Political Participation

I would like to thank Aina Gallego for her assistance and the editors for their comments on a draft of this chapter.

1 Some studies use "voting age population" as the denominator, but this has the disadvantage of including people who do not have the right to vote (Blais and Dobrzynska 1998; Franklin 2004). The United States is not included because people (mostly) have to register themselves, contrary to almost every other country.

2 Franklin (2004: 187), for instance, shows a slight reduction in average margin of victory between 1965 and 1999.

3 A similar definition is proposed by Parry et al. (1992: 19–20).

4 I leave aside campaign activity, which is also decreasing in most advanced industrial democracies (Dalton and Wattenberg 2000: ch. 3).

5 For the positive correlation between age and voting see Wolfinger and Rosenstone (1980) and Blais (2000). Dalton (2006b: 72) shows a negative correlation between age and protest activity in the US, the UK, Germany, and France.

6 For contacting, see Verba et al. (1995).

Chapter 9   Elections and the Economy

1 These points of debate are taken up in more detail in two recently published books on individual-level economic voting by van der Brug, van der Eijk, and Franklin (2007) and by Duch and Stevenson (2008). While both studies examine the economic vote in advanced industrial democracies, Duch and Stevenson examine the effect of perceptions of the national economy on actual party choice, while van der Brug et al. look at the influence of aggregate economic indicators on a measure of the utility a voter would get from choosing one party over another (discussed below). The two books also have different points of departure: van der Brug et al. provide readers with a set of shortcomings in empirical work on economic voting and show how their approach corrects for them. Duch and Stevenson, however, begin by developing a competency-based theory for how voters decide in complex environments.

2   The party of the incumbent chief executive is the party of the prime minister in parliamentary systems and the party of the president in presidential regimes. Parties in government are identical to the party of the chief executive except in cases where the incumbent is composed of a coalition of parties. There are arguments on both sides for which measure is preferred; one might argue, for instance, that "party in government" is better because it does not make sense to treat junior coalition partners as being part of the opposition. On the other hand, it has been shown that voters evaluate parties differently in terms of the economy based on whether or not the party holds the prime minister's office (see, e.g., Anderson 1995).

3   Complete descriptions of variables and codes used, along with the logistic regression results for each country, are found in Appendix 9.A, available from the *Comparing Democracies 3* website www.sagepub.co.uk/leduc3).

4   Here a positive economic vote means that a worsening economic perception increases the incumbent's standing in the polls beyond what it would otherwise be.

5   Indeed, herein lies much of the attraction of economic voting in general: by only knowing two pieces of information, the state of the economy and the incumbent party, voters can cast their ballots in a fashion that serves to hold elected officials accountable.

6   This may be due to a culture of individualism in the UK or the broad social protections in Denmark that desensitize voters to national economic cycles. Similarly, Feldman (1982: 446) writes that American voters' "belief in economic individualism leads people to accept personal responsibility for their economic conditions, which in turn eliminates any connection between personal well-being and political evaluation."

7   As part of their comprehensive study of the American macro-political economy, Erikson et al. (2002: 98) demonstrate that "the subjective economy is somewhat different from the one objectively measured."

8   Still more troubling is that the difficulty with separating *political* evaluations from *economic* ones increases opportunities for voter manipulation – a point taken up below.

9   These data are an updated version of those used in Hellwig and Samuels (2008). I thank Eva Coffey and Anna Mikulska for assisting in data collection. A listing of the cases and data sources is found in Appendix 9. B, available from the *Comparing Democracies 3* website (www.sagepub.co.uk/leduc3).

10   In cases of coalition governments in parliamentary systems, the head of government's party is that of the prime minister. For executive elections we use results from the first or only round of elections.

11   The source is the Penn World Tables v6.2, http://pwt.econ.upenn.edu/, last accessed 06/08. I use GDP change in year "t-1" if the election was held in the first six months of the year, and the change in year "t" if the election was held later in the year. While other macro studies have used measures such as unemployment or inflation, only GDP data are available for our larger global sample.

12   Age of Democracy is equal to the election year minus the year in which the country first scores +6 or above on Polity IV's −10 to +10 democracy measure. The expectation is that the coefficient on the variable is positive since in older democracies elections are less volatile and, therefore, the incumbent should

be better able to maintain a level of votes. Following Hellwig and Samuels (2008), I also include the variable squared to account for the declining marginal impact of years of democratic experience.

13   To control for possible heteroscedasticity within country-groups, all models are estimated with Huber–White robust standard errors clustered within country-units. This approach is appropriate for data sets where the number of observations exceeds the number of non-missing within-panel time periods. The errors are robust to any type of error correlation within each country-group and assume only that observations are independent across country-groups.

14   Semi-presidential regimes are those in which there is a head of state (president) and head of government (prime minister), both are directly elected, and the prime minister is accountable to the legislature.

15   In examining the semi-presidential French case, Lewis-Beck (1997) shows the electoral consequences of the economy depending on whether the executive is unified or divided. Hellwig and Samuels (2008) report similar evidence in cross-national perspective.

16   An exception are partisan, or issue-priority models of economic voting which assert that voters evaluate parties differently according to the preferences of their key constituents in the electorate – e.g., preferences for curbing inflation relative to lowering unemployment (Hibbs 1977; see also Anderson 1995).

17   That is, these elections are "opportunistic" in that they are due to government calls. Opportunistic elections are distinguished from those held early for other reasons, such as due to a split in the government's coalition or an election following a failed vote of no-confidence. Following Kayser (2006), I classify an election as occurring early if it takes place before the quarter of the constitutionally mandated end of term.

18   To see this, we combine the coefficients on *Economy* and the *Economy* × *Opportunistic* interaction term (+0.32 and −0.29) to get a conditional coefficient of 0.03. The large conditional standard error (0.42) makes clear that the economy, on average, has no effect on incumbent vote shares when the government calls an early election.

19   Though the coefficient on the *Economy* × *Polarization* term is not statistically significant, the reported standard error pertains only to two specific combinations of values: the effect of *Economy* on *Incumbent Vote* when *Polarization* equals zero or the effect of *Polarization* on *Incumbent Vote* when *Economy* equals zero.

20   The KOF Index of Globalization develops indices for three forms of globalization: economic, social, and political. The measure used here is the *restrictions* sub-component of the economic globalization index, consisting of scores for hidden import barriers, tariff rates, taxes on international trade, and capital account restrictions. Data are available at http://globalization. kof.ethz.ch/

21   This claim is supported by a comparison of means between old and new democracies. The data show that old democracies (those greater than 10 years) more frequently are subjected to early election calls, score higher on the liberalization index, and have more polarized parties than young

democracies. Regarding the last of these, some scholars (e.g., Dalton, see Chapter 7) have argued that partisan attachments are a sign of democratic consolidation. Similarly, it may be the case that coherent and *distinct* policy positions held by elites are part and parcel with democratic consolidation. With consolidation, then, comes a divergence of issue positions and thus greater polarization and less economic voting.

Chapter 10   Women and Elections

My thanks to Donley Studlar, Merrindahl Andrew, and Peter Brent for helpful comments and assistance.

1   The IPU data here are aggregated from those OECD countries that have been continuous democracies since 1949, with universal suffrage (Sweden, Finland, Norway, Denmark, the Netherlands, Germany, Austria, Iceland, New Zealand, Belgium, Luxembourg, Israel, Canada, Italy, the United Kingdom, Australia, Ireland, the United States, France, Japan). As elsewhere in the chapter, figures for the parliamentary representation of women refer to the percentage of women in the lower house or the only house of national parliaments/legislatures.
2   The right of women to participate in public life on an equal basis with men had also been inscribed in Article 25 of the International Covenant on Civil and Political Rights but indirectly and without nearly as much impact as Article 7 of CEDAW.
3   For more detailed discussion of the effects of different types of electoral system on women's representation see Tremblay (2008).
4   Matland (2006) argues that what is more important is the related factor of party magnitude – how many seats a party expects to fill.
5   The Women's List merged into a new Social Democratic Alliance in 1998 of which Sólrún became Chair and, in 2007, Minister of Foreign Affairs.
6   Legislated quotas were introduced in Argentina (1991), Bolivia (1997), Brazil (1997), Costa Rica (1997), the Dominican Republic (1997), Ecuador (1997), Mexico (1996), Panama (1997), Paraguay (1996), Peru (1997), and Venezuela (1998).
7   France's parity legislation was much more successful in municipal elections, where PR is used for the larger units. In Belgium, the effectiveness of the party list system was enhanced by the introduction of larger district magnitudes at the same time as the parity legislation.

Chapter 11   Consequences of Elections

1   There is also a complex and growing literature on the implications of democratic regimes for citizen welfare, especially in its redistributive dimension. Dreze and

Sen (1989) argue that no democracy has suffered a real famine. But it seems to be independent media and information that are the causal mechanism, rather than elections as such. Blaydes and Kayser (2008) find the empirical literature on the effects of democratic regimes on income redistribution to be highly mixed; their work suggests that democratic regimes have some redistributive effect on caloric consumption, maybe income generally, under conditions of economic growth. However, works in this literature, including theirs, don't try to disentangle the role of elections *per se* from other features of democratic regimes.

2   A famous example is the British electorate's eviction of Winston Churchill as prime minister immediately after World War II, despite his magnificent war leadership. Shortly thereafter Churchill, ostensibly writing about France and Clemenceau after World War I, quoted Plutarch as saying that "Ingratitude towards their great men is the mark of strong peoples" (Churchill, *World War II*, vol. 1: *The Gathering Storm*, p. 11).

Bibliography

Aarts, Kees, André Blais, and Hermann Schmitt, eds 2010. *Political Leaders and Democratic Elections*. Oxford: Oxford University Press.

Abramowitz, Alan I. 1988. "Explaining Senate Election Outcomes." *American Political Science Review* 83: 385–403.

Abramowitz, Alan I. 1991. "Incumbency, Campaign Spending, and the Decline of Competition in the U.S. House Elections." *Journal of Politics* 53: 35–58.

Abramson, Paul R., John H. Aldrich, and David W. Rohde. 2007. *Change and Continuity in the 2004 and 2006 Elections*. Washington, DC: CQ Press.

Achen, Christopher, and Richard Sinnott. 2007. "The Rational Learning Model." In *Voting Turnout in Multi-Level Systems*, eds Christopher Achen and Richard Sinnott. Typescript.

Ackerman, Bruce, and Ian Ayres. 2002. *Voting with Dollars: A New Paradigm for Campaign Finance*. New Haven, CT: Yale University Press.

Alcañiz, Isabella, and Timothy Hellwig. Forthcoming. "Who's to Blame? The Distribution of Responsibility in Developing Democracies." *British Journal of Political Science*.

Aldrich, John H. 1993. "Rational Choice and Turnout." *American Journal of Political Science* 37: 246–78.

Aldrich, John. 1995. *Why Parties?* Chicago, IL: University of Chicago Press.

Alexander, Herbert E. 2001. "Approaches to Campaign and Party Finance Issues." In *Foundations for Democracy: Approaches to Comparative Political Finance*, ed. Karl-Heinz Nassmacher. Baden-Baden: Nomos.

Alexander, Herbert E., and Rei Shiratori, eds 1994. *Comparative Political Finance among the Democracies*. Boulder, CO: Westview.

Almond, Gabriel, and Sidney Verba. 1963. *The Civic Culture*. Princeton, NJ: Princeton University Press.

Alt, James E., and David Dreyer Lassen. 2006. "Transparency, Political Polarization, and Political Budget Cycles in OECD Countries." *American Journal of Political Science* 50: 530–50.

Altheide, David L., and Robert P. Snow. 1979. *Media Logic*. Beverly Hills, CA: Sage.

Alvarez, R. Michael, and Jonathan Nagler. 1995. "Economics, Issues, and the Perot Candidacy: Voter Choice in the 1992 Election." *American Journal of Political Science* 39: 714–44.

Anderson, Christopher J. 1995. "The Dynamics of Support for Coalition Governments." *Comparative Political Studies* 28: 350–83.

Anderson, Christopher J. 2007. "The End of Economic Voting? Contingency Dilemmas and the Limits of Democratic Accountability." *Annual Review of Political Science* 10: 271–96.

Ansolabehere, Stephen D., Shanto Iyengar, and Adam Simon. 1999. "Replicating Experiments Using Aggregate and Survey Data: The Case of Negative Advertising and Turnout." *American Political Science Review* 93: 901–9.

Arceneaux, Kevin. 2005. "Do Campaigns Help Voters Learn: A Cross-National Analysis." *British Journal of Political Science* 36: 159–73.

Armony, Ariel C., and Hector E. Schamis. 2005. "Babel in Democratization Studies." *Journal of Democracy* 16: 113–28.

Asher, Herbert. 1998. *Polling and the Public: What Every Citizen Should Know*, 4th edn. Washington, DC: CQ Press.

Asp, Kent. 1983. "The Struggle for the Agenda: Party Agenda, Media Agenda, and Voter Agenda in the 1979 Swedish Election Campaign." *Communication Research* 10: 333–55.

Austin, Reginald, and Maja Tjernström. 2003. *Funding of Political Parties*. Stockholm: International Institute for Democracy and Electoral Assistance.

Aye, Joseph. 2000. *Deepening Democracy in Ghana*. Oxford: Freedom Publications.

Bakke, Elizabeth, and Nick Sitter. 2005. "Patterns of Stability: Competition and Strategy in Central Europe since 1989." *Party Politics* 11: 243–63.

Baldini, Gianfranco and Adriano Pappalardo. 2009. *Elections, Electoral Systems and Volatile Voters*. Basingstoke: Palgrave Macmillan.

Ballington, Julie, and Drude Dahlerup. 2006. "Gender Quotas in Post-Conflict States: East Timor, Afghanistan and Iraq." In *Women, Quotas and Politics*, ed. Drude Dahlerup. London: Routledge.

Ballington, Julie, and Azza Karam. 2005. *Women in Parliament: Beyond Numbers*, rev. edn. Stockholm: International Institute for Democracy and Electoral Assistance.

Banducci, Susan A., and Jeffrey A. Karp. 2003. "How Elections Change the Way Citizens View the Political System: Campaigns, Media Effects and Electoral Outcomes in Comparative Perspective." *British Journal of Political Science* 33: 443–67.

Bargsted, Matias. 2007. *Macro Level Data Codebook for CSES Module 1 and 3 Countries*. Available from the CSES website: www.cses.org

Barisione, Mauro. Forthcoming. "So, What Difference Do Leaders Make? Candidates' Images and the 'Conditionality' of Leader Effects on Voting." *Journal of Elections, Public Opinion and Parties*.

Barnes, Samuel H. 1977. *Representation in Italy: Institutionalized Tradition and Electoral Choice*. Chicago, IL: University of Chicago Press.

Barnes, Samuel, M. Kent Jennings, Ronald Inglehart, and Barbara Farash. 1988. "Party Identification and Party Closeness in Comparative Perspective." *Political Behavior* 10: 215–31.

Barro, Robert J. 1999. "Determinants of Democracy." *Journal of Political Economy* 107: 158–83.

Barry, Brian. 1978. *Sociologists, Economists, and Democracy*. Chicago, IL: University of Chicago Press.

Bartels, Larry M. 1988. *Presidential Primaries and the Dynamics of Public Choice*. Princeton, NJ: Princeton University Press.

Bartels, Larry M. 1996. "Uninformed Votes: Information Effects in Presidential Elections." *American Journal of Political Science* 40: 194–230.

Bartels, Larry M. 2000. "Partisanship and Voting Behavior, 1952–1996." *American Journal of Political Science* 44: 25–50.

Bartolini, Stefano. 2000. *The Political Mobilization of the European Left*. Cambridge: Cambridge University Press.

Bartolini, Stefano, and Peter Mair. 1990. *Identity, Competition and Electoral Availability*. Cambridge: Cambridge University Press.

Bell, Daniel. 1970. *The End of Ideology: On the Exhaustion of Political Ideas in the Fifties*. Glencoe, IL: Free Press.

Bell, Daniel. 2000. "The Resumption of History in the New Century." In Daniel Bell, *The End of Ideology*, rev. edn. Cambridge, MA: Harvard University Press.

Bennett, Stephen Earl, Staci L. Rhine, Richard S. Flickinger, and Linda L.M. Bennett. 1999. "'Video Malaise' Revisited: Public Trust in the Media and Government." *Harvard International Journal of Press/Politics* 4: 8–23.

Benoit, Kenneth. 2004. "Models of Electoral System Change." *Electoral Studies* 23: 363–89.

Benoit, Kenneth. 2005. "Hungary: Holding Back the Tiers." In *The Politics of Electoral Systems*, eds Michael Gallagher and Paul Mitchell. Oxford: Oxford University Press.

Benoit, Kenneth, and Michael Laver. 2006. *Party Policy in Modern Democracies*. London: Routledge.

Berelson, Bernard, Paul F. Lazarsfeld, and William N. McPhee. 1954. *Voting*. Chicago, IL: University of Chicago Press.

Berglund, Frode, Sören Holmberg, Hermann Schmitt, and Jacques Thomassen. 2005. "Party Identification and Party Choice." In *The European Voter*, ed. Jacques Thomassen. Oxford: Oxford University Press.

Birch, Sarah, Frances Millard, Marina Popescu, and Kieran Williams. 2002. *Embodying Democracy: Electoral System Design in Post-Communist Europe*. Houndmills, Basingstoke: Palgrave Macmillan.

Blais, André. 1988. "The Classification of Electoral Systems." *European Journal of Political Research* 16: 99–110.

Blais, André. 2000. *To Vote or Not to Vote: The Merits and Limits of Rational Choice Theory*. Pittsburgh, PA: University of Pittsburgh Press.

Blais, André. 2006. "What Affects Voter Turnout?" *Annual Review of Political Science* 9: 111–25.

Blais, André, and Kees Aarts. 2006. "Electoral Systems and Turnout." *Acta Politica* 41: 180–96.

Blais, André, and Marc A. Bodet. 2006. "Does Proportional Representation Foster Closer Congruence between Citizens and Policymakers?" *Comparative Political Studies* 9: 1243–63.

Blais, André, and R. Kenneth Carty. 1991. "The Psychological Impact of Electoral Laws: Measuring Duverger's Elusive Factor." *British Journal of Political Science* 21: 79–93.

Blais, André, and Agniezska Dobrzynska. 1998. "Turnout in Electoral Democracies." *European Journal of Political Research* 33: 239–61.

Blais, André, Agnieszka Dobrzynska, and Indridi Indridason. 2004. "To Adopt or Not to Adopt Proportional Representation: the Politics of Institutional Choice." *British Journal of Political Science* 35: 182–90.

Blais, André, Elisabeth Gidengil, Neil Nevitte, and Richard Nadeau. 2004. "Where Does Turnout Decline Come From?" *European Journal of Political Research* 43: 221–36.

Blais, André, Elisabeth Gidengil, Richard Nadeau, and Neil Nevitte. 2003. "Campaign Dynamics in the 2000 Canadian Election: How the Leader Debates Salvaged the Conservative Party." *PS: Political Science and Politics* 36: 45–50.

Blais, André, and Ignacio Lago. 2009. "A General Measure of District Competitiveness." *Electoral Studies* 28: 94–100.

Blais, André, and Louis Massicotte. 2002. "Electoral Systems." In *Comparing Democracies 2*, eds Lawrence LeDuc, Richard G. Niemi, and Pippa Norris. London and Thousand Oaks, CA: Sage.

Blaydes, Lisa, and Mark Andreas Kayser. 2008. "Counting Calories: Democracy and Distribution in the Developing World." Unpublished ms, University of Rochester.

Blechinger, Verena, and Karl-Heinz Nassmacher. 2001. "Political Finance in Non-Western Democracies: Japan and Israel." In *Foundations for Democracy: Approaches to Comparative Political Finance*, eds Karl-Heinz Nassmacher. Baden-Baden: Nomos.

Blondel, Jean. 1968. "Party Systems and Patterns of Government in Western Democracies." *Canadian Journal of Political Science* 1: 180–203.

Blumler, Jay G., and Michael Gurevitch. 1995. *The Crisis of Public Communication*. London: Routledge.

Blumler, Jay G., and Michael Gurevitch. 1998. "Change in the Air: Campaign Journalism at the BBC, 1997." In *Political Communication: Why Labour Won the General Election of 1997*, eds Ivor Crewe, Brian Gosschalk, and John Bartle. London: Frank Cass.

Blumler, Jay G., and Michael Gurevitch. 2000. "'Americanization' Reconsidered: UK–US Campaign Communication Comparisons across Time." In *Mediated Politics: Communication and the Future of Democracy*, eds L. Bennett and B. Entman. Cambridge: Cambridge University Press.

Boafo-Arthur Kwame, ed. 2007. *Ghana: One Decade of the Liberal State*. London: Zed Books.

Boas, Taylor. 2008. "Varieties of Electioneering: Success Contagion and Presidential Campaigns in Latin America." Paper presented at the annual meeting of the American Political Science Association, Boston, MA.

Bogdanor, Vernon. 1983. "Introduction." In *Democracy and Elections: Electoral Systems and Their Political Consequences*, eds Vernon Bogdanor and David Butler. Cambridge: Cambridge University Press.

Boix, Carles. 1999. "Setting the Rules of the Game: The Choice of Electoral Systems in Advanced Democracies." *American Political Science Review* 93: 609–24.

Bollen, Kenneth A. 1990. "Political Democracy: Conceptual and Measurement Traps." *Studies in International Development* 25: 7–24.

Bowler, Shaun, Elisabeth Carter, and David Farrell. 2003. "Changing Party Access to Elections." In *Democracy Transformed? Expanding Political Opportunities in Advanced Industrial Democracies*, eds Bruce Cain, Russell J. Dalton, and Susan Scarrow. Oxford: Oxford University Press.

Bowler, Shaun, Todd Donovan, and David Brockington. 2003. *Electoral Reform and Minority Representation: Local Experiments with Alternative Elections*. Columbus, OH: Ohio State University Press.

Bowler, Shaun, and David M. Farrell, eds 1992. *Electoral Strategies and Political Marketing*. London: St. Martin's Press.

Bowler, Shaun, and David Farrell. 2008. "Just Because They Are 'Second-order' Doesn't Mean You Can Put Your Feet Up: Campaign Activity in European Parliament Elections." *DCERN Working Paper*, University of Manchester. www.dcern.org.uk/research/working_papers/index.htm

Bowler, Shaun, David M. Farrell, and Richard S. Katz, eds 1999. *Party Discipline and Parliamentary Government*. Columbus, OH: Ohio State University Press.

Bowler, Shaun, and Bernard Grofman, eds 2000. *Elections in Australia, Ireland, and Malta under the Single Transferable Vote*. Ann Arbor, MI: University of Michigan Press.

Brader, Ted, and Joshua Tucker. 2001. "The Emergence of Mass Partisanship in Russia, 1993–1996." *American Journal of Political Science* 45: 69–83.

Brady, Henry E., and Richard Johnston, eds 2006. *Capturing Campaign Effects*. Ann Arbor, MI: University of Michigan Press.

Brady, Henry E., Sidney Verba, and Kay Lehman Schlozman. 1995. "Beyond SES: A Resource Model of Political Participation." *American Political Science Review* 89: 271–95.

Bratton, Michael, Robert Mattes, and E. Gyimah-Boadil. 2004. *Public Opinion, Democracy, and Market Reform in Africa*. New York: Cambridge University Press.

Bratton, Michael, and Nicolas Van de Walle. 1997. *Democratic Experiments in Africa*. Cambridge: Cambridge University Press.

Briffault, Richard. 2006. "Soft Money, Congress and the Supreme Court." In *Party Funding and Campaign Financing in International Perspective*, eds K.D. Ewing and Samuel Issacharoff. Oxford and Portland, OR: Hart Publishing.

Brownlee, Jason. 2007. *Authoritarianism in an Age of Democratization*. New York: Cambridge University Press.

Brudny, Yitzhak M. 1997. "In Pursuit of the Russian Presidency: Why and How Yeltsin Won the 1996 Presidential Election." *Communist and Post-Communist Studies* 30: 255–75.

Budge, Ian, Ivor Crewe, and Dennis J. Farlie. 1976. *Party Identification and Beyond*. New York: Wiley.

Budge, Ian, and Dennis Farlie. 1983. *Explaining and Predicting Elections: Issue Effects and Party Strategies in Twenty-three Democracies*. London: George Allen and Unwin.

Budge, Ian, Hans-Dieter Klingemann, Andrea Volkens, Judith Bara, and Eric Tanenbaum. 2001. *Mapping Policy Preferences*. New York: Oxford University Press.

Bunce, Valerie. 2003. "Rethinking Recent Democratization: Lessons from the Postcommunist Experience." *World Politics* 55: 167–92.

Burnell, Peter. 2005. "Political Strategies of External Support for Democratization." *Foreign Policy Analysis* 1: 361–84.

Butler, David and Austin Ranney. 1992. *Electioneering: A Comparative Study of Continuity and Change*. Oxford: Clarendon Press.

Cain, Bruce E., John A. Ferejohn, and Morris P. Fiorina. 1984. "The Constituency Service Basis of the Personal Vote for U.S. Representatives and British Members of Parliament." *American Political Science Review* 78: 110–25.

Campbell, Angus, Philip Converse, Warren E. Miller, and Donald E. Stokes. 1960. *The American Voter*. New York: Wiley.

Campbell, David E. 2006. *Why We Vote: How Schools and Communities Shape Our Civic Life*. Princeton, NJ: Princeton University Press.

Campbell, James E. 2000. *The American Campaign: U.S. Presidential Campaigns and the National Vote*. College Station: Texas A&M University Press.

Campbell, James E., and James C. Garand. 2000. *Before the Vote: Forecasting American National Elections*. Thousand Oaks, CA: Sage.

Campbell, Rosie, Sarah Childs, and Joni Lovenduski. 2007. "Do Women Need Women MPs?" Paper to ECPR Workshop on Substantive Representation, Helsinki.

Cappella, Joseph N., and Kathleen Hall Jamieson. 1997. *Spiral of Cynicism: The Press and the Public Good*. New York: Oxford University Press.

Caramani, Daniele. 2005. "The Formation of National Party Systems in Europe: A Comparative-Historical Analysis." *Scandinavian Political Studies* 28: 295–322.

Carothers, Thomas. 2002. "The End of the Transition Paradigm." *Journal of Democracy* 13: 5–21.

Carroll, Susan J. 2002. "Have Women Legislators in the United States Become More Conservative? A Comparison of State Legislators in 2001 and 1988." *Atlantis* 27: 128–39.

Carstairs, Andrew McLaren. 1980. *A Short History of Electoral Systems in Western Europe*. London: George, Allen and Unwin.

Casas-Zamora, Kevin. 2005. *Paying for Democracy: Political Finance and State Funding for Parties*. Colchester: ECPR Press.

Castles, Francis, and Peter Mair. 1984. "Left–Right Political Scales: Some 'Expert' Judgments." *European Journal of Political Research* 12: 73–88.

Caul, Miki. 2001. "Political Parties and the Adoption of Candidate Gender Quotas: A Cross-National Analysis." *Journal of Politics* 63: 1214–29.

Chazan, Naomi, Peter Lewis, Robert Mortimer, Donald Rothchild, and Steven Stedman. 1999. *Politics and Society in Contemporary Africa*. Boulder, CO: Lynne Rienner.

Cheibub, Jose Antonio and Adam Przeworski. 1999. "Democracy, Elections and Accountability for Economic Outcomes." In *Democracy, Accountability and Representation*, eds Adam Przeworski, Susan C. Stokes and Bernard Manin. New York: Cambridge University Press.

Cheibub, Jose, and Jennifer Gandhi. 2004. "A Six-fold Measure of Democracies and Dictatorships." Paper presented at the annual meeting of the American Political Science Association.

Chhibber, Pradeep. 1999. *Democracy without Associations*. Ann Arbor, MI: University of Michigan Press.

Chhibber, Pradeep, and Ken Kollman. 2004. *The Formation of National Party Systems: Federalism and Party Competition in Canada, Great Britain, India and the United States*. Princeton, NJ: Princeton University Press.

Chhibber, Pradeep, and Geetha Murali. 2006. "Duvergerian Dynamics in the Indian States: Federalism and the Number of Parties in the State Assembly Elections." *Party Politics* 12: 5–34.

Childs, Sara, and Mona Lena Krook. 2006. "Should Feminists Give Up on Critical Mass? A Contingent Yes." *Politics and Gender* 2: 522–30.

Clarke, Harold, Allan Kornberg, and Thomas J. Scotto. 2009. *Making Political Choices: Canada and the United States*. Toronto: University of Toronto Press.

Clarke, Harold, David Sanders, Marianne Stewart and Paul Whiteley. 2004. *Political Choice in Britain*. Oxford: Oxford University Press.

Clarke, Harold, David Sanders, Marianne Stewart and Paul Whiteley. 2008. Special Issue on Internet Surveys and National Election Studies. *Journal of Elections, Public Opinion and Parties* 18: 325–448.

Clarke, Harold D., and Marianne Stewart. 1998. "The Decline of Parties in the Minds of Citizens." *Annual Review of Political Science* 1: 357–78.

Clarke, Harold D., Marianne C. Stewart, Mike Ault, and Euel Elliott. 2004. "Men, Women, and the Dynamics of Presidential Approval." *British Journal of Political Science* 35: 31–51.

Collier, David, and Robert Adcock. 1999. "Democracy and Dichotomies: A Pragmatic Approach to Choices about Concepts." *Annual Review of Political Science* 1: 537–65.

Colomer, Josep M. 2001. *Political Institutions*. Oxford: Oxford University Press.

Colomer, Josep, ed. 2004. *Handbook of Electoral System Choice*. London: Palgrave.

Colomer, Josep. 2005. "It's Parties that Choose Electoral Systems or, Duverger's Laws Upside Down." *Political Studies* 53: 1–21.

Colton, Timothy J., and Michael McCaul. 2003. *Popular Choice and Managed Democracy*. Washington, DC: Brookings.

CEDAW (Committee on the Elimination of Discrimination against Women). 1997. General Recommendation No. 23. http://www.un.org/womenwatch/daw/cedaw/recommendations (accessed 8 January 2009).

Converse, Philip E. 1964. "The Nature of Belief Systems in Mass Publics." In *Ideology and Discontent*, ed. David Apter. New York: Free Press.

Converse, Philip E., and Roy Pierce. 1986. *Political Representation in France*. Cambridge, MA: Harvard University Press.

Cox, Gary. 1987. *The Efficient Secret*. Cambridge: Cambridge University Press.

Cox, Gary W. 1997. *Making Votes Count: Strategic Coordination in the World's Electoral Systems*. Cambridge: Cambridge University Press.

Cross, William. 2005. "The Rush to Electoral Reform in the Canadian Provinces: Why Now?" *Representation* 41: 75–84.

Curtin, Jennifer. 2008a. "Gendering Parliamentary Representation: A Mixed System Producing Mixed Results?" In *Women and Legislative Representation: Electoral Systems, Political Parties and Sex Quotas*, ed. Manon Tremblay. Houndmills, Basingstoke: Palgrave Macmillan.

Curtin, Jennifer. 2008b. "Women, Political Leadership and the Substantive Representation of Women." *Parliamentary Affairs* 61: 490–504.

D'Alessio, Dave, and Mike Allen. 2000. "Media Bias in Presidential Elections: A Meta-analysis." *Journal of Communication* 50: 133–56.

D'Angelo, Paul. 2002. "News Framing as a Multiparadigmatic Research Program: A Response to Entman." *Journal of Communication* 52: 870–88.

Dahl, Robert A. 1989. *Democracy and Its Critics*. New Haven, CT: Yale University Press.

Dahl, Robert A. 1966. "Patterns of Opposition." In *Political Oppositions in Western Democracies*, ed. Robert Dahl. New Haven, CT: Yale University Press.

Dahlerup, Drude. 1988. "From a Small to a Large Minority: Women in Scandinavian Politics." *Scandinavian Political Studies* 11: 275–97.

Dahlerup, Drude, ed. 2006. *Women, Quotas and Politics*. London: Routledge.

Dalton, Russell. 1985. "Political Parties and Political Representation: Party Supporters and Party Elites in Nine Nations." *Comparative Political Studies* 18: 267–99.

Dalton, Russell. 2002. "The Decline of Party Identifications." In *Parties without Partisans: Political Change in Advanced Industrial Democracies*, eds Russell Dalton and Martin Wattenberg. Oxford: Oxford University Press.

Dalton, Russell. 2006a. "Social Modernization and the *End of Ideology* Debate: Patterns of Ideological Polarization." *Japanese Journal of Political Science* 7: 1–22

Dalton, Russell. 2006b. *Citizen Politics: Public Opinion and Political Parties in Advanced Industrial Democracies*, 5th edn. Washington, DC: CQ Press.

Dalton, Russell. 2007a. "Partisan Mobilization, Cognitive Mobilization and the Changing American Electorate." *Electoral Studies* 26: 274–86.

Dalton, Russell. 2007b. *The Good Citizen: How a Younger Generation is Reshaping American Politics*. Washington, DC: CQ Press.

Dalton, Russell. 2008. "The Quantity and the Quality of Party Systems: Party System Polarization, Its Measurement and Its Consequences." *Comparative Political Studies* 41: 899–920.

Dalton, Russell J., and Martin Wattenberg, eds 2000. *Parties without Partisans: Political Change in Advanced Industrial Democracies*. Oxford: Oxford University Press.

Dalton, Russell J., and Steven A. Weldon. 2005. "Public Images of Political Parties: A Necessary Evil?" *West European Politics* 28: 931–51.

Dalton, Russell, and Steven Weldon. 2006. "Partisan Attachments in New and Old Democracies." *Party Politics* 13: 179–96.

Dalton, Russell, and Steven Weldon. 2007. "Partisanship and Party System Institutionalization." *Party Politics* 13: 179–96.

Darras, Eric. 2008. "Free Journalism under Control: Election Coverage in France." In *Handbook of Election News Coverage around the World*, eds Jesper Strömback and Lynda Lee Kaid. London: Routledge.

Davenport, Christian. 2007. *State Repression and the Domestic Democratic Peace*. New York: Cambridge University Press.

Dawood, Yasmin. 2006. "Democracy, Power, and the Supreme Court: Campaign Finance Reform in Comparative Context." *International Journal of Constitutional Law* 4: 269–93.

De Vreese, Claes H. 2001. "Election Coverage – New Directions for Public Broadcasting: The Netherlands and Beyond." *European Journal of Communication* 16: 155–80.

De Vreese, Claes H. 2002. *Framing Europe: Television News and European Integration*. Amsterdam: Aksant/Transaction.

De Vreese, Claes H. 2009a. "Second-rate Election Campaigning? An Analysis of Campaign Styles in European Parliamentary Elections." *Journal of Political Marketing*, 8 (1), 7–19.

De Vreese, Claes H. 2009b. "Framing the Economy: Effects of Journalistic News Frames." In *Doing Framing Research*, ed. Paul d'Angelo and Jim Kuipers. London: Routledge.

De Vreese, Claes H., Susan A. Banducci, Holli A. Semetko, and Hajo G. Boomgaarden. 2006a. "The News Coverage of the 2004 European Parliamentary Election Campaign in 25 Countries." *European Union Politics* 7: 477–504.

De Vreese, Claes H., and Hajo G. Boomgaarden. 2006b. "How Content Moderates the Effects of Television News on Political Knowledge and Engagement." *Acta Politica: International Journal of Political Science* 41: 317–41.

De Vreese, Claes H., Jochen Peter, and Holli A. Semetko. 2001. "Framing Politics at the Launch of the Euro: A Cross-National Comparative Study of Frames in the News." *Political Communication* 18: 107–122.

De Vreese, Claes H., and Holli A. Semetko. 2004. "News Matters: Influences on the Vote in the Danish 2000 Euro Referendum Campaign." *European Journal of Political Research* 43: 699–722.

Deegan-Krause, Kevin. 2007. "New Dimensions of Political Cleavage." In *Oxford Handbook of Political Behavior*, eds Russell Dalton and Hans-Dieter Klingemann. Oxford: Oxford University Press.

Denny, Kevin, and Orla Doyle. 2009. "Does Voting History Matter? Analyzing Persistence in Turnout." *American Journal of Political Science*. 53: 17–35.

Denver, David, and Gordon Hands. 1997. *Modern Constituency Electioneering*. London: Frank Cass.

Diamond, Larry. 1996. *Developing Democracy: Toward Consolidation*. Baltimore, MD: Johns Hopkins University Press.

Diamond, Larry. 2002. "Thinking about Hybrid Regimes." *Journal of Democracy* 13: 21–35.

Diamond, Larry. 2008. The Spirit of Democracy: The Struggle to Build Free Societies throughout the World. New York: Times Books.

Dix, Robert. 1989. "Cleavage Structures and Party Systems in Latin America." *Comparative Politics* 22: 23–37.

Downs, Anthony. 1957. *An Economic Theory of Democracy*. New York: Harper and Row.

Dreher, Axel, Noel Gaston, and Pim Martens. 2008. *Measuring Globalization – Gauging Its Consequences*. New York: Springer.

Drew, Dan, and David Weaver. 2006. "Voter Learning in the 2004 Presidential Election: Did the Media Matter?" *Journalism and Mass Communication Quarterly* 83: 25–42.

Dreze, Jean, and Amartya Sen. 1989. *Hunger and Public Action*. New York, NY: Oxford University Press.

Duch, Raymond M., and Randy Stevenson. 2008. *The Economic Vote: How Political and Economic Institutions Condition Election Results*. Cambridge: Cambridge University Press.

Duverger, Maurice. 1959 [1954]. *Political Parties: Their Organization and Activity in the Modern State* (revised 2nd edn). trans. Barbara and Robert North. New York: Wiley.

Duverger, Maurice. 1980. "A New Political System Model: Semi-Presidential Government." *European Journal of Political Research* 8: 165–87.

Edlin, Aron, Andrew Gelman, and Noha Kaplan. 2007. "Voting as a Rational Choice: Why and How People Vote to Improve the Well-Being of Others." *Rationality and Society* 19: 293–314.

Ejima, Akiko. 2006. "Revisiting Transparency and Disclosure in Japanese Political Reform." In *Party Funding and Campaign Financing in International Perspective*, ed. K.D. Ewing and Samuel Issacharoff. Oxford and Portland, OR: Hart Publishing.

Eke, S.M. 2000. "Sultanism in Eastern Europe: The Socio-political Roots of Authoritarian Populism in Belarus." *Europe-Asia Studies* 52: 523.

Elkins, Zachary. 2000. "Gradations of Democracy? Empirical Tests of Alternative Conceptualizations." *American Journal of Political Science* 44: 293–300.

Epstein, Leon. 1967. *Political Parties in Western Democracies* (rev. edn. 1980). New Brunswick, NJ: Transaction Publishers.

Erickson, Lynda. 1997. "Might More Women Make a Difference? Gender, Party and Ideology among Canada's Parliamentary Candidates." *Canadian Journal of Political Science* 30: 663–88.

Erikson, Robert S., Michael B. MacKuen, and James A. Stimson. 2002. *The Macro Polity*. Cambridge: Cambridge University Press.

Erikson, Robert S., Costas Panagopoulos, and Christopher Wlezien. 2004. "Likely and Unlikely Voters and the Assessment of Campaign Dynamics." *Public Opinion Quarterly* 68: 588–601.

Erikson, Robert S., and Lee Sigelman. 1996. "Poll-Based Forecasts of the House Vote in Presidential Election Years." *American Politics Research* 24: 520–31.

Erikson, Robert S., and Christopher Wlezien. 2008. "Leading Economic Indicators, the Polls and the Presidential Vote." *PS: Political Science and Politics* 41: 703–7.

Esmer, Yilmaz, and Thorleif Pettersson. 2007. "The Effects of Religion and Religiosity on Voting Behavior." In *Oxford Handbook of Political Behavior*, eds Russell Dalton and Hans-Dieter Klingemann. Oxford: Oxford University Press.

Esser, Frank, and Paul D'Angelo. 2006. "Framing the Press and Publicity Process in U.S., British, and German General Election Campaigns: A Comparative Study of Metacoverage." *Harvard International Journal of Press/Politics* 11: 44–66.

Esser, Frank, and Katharina Hemmer. 2008. "Characteristics and Dynamics of Election News Coverage in Germany." In *Handbook of Election News Coverage around the World*, eds Jesper Strömback and Lynda Lee Kaid. London: Routledge.

Esser, Frank, Carsten Reinemann, and David Fan. 2000. "Spin Doctoring in British and German Election Campaigns: How the Press is Being Confronted with a New Quality of Political PR." *European Journal of Communication* 15: 209–39.

Evans, Geoffrey, and Robert Andersen. 2005. "The Impact of Party Leaders: How Blair Lost Labour Votes." In *Britain Votes*, eds Pippa Norris and Christopher Wlezien. Oxford: Oxford University Press.

Evans, Geoffrey, and Robert Andersen. 2006. "The Political Conditioning of Economic Perceptions." *Journal of Politics* 68: 194–207.

Evans, Geoffrey. 2006. "The Social Bases of Political Divisions in Post-Communist Eastern Europe." *Annual Review of Sociology* 32: 245–70.

Ewing, K.D. 2002. *Trade Unions, the Labour Party and Political Funding*. London: Catalyst Press.

Ezrow, Lawrence. 2007. "The Variance Matters: How Party Systems Represent the Preferences of Voters." *Journal of Politics* 69: 182–192.

Farrell, David M. 1996. "Campaign Strategies and Tactics." In *Comparing Democracies: Elections and Voting in Global Perspective*, eds Lawrence LeDuc, Richard G. Niemi, and Pippa Norris. Thousand Oaks, CA: Sage.

Farrell, David. 2001a. *Electoral Systems: A Comparative Introduction*. Houndmills, Basingstoke: Palgrave Macmillan.

Farrell, David. 2001b. "The United Kingdom Comes of Age: The British Electoral Reform 'Revolution' of the 1990s." In *Mixed-Member Electoral Systems: The Best of Both Worlds?* ed. Matthew Shugart and Martin Wattenberg. Oxford: Oxford University Press.

Farrell, David. 2010. *Electoral Systems: A Comparative Introduction*, 2nd edn. Houndmills, Basingstoke: Palgrave Macmillan.

Farrell, David, and Ian McAllister. 2006. *The Australian Electoral System: Origins, Variations and Consequences*. Sydney: University of New South Wales Press.

Farrell, David M., and Rudiger Schmitt-Beck, eds 2002. *Do Political Campaigns Matter? Campaign Effects in Elections and Referenda*. London: Routledge.

Farrell, David, and Roger Scully. 2007. *Representing Europe's Citizens? Electoral Institutions and the Failure of Parliamentary Representation*. Oxford: Oxford University Press.

Farrell, David, and Paul Webb. 2000. "Political Parties as Campaign Organisations." In *Parties without Partisans*, ed. Russell J. Dalton and Martin Wattenberg. Oxford: Oxford University Press.

Farrell, Henry, and Daniel Drezner. 2008. "The Power and Politics of Blogs." *Public Choice* 134: 15–30.

Fearon, James D. 1999. "Electoral Accountability and the Control of Politicians: Selecting Good Types versus Sanctioning Poor Performance." In *Democracy, Accountability, and Representation*, eds Adam Przeworski, Susan Stokes, and Bernard Manin. Cambridge: Cambridge University Press.

Feasby, Colin. 2006. "The Supreme Court of Canada's Political Theory and the Constitutionality of the Political Finance Regime." In *Party Funding and Campaign Financing in International Perspective*, eds K.D. Ewing and Samuel Issacharoff. Oxford and Portland, OR: Hart Publishing.

Feldman, Stanley. 1982. "Economic Self-Interest and Political Behavior." *American Journal of Political Science* 26: 446–66.

Fenno, Richard F. 1978. *Home Style: House Members in Their Districts*. Boston, MA: Little, Brown.

Ferdinand, Peter. 1998. "Building Democracy on the Basis of Capitalism: Towards an East Asian Model of Party Funding." In *Funding Democratization*, eds Peter Burnell and Alan Ware. Manchester: Manchester University Press.

Ferejohn, John. 1986. "Incumbent Performance and Electoral Control." *Public Choice* 50: 5–25.

Finkel, Steven E., Edward N. Muller, and Karl-Dieter Opp. 1989. "Personal Influence, Collective Rationality and Mass Political Action." *American Political Science Review* 83: 885–903.

Fiorina, Morris. 1981. *Retrospective Voting in American National Elections*. New Haven, CT: Yale University Press.

Fisher, Justin, and Todd A. Eisenstadt. 2004. "Introduction: Comparative Party Finance. What Is to Be Done?" *Party Politics* 10: 619–26.

Fisher, Justin, David Denver, and Gordon Hands. 2005. "The Relative Electoral Impact of Central Party Co-ordination and Size of Party Membership at Constituency Level." *Electoral Studies* 25: 664–76.

Flanagan, Scott, Shinsaku Kohei, Ichiro Miyake, Bradley M. Richardson, and Joji Watanuki. 1991. *The Japanese Voter*. New Haven, CT: Yale University Press.

Fornos, Carolina A., Timothy J. Power, and James C. Garand. 2004. "Explaining Voter Turnout in Latin America, 1980–2000." *Comparative Political Studies* 37: 909–40.

Fournier, Patrick, Richard Nadeau, Andre Blais, Elisabeth Gidengil, and Neil Nevitte. 2004. "Time of Voting Decision and Susceptibility to Campaign Effects." *Electoral Studies* 23: 661–81.

Fowler, James H. 2006. "Altruism and Turnout." *Journal of Politics* 68: 674–83.

Fowler, James, Laura A. Baker, and Christopher T. Dawes. 2008. "Genetic Variation in Political Participation." *American Political Science Review* 102: 233–48.

Fowler, James H., and Christopher T. Dowes. 2008. "Two Genes Predict Voter Turnout." *Journal of Politics* 70: 579–94.

Fowler, James H., and Cindy D. Kam. 2007. "Beyond the Self: Altruism, Social Identity, and Political Participation." *Journal of Politics* 69: 813–27.

Fowler, James H., and Oleg Smirnov. 2007. *Mandates, Parties, and Voters: How Elections Shape the Future*. Philadelphia, PA: Temple University Press.

Franklin, Mark N. 2004. *Voter Turnout and the Dynamics of Electoral Competition in Established Democracies since 1945*. New York: Cambridge University Press.

Franklin, Mark, Tom Mackie, and Henry Valen, eds 1992. *Electoral Change*. New York, NY: Cambridge University Press.

Frear, M. 2008. "The Lukashenka Phenomenon: Elections, Propaganda and the Foundations of Political Authority in Belarus." *Europe–Asia Studies* 60: 1274–6.

Freedman, Paul, Michael Franz, and Kenneth Goldstein. 2004. "Campaign Advertising and Democratic Citizenship." *American Journal of Political Science* 48: 723–41.

Freedom House. 2008a. *Freedom in the World 2008.* Washington, DC: Freedom House. http://www.freedomhouse.org

Freedom House. 2008b. "Freedom of the Press World Ranking." www.freedomhouse. org/template.cfm?page=251&year=2008 (accessed 15.03.2009).

Freedom House. 2009. *Freedom in the World 2009.* Washington, DC: Freedom House. www.freedomhouse.org

Fuchs, Dieter, and Hans-Dieter Klingemann. 1989. "The Left–Right Schema." In *Continuities in Political Action,* ed M. Kent Jennings and Jan van Deth. Berlin: de Gruyter.

Gaines, Brian. 1999. "Duverger's Law and Canadian Exceptionalism." *Comparative Political Studies* 32: 835–61.

Gallagher, Michael. 1991. "Proportionality, Disproportionality and Electoral Systems." *Electoral Studies* 10: 33–51.

Gallagher, Michael and Paul Mitchell, eds 2005. *The Politics of Electoral Systems.* Oxford: Oxford University Press.

Gambetta, Diego. 2002. "Corruption: An Analytical Map." In *Political Corruption in Transition: A Sceptic's Handbook,* ed. Stephen Kotkin and András Sajó. Budapest: Central European University Press.

Geddes, Barbara. 1999. "What Do We Know about Democratization after Twenty Years?" *Annual Review of Political Science* 2: 115–44.

Geer, John. 1998. *In Defense of Negativity.* Chicago, IL: Chicago University Press.

Gelman, Andrew, and Gary King. 1993. "Why are American Presidential Election Polls so Variable When Votes are so Predictable?" *British Journal of Political Science* 23: 409–51.

Gelman, Andrew, and Gary King. 1994. "Enhancing Democracy through Legislative Redistricting." *American Political Science Review* 88: 541–59.

Gerber, Alan, and Donald Green. 2004. *Get Out the Vote: How to Increase Voter Turnout.* Washington, DC: Brookings.

Gerber, Alan S., Donald P. Green, and Ron Shachar. 2003. "Voting May Be Habit-Forming: Evidence from a Randomized Field Experiment." *American Journal of Political Science* 47: 540–50.

Gibson, Rachel K., and Ian McAllister. 2006. "Does Cyber-Campaigning Win Votes? Online Communication in the 2004 Australian Election." *Journal of Elections, Public Opinion and Parties* 16: 243–63.

Gibson, Rachel K., Michael Margolis, David Resnick, and Stephen J. Ward. 2003. "Election Campaigning on the WWW in the USA and UK: A Comparative Analysis." *Party Politics* 9: 47–75.

Gibson, Rachel, Paul Nixon, and Stephen Ward, eds 2003. *Political Parties and the Internet – Net Gain?* London: Routledge.

Gidlund, Gullan, and Ruud Koole. 2001. "Political Finance in the North of Europe: The Netherlands and Sweden." In *Foundations for Democracy: Approaches to Comparative Political Finance,* ed. Karl-Heinz Nassmacher. Baden-Baden: Nomos.

Gillespie, Richard. 1998. "Party Funding in a New Democracy: Spain." In *Funding Democratization,* eds Peter Burnell and Alan Ware. Manchester: Manchester University Press.

Githens, Marianne. 2003. "Accounting for Women's Political Involvement: The Perennial Problem of Recruitment." In *Women and American Politics*, ed. Susan J. Carroll. *New Questions, New Directions*. Oxford: Oxford University Press.

Goetz, Anne-Marie, and Shireen Hassim. 2002. "In and Against the Party: Women's Representation and Constituency Building in Uganda and South Africa." In *Gender, Justice, Development and Rights*, eds Maxine Molyneux and Shahrashoub Razavi. Oxford: Oxford University Press.

Golder, Matt, and Jacek Stramski. 2007. "Ideological Congruence and Two Visions of Democracy." Paper presented at the annual meeting of the American Political Science Association, Chicago.

Golder, Matt and Jacek Stramski. Forthcoming. *American Journal of Political Science* 54.

Golder, Sona. 2006a. "Pre-Electoral Coalition Formation in Parliamentary Democracies." *British Journal of Political Science* 36: 193–212.

Golder, Sona Nadenichek. 2006b. *The Logic of Pre-Electoral Coalition Formation.* Columbus, OH: Ohio State University Press.

Gomez, Brad T., and J. Matthew Wilson. 2001. "Political Sophistication and Economic Voting in the American Electorate." *American Journal of Political Science* 45: 899–914.

Gomez, Brad T., and J. Matthew Wilson. 2006. "Cognitive Heterogeneity and Economic Voting: A Comparative Analysis of Four Democratic Electorates." *American Journal of Political Science* 50: 127–45.

Goodin, Robert, ed. 1996. *The Theory of Institutional Design.* Cambridge: Cambridge University Press.

Granberg, Donald, and Sören Holmberg. 1988. *The Political System Matters: Social Psychology and Voting Behavior in Sweden and the United States.* New York, NY: Cambridge University Press.

Grant, Alan. 2005. "Party and Election Finance in Britain and America: A Comparative Analysis." *Parliamentary Affairs* 58: 71–88.

Green, Donald, Sunshine Hillygus, John Sides, and Daron Shaw. 2008. "The Influence of Television and Radio Advertising on Candidate Evaluation: Results from a Large-Scale Randomized Experiment." Paper presented at the annual meeting of the Midwest Political Science Association, Chicago, IL.

Green, Donald, Bradley Palmquist, and Eric Schickler. 2002. *Partisan Hearts and Minds: Political Parties and the Social Identities of Voters.* New Haven, CT: Yale University Press.

Grey, Sandra. 2002. "Does Size Matter? Critical Mass and New Zealand's Women MPs." *Parliamentary Affairs* 55: 19–29.

Griner, Steven, and Daniel Zovatto, eds 2005. *The Delicate Balance between Political Equality and Freedom of Expression: Political Party and Campaign Financing in Canada and the United States.* Washington, DC: Organization of American States and International IDEA.

Grofman, Bernard, Sung-Chull Lee, Edwin Winckler, and Brian Woodall, eds 1999. *Elections in Japan, Korea and Taiwan under the Single Non-Transferable Vote: The Comparative Study of an Embedded Institution.* Ann Arbor, MI: University of Michigan Press.

Gryzymala-Busse, Anna. 2006. "Authoritarian Determinants of Democratic Party Competition." *Party Politics* 12: 415–37.

Gunther, Richard, and Anthony Mughan, eds 2000. *Democracy and the Media: A Comparative Perspective.* Cambridge: Cambridge University Press.

Gurevitch, Michael, and Jay G. Blumler. 1993. "Longitudinal Analysis of an Election Communication System: Newsroom Observation at the BBC, 1966–92." *Oesterreichische Zeitschrift für Politikwissenschaft* 22: 427–44.

Hagen, Michael, and Robin Kolodny. 2008 "Slicing and Dicing the Electorate: Heterogeneity and Campaign Strategy." Paper presented at the conference on Homogeneity and Heterogeneity of Public Opinion. Ithaca, NY: October.

Hagopian, Frances. 1998. "Democracy and Political Representation in Latin America in the 1990s." In *Fault Lines of Democracy in Post-Transition Latin America*, eds Felipe Agüero and Jeffrey Stark. Coral Gables, FL: North/South Center Press, University of Miami.

Hallin, Daniel C. 1992. "Sound Bite News: Television Coverage of Elections, 1968–1988." *Journal of Communication* 42: 5–24.

Hallin, Daniel C., and Paolo Mancini. 2004. *Comparing Media Systems: Three Models of Media and Politics*. Cambridge: Cambridge University Press.

"Has Labour Kept Its Promises?" BBC News, May 3, 2002, http://news.bbc.co.uk/1/hi/uk_politics/1961522.stm

Hazan, Reuven. 2001. "The Israeli Mixed Electoral System: Unexpected Reciprocal and Cumulative Consequences." In *Mixed-Member Electoral Systems*, eds Matthew Shugart and Martin Wattenberg. Oxford: Oxford University Press.

Hellwig, Timothy, Eve Ringsmuth, and John R. Freeman. 2008. "The American Public and the Room to Maneuver: Responsibility Attributions and Policy Efficacy in an Era of Globalization." *International Studies Quarterly* 52: 855–80.

Hellwig, Timothy, and David Samuels. 2007. "Voting in Open Economies: The Electoral Consequences of Globalization." *Comparative Political Studies* 40: 283–306.

Hellwig, Timothy, and David Samuels. 2008. "Electoral Accountability and the Variety of Democratic Regimes." *British Journal of Political Science* 38: 65–90.

Hibbing, John R., and Elizabeth Theiss-Morse. 2002. *Stealth Democracy: Americans' Beliefs about How Government Should Work*. Cambridge: Cambridge University Press.

Hibbs, Douglas A., Jr. 1977. "Political Parties and Macroeconomic Policy." *American Political Science Review* 71: 1467–87.

Hicken, Allen. 2006. "Stuck in the Mud: Parties and Party Systems in Democratic Southeast Asia." *Taiwan Journal of Democracy* 2: 23–46.

Hillygus, D. Sunshine. 2005. "Campaign Effects and the Dynamics of Turnout Intention in Election 2000." *Journal of Politics* 67: 50–68.

Hobolt, Sara Binzer. 2005. "When Europe Matters: The Impact of Political Information on Voting Behaviour in EU Referendums." *Journal of Elections, Public Opinion and Parties* 15: 85–109.

Holbrook, Thomas. 1996. *Do Campaigns Matter?* Thousand Oaks, CA: Sage.

Holmberg, Sören. 2000. "Issue Agreement." In *Beyond Westminster and Congress: The Nordic Experience,* eds Peter Esaiasson and Knut Heidar. Columbus, OH: Ohio State University Press.

Holmberg, Sören. 2007. "Partisanship Reconsidered." In *Oxford Handbook of Political Behavior*, eds Russell J. Dalton and Hans-Dieter Klingemann. Oxford: Oxford University Press.

Hopkin, Jonathan. 2004. "The Problem with Party Finance: Theoretical Perspectives on the Funding of Party Politics." *Party Politics* 10: 627–51.

Horowitz, Donald. 2000. *Ethnic Groups in Conflict: Theories, Patterns, and Policies*, 2nd edn. Berkeley, CA: University of California Press.

Howard, Morje Marc, and Philip G. Roessler. 2006. "Liberalizing Electoral Outcomes in Competitive Authoritarian Regimes." *American Journal of Political Science* 50: 365–81.

Huber, Gregory, and Kevin Arceneaux. 2008. "Uncovering the Persuasive Effects of Presidential Advertising." *American Journal of Political Science* 51: 957–77.

Huber, John D., and G. Bingham Powell. 1994. "Congruence between Citizens and Policymakers in Two Visions of Liberal Democracy." *World Politics* 46: 291–326.

Huff, Barbara. 2003. "No Lessons Learned from the Holocaust? Assessing Risks of Genocide and Political Mass Murder since 1955." *American Political Science Review* 97: 57–74.

Huntington, Samuel P. 1991. *The Third Wave: Democratization in the Late Twentieth Century*. Norman, OK: University of Oklahoma Press.

Inglehart, Ronald. 1990. *Culture Shift in Advanced Industrial Society*. Princeton, NJ: Princeton University Press.

Inglehart, Ronald, and Hans-Dieter Klingemann. 1976. "Party Identification, Ideological Preference and the Left–Right Dimension among Western Mass Publics." In *Party Identification and Beyond*, eds Ian Budge, Ivor Crewe, and Dennis Farlie. New York: Wiley.

Inglehart, Ronald, and Pippa Norris. 2003. *Rising Tide: Gender Equality and Cultural Change around the World*. New York: Cambridge University Press.

Inglehart, Ronald, and Christopher Wlezien. 2005. *Modernization, Cultural Change, and Democracy: The Human Development Sequence*. New York: Cambridge University Press.

International Institute for Democracy and Electoral Assistance. 2001. *Handbook on Funding of Parties and Election Campaigns*. Stockholm: International IDEA.

International Institute for Democracy and Electoral Assistance. 2002. *International Electoral Standards Guidelines for Reviewing the Legal Framework of Elections*. Stockholm: International IDEA.

International Telecommunications Union (ITU). 2003. *World Telecommunications Development Report*. Geneva: ITU.

IPU. 1997. *Men and Women in Politics: Democracy Still in the Making*. Geneva: Inter-Parliamentary Union.

IPU. 2007. *The Role of Parliamentary Committees in Mainstreaming Gender and Promoting the Status of Women*. Geneva: Inter-Parliamentary Union.

IPU. 2008a. Women in National Parliaments. 31 October, www.ipu.org/wmn-e/classif.htm

IPU. 2008b. *Equality in Politics: A Survey of Women and Men in Parliaments*. Geneva: Inter-Parliamentary Union.

Irwin, Galen A., and Jacques, Thomassen. 1975. "Issue-consensus in a Multi-party System: Voters and Leaders in the Netherlands." *Acta Politica* 10: 389–420.

Jackman, Robert W. 1987. "Political Institutions and Voter Turnout in the Industrialized Democracies." *American Political Science Review* 8: 405–24.

Jamieson, Katheleen Hall. 1992. *Dirty Politics: Distraction, Deception and Democracy*. New York, NY: Oxford University Press.

Janda, Kenneth. 2005. *Adopting Party Law*. Washington, DC: National Democratic Institute.

Jennings, M. Kent, and Richard G. Niemi. 1981. *Generations and Politics*. Princeton, NJ: Princeton University Press.

Johnson, Thomas J., Barabara K. Kaye, Shannon L. Bichard, and W. Joann Wong. 2007. "Every Blog Has Its Day: Politically-interested Internet Users' Perceptions of Blog Credibility." *Journal of Computer Mediated Communication* 13: 100–22.

Johnston, Richard. 2008. "Polarized Pluralism in the Canadian Party System: Presidential Addresses to the Canadian Political Science Association." *Canadian Journal of Political Science* 41: 815–34.

Johnston, Richard, André Blais, Henry E. Brady, and Jean Crete. 1992. *Letting the People Decide: Dynamics of a Canadian Election*. Kingston, Canada: McGill-Queen's Press.

Johnston, Richard, Michael G. Hagen, and Kathleen Hall Jamieson. 2004. *The 2000 Presidential Election and the Foundations of Party Politics*. Cambridge: Cambridge University Press.

Johnston, Richard, and Jack Vowles. 2006. "Strategic Learning in Campaigns with Proportional Representation: Evidence from New Zealand." In *Capturing Campaign Effects*, eds Henry E. Brady and Richard Johnston. Ann Arbor, MI: University of Michigan Press.

Jones, Mark. 1995. *Electoral Rules and the Survival of Presidential Democracies*. Notre Dame, IN: Notre Dame University Press.

Kabeer, Naila. 2005. "The Beijing Platform for Action and the Millennium Development Goals: Different Processes, Different Outcomes." UNDAW Expert Group Meeting, Baku, Azerbaijan, February.

Kaid, Lynda Lee. 1999. "Political Advertising: A Summary of Research Findings." In *The Handbook of Political Advertising*, ed. Bruce Newman. Thousand Oaks, CA: Sage.

Kaid, Lynda Lee, and Christina Holtz-Bacha, eds 2006. *The Sage Handbook of Political Advertising*. Thousand Oaks, CA: Sage.

Kanter, Rosabeth Moss. 1977. *Men and Women of the Corporation*. New York: Basic Books.

Karam, Azza. 1998. *Women in Parliament: Beyond Numbers*. Stockholm: International Institute for Democracy and Electoral Assistance.

Katz, Richard S. 1996 "Party Organizations and Finance." In *Comparing Democracies: Elections and Voting in Global Perspective*, eds Lawrence LeDuc, Richard G. Niemi, and Pippa Norris. London: Sage.

Katz, Richard S. 1997. *Democracy and Elections*. New York: Oxford University Press.

Katz, Richard S. 2002. "The Internal Life of Parties." In *Political Challenges in the New Europe: Political and Analytical Challenges*, eds Kurt Richard Luther and Ferdinand Müller-Rommel. Oxford: Oxford University Press.

Katz, Richard. 2005. "Why Are There so Many or so Few Electoral Reforms?" In *The Politics of Electoral Systems*, eds Michael Gallagher and Paul Mitchell. Oxford: Oxford University Press.

Katz, Richard S., and Peter Mair. 1995. "Changing Models of Party Organization and Party Democracy: The Emergence of the Cartel Party." *Party Politics* 1: 5–28.

Kayser, Mark Andreas. 2006. "Trade and the Timing of Elections." *British Journal of Political Science* 36: 437–57.

Kayser, Mark, and Christopher Wlezien. 2006. "Performance Pressure: Patterns of Partisanship and the Economic Vote." Paper presented at the annual meeting of the American Political Science Association, Philadelphia.

Key, V.O., Jr. 1964. *Politics, Parties and Pressure Groups*, 5th edn. New York: Crowell.

Key, V.O., Jr. 1966. *The Responsible Electorate*. New York: Vintage Books.

Kim, HeeMin, and Richard C. Fording. 1998. "Voter Ideology in Western Democracies." *European Journal of Political Research* 33: 73–97.

Kim, HeeMin, and Richard C. Fording. 2002. "Government Partisanship in Western Democracies, 1945–1998." *European Journal of Political Research* 41: 187–206.

Kim, HeeMin, G. Bingham Powell, and Richard C. Fording. Forthcoming. "Electoral Systems, Party Systems, and Ideological Representation: Ideological Distortion in Western Democracies." *Comparative Politics*.

King, Gary, James Alt, Nancy Burns, and Michael Laver. 1990. "A Unified Model of Cabinet Dissolution in Parliamentary Democracies." *American Journal of Political Science* 34: 846–71.

Kirchheimer, Otto. 1966. "The Transformation of the Western European Party Systems." In *Political Parties and Political Development*, ed. Joseph LaPalombara and Myron Weiner. Princeton: Princeton University Press.

Kitschelt, Herbert, Zdenka Mansfeldova, Radoslaw Markowski, and Gábor Tóka. 1999. *Post-Communist Party Systems: Competition, Representation and Inter-Party Cooperation*. New York: Cambridge University Press.

Klapper, Joseph T. 1960. *The Effects of Mass Communication*. New York, NY: Free Press.

Klingemann, Hans-Dieter, Richard I. Hofferbert, and Ian Budge. 1994. *Parties, Policies and Democracy*. Boulder, CO: Westview.

Klingemann, Hans-Dieter, Andrea Volkens, Judith Bara, Ian Budge, and Michael D. McDonald. 2006. *Mapping Policy Preferences II*. Oxford: Oxford University Press.

Knutsen, Oddbøjrn. 1995. "Left–Right Materialist Value Orientations." In *The Impact of Values*, eds J. Van Deth and E. Scarbrough. New York: Oxford University Press.

Knutsen, Oddbøjrn. 2006. *Class Voting in Western Europe: A Comparative Longitudinal Study*. Latham, MD: Lexington Books.

Knutsen, Oddbjørn. 2007. "The Decline of Social Class?" In *Oxford Handbook of Political Behavior*, eds Russell J. Dalton and Hans-Dieter Klingemann. Oxford: Oxford University Press.

Kopecký, Petr. 2006, "Political Parties and the State in Post-Communist Europe: The Nature of Symbiosis." *Journal of Communist Studies and Transition Politics* 22: 251–73.

Kopecký, Petr, and Peter Mair. 2003. "Political Parties and Government." In *Political Parties in Africa*, ed. Mohamed A. Salih. London: Pluto.

Kostadinova, Tatiana, and Timothy J. Power. 2007. "Does Democratization Depress Participation? Voter Turnout in the Latin American and Eastern European Transitional Democracies." *Political Research Quarterly* 60: 363–77.

Krook, Mona Lena. 2008. "Campaigns for Candidate Gender Quotas: A New Global Women's Movement?" In *Women's Movements: Flourishing or in Abeyance?*, eds Sandra Grey and Marian Sawer. London: Routledge.

Krosnick, Jon A., and Donald R. Kinder. 1990. "Altering the Foundations of Support for the President through Priming." *American Political Science Review* 84: 497–512.

Kuenzi, Michelle, and Gina Lambright. 2001. "Party System Institutionalization in 30 African Countries." *Party Politics* 7: 437–68.

Laakso, Markku, and Rein Taagepera. 1979. "The Effective Number of Parties: A Measure with Application to West Europe." *Comparative Political Studies* 12: 3–27.

Ladner, Matthew, and Christopher Wlezien. 2007. "Partisan Preferences, Electoral Prospects, and Economic Expectations." *Comparative Political Studies* 40: 571–96.

Lau, Richard R., Lee Sigelman, and Ivy Brown Rovner. 2007. "The Effects of Negative Political Campaigns: A Meta-Analytic Reassessment." *Journal of Politics* 69: 1176–209.

Laver, Michael. 2003. "Government Termination." *Annual Review of Political Science* 6: 23–40.

Laver, Michael, and Norman Schofield. 1990. *Multiparty Government: The Politics of Coalition in Europe.* Oxford: Oxford University Press.

Lawson, Chappell. 2008. "Election Coverage in Mexico: Regulation Meets Crony Capitalism." In *Handbook of Election News Coverage around the World*, eds Jesper Strömback and Lynda Lee Kaid. London: Routledge.

Lawson, Kay, Andrea Römmele, and Georgi Karasimeonov, eds 1999. *Cleavages, Parties, and Voters: Studies from Bulgaria, the Czech Republic, Hungary, Poland, and Romania.* Westport, CT: Praeger.

Lazarsfeld, Paul F., Berelson Bernard, and Gaudet Hazel. 1944. *The People's Choice: How the Voter Makes Up His Mind in a Presidential Campaign.* New York: Duell, Sloan and Pearce.

LeDuc, Lawrence. 2003. *The Politics of Direct Democracy: Referendums in Global Perspective.* Peterborough, Ontario, and Orchard Park, NY: Broadview Press.

LeDuc, Lawrence, Richard G. Niemi, and Pippa Norris, eds 1996. *Comparing Democracies: Elections and Voting in Global Perspective.* Thousand Oaks, CA: Sage.

Lee, Aie-Rie. 2008. "Value Cleavages, Issues and Partisanship in East Asia." In *Party Politics in East Asia*, eds Russell Dalton, Doh Chull Shin and Yun-han Chu. Boulder, CO: Lynne Rienner.

Levitsky, Steven, and Lucan A. Way. 2002. "The Rise of Competitive Authoritarianism." *Journal of Democracy* 13: 51–65.

Lewis-Beck, Michael S. 1988. *Economics and Elections: The Major Western Democracies.* Ann Arbor, MI: University of Michigan Press.

Lewis-Beck, Michael S. 1991. "Introduction." In *Economics and Politics: The Calculus of Support*, eds Helmut Norpoth, Michael S. Lewis-Beck, and Jean-Dominique Lafay. Ann Arbor, MI: University of Michigan Press.

Lewis-Beck, Michael S. 1997. "Who's the Chef? Economic Voting under a Dual Executive." *European Journal of Political Research* 31: 315–25.

Lewis-Beck, Michael S. 2005. "Election Forecasting: Principles and Practice." *British Journal of Politics and International Relations* 7: 145–64.

Lewis-Beck, Michael, William G. Jacoby, Helmut Norpoth, and Herbert F. Weisberg. 2008. *The American Voter Revisited.* Ann Arbor, MI: University of Michigan Press.

Lewis-Beck, Michael S., and Mary Stegmaier. 2000. "Economic Determinants of Electoral Outcomes." *Annual Review of Political Science* 3: 183–219.

Lijphart, Arend. 1994. *Electoral Systems and Party Systems: A Study of Twenty-Seven Democracies, 1945–1990.* New York: Oxford University Press.

Lijphart, Arend. 1999. Patterns of Democracy: *Government Forms and Performance in Thirty-Six Countries.* New Haven, CT: Yale University Press.

Lindberg, Staffan I. 2006. *Democracy and Elections in Africa.* Baltimore, MD: Johns Hopkins University Press.

Linz, Juan J. 1990. "The Perils of Presidentialism." *Journal of Democracy* 1: 51–69.

Lippmann, Walter. 1922. *Public Opinion.* New York: Harcourt.

Lipset, Seymour Martin, and Stein Rokkan. 1967. *Party Systems and Voter Alignments.* New York: Free Press.

Lodge, Milton, Marco Steenbergen, and Shawn Brau. 1995. "The Responsive Voter: Campaign Information and the Dynamics of Candidate Evaluation." *American Political Science Review* 89: 309–26.

López-Escobar, Esteban, Teresa Sádaba, and Ricardo Zugasti. 2008. "Election Coverage in Spain: From Franco's Death to the Atocha Massacre." In *Handbook of Election News Coverage around the World*, eds Jesper Strömback and Lynda Lee Kaid. London: Routledge.

López-Pintor, Rafael. 2000. *Electoral Management Bodies as Institutions of Governance.* New York, NY: Bureau for Development Policy, United Nations Development Programme, www.undp.org/governance/docs/Elections-Pub-EMBbook.pdf

Lösche, Peter. 1993. "Problems of Party and Campaign Financing in Germany and the United States – Some Comparative Reflections." In *Campaign and Party Finance in North America and Western Europe*, ed. Arthur B. Gunlicks. Boulder, CO: Westview.

Lovenduski, Joni. 2005. *Feminizing Politics.* Cambridge: Polity Press.

Lovenduski, Joni, and Pippa Norris. 1993. *Gender and Party Politics.* London: Sage.

Lowell, A. Lawrence. 1897. *Government and Parties in Continental Europe.* Vol 1, 2nd edn. Boston, MA: Houghton, Mifflin and Co.

Lutz, Georg, and Michael Marsh. 2007. "Introduction: Consequences of Low Turnout." *Electoral Studies* 26: 539–47.

Lyons, William, and Robert Alexander. 2000. "A Tale of Two Electorates: Generational Replacement and the Decline of Voting in Presidential Elections." *Journal of Politics* 62: 1014–34

Mackay, Fiona. 2004. "Gender and Political Representation in the UK: The State of the Discipline." *British Journal of Politics and International Relations* 6: 99–120.

Mackay, Fiona. 2006. "Descriptive and Substantive Representation in New Parliamentary Spaces: The Case of Scotland." In *Representing Women in Parliament: A Comparative Study*, eds Marian Sawer, Manon Tremblay, and Linda Trimble. London: Routledge.

MacKuen, Michael B., Robert S. Erikson, and James A. Stimson. 1992. "Peasants or Bankers? The American Electorate and the U.S. Economy." *American Political Science Review* 86: 597–611.

Madrid, Raúl. 2005. "Indigenous Voters and Party System Fragmentation in Latin America." *Electoral Studies* 24: 689–707.

Mainwaring, Scott. 1999. *Rethinking Party Systems in the Third Wave of Democratization: The Case of Brazil.* Palo Alto, CA: Stanford University Press.

Mainwaring, Scott, and Mark Jones. 2003. "The Nationalization of Parties and Party Systems: An Empirical Measure and an Application to the Americas." *Party Politics* 9: 139–66.

Mainwaring, Scott, and Timothy R. Scully. 1995. "Introduction: Party Systems in Latin America." In *Building Democratic Institutions*, ed. Scott Mainwaring and Timothy Scully. Stanford, CA: Stanford University Press.

Mainwaring, Scott, and Matthew Shugart. 1997. *Presidentialism and Democracy in Latin America.* Cambridge: Cambridge University Press.

Mainwaring, Scott, and Mariano Torcal. 2006. "Party System Institutionalization and Party System Theory after the Third Wave of Democratization." In *Handbook of Party Politics*, eds Richard S. Katz and William Crotty. London: Sage.

Mainwaring, Scott, and Edurne Zoco. 2007. "Political Sequences and the Stabilization of Interparty Competition." *Party Politics* 13: 155–78.

Mair, Peter. 2002. "Comparing Party Systems." In *Comparing Democracies 2*, eds Lawrence LeDuc, Richard G. Niemi, and Pippa Norris. London: Sage.

Mair, Peter, and Ingrid van Biezen. 2001. "Party Membership in Twenty European Democracies, 1980–2000." *Party Politics* 7: 5–21.

Mair, Stefan. 2000. "Germany's *Stiftungen* and Democracy Assistance: Comparative Advantages, New Challenges." In *Democracy Assistance: International Co-operation for Democratization*, ed. Peter Burnell. London: Frank Cass.

Malbin, Michael. 2008. "Rethinking the Campaign Finance Agenda." *The Forum* 6/1, article 3.

Manion, Melanie. 1996. "The Electoral Connection in the Chinese Countryside." *American Political Science Review* 90: 736–48.

Mansbridge, Jane. 2003. "Rethinking Representation." *American Political Science Review* 97 (3): 515–28.

Massicotte, Louis, André Blais, and Antoine Yoshinaka. 2004. *Establishing the Rules of the Game: Election Laws in Democracies*. Toronto: University of Toronto Press.

Mateo Diaz, Mercedes. 2005. *Representing Women? Female Legislators in West European Parliaments*. Colchester: ECPR Press.

Matland, Richard E. 2006. "Electoral Quotas: Frequency and Effectiveness." In *Women, Quotas and Politics*, ed. Drude Dahlerup. London: Routledge.

Matland, Richard E., and Donley T. Studlar. 1996. "The Contagion of Women Candidates in Single-Member District and Proportional Representation Electoral Systems: Canada and Norway." *Journal of Politics* 58: 707–33.

Matthews, Donald R., and Henry Valen. 1999. *Parliamentary Representation: The Case of the Norwegian Storting*. Columbus, OH: Ohio State University Press.

Mazzoleni, Gianpietro. 1987. "Media Logic and Party Logic in Campaign Coverage: The Italian General Election of 1983." *European Journal of Communication* 2: 81–103.

McAllister, Ian. 1991. "Party Elites, Voters and Political Attitudes: Testing Three Explanations of Mass-Elite Differences." *Canadian Journal of Political Science* 24: 237–68.

McAllister, Ian. 2008. "Social Structure and Party Choice." In *Party Politics in East Asia*, eds Russell Dalton, Doh Chull Shin, and Yun-han Chu. Boulder, CO: Lynne Rienner.

McCombs, Maxwell E. 2004. *Setting the Agenda: The Mass Media and Public Opinion*. Cambridge: Polity Press.

McCombs, Maxwell E., Esteban Lopez-Escobar, and Juan Pablo Llamas. 2000. "Setting the Agenda of Attributes in the 1996 Spanish General Elections." *Journal of Communication* 50: 77–92.

McCombs, Maxwell E., and Donald L. Shaw. 1972. "The Agenda-Setting Function of Mass Media." *Public Opinion Quarterly* 36: 176–87.

McDonald, Michael D., and Ian Budge. 2005. *Elections, Parties, Democracy: Conferring the Median Mandate*. New York: Oxford University Press.

McDonald Michael D., Silva M. Mendes, and Ian Budge. 2004. "What Are Elections For? Conferring the Median Mandate." *British Journal of Political Science* 34: 1–26.

McDonough, Peter, Samuel H. Barnes, and Antonio López Pina. 1998. *The Cultural Dynamics of Democratization in Spain*. Ithaca, NY: Cornell University Press.

McFaul, Michael. 1997. Russia's 1996 Presidential Election. Stanford, CA: Hoover Institution.

McKenna, Laura, and Antoinette Pole. 2008. "What Bloggers Do: An Average Day on an Average Political Blog." *Public Choice* 134: 97–108.

McKinney, Mitchell, S., and Diana B. Carlin. 2004. "Political Campaign Debates." In *Handbook of Political Communication Research*, ed. Lynda Lee Kaid. London: Routledge.

McLeod, Douglas M., Gerald M. Kosicki, and Jack M. McLeod. 1994. "The Expanding Boundaries of Political Communication Effects." In *Media Effects: Advances in Theory and Research*, eds Jennings Bryant and Dolf Zillmann. Hillsdale, NJ: Lawrence Erlbaum.

Milbrath, Lester W. 1965. *Political Participation*. Chicago, IL: Rand McNally.

Miller, Arthur H., Edie N. Goldenberg, and Lutz Erbring. 1979. "Type-Set Politics: Impact of Newspapers on Public Confidence." *American Political Science Review* 73: 67–84.

Miller, Joanne M., and Jon A. Krosnick. 2000. "News Media Impact on the Ingredients of Presidential Evaluations: Politically Knowledgeable Citizens Are Guided by a Trusted Source." *American Journal of Political Science* 44: 301–15.

Miller, Warren E., and Donald Stokes. 1963. "Constituency Influence in Congress." *American Political Science Review* 57: 165–77.

Miller, Warren E., and J. Merrill Shanks. 1996. *The New American Voter*. Cambridge, MA: Harvard University Press.

Miller, Warren E., Roy Pierce, Jacques Thomassen, Richard Herrera, Sören Holmberg, Peter Esaisson, and Bernhard Wessels. 1999. *Policy Representation in Western Democracies*. Oxford: Oxford University Press.

Miller, William L. 1991. *Media and Voters: The Audience, Content, and Influence of Press and Television at the 1987 General Election*. Oxford: Clarendon Press.

Milner, Henry. 2002. *Civic Literacy: How Informed Citizens Make Democracy Work*. Medford, MA: Tufts University Press.

Molomo, Mpho, and David Sebudubudu. 2005. "Funding of Political Parties: Levelling the Political Playing Field." In *40 Years of Democracy in Botswana, 1965–2005*, ed. Zibani Maundeni. Gaborone: Mmegi Publishing House.

Mozaffar, Shaheen, and James Scarritt. 2005. "The Puzzle of African Party Systems." *Party Politics* 11: 399–422.

Mughan, Anthony. 2000. *Media and the Professionalization of Parliamentary Campaigns*. Houndmills, Basingstoke: Palgrave.

Muller, Edward N., and Karl-Dieter Opp. 1986. "Rational Choice and Rebellious Collective Action." *American Political Science Review* 80: 471–89.

Munck, Geraldo L., and Jay Verkuilen. 2002a. "Conceptualizing and Measuring Democracy: Evaluating Alternative Indices." *Comparative Political Studies* 35: 5–34.

Munck, Geraldo L., and Jay Verkuilen. 2002b. "Generating Better Data: A Response to Discussants." *Comparative Political Studies* 35: 52–7.

Nadeau, Richard, and Michael S. Lewis-Beck. 2001. "National Economic Voting in U.S. Presidential Elections." *Journal of Politics* 63: 159–81.

Nadeau, Richard, Richard G. Niemi, and Antoine Yoshinaka. 2002. "A Cross-National Analysis of Economic Voting: Taking Account of the Political Context across Time and Nations." *Electoral Studies* 21: 403–23.

Nassmacher, Karl-Heinz. 2003. "Monitoring, Control and Enforcement of Political Finance Regulation." In *Funding of Political Parties and Election Campaigns*, ed. Reginald Austin and Maja Tjernström. Stockholm: International IDEA.

Nannestad, Peter, and Martin Paldam. 1997. "From the Pocketbook to the Welfare Man: A Pooled Cross-section Study of Economic Voting in Denmark." *British Journal of Political Science* 27: 119–37.

Neumann, Sigmund. 1956. "Towards a Comparative Study of Political Parties." In *Modern Political Parties*, Sigmund Neumann. Chicago, IL: University of Chicago Press.

Newman, Bruce I. 1999. *Handbook of Political Marketing*. Thousand Oaks, CA: Sage.

Nie, Norman H., Sidney Verba, and John R. Petrocik. 1979. *The Changing American Voter*. Cambridge, MA: Harvard University Press.

Nieuwbeerta, Paul, and Nan Dirk De Graaf. 1999. "Traditional Class Voting in 20 Postwar Societies." In *The End of Class Politics?*, ed. Geoffrey Evans. New York: Oxford University Press.

Nohlen, Dieter. 1984. "Chances and Choices in Electoral Systems." In *Choosing an Electoral System*, eds Arend Lijphart and Bernard Grofman. New York: Praeger.

Nohlen, Dieter. 1997. "Electoral Systems in Eastern Europe: Genesis, Critique, Reform." In *Electoral Systems for Emerging Democracies: Experiences and Suggestions*, ed. J. Elklit. Copenhagen: Danish Ministry of Foreign Affairs.

Norpoth, Helmut. 1996. "The Economy." In *Comparing Democracies: Elections and Voters in Comparative Perspective*, eds Lawrence LeDuc, Richard G. Niemi, and Pippa Norris. Thousand Oaks, CA: Sage.

Norris, Pippa. 1985. "Women's Legislative Participation in Western Europe." *West European Politics* 8: 90–101.

Norris, Pippa. 1995. "Introduction: The Politics of Electoral Reform." *International Political Science Review* 16: 3–8.

Norris, Pippa. 1997. *Passages to Power: Legislative Recruitment in Advanced Democracies*. Cambridge: Cambridge University Press.

Norris, Pippa. 1999. *A Virtuous Circle: Reinventing Political Activism*. Cambridge: Cambridge University Press.

Norris, Pippa. 2000. *A Virtuous Circle: Political Communications in Postindustrial Societies*. Cambridge: Cambridge University Press.

Norris, Pippa. 2001. *Digital Divide: Civic Engagement, Information Poverty, and the Internet Worldwide*. Cambridge: Cambridge University Press.

Norris, Pippa. 2002. "Campaigns Communications." In *Comparing Democracies 2*, eds Larry LeDuc, Richard G. Niemi, and Pippa Norris. London: Sage.

Norris, Pippa. 2003. "Preaching to the Converted." *Party Politics* 9: 21–45.

Norris, Pippa. 2004. *Electoral Engineering: Electoral Rules and Voting Behavior*. New York: Cambridge University Press.

Norris, Pippa, and Ronald Inglehart. 2004. *Sacred and Secular: Religion and Politics Worldwide*. New York: Cambridge University Press.

Norris, Pippa, Joni Lovenduski, and Rosie Campbell. 2004. *Gender and Political Participation*. Research Report. London: UK Electoral Commission.

Norris, Pippa, and Christopher Wlezien. 2005. *Britain Votes*. Oxford: Oxford University Press.

Oates, Sarah. 2008. "Election Coverage in the Russian Federation." In *The Handbook of Election News Coverage around the World*, eds Jesper Strömbäck and Lynda Lee Kaid. London: Routledge.

O'Dwyer, Conor, and Branislav Kovalčik. 2007. "And the Last Shall Be First: Party System Institutionalization and Second-Generation Economic Reform in Postcommunist Europe." *Studies in Comparative International Development* 41: 3–26.

Olson, Mancur. 1965. *The Logic of Collective Action: Public Goods and the Theory of Groups*. Cambridge, MA: Harvard University Press.

Opp, Karl-Dieter. 1986. "Soft Incentives and Collective Action: Participation in the Anti-Nuclear Movement." *British Journal of Political Science* 16: 87–112.

Opp, Karl-Dieter, Käte Burow-Auffarth, and Uwe Heinrichs. 1981. "Conditions for Conventional and Unconventional Political Participation: An Empirical Test of Economic and Sociological Hypotheses." *European Journal of Political Research* 9: 147–68.

Opp, Karl-Dieter, Peter Voss, and Christian Gern. 1995. *Origins of a Spontaneous Revolution: East Germany 1989*. Ann Arbor, MI: University of Michigan Press.

Pacek, Alexander, and Benjamin Radcliff. 1995. "Economic Voting and the Welfare State: A Cross-National Analysis." *Journal of Politics* 57: 44–61.

Page, Benjamin I. and Robert Y. Shapiro. 1992. *The Rational Public: Fifty Years of Trends in Americans' Policy Preferences*. Chicago, IL: University of Chicago Press.

Parry, Garaint, George Moyser, and Neil Day. 1992. *Political Participation and Democracy in Britain*. Cambridge: Cambridge University Press.

Pastor, Robert A. 2006. "The US Administration of Elections: Decentralized to the Point of Being Dysfunctional." In *Electoral Management Design: The International Idea Handbook*, ed. Alan Wall, et al. Stockholm: International Institute for Democracy and Electoral Assistance.

Pateman, Carole. 1970. *Participation and Democratic Theory*. Cambridge: Cambridge University Press.

Patterson, Thomas. 1993. *Out of Order*. New York: Alfred Knopf.

Patterson, Thomas. 1998. "Political Roles of the Journalist." In *The Politics of News, the News of Politics*, eds Doris A. Graber, Denis McQuail, Pippa Norris, and Joseph N. Cappella. Washington, DC: CQ Press.

Paterson, William E., and James Sloam. 2005. "Gerhard Schröder and the Unlikely Victory of the German Social Democrats." In *Precarious Victory: The 2002 German Federal Election and Its Aftermath*, eds David P. Conradt, Gerald R. Kleinfeld, and Christian Soe. New York: Berghahn Books.

Payne, J. Mark. 2007. "Party Systems and Democratic Governability." In *Democracies in Development: Politics and Reform in Latin America*, eds J. Mark, Payne, Daniel Zovatto, and Mercedes Mateo Díaz. Washington, DC: InterAmerican Development Bank.

Pedersen, K., and J. Saglie. 2005. "New Technology in Ageing Parties. Internet Use in Danish and Norwegian Parties." *Party Politics* 11: 359–77.

Persson, Torsten, Gérard Roland, and Guido Tabellini. 1997. "Separation of Powers and Political Accountability." *Quarterly Journal of Economics* 112: 1163–203.

Pew Research Center. 2006. Pew Research Center Biennial News Consumption Survey, http://people-press.org/reports/pdf/282.pdf

Pew Research Centre for People and the Press. 2008. http://people-press.org/report/468/obama-leads-mccain-in-final-days

Phillips, Anne. 1995. *The Politics of Presence*. Oxford: Clarendon Press.

Pickup, Mark, and Richard Johnston. 2007. "Campaign Trial Heats as Electoral Information: Evidence from the 2004 and 2006 Canadian Federal Elections." *Electoral Studies* 26: 460–76.

Pierre, Jon, Lars Svåsand, and Anders Widfeldt. 2000. "State Subsidies to Political Parties: Confronting Rhetoric with Reality." *West European Politics* 23: 1–24.

Pinto-Duschinsky, Michael. 2002. "Financing Politics: A Global View." *Journal of Democracy* 13: 69–86.

Pitkin, Hanna F. 1967. *The Concept of Representation.* Berkeley, CA: University of California Press.

Plasser, Fritz, and Gunda Plasser. 2002. *Global Political Campaigning: A Worldwide Analysis of Campaign Professionals and Their Practices.* Westport, CT: Praeger.

Platform for Action (PFA). 1995. *Report of the Fourth World Conference on Women.* A/CONF.177/20. New York: United Nations.

Plutzer, Eric. 2002. "Becoming a Habitual Voter: Inertia, Resources, and Growth in Young Adulthood." *American Political Science Review* 96: 41–56.

Poe, Steven C., C. Neal Tate, and Linda Camp Keith. 1999. "Repression of the Human Right to Personal Integrity Revisited." *International Studies Quarterly* 43: 291–313.

Poguntke, Thomas, and Paul Webb, eds 2005. *The Presidentialization of Politics.* Oxford: Oxford University Press.

Posada-Carbó, Eduardo. 2008. "Democracy, Parties and Political Finance in Latin America." Kellogg Institute Working Papers, No. 346.

Pottie, David. 2003. "Party Finance and the Politics of Money in Southern Africa." *Journal of Contemporary African Studies* 21: 5–26.

Powell, G. Bingham. 1982. *Contemporary Democracies: Participation, Stability and Violence.* Cambridge, MA: Harvard University Press.

Powell, G. Bingham. 2000. Elections as Instruments of Democracy: Majoritarian and Proportional Visions. New Haven, CT: Yale University Press.

Powell, G. Bingham. 2004. "Political Representation in Comparative Politics." *Annual Review of Political Science* 7: 273–96.

Powell, G. Bingham. 2009. "The Ideological Congruence Controversy." *Comparative Political Studies* 42.

Powell, G. Bingham, and Georg Vanberg. 2000. "Election Laws, Disproportionality and the Left–Right Dimension." *British Journal of Political Science* 30: 383–411.

Powell, G. Bingham, and Guy D. Whitten. 1993. "A Cross-National Analysis of Economic Voting: Taking Account of the Political Context." *American Journal of Political Science* 37: 391–414.

Przeworski, Adam, Michael E. Alvarez, Jose Antonio Cheibub, and Fernando Limongi. 2000. *Democracy and Development: Political Institutions and Well-Being in the World, 1950–1990.* New York: Cambridge University Press.

Puddington, Arch. 2008. *Freedom in Retreat: Is the Tide Turning? Findings of Freedom in the World 2008.* Washington, DC: Freedom House. http://www. freedomhouse.org

Putnam, Robert D. 2000. *Bowling Alone: The Collapse and Revival of American Community.* New York: Simon and Schuster.

Rae, Douglas. 1967, 1971. *The Political Consequences of Electoral Laws.* New Haven, CT: Yale University Press.

Rahat, Gideon. 2004. "The Study of the Politics of Electoral Reform in the 1990s: Theoretical and Methodological Lessons." *Comparative Politics* 36: 461–79.

Rahat, Gideon. 2008. *The Politics of Regime Structure Reform in Democracies: Israel in Comparative and Theoretical Perspective.* New York: State University of New York Press.

Rahat, Gideon, and Reuven Hazan. 2005. "Israel: The Politics of an Extreme Electoral System." In *The Politics of Electoral Systems*, eds Michael Gallagher and Paul Mitchell. Oxford: Oxford University Press.

Rai, Shirin M., Farzana Bari, Nazmunnessa Mahtab, and Bidyut Mohanty. 2006. "South Asia: Gender Quotas and the Politics of Empowerment: A Comparative Study." In *Women, Quotas and Politics*, ed. Drude Dahlerup. London: Routledge.

Randall, Vicky, and Lars Svåsand, 2002. "Party Institutionalization in New Democracies." *Party Politics* 8: 5–29.

Ranney, Austin. 1954. *The Doctrine of Responsible Party Government*. Urbana, IL: University of Illinois Press.

Reilly, Ben. 2001. *Democracy in Divided Societies*. Cambridge: Cambridge University Press.

Reilly, Ben, and Andrew Reynolds. 1999. "Electoral Systems and Conflict in Divided Societies." *Papers on International Conflict Resolution,* No. 2. Washington, DC: National Academy Press.

Renwick, Alan. 2009. *Changing the Rules of Democracy: The Politics of Electoral Reform*. Cambridge: Cambridge University Press.

Reynolds, Andrew. 1999. *Electoral Systems and Democratization in Southern Africa*. Oxford: Oxford University Press.

Reynolds, Andrew, ed. 2002. *The Architecture of Democracy: Constitutional Design, Conflict Management and Democracy*. Oxford: Oxford University Press.

Reynolds, Andrew, Ben Reilly, and Andrew Ellis. 2005. *Electoral Systems Design: The New International IDEA Handbook*. Stockholm: International IDEA.

Rice, Ron, and Charles Atkin, eds 2001. *Public Communication Campaigns*, 3rd edn. Thousand Oaks, CA: Sage.

Richards, David L. 1999. "Perilous Proxy: Human Rights and the Presence of National Elections." *Social Science Quarterly* 80: 648–65.

Richards, David, and Ronald P. Gelleny. 2007. "Good Things to Those Who Wait? National Elections and Government Respect for Human Rights." *Journal of Peace Research* 44: 505–23.

Riker, William H. 1982a. "The Two-Party System and Duverger's Law: An Essay on the History of Political Science." *American Political Science Review* 76: 753–66.

Riker, William H. 1982b. *Liberalism against Populism*. San Francisco, CA: W.H. Freeman.

Riker, William H., and Peter C. Ordeshook. 1968. "A Theory of the Calculus of Voting." *American Political Science Review* 62: 25–42.

Rohrschneider, Robert, and Stephen Whitefield. 2009. "Understanding Cleavages in Party Systems: Issue Position and Issue Salience in 13 Post-Communist Democracies." *Comparative Political Studies* 42: 280–313.

Rokkan, Stein. 1970. *Citizens, Elections, and Parties: Approaches to the Comparative Study of the Process of Development*. Oslo: Universitetsforlaget.

Rommele, Andrea. 2003. "Political Parties, Party Communication and New Information and Communication Technologies." *Party Politics* 9: 7–20.

Rose, Richard, and Doh Chull Shin. 1999. "Democratization Backwards: The Problem of Third Wave Democracies." *Studies in Public Policy* 314, Glasgow: Centre for the Study of Public Policy.

Royed, Terry J. 1996. "Testing the Mandate Model in Britain and the United States." *British Journal of Political Science* 26: 45–80.

Rucht, Dieter. 2007. "Social Movements." In *The Oxford Handbook of Political Behavior*, eds Russell J. Dalton and Hans-Dieter Klingemann. Oxford: Oxford University Press.

Rule, Wilma. 1981. "Why Women Don't Run: The Critical Contextual Factors in Women's Legislative Recruitment." *Political Research Quarterly* 34: 60–77.

Rule, Wilma. 1987. "Electoral Systems, Contextual Factors and Women's Opportunity for Election to Parliament in Twenty-Three Democracies." *Western Political Quarterly* 40: 477–98.

Saffu, Yaw. 2003. "The Funding of Political Parties and Election Campaigns in Africa." In *Funding of Political Parties and Election Campaigns*, eds Reginald Austin and Maja Tjernström. Stockholm: International IDEA.

Saggar, Shamit. 2007. "Race and Political Behavior." In *Oxford Handbook of Political Behavior*, eds Russell Dalton and Hans-Dieter Klingemann. Oxford: Oxford University Press.

Samuels, David. 2004. "From Socialism to Social Democracy: Party Organization and the Transformation of the Workers' Party in Brazil." *Comparative Political Studies* 37: 999–1024.

Sánchez, Fernando. 2003. "Dealignment in Costa Rica: A Case Study of Electoral Change." PhD Thesis. St Anthony's College, University of Oxford.

Sanders, David. 1996. "Economic Performance, Management Competence, and the Outcome of the Next General Election." *Political Studies* 44: 203–231.

Sanders, David. 2000. "The Real Economy and the Perceived Economy in Popularity Functions: How Much Do the Voters Need to Know?" *Electoral Studies* 19: 275–94.

Sanders, David, David Marsh, and Hugh Ward. 1987. "Government Popularity and the Falklands War." *British Journal of Political Science* 17: 281–313.

Sapiro, Virginia. 1981. "When Are Interests Interesting? The Problem of the Political Representation of Women." *American Political Science Review* 75: 701–21.

Sapiro, Virginia, W. Philips Shively, and the Comparative Study of Electoral Systems. 2003. Comparative Study of Electoral Systems, 1996–2001: Module I Micro-District Macro Data [dataset]. Ann Arbor, MI: University of Michigan, Center for Political Studies [producer and distributor].

Sarakinsky, Ivor. 2007. "Political Party Finance in South Africa: Disclosure versus Secrecy." *Democratization* 14: 111–28.

Sartori, Giovanni. 1976. *Parties and Party Systems: A Framework for Analysis.* Cambridge: Cambridge University Press.

Sartori, Giovanni. 1997. *Comparative Constitutional Engineering: An Inquiry into Structures, Incentives and Outcomes*, 2nd edn. London: Palgrave Macmillan.

Sawer, Marian. 2006. "When Women Support Women ... EMILY's List and the Substantive Representation of Women in Australia." In *Representing Women in Parliament: A Comparative Study*, eds Marian Sawer, Manon Tremblay, and Linda Trimble. London: Routledge.

Sawer, Marian. 2007. "Gender Divisions: Crossing the Floor for Women." Paper to ECPR Workshop on Substantive Representation, Helsinki.

Sawer, Marian, Manon Tremblay, and Linda Trimble, eds 2006. *Representing Women in Parliament: A Comparative Study.* London: Routledge.

Scammell, Margaret, and Holli Semetko. 1995. "Political Advertising in Television: The British Experience." In *Political Advertising in Western Democracies*, eds Lynda Lee Kaid and Christina Holtz-Bacha. London: Sage.

Scammell, Margaret, and Holli A. Semetko. 2008. "Election News Coverage in the U.K." In *Handbook of Election News Coverage around the World*, eds Jesper Strömback and Lynda Lee Kaid. London: Routledge.

Scarrow, Susan. 2002. *Perspectives on Political Parties*. New York: Palgrave.

Scarrow, Susan E. 2007. "Political Finance in Comparative Perspective." *Annual Review of Political Science* 10: 193–210.

Schattschneider, E.E. 1942. *Party Government*. New York: Holt, Rinehart and Winston.

Schedler, Andreas. 2002. "The Menu of Manipulation." *Journal of Democracy* 13: 35–50.

Schleiter, Petra, and Edward Morgan-Jones. Forthcoming. "Citizens, Presidents, and Assemblies: The Study of Semi-Presidentialism beyond Duverger and Linz." *British Journal of Political Science*.

Schlesinger, Joseph. 1994. *Political Parties and the Winning of Office*. Ann Arbor, MI: University of Michigan Press.

Schmitt, Hermann, and Jacques Thomassen. 1999. *Political Representation and Legitimacy in the European Union*. Oxford: Oxford University Press.

Schmitt-Beck, Rudiger. 2007. "New Modes of Campaigning." In *Oxford Handbook of Political Behavior*, eds Russell J. Dalton and Hans-Dieter Klingemann. Oxford: Oxford University Press.

Schofield, Norman, and Itai Sened. 2006. *Multiparty Democracy: Elections and Legislative Politics*. Cambridge: Cambridge University Press.

Schumpeter, Joseph A. 1950. *Capitalism, Socialism and Democracy*, 3rd edn. New York: Harper and Row.

Selolwane, Onalenna Doo. 2002. "Monopoly Politikos: How Botswana's Opposition Parties Have Helped Sustain One-Party Dominance." *African Sociological Review* 6: 68–90.

Semetko, Holli. 1996. "The Media." In *Comparing Democracies: Elections and Voting in Global Perspective*, eds Lawrence LeDuc, Richard G. Niemi, and Pippa Norris. Thousand Oaks, CA: Sage.

Semetko, Holli A., Jay G. Blumler, Michael Gurevitch, and David Weaver. 1991. *The Formation of Campaign Agendas: A Comparative Analysis of Party and Media Roles in Recent American and British Elections*. Hillsdale, NJ: Lawrence Erlbaum.

Shaefer, Tamir, Gabriel Weimann, and Yariv Tsfati, 2008. "Campaigns in the Holy Land: The Content and Effects of Election News Coverage in Israel." In *Handbook of Election News Coverage around the World*, eds Jesper Strömback and Lynda Lee Kaid. London: Routledge.

Shaw, Daron R. 1999. "A Study of Presidential Campaign Event Effects from 1952 to 1992." *Journal of Politics* 6: 387–422.

Shugart, Matthew S. 2001. "Electoral 'Efficiency' and the Move to Mixed-Member Systems." *Electoral Studies* 20: 173–93.

Shugart, Matthew S. 2005a. "Semi-Presidential Systems: Dual Executive and Mixed Authority Patterns." *French Politics* 3: 323–51.

Shugart, Matthew S. 2005b. "Comparative Electoral Systems Research: The Maturation of a Field and New Challenges Ahead." In *The Politics of Electoral Systems*, eds Michael Gallagher and Paul Mitchell. Oxford: Oxford University Press.

Shugart, Matthew, and John Carey. 1992. *Presidents and Assemblies*. Cambridge: Cambridge University Press.

Shugart, Matthew Soberg, Melody Ellis Valdini, and Kati Suominen. 2005. "Looking for Locals: Voter Information Demands and Personal Vote-Earning Attributes of Legislators under Proportional Representation." *American Journal of Political Science* 49: 437–49.

Shugart, Matthew, and Martin P. Wattenberg, eds 2001. *Mixed-Member Electoral Systems: The Best of Both Worlds?* Oxford: Oxford University Press.

Smith, Alastair. 2004. *Election Timing.* Cambridge: Cambridge University Press.

Snyder, Jack. 2000. *From Voting to Violence: Democratization and Nationalist Conflict.* New York: Norton.

Somolekae, Gloria. 2005. *Political Parties in Botswana.* EISA Research Report No. 27. Johannesburg: EISA.

Southall, Roger. 2006. "Party Assistance and the Crisis of Democracy in Southern Africa." In *Globalising Party Democracy: Party Politics in Emerging Democracies,* eds Peter Burnell. London: Routledge.

Stanley, Harold W., and Richard G. Niemi, 2007. *Vital Statistics on American Politics 2007–2008.* Washington, DC: CQ Press.

Stevens, Anne. 2007. *Women, Power and Politics.* Houndmills, Basingstoke: Palgrave Macmillan.

Stevenson, Randolph, and Lynn Vavreck. 2000. "Does Campaign Length Matter? Testing for Cross-National Effects." *British Journal of Political Science* 30: 217–35.

Stolle, Dietlind. 2007. "Social Capital." In *The Oxford Handbook of Political Behavior,* eds. Russel J. Dalton and Hans-Dieter Klingemann. Oxford: Oxford University Press.

Stolle, Dietlind, and Marc Hooghe. 2004. "Consumers as Political Participants? Shifts in Political Action Repertoires in Western Societies." In *Politics, Products, and Markets: Exploring Political Consumerism Past and Present,* eds Michele Micheletti, Andreas Follesdal, and Dietlind Stolle. New Brunswick, NJ: Transaction.

Stolle, Dietlind, and Marc Hooghe. 2005. "Inaccurate, Exceptional, One-Sided or Irrelevant? The Debate about the Alleged Decline of Social Capital and Civic Engagement in Western Societies." *British Journal of Political Science* 34: 703–21.

Strom, Kaare. 1997. "Democracy, Accountability and Coalition Bargaining." *European Journal of Political Research* 31: 47–62.

Strömback, Jesper, and Lynda Lee Kaid. 2008a. "Election News Coverage around the World: A Comparative Perspective." In *Handbook of Election News Coverage around the World,* ed. Jesper Strömback and Lynda Lee Kaid. London: Routledge.

Strömbäck, Jesper and Lynda Lee Kaid, eds 2008b. *The Handbook of Election News Coverage around the World.* London: Routledge.

Studlar, Donley T., and Ian McAllister. 2002. "Does a Critical Mass Exist? A Comparative Analysis of Women's Legislative Representation since 1950." *European Journal of Political Research* 41: 233–53.

Swanson, David L., and Paolo Mancini. 1996. *Politics, Media, and Democracy: International Study of Innovations in Electoral Campaigning and Their Consequences.* Westport, CT: Praeger.

Swers, Michele L. 2002. *The Difference Women Make: The Impact of Women on Congress.* Chicago, IL: University of Chicago Press.

Taagepera, Rein. 1998. "How Electoral Systems Matter for Democratization." *Democratization* 5: 69–91.

Taagepera, Rein. 2007. *Predicting Party Sizes: The Logic of Simple Electoral Systems.* Oxford: Oxford University Press.

Taagepera, Rein, and Matthew S. Shugart. 1989. *Seats and Votes*. New Haven, CT: Yale University Press.

Taylor, Peter J. and Ron Johnston. 1979. *Geography of Elections*. London: Penguin.

Teorell, Jan, Mariano Torcal, and José Ramón Montero. 2007. "Political Participation: Mapping the Terrain." In *Citizenship and Involvement in European Democracies: A Comparative Analysis*, eds Jan Van Deth, José Ramón Montero, and Anders Westholm. London: Routledge.

Thomassen, Jacques. 1994. "Introduction: The Intellectual History of Election Studies." *European Journal of Political Research* 25: 239–45.

Thomassen, Jacques, and Hermann Schmitt 1997. "Policy Representation." *European Journal of Political Research* 32: 165–84.

Thomson, Robert. 2001. "The Programme to Policy Linkage: The Fulfillment of Election Pledges on Socio-economic Policy in the Netherlands, 1986–1998." *European Journal of Political Research* 40: 171–97.

Tóka, Gábor. 1998. "Party Appeals and Voter Loyalty in New Democracies." In *Parties and Democracy*, ed. Richard Hofferbert. Oxford: Blackwell.

Towns, Ann. 2003. "Understanding the Effects of Larger Ratios of Women in National Legislatures. Proportions and Gender Differentiation in Sweden and Norway." *Women and Politics* 25: 1–29.

Tremblay, Manon. 1998. "Do Female MPs Substantively Represent Women? A Study of Legislative Behaviour in Canada's Thirty-fifth Parliament." *Canadian Journal of Political Science* 3: 435–65.

Tremblay, Manon, ed. 2008. W*omen and Legislative Representation: Electoral Systems, Political Parties and Sex Quotas*. Houndmills, Basingstoke: Palgrave Macmillan.

Trenaman, Joseph M., and Denis McQuail. 1961. *Television and the Political Image: A Study of the Impact of Television on the 1959 General Election*. London: Methuen.

Trimble, Linda. 1997. "Feminist Politics in the Alberta Legislature, 1972–1994." In *In the Presence of Women: Representation in Canadian Governments*, ed. Jane Arscott and Linda Trimble. Toronto: Harcourt Brace.

Trimble, Linda. 2006. "When Do Women Count? Substantive Representation of Women in Canadian Legislatures." In *Representing Women in Parliament: A Comparative Study*, eds Marian Sawer, Manon Tremblay, and Linda Trimble. London: Routledge.

UNDP. 2008. Human Development Indices 2008. http://hdr.undp.org/en/statistics/data/

Uslaner, Eric M. 1989. "Looking Forward and Looking Backward: Prospective and Retrospective Voting in the 1980 Federal Elections in Canada." *British Journal of Political Science* 19: 495–513.

van Biezen, Ingrid. 2003. *Political Parties in New Democracies: Party Organization in Southern and East-Central Europe*. Houndmills, Basingstoke: Palgrave.

van Biezen, Ingrid. 2008. "State Intervention in Party Politics: The Public Funding and Regulation of Political Parties." *European Review* 16: 337–53.

van Biezen, Ingrid, and Petr Kopecký. 2007. "The State and the Parties: Public Funding, Public Regulation and Rent-Seeking in Contemporary Democracies." *Party Politics* 13: 235–54.

van der Brug, Wouter, Cees van der Eijk, and Mark Franklin. 2007. *The Economy and the Vote: Economic Condition and Elections in Fifteen Countries*. Cambridge: Cambridge University Press.

van der Eijk, Cees, and Mark Franklin. 1996. *Choosing Europe? The European Electorate and National Politics in the Face of Union*. Ann Arbor, MI: University of Michigan Press.

van der Eijk, Cees, and Mark N. Franklin. 2009. *Elections and Voters*. Houndmills, Basingstoke: Palgrave Macmillan.

Van Deth, Jan, José Ramón Montero, and Anders Westholm, eds. 2007. *Citizenship and Involvement in European Democracies: A Comparative Analysis*. London: Routledge.

van de Walle, Nicolas. 2003, "Presidentialism and Clientelism in Africa's Emerging Party Systems." *Journal of Modern African Studies* 41: 297–321.

Van Praag, Philip, and Kees Brants. 1999. "The 1998 Campaign: An Interaction Approach." *Acta Politica* 34: 179–200.

Verba, Sidney, Kay Lehman Schlozman, and Henry E. Brady. 1995. *Voice and Equality: Civic Voluntarism in American Politics*. Cambridge, MA: Harvard University Press.

Vickers, Jill. 2006. "The Problem with Interests: Making Political Claims for 'Women.'" In *The Politics of Women's Interests: New Comparative Perspectives*, ed. Louise Chappell and Lisa Hill. London: Routledge.

Wahl-Jorgensen, Karin. 2002. "Understanding the Conditions for Public Discourse: Four Rules for Selecting Letters to the Editor." *Journalism Studies* 3: 69–81.

Wall, Alan, Andrew Ellis, Ayman Ayoub, Carl W. Dundas, Joram Rukambe, and Sara Staino. 2006. *Electoral Management Design: The International IDEA Handbook*. Stockholm: International Institute for Democracy and Electoral Assistance.

Wallsten, Kevin. 2007. "Agenda Setting and the Blogosphere: An Analysis of the Relationship between Mainstream Media and Political Blogs." *Review of Policy Research* 24: 567–87.

Wängnerud, Lena. 2000. "Testing the Politics of Presence: Women's Representation in the Swedish Riksdag." *Scandinavian Political Studies* 23: 67–91.

Ward, Stephen, Diana Owen, Richard Davis, and David Tars, eds. 2008. *Making a Difference: A Comparative View of the Role of the Internet in Election Politics*. Lanham, MD: Lexington Books.

Waring, Marilyn. 2000. *Politics: Women's Insight*. Geneva: IPU.

Warwick, Paul V. 1994. *Government Survival in Parliamentary Democracies*. New York, NY: Cambridge University Press.

Wass, Hanna. 2007. "The Effects of Age, Generation, and Period on Turnout in Finland, 1975–2003." *Electoral Studies* 26: 648–59.

Wattenberg, Martin. 1991. *The Rise of Candidate-Centered Politics*. Cambridge, MA: Harvard University Press.

Wattenburg, Martin P. 1994. *The Decline of American Political Parties, 1952–1992*. Cambridge, MA: Harvard University Press.

Wattenberg, Martin P. 2007. *Is Voting for Young People?* New York: Pearson Longman.

Way, Lucian A. 2005. "Authoritarian State Building and the Sources of Regime Competitiveness in the Fourth Wave: The Cases of Belarus, Moldova, Russia, and Ukraine." *World Politics* 57: 231–61.

Way, Lucian A., and Steven Levitsky. 2006. "The Dynamics of Autocratic Coercion after the Cold War." *Communist and Post-Communist Studies* 39: 387–410.

Waylen, Georgina. 2008. "Enhancing the Substantive Representation of Women: Lessons from Transitions to Democracy." *Parliamentary Affairs* 61: 518–34.

Weaver, David G., Maxwell E. McCombs, Doris A. Graber, and Chaim H. Eyal. 1981. *Media Agenda-setting in a Presidential Election: Issues, Images, and Interests.* New York: Praeger.

Weisberg, Herbert, and Steve Greene. 2003. "The Political Psychology of Party Identification." In *Electoral Democracy*, eds Michael MacKuen and George Rabinowitz. Ann Arbor, MI: University of Michigan Press.

West, Darrell. 2000. *Checkbook Democracy.* Boston, MA: Northeastern University Press.

Whitten, Guy D., and Harvey D. Palmer. 1999. "Cross-National Analysis of Economic Voting." *Electoral Studies* 18: 49–67.

Wilkinson, Steven. 2004. *Votes and Violence: Electoral Competition and Ethnic Riots in India.* New York: Cambridge University Press.

Williams, Andrew Paul, and John C. Tedesco, eds 2006. *The Internet Election: Perspectives on the Web in Campaign 2004.* Lanham, MD: Rowman and Littlefield.

Wlezien, Christopher, and Robert S. Erikson. 2001. "Campaign Effects in Theory and Practice." *American Politics Research* 29: 419–37.

Wlezien, Christopher, and Robert S. Erikson. 2002. "The Timeline of Presidential Election Campaigns." *Journal of Politics* 64: 969–93.

Wlezien, Christopher, Mark Franklin, and Daniel Twiggs. 1997. "Economic Perceptions and Vote Choice: Disentangling the Endogeneity." *Political Behavior* 19: 7–17.

Wolfinger, Raymond and Steven Rosenstone. 1980. *Who Votes?* New Haven: Yale University Press.

Women's Environment and Development Organization (WEDO). 2007. *Getting the Balance Right in National Cabinets.* www.wedo.org/files/5050_Cabinets Factsheet02.pdf

Young, Iris Marion. 2000. *Inclusion and Democracy.* Oxford: Oxford University Press.

Young, Lisa. 2004. "Regulating Campaign Finance in Canada: Strength and Weaknesses." *Election Law Journal* 3: 444–62.

Zakaria, Fareed. 1997. "The Rise of Illiberal Democracy." *Foreign Affairs* 76: 22–41.

Zaller, John. 1998. "Politicians as Prize Fighters: Electoral Selection and Incumbency Advantage." In *Party Politics and Politicians*, ed. John Geer. Baltimore, MD: Johns Hopkins University Press.

Zaller, John. 2002. "Assessing the Statistical Power of Election Studies to Detect Communication Effects in Political Campaigns." *Electoral Studies* 21: 297–329.

Zaller, John. 2004. "Floating Voters in U.S. Presidential Elections, 1948–2000." In *The Issue of Belief: Essays in the Intersection of Non-Attitudes and Attitude Change*, ed. Paul Sniderman and Willem Saris. Princeton, NJ: Princeton University Press.

Zielinski, Jakub, Kazimierz M. Slomczynski, and Goldie Shabad. 2005. "Electoral Control in New Democracies: The Perverse Incentives of Fluid Party Systems." *World Politics* 57: 365–95.

Zovatto, Daniel. 2003. "The Legal and Practical Characteristics of the Funding of Political Parties and Election Campaigns in Latin America." In *Funding of Political Parties and Election Campaigns*, eds Reginald Austin and Maja Tjernström. Stockholm: International Institute for Democracy and Electoral Assistance.

Author Index

Subject Index

women's movement, 203, 208,
216−19
World Values Survey (WVS),
54, 64, 146, 149, 153, 155−6,
174−8

Yeltsin, Boris, 10, 114−15

Zimbabwe, 17
"zipping", 210
Zyuganov, Gennady, 115

Supporting researchers for more than forty years

Research methods have always been at the core of SAGE's publishing. Sara Miller McCune founded SAGE in 1965 and soon after, she published SAGE's first methods book, *Public Policy Evaluation*. A few years later, she launched the Quantitative Applications in the Social Sciences series – affectionately known as the 'little green books'.

Always at the forefront of developing and supporting new approaches in methods, SAGE published early groundbreaking texts and journals in the fields of qualitative methods and evaluation.

Today, more than forty years and two million little green books later, SAGE continues to push the boundaries with a growing list of more than 1,200 research methods books, journals, and reference works across the social, behavioural, and health sciences.

From qualitative, quantitative and mixed methods to evaluation, SAGE is the essential resource for academics and practitioners looking for the latest in methods by leading scholars.

www.sagepublications.com